TH INCREDIBLE KEY

The Key that Unlocks the
BOOK OF REVELATION
and the
ENDTIMES
for Christians Living
in a Hostile
and
Chaotic World

END TIMES
FIRST PLACE
AWARD

JOE LUTZ

CS Version
Copyright © 2017 Joe Lutz
ISBN: 978-1979343183
Published in the United States of America

All rights reserved. This book may not be used or reproduced by any means, graphic, electronic, or mechanical, including photocopying, recording, taping or by any information storage retrieval system for commercial gain or profit. The use of short quotations or occasional page copying for personal, group study, critical articles or reviews is permitted and encouraged. Written permission will be granted upon request.

Print Version
Copyright © 2017 Joe Lutz
ISBN: 978-1-940359-49-6
Library of Congress Number: 2042475

Unless otherwise noted, Scripture quotations are taken from the *New King James Version*®, Copyright © 1982 by Thomas Nelson, Inc. www.thomasnelson.com/consumer. Used by permission. All rights reserved.

Scripture quotations marked KJV are taken from *The King James Version* of the Bible unless marked otherwise.

Scripture quotations marked NASB95 are taken from the *New American Standard Bible*®, Copyright © 1960, 1962, 1963, 1968, 1971, 1972, 1973, 1975, 1977, 1995 by The Lockman Foundation Used by permission. www.Lockman.org"

Scripture quotations taken from the *Amplified® Bible* (AMPC), Copyright © 1954, 1958, 1962, 1964, 1965, 1987 by The Lockman Foundation Used by permission. www.Lockman.org.

Scripture quotations marked NCV are taken from the *New Century Version*®. Copyright © 2005 by Thomas Nelson. Used by permission. All rights reserved.

Scripture quotations marked NIV84 are taken from THE HOLY BIBLE, NEW INTERNATIONAL VERSION®, NIV® 1984 version, Copyright © 1973, 1978, 1984, 2011 by Biblica, Inc.® Used by permission. All rights reserved worldwide.

Scripture quotations marked ESV are taken from *The ESV® Bible* (*The Holy Bible, English Standard Version*®). ESV® Permanent Text Edition® (2016). Copyright © 2001 by Crossway, a publishing ministry of Good News Publishers. The ESV® text has been reproduced in cooperation with and by permission of Good News Publishers. Unauthorized reproduction of this publication is prohibited. All rights reserved

Cover by Joe Lutz and Amanda Grace Butt

Bedford, Texas

During the days of the sounding of the seventh trumpet,
"the MYSTERY OF GOD will be fulfilled ..."

Revelation 10:7

DEDICATION

To Jesus Christ, the Lamb of God—our Bridegroom!

If our Lord chooses to use this book to draw hearts closer to Him, to Him alone is honor due. If there was only one believer drawn nearer to Him, the privilege of writing this book will have been well worth it. On the other hand He doesn't deserve any scorn that could accompany any failure on my part in presenting His Word. Any failure, mistake, or erroneous idea found in this book is mine, and mine alone. I am utterly aware of my inability to spiritually see, hear, or learn His truths through the means of my own fleshly efforts, as far as any eternal value is concerned. I am also aware, thankfully, of His ability to open the eyes of the blind and the ears of the deaf, and to enlighten any hungry heart who pursues intimacy with Him; I know this delights His heart. Concerning study, research, reading and writing this book, my dependence has been rooted in the reality that the Holy Spirit is our Teacher and Helper. Therefore, with His help, I trust that my desire to honor Christ and His Word is a joy to Him and a help to others who want to know Him more intimately.

My feeling is that it would be difficult to imagine how anyone could receive more benefit by reading this book than I have been by writing it. Perhaps, that suggests that no one needs these truths in their lives more than I do. As far as I am concerned, that is the case.

I deeply desire that each reader will see more clearly than ever that Christ, our Savior, and Bridegroom, is our individual and collective "joy unspeakable, full of glory"! While we want to know Him during our short lives in our present bodies, there is coming a more glorious day when those who love Him will experience the *Marriage of the Lamb*; Christ will marry His bride! Because of that reality, it is our privilege to **dedicate** our lives as a living sacrifice to Him on a moment by moment basis. To **dedicate** this book to Him is a part of my own desire to allow His life to be lived through me by His Spirit. *"He must increase; I must decrease,"* as our brother, John the Baptist, testified.

When all is said and done, it is all about Him.

*"For **by Him**, all things were created that are in heaven and that are on earth, visible and invisible, whether thrones or dominions or principalities or powers. All things were created **through Him** and **for Him**. And He is **before all things**, and **in Him, all things consist**. And **He is the head** of the body, the church, who is the beginning, the firstborn from the dead, **that in all things He may have the preeminence**." (emphasis mine)*

Colossians 1:16–18

Acknowledgments

Above all other people in my life, I wish to acknowledge my wife, **Colleen**, who rejoices in the truths in this book, just as much I do, and who has taught me many things that God has shown her in His Word. I cannot fully express the incredible example she has been to me in her personal pursuit to know Christ *"in the power of His resurrection."* She is a true student of God's Word and a faithful intercessor in prayer. She is a woman with a passion for truth, who has played a major role in my walk with God. I thank God for you, a million times over, Colleen!

I wish to acknowledge my father and mother, **Dr. Stanley and Virginia Lutz**, both of whom are already privileged to be in the presence of the Lord. They left my siblings and me with a great legacy in Christ. I thank God for their love and their eternal impact in my life. One of the songs my mother wrote was titled, *"In the Twinkling of an Eye"*! (He will appear). It won't be long.

I rejoice in our **five children and the six grandchildren**. Also, for the love and friendship of all of **my siblings**, some of whom are with the Lord, and all of whom have a testimony that we will be together with Christ for eternity. May God bless you, one and all!

Dr. Stephen and Lauren Tucker have walked with me every step of the way through two-and-a-half years of writing, offering encouragement, support, great suggestions, prayer—and reading and more reading of the manuscript. God has blessed Colleen and me with your friendship and love. As a member of the board of our organization, *Endlighten Ministries*, Steve, you have been, and are a friend, and an indispensable encourager, helpful hand supporter, and brother. Your ideas and suggestions have played a key role in the direction this book has taken. The past ten years of weekly fellowship together has been an incredible journey in the Spirit of Christ and His Word. What would I have done without you? To God be the glory, "Bro"!

What very special friends **Marvin and Pat Carter** are to Colleen and me. Marvin, as a member of the board of our *Endlighten Ministries*, you have been and are a true supporter from day one. Thank you for the myriad of corrections and suggestions, and the time and support invested. Thank you for opening your arms of love and your home to me on so many occasions allowing me to sequester myself and write on your beautiful enclosed back porch overlooking the golf course.

To **Pastor Marvin Byers**, who introduced Colleen and me to the fundamental truths about which this book is written. Marvin, it is impossible to express the impact your life, ministry, and example continues to have. Thank you for being an exemplary *lover of the Lamb*; and thanks to you and Barb for your faithfulness these many years as friends and as a brother and sister in Christ. A very special thank you for allowing me to utilize many important quotes from a few of your many books, without which this book would not be complete.

Early in this project, **Karmon Wright** did a great job researching for me, and encouraging the project. Thank you Karmon for a super attitude, and for your love for Christ.

My long-distance and long-term friend, **Brent Rutledge**, has been a student of the truths in this book for many years. Your knowledge, suggestions, and feedback have helped me to get clarity for explaining a thing time and again. You have been and remain a faithful listening ear. Perhaps, you would be willing to move closer to where I live, selfishly speaking! No, Brent, I am not moving out there, as beautiful as that part of the country is!

There was a pivotal time in the writing of this book, during which I knew I needed complete isolation in a desirable environment. I asked the Lord for a window of time, several weeks. God made that possible through our *Endlighten Ministries* supportive board members, who encouraged me to take time off to write. The Lord further used my brother and his wife, **Courtney and Janet Lutz** whose Tennessee countryside home is on ten acres with a barn and three horses, a beautiful lake, and a large, covered back porch, along with a lock-away guest bedroom with a desk, which was perfect for writing in quiet. Also **Mark and Joan Krupicka** are absolute treasures. Mark and Joan extended to me a perfect hide-a-way in their guest apartment in their home; a place of solace and quiet to write on many occasions. Their's is a place dedicated to and blessed of the Lord.

For my brothers-in-Christ in our Monday night study, **Steve, Roger, and Michael**, *(and our newest member of our band of brothers,* **Vic**) who have stayed by my side, and listened to my meanderings during many of our evenings together. They are always encouraging, plus they know how to jerk my chains; what are brothers for, after all! *"Iron sharpens iron!"* Now, you guys can stop asking me, *"When will the book be finished?"* By the way, let's not forget about Mama and Martha. I'll leave it at that. Love you guys.

To **Aris, Jackson, Mike, Tom and Gaye, and Bob and Judy**. Each of you has added more to this project than you would be willing to believe. I so appreciate your friendship and fellowship in Christ. To **the men of the Saturday morning Men's Breakfast and Bible Study**, whose fellowship and encouragement continue adding to my life. Thank you for your brotherhood, friendship, and encouragement to write.

To the **pastors and members of the churches** where I have been greatly honored and privileged to present our *Endlighten Ministries* seminars. Thank you for your love, friendship, and the tremendous response to the message of the seminar.

Contents

Dedication
Acknowledgments
Preface — xi
Introduction — xv

PART I - THE MYSTERY OF GOD UNLOCKS THE BOOK OF REVELATION
Chapter 1: The Mystery Will Be Completed During the Days of the Last Trumpet — 43
Chapter 2: The Big Picture in Revelation — 61
Chapter 3: The Revelation Divide — 77
Chapter 4: 42 Unmistakable Similarities: Comparing Revelation 4-13 With 14-19 — 101

PART II - THE MYSTERY OF GOD: THE INCREDIBLE KEY
Chapter 5: Waiting! — 115
Chapter 6: The Scope of the Mystery — 119
Chapter 7: Overview of the Mystery — 133
Chapter 8: Six-Thousand-Year-Old Truth — 135
Chapter 9: The Mystery of God: Planned Before the Beginning — 153
Chapter 10: The Transition of the Jewish-Only Early Church — 171
Chapter 11: The Apostle Paul Brings Clarity — 179
Chapter 12: A Glorious Revelation — 197

PART III - THE BRAIDED, MULTI-THREADED, UNBREAKABLE, PROPHETIC CORD
Chapter 13: In The Beginning Was the Beginning and the End — 213
Chapter 14: The Serpent, The Seed, and Adam and Eve — 221
Chapter 15: The Promised Seed: Cain or Abel? — 237
Chapter 16: The Mystery of God and the Revelation of Jesus Christ Throughout the Bible — 245

PART IV - THE LAMB AND HIS BRIDE
Chapter 17: The Last Eve and the Great Mystery — 261
Chapter 18: The Perfect Wedding Planner and His Plan — 277
Chapter 19: Betrothal — 287
Chapter 20: Only One Bridegroom and Only One Bride — 305
Chapter 21: Old Testament Saints and the Bride of Christ — 311
Chapter 22: I Go to Prepare a Place for You — 337

PART V - THE BRIDEGROOM IS COMING
Chapter 23: We Can Know The Times and Seasons of His Coming — 349
Chapter 24: The Bridegroom Ties the Knot! — 363

SIGNIFICANT CLOSING THOUGHTS TO MY READERS — 373

Works Cited — 377
APPENDIX A - Mystery Details 1 through 12 — 379
APPENDIX A - Mystery Details 13 through 25 — 380
APPENDIX A - Mystery Details 26 through 31 — 381
APPENDIX A - Mystery Details 32 through 35 — 382
APPENDIX B - Christ the Mystery in the Old Testament — 383
APPENDIX C - Division Theology and Replacement Theology — 391

About the Author

PREFACE

I will always cherish the memory of a certain life-changing moment.

As a sixteen-year-old teenage boy, I had recently been born again. I noticed a change in my mother's interactions with me. Little by little, she had wanted to spend more time in spiritual conversation. I knew quite well that this meant talking about God and His Word! You would need to have known my mother to appreciate that fully.

The life-changing moment came after having come home from basketball practice, one evening late.

"Joe! Is that you?"

I was tired. I was impatient. I was youthfully selfish and really didn't want to take the time.

"Yes, Mama! It's me!"

She was quick to continue. *"Come in here a minute. I want to show you something!"*

Her minute was, typically, more like an hour—or, maybe, three. When it came to talking about that which she loved, God and His Word, she was like a bottle of unchilled, shaken-up Coca-Cola on a hot, sunny day. Just pop the top, and the gushing flow was amazing! That's just who she was.

That night, I wasn't really up to a long discussion. I voiced my meager appeal from down the hallway, as I kept walking in the direction of her room admitting defeat!

"Hi, Mama! What ya' got?"

More than I realized at the time, the Spirit of God had leveraged her love and patience toward me to kindle a spiritual fire in me. It seems He had shown her what I needed, and she was more than happy to follow His leading to meet that need. Months of our regular late-night conversations had been feeding into my soul. Learning about Christ and His return filled my young, hungry heart. I was hungrier than I had fully understood, or admitted at the time.

She was graciously formidable and hard to resist; not that I tried too often. At the time, I had thought that she could be quite stubborn. I now know that it wasn't about her personality; rather it was her godly diligence, overflowing in the Holy Spirit, that had generated a meek, yet strong heart—a heart in pursuit of mine. It was the fruit of the Spirit, the life of Christ flowing through her that I had been experiencing. Kindled by the Spirit in the example of her passionate love for Jesus, a fire began to burn deep within me. I did not understand that fire; not yet.

So, there I was sitting on the side of her bed, not daring to lay over on my side because sleep would have doubtless found its prey. After settling in for her "minute," my heart began to warm up that night as she talked. My interest in what she had to say had once again peaked—as usual.

How she loved to speak about the glorious Lord Jesus, His finished work on the cross, His resurrection, His return, His love and mercies, and whatever else her meditations had been that day. Invariably, however, she would end up talking about Endtime prophecy and the return of Christ for His Bride.

That night, as part of what she had come to understand about biblical Endtime prophecy, she alerted me that I should keep my eye on Persia (Iran) and Turkey during my personal Endtimes studies. She proceeded to offer support in the prophetic Scriptures for the ideas she was sharing. Those two countries, she explained, would play major roles concerning God's dealings with Israel and the world in the end before Jesus returns. She continued for a few minutes. Then she took a sharp turn.

"*Your Daddy was a great man of God, Joe. He started, and for twenty years, pastored our church in South Memphis, before he went 'Home' to be with the Lord.*" She went on to explain that because I had been "*only seven years old, nearly eight when he died, you will want to know something very special he told me about you children.*" She had my attention. I was always hungry to hear anything about Daddy because I had *very few personal memories of him.*"

"*Your father was a lover of God, His Word, and of people. He had a special love for the study of Endtime prophecies. He taught me to love it. One day, he told me something that was breathtaking. He said, 'Ginny, I believe some of our children will live to see the return of Christ!'*"

"*Joe, back then, when he had said that to me, Israel had only recently become a sovereign nation again in 1948. That fact, he told me, was a major sign of the endtimes and the return of Jesus. Think about that! Israel became a nation again only eighteen years ago.*

"*You are the next to the youngest of the eight children—the last of the four boys. I want this to hold special meaning for you. I hope it will stick with you for the rest of your life.*"

Looking in the rearview mirror at that sixteen-year-old boy, I now know that the weight of what she had said to me did not fully register at that time. But I received her words with as much grace and gravity as a young, sports-addicted, teenage boy could. As she had hoped, and no doubt had prayed, it has stuck with me to this day.

We talked a while longer, and off to bed, I went, comforting myself that although some school homework had been left undone, I had done the important homework. I have also often wondered what had gone through my mother's mind after I left her room that night. About one thing, I am certain. She was in prayer before she ended her night.

That particular life-changing moment was in 1966, and never forgotten! But it wasn't the last such conversation, and it was not the last of special moments.

Fast forward to 1995, twenty-nine years later. I was forty-five.

My mother was within a few days of finally getting to go Home to be with the Lord. I had flown to be with her and the rest of the family. Those few, fleeting nights with her just before she left us, I had slept in a chair by her hospital bed. Early, on my last morning with her, in this life, she woke up from her induced sleep and had called out my name, waking me.

Clear mindedness had been escaping her over the previous two days. Medications had seemed in control, due to her discomfort and pain. But that morning, she had awakened with a clear mind. She wanted to talk. A few bites of crushed ice, periodically, and she was back in business. Her spiritual Coca-Cola bottle was full, and the top had popped open once again!

For the next few hours, even though her body was fading, her mind engaged fully—one last time together. It was as though we were in her room back at home, once again, digging in the Scriptures together. And this one last time, she wanted to talk about *things to come in the Endtimes.*

During the previous years before I found myself sitting by her hospital bedside, my understanding of the prophetic Endtime Scriptures had been changing. In fact, they had been changing dramatically. Until that very moment at her bedside, I had wondered if I would ever get the opportunity to fully share the things I had been learning, even though we had touched on it over the phone on several occasions. Given her condition, I was uncertain if that current moment was the best time, or even necessary. But she would have none of that. She insisted that we talk.

There we were, talking about the things of God, just two days before she would leave us! She was excited to hear what had changed in my understanding. *"Tell me everything, Joe! I want to know what the Lord has taught you!"*

This time, it was my Coca-Cola top that popped. I did just what she asked. I shared everything. From time to time, she would eagerly interrupt quoting confirmation with this Scripture verse or that, or adding some thoughtful insight. She had truly gotten what I was sharing, connecting dot to dot, all the way through! She was excited about it.

I was thrilled. My mother was thrilled. She was so happy to have heard the things I shared. While overflowing with a delighted tone, she said: *"I cannot believe that I have not seen this before! God is opening His prophetic Word more and more to His people, as we draw nearer to Jesus' return!"* That heartfelt attitude in and from her was similar to what it had been when I had been a teenager. Her desire and love of the truth had never faded; rather, it had obviously intensified, to which I was witness, once again. It was that intense desire and love of God and truth that had initially inspired my study of Endtime prophecy decades before.

There we were, enjoying each other, loving each other, and mutually delighting in the refreshed insights God was showing both of us! One of the great joys in my life, since that moment, has been to reminisce, basking in the warmth, and instructiveness, of and from her heart. Those hours felt like mere seconds, and then it was over.

That was the last of my *minutes* with her. Selfishly, I have wished those minutes could have been days longer! She slipped away Home within a couple of days, and finally, saw her Lord and Savior face to face. I still have lasting joy for having witnessed her passion in those precious moments, and for the assurance in knowing that she had finally been able to be with the One she loved and longed for!

Fast forward again, to today, another twenty-two years later in 2017. A lot of water has flowed under my bridge during these past fifty-one years since the Lord drew me to Himself and saved me as a teenager. God has been merciful in every way, absolutely undeserving as I am. Looking in the rear-view mirror again, I know that His mercies have spared my life and opened my eyes to so much more, since those early, life-changing moments in her room; and even more so, since those few moments with her at the end of her earthly life. My borrowed passion for God and His Word garnered from her example, has never been more on fire in me, than it is today. I owe her so much because she allowed His life to overflow through her own into mine!

And now, it is a true joy and privilege to share *everything* I had shared with my mother twenty-two years ago in this book.

The bottle top has popped!

INTRODUCTION

Typically, a book begins at the Introduction. However, for greatest advantage, I am asking the reader to begin at the ending, which is APPENDIX A. This appendix is fundamental to your clearer understanding of this book.

"Blessed is he who reads and those who hear the words of this prophecy, and keep those things which are written in it; for the time is near."

Revelation 1:3

The first five words of the Book of Revelation tell us why we will be "blessed" by reading, hearing and keeping the words of this prophecy: "The revelation of Jesus Christ." Yet, even greater than any knowledge we might learn about the events found in Revelation, we will gain an increasing intimacy with Jesus as He is revealed to us in great glory. The Book of Revelation is, in fact, the revelation of Jesus Christ. It is about Jesus being revealed in a deeper and glorious way!

If we truly want to understand prophecy, then we should give our hearts attention to Jesus Himself, and what God's written Word reveals about Him. Focusing on prophecy for prophecy's sake is not the singular objective; it is not even the primary objective. If you want to understand what is coming in the future, grow in knowing Him. Focusing on Jesus will reveal His prophetic perspective and the events and details that come through knowing Him. *"The testimony of Jesus is the spirit of prophecy"* (Revelation 19:10).

Didn't Jesus say about Himself that He is "the Beginning and **the End**" in Revelation 1:8? When He said that He is **"the End,"** that identification was more than a hint; it was a declaration of who He is. And what is it that bridges the distance between the "Beginning" and the "End?"

Prophecy does!

Yes, there are events that we can learn about in prophecy, and we will. But those events find their reason for existence in the central figure and purpose of prophecy, which is Jesus Christ and His glorification.

From the beginning to the end of the Bible, He and His plans are foretold. *"Surely the Lord God does nothing unless He reveals His secret to His servants the prophets"* (Amos 3:7).

The revealing of Jesus begins in Genesis and ends in the Book of Revelation. "... *For I am God, and there is no other; I am God, and there is none like Me, Declaring the end from the beginning ...*" (Isaiah 46:9–10).

We could rightly describe the entire Bible as *The Revelation of Jesus Christ*. Therefore, it should not be surprising to us that the first five words of the Book of Revelation are, in fact, "*The Revelation of Jesus Christ.*" Nor should it be any surprise to us when we read that He was not only "*in the beginning,*" but that He *made the beginning*:

"*In the beginning was the Word [Jesus], and the Word was with God, and the Word was God. He was in the beginning with God. All things were made through Him, and without Him, nothing was made that was made.*"

John 1:1–3

Or, this from the apostle Paul:

"*For **by Him all things were created** that are in heaven and that are on earth, visible and invisible, whether thrones or dominions or principalities or powers. **All things were created through Him and for Him**. And <u>**He is before all things**</u>, and in Him, all things consist.*"

Colossians 1:16–17

As we will see in this book, the basic reason for our deficient understanding of the prophetic Endtimes is that we fail to view the Endtimes through the eternal paradigm of Jesus Himself. This book is first and foremost about Jesus! In knowing Jesus in and through this *Mystery of God*, He has given us a way to unlock and understand *the Endtimes*! The approach to understanding Revelation and the Endtimes in this book is to see and know Jesus more intimately, and thereby unlock the Endtimes with a key, specially designed by the Creator Himself. This key is revealed to us in His Word. I call it **The Incredible Key**.

The **"*Mystery of God,*"** as found in Revelation 10:7, is ***The Incredible Key That Unlocks the Book of Revelation and the Endtimes for Christians Living in a Hostile and Chaotic World***:

"*... in the days of the trumpet call to be sounded by the seventh angel, the mystery of God would be fulfilled [finished, completed], just as he announced to his servants the prophets.*"[1]

Revelation 10:7

I want to see with you what this *Mystery* is, and why it unlocks the Endtimes and the Book of Revelation. The *Mystery of God* is far more than merely a short phrase found in Revelation. Far from this being an incidental subject, the *Mystery of God* reveals the overall plan of God in His desired and planned relationship with humanity, beginning in Genesis and culminating in the Book of Revelation. This is specifically because God's overall plan is about Jesus, and this *Mystery*, in every sense of the word, is about Jesus.

When it comes to the Book of Revelation, I think it is fair to say that there are a handful of special Endtime events, which are of greatest interest to most believers. It is no little coincidence that the list of those most commonly discussed Endtime events are inextricably interwoven into the fabric of the *Mystery of God*, as this book makes clear through a myriad of specific biblically-referenced details.

Amazingly, though many of us read right past these references, we will learn that the *Mystery of God* is specifically referred to, by name, nearly 20 times in 13 different chapters in 7 of the New Testament books written by the apostles John and Paul. The truths of the *Mystery* are contained and described in 10 major factors. Those factors are further amplified into 35 details.

Some of the commonly discussed Endtime events inextricably connected to the *Mystery of God* are these:

- The sounding of the last trumpet;
- The resurrection and the rapture;
- The judgment at the Judgment Seat of Christ
- The rewarding of the saints and prophets;
- The *Marriage* and *the Marriage Supper of the Lamb*.

All the above are intrinsically part of the *Mystery of God* truth. The additional events, below, chronologically follow after the fulfillment of the *Mystery of God* events, yet, they are affected by the *Mystery's* fulfillment.

- The Second Coming of Christ;
- The Millennial Reign of Christ
- The Great White Throne Judgment;
- The making of a *New Heaven and a New Earth*;
- And the *eternal Kingdom of God*.

The chronology, meaning, and purpose of all of these events, referred to in the Book of Revelation, cannot be understood without unlocking them with *The Incredible Key—the Mystery of God*.

In one sense, this *Incredible Key* unlocks and reveals the very heart of God's love for all to see. We say that the Bible is God's *love story*, in which He tells of His love for His created beings, as divinely demonstrated in Jesus' sacrifice on the cross for sin.

"For God so loved the world that He gave His only begotten Son, that whoever believes in Him should not perish but have everlasting life."

John 3:16

It's true; the Bible is His *love story*. His *love* is expressed in the most elegant and profound terms of endearment, extending even more deeply and broadly than that of John 3:16. From the Garden of Eden, and all the way through history to the sounding of the last trumpet, the resurrection and rapture, judgment and rewarding of the saints, Jesus, our Bridegroom, has a plan, a goal, an objective, and a divine appointment. His eyes and heart are focused like a laser on the *"... joy set before Him"* (Hebrews 12:2). His preeminent joy, beyond pleasing His Father, is Christ's own wedding and supper at the *Marriage of the Lamb*!

I began this Introduction by saying that this book is about Jesus. Jesus is the *Lamb, the Lamb of God*. The *Marriage of the Lamb* is about Jesus' marriage to His bride, the Church. Once we reach the end of this book, we will have basically seen God's plan for His Son's *Marriage* chronicled throughout the Bible. We will have seen Him gathering His bride, from Genesis to Revelation. That story is the heart and soul of the *Mystery of God*. It shows us the desire of the Bridegroom's heart for His bride, the Church.

This doctrine of the *Marriage of the Lamb* was taught by Jesus and His apostles. In this book, we see the inseparable relationship between the *Mystery* and the *Marriage*, which brings the greatest clarity to the subject of the *Marriage*. Many well-known teachers and preachers have written on this subject. For example, Billy Graham wrote the Forward to the First Edition of the popular book by Paul E. Billheimer, which was entitled, *Destined for the Throne*; subtitled *How Spiritual Warfare Prepares the Bride of Christ for Her Eternal Destiny*.

In the first paragraph of his Introduction, Mr. Billheimer stated:

> "The author's thesis is that the primary purpose of the universe from all eternity is the production and preparation of an Eternal Companion for the Son, called the Bride, the Lamb's Wife. Since she is to share the throne of the universe with her Divine Lover and Lord, privileged to judge the world with Him, she must be trained, educated, and prepared for her role."[2]

He continues:

> "From before the foundation of the world until the dawn of eternal ages God has been working toward one grand event, one supreme end—the glorious wedding of His Son, the *Marriage of the Lamb*. Therefore, from all eternity, all that precedes the Marriage Supper of the Lamb is preliminary and preparatory."

One of the Bible passages Mr. Billheimer uses to support his introductory remarks would be Ephesians 5:22-32, which he refers to early in his book. In this passage in Ephesians, which I refer to regularly throughout this book, the Apostle Paul uses profound language in describing what Billheimer is saying:

*"... Christ also **loved the church** and **gave Himself for her**, that He might **sanctify and cleanse** her with the washing of water by the word, that He might **present her to Himself** a glorious church, **not having spot or wrinkle** or any such thing, but that she should be holy and without blemish."*

Ephesians 5:25–27

The Apostle Paul, then, removes all doubt in his explosive declaration that the Ephesians 5:22-32 passage is about nothing less that the "great *Mystery*," which specifically speaks to the *Marriage of the Lamb* to the Church, His bride!

*"This is a **great mystery**, but I speak concerning **Christ and the church.**"*

Ephesians 5:32

This matter of Jesus presenting His bride to Himself as a glorious Church is specifically about our Bridegroom's love for us; His goal for us. The connection, between the **"great Mystery"** and the **"Marriage of the Lamb"** in this Ephesians passage, is God's declaration that these *cannot be and must not be separated from the Endtimes.*

For some reason, some believers have a mistaken perception that the current prophetic era will conclude at the rapture, the snatching away of the Church from this earth. By knowing that the rapture will actually take place, they now feel that knowing that fact is all they need to know and understand about the Endtimes. Tragically, an astounding number of other believers maintain a somewhat fantasized concept, or misconception, of what will take place following the rapture. Their view might sound something like this, in simple terms: *Jesus is coming to rapture us, to take us out of this mess, and then we will be with Jesus **in heaven forever**. There will be a judgment and rewards, but we will be with Him in heaven, and we'll be with Him there forever and ever and ever!*

That kind of perspective is, at a minimum, incomplete. What is really sad about that outlook is that those who view the Endtimes in such a limited way are missing out on what is meant by what is quoted so often about Jesus' return. We say that His return is the "Blessed Hope." It is, indeed, a blessed hope. But the *Blessed Hope* is far more than just being raptured out of this world into the presence of God forever in heaven.

Do we not know that there is going to be a *heavenly Marriage*? Do we not even consider the fact that after the rapture, judgment, rewards, and *Marriage*, Jesus and His "wife" are going to return to the earth, and He is going to rule for 1,000 years on this earth in what is called the *Millennial Reign of Christ*? We will **not be in heaven** at that juncture. We will have a thousand years more of life on this earth. I have a name for this gaping hole in the Church's eschatological teaching. I call it *The Missing Millennium*! Christian leaders, if asked, would typically quickly agree that there will be a *Millennium* lived out on this earth. Nevertheless, it's almost as though some pastors and Bible teachers lead their congregations to believe that there will be a *rapture*, as well they should, only to explain the rest of the picture, leaving their flock missing the details of what is ahead of them.

The point I am making is not intended to criticize pastors and teachers; absolutely not. God bless every faithful leader, who is teaching the Word. However, I think the biblical requirement in the body of Christ involves the word *provoke*. Loving one another requires willingness to provoke one another toward love and good works, as the writer of Hebrews teaches us. Furthermore, *iron sharpens iron*. Each of us needs it.

Please understand it's not that leadership in the Church does not acknowledge the *Marriage* and the reign of Christ for one-thousand-years on the earth; almost all do. The problem is that the leadership is completely aware of the *Marriage* and the *Millennium*, yet rarely, if ever, teach the intricate details of the actual *post-rapture* events, and the importance of those events for the success or failure of our current Christian walk. The apostles and early church saints would be astounded and appalled at our lack of teaching on these things. And so is our Lord! This lack is doubtless one of the reasons Jesus looked forward to our day and gave commentary:

"When the son of man comes, will He really find faith on the earth?"

Luke 18:8

Likewise, in Jesus' story of the ten virgins, who were waiting for their Bridegroom to come, all ten were found sleeping and slumbering, when the Bridegroom showed up! Are we awake, ready, and looking for His coming with understanding?

A complete study of some of the previously listed prophesied events, beginning with the *Second Coming of Christ and Millennial Reign of Christ*, is outside of the scope of this book, even though I refer to the *Second Coming* nearly twenty times, and the *Millennium* over thirty times. However, those mentions are incidental to the purpose of this book. Our scope concludes with the *Marriage* and *Supper of the Lamb*, for reasons that will become crystal clear, as we go along.

Nevertheless, it's worth noting that immediately following the *Marriage and the Marriage Supper of the Lamb*, a new era will begin, initiated at the Second Coming of Jesus with His saints to this earth. The Second Coming of Christ will signal the beginning of that One-Thousand-Year Reign of Christ. I find it interesting that if you or I were to live to be a hundred-years-old, we would say that we lived a very long life. But what about the fact that His saints will live, once again on this earth, another one-thousand-years before we segue into the next part of God's eternal plan in the eternal Kingdom of God?

What will you be doing during that one-thousand-years on earth? What role will you be privileged to play; or perhaps, lack the privilege to play in the coming Kingdom? Our assignments and privileges in the Millennial Kingdom will reflect how well we did at allowing the Holy Spirit to fulfill God's purpose in and through us during our current, earthly lifetime. Or, putting it another way, how well we did in choosing to allow the Holy Spirit to live the life of Jesus in and through us. This is a big deal, to say the least! This should cause us to stop and consider the priorities of our lives today and going forward. After all, what did Jesus mean when he distinguished between "good and faithful servants" and "wicked servants," and the consequences of each judgment. He was not talking about servants going to heaven or hell in that parable. He was talking about the *quality of life in the Millennium and the eternal Kingdom of God*. Beware! This is not some little game.

It is not the ultimate objective of this book to simply disclose facts throughout the Bible about *The Incredible Key, the Mystery of God*. It's much more practical than that. Like any other key, this *Incredible Key* exists for the purpose of unlocking something. By having *The Incredible Key* in our spiritual hands, we will be able to unlock the Endtimes and the Book of Revelation, which is essential to sanctification today, and in our preparations for eternity. To the surprise of some believers, if we do not pursue understanding of the prophetic Endtimes, we are being offensive to the heart of our Bridegroom, and we are grieving His Spirit. Are we the bride of Christ, or not? It is ludicrous even to try to imagine a wedding day arriving, only to discover that the bride has forgotten, disregarded, taken lightly, and did not use well what time she had to prepare. What if, in fact, she didn't even get a wedding dress? Who are we kidding? Again: *This is a big deal*. It is an eternally big deal to the heart of Jesus, our Bridegroom; and He will not take lightly our being ill-prepared for the *Marriage of the Lamb*.

By unlocking the critical truths in the *Mystery of God*, it is my intent, and I believe it is God's desire, for the reader to see Jesus in a more glorious light. The hope is that our love for our Bridegroom will abound in a way that reflects how a bride would love her Bridegroom.

For those reasons and more, it matters what you believe about the Endtimes. A majority of Christians I speak with, asking about the Endtimes, acknowledge they are "coasting toward the rapture."[3] They are not necessarily saying that they don't really care about it. They care about it, but their common response is that since they have no idea when Christ is coming, and since they can't "do anything about it anyhow," they "coast." Without condemning anyone in that condition of mind and heart, it is tragic and sad that we break the heart of our Bridegroom, the One who purchased us to be His bride by means of His suffering and the shedding of His own blood! It's no wonder why the Apostle Paul wrote the following verses. You will notice that I refer to them numerous times throughout this book, and for very good reasons.

> "… *Christ also loved the church and gave Himself for her, that He might sanctify and cleanse her with the washing of water by the word, that He might present her to Himself a glorious church, not having spot or wrinkle or any such thing, but that she should be holy and without blemish.*"
>
> Ephesians 5:25–27

This is the heart of Jesus for His bride! We would do well to learn what happens when those in His Bride-Church do not love Him enough to prepare themselves for His special day.

Earlier, I said that what we believe about the Endtimes really does matter. What we know matters, because what we know and meditate on in our hearts directly affects how we live."

As a man thinks in his heart; so is he."

Proverbs 23:7

As the reader may be aware, there are a number of differing opinions among believers as to the order of events surrounding the rapture of the Church, the timing of the rapture, and where the rapture is shown to occur within the Book of Revelation. To understand whether the rapture will occur before, or during, or near the end of, or after the Tribulation Period, we must, once again, understand the role of the *Mystery of God*. To test whether or not a particular teaching about the chronology of the Book of Revelation is correct, we must know the placement, context, and fundamental importance of the *Mystery of God* within the Book of Revelation and we must include all references to this *Mystery* throughout the New Testament. Only then, can we see events clearly.

The pursuit of understanding prophecy is a holy task. The Apostle Peter tells us that the prophets "inquired and searched diligently" to understand the events surrounding Jesus' first coming, ministry, and the salvation He would bring. He goes on to say that those things, for which the prophets so diligently sought to understand were for us to know. Therefore, we are privileged to *"inquire and search diligently"* to know and understand (1 Peter 1:6-12). Furthermore, why does Jesus tell us this? "Blessed is he who reads and those who hear the words of this prophecy, and keep those things which are written in it; for the time is near" (Revelation 1:3). And this? "Behold, I am coming quickly! Blessed is he who keeps the words of the prophecy of this book" (Revelation 22:7).

In this book, our *Key*, the *Mystery of God*, is introduced, highlighted, and described. The *Mystery of God* is like God's traffic officer, standing in the middle of the Book of Revelation. If we keep our eye on the *Mystery of God*-officer, he will direct us. The biblical truth of the *Mystery of God* is the litmus test for rightly understanding Endtimes truth. It is the paradigm through which our personal understanding is to be examined and determined. It is primary, not secondary. It is essential, as we will see together.

When I was first introduced to the biblical truth of the "*Mystery of God*," I was bewildered as to why I had been unfamiliar with it up to that point. I had read the Bible many times, so I was completely aware that there were *mysteries* mentioned in the Bible. Nevertheless, I had somehow passed right over the *Mystery of God* without so much as even pausing to research or ponder it. But soon, I learned that the *Mystery of God* is central, not only for understanding the Book of Revelation, but for more fully comprehending the overall plan of God, especially in the End, and concerning my own ending. *The Mystery of God has been and is a profound and eye-opening "revelation!"*

The Holy Spirit is the One who highlighted this pivotal Revelation 10:7 passage about the *Mystery of God*. This passage provokes a question, which begs for an answer—a biblically sound answer! So, let's read Revelation 10:7 one phrase at a time, pausing for meditative impact and clearer comprehension.

> "... *in the days of the trumpet call.*
> ... *to be sounded by the seventh angel.*
> ... the *Mystery of God* would be *fulfilled* [**finished, completed**].
> ... just as **he announced to his servants the prophets.**"

This provokes numerous questions: What does God mean when He says: "... *the Mystery of God will be completed ...*?" And what is this *Mystery of God*; and what in this Mystery needs to be *"finished"*? Since this verse doesn't define the *Mystery of God*, does the general context define or describe it? Do other Scripture passages describe or define it? Since this Mystery will begin to be completed at the sounding of the trumpet, in what way does the completion of this *Mystery of God* affect the Endtimes? When and how will the *Mystery of God* be completed? What else has to happen before it is completed? Does the Bible specifically answer these questions? The answer is *yes, the Bible answers those things, and many other important questions connected to them!*

We will learn that the key factors, about which Christians are often most interested regarding the Endtimes, are each found in the immediate context of this specific trumpet. Note that this seventh trumpet is the last "trumpet" in Revelation and the last trumpet in the entire Bible.

Here are the key factors in the immediate context of Revelation 10:7 and Revelation 11:15-18.

- The full context of the **seventh** [**last**] **trumpet** involves the two chapters, Revelation 10 and 11;
- *the resurrection* [with the rapture following, based on many proofs] (11:18);
- *the judgment of the saints and prophets* (11:18);
- *the rewarding of the saints and prophets* (11:18);
- and later, we will see that the events found in Revelation 10 and 11 are chronologically inseparable from the *Marriage of the Lamb* to His bride (19:7-10).

I am not foolish enough to believe that every Christian passionately cares about the Endtimes. But I **am** foolish enough to believe that we should, even must, care, if we are going to walk in the will of God and if we are going to give attention to the same things God is currently giving attention to in our world! I **am** foolish enough to believe the words of Jesus and His apostles, all of whom confirm our need to care greatly. For instance, concerning the condition of faith at the time of His return, Jesus said:

*"... when the Son of Man [Jesus] comes, **will He really find faith on the earth?**"*

Luke 18:8

Will faith be lacking throughout the earth? Do I, do you, lack faith that pleases Him. This should cause any sincere believer to pause and consider the condition of their own life of faith, as the time of His return draws very close; and for that matter, the condition of our faith at the time of our death, if we die before His return.

The Apostle Paul wrote:

*"For the time will come when **they will not endure sound doctrine**, but according to their own desires, because they have itching ears, they will heap up for themselves teachers; and they will turn their ears away from the truth, and be turned aside to fables (unbiblical, fictional ideas)."*

2 Timothy 4:3-4

The apostle had stated just a few verses before that many in the last days will have …

"… the appearance of godliness, but denying its power. Avoid such people."

2 Timothy 3:5, ESV

In Paul's first letter to Timothy, he gave an extremely stern warning for those of us who will be living in the last of the last days before Christ's return, when he wrote:

"Now the Spirit expressly says that in latter times some will depart from the faith, giving heed to deceiving spirits and doctrines of demons …"

1 Timothy 4:1

Some might protest this idea, because after all, they know that they *"are not giving heed to deception and false doctrines."* But if that same protesting believer has little to no interest or knowledge of the Endtimes teachings of Scripture, that lack of knowledge inherently leaves that believer vulnerable. Ignorance is our enemy. To throw up our hands about the subject of the Endtimes is not a valid option. We should cry out to God to receive a *"love of the truth,"* and to pursue Him for greater understanding (2 Thessalonians 2:10.)

The tragic truth is that many who are already poised for becoming deceived say they are too busy to worry about the Endtimes, the Book of Revelation, and such. Those folks horrify me; they do not know what they are saying! (I didn't say that I don't love them; I said they horrify me, and it is for their sakes that I am horrified!) Having an apathetic attitude about the Endtimes and the Book of Revelation flies in the face of Christ Himself, because the Endtimes is near and dear to His heart and plans. ***"The testimony of Jesus is the spirit of prophecy"*** (Revelation 19:10). Do we not understand that the Endtimes is so closely identified with Jesus that the very words, "The End," are one of His many names given to us in Scripture to describe who Jesus is? In Revelation 1:8, Jesus is quoted: *"I am ... the Beginning and the End."* That is not a lighthearted play on words. The *End* is rich with truth about who He is. (We will expand on this in **Part III.**)

If you have the least bit of desire and interest in knowing, understanding, and having a truly biblical revelation or understanding concerning the Endtimes, then count yourself greatly blessed by God's mercy and grace. Having an active desire for a clearer understanding of the Endtimes is a remarkable advantage in these last days. May God pity those who do not have that. With such a desire and vision, we are more prone to receive His wisdom for living out His priorities in our words and actions "as the Day approaches." We will listen more intently to His *"small still voice,"* living a life of restraint concerning the temptations of our flesh, the world, and the devil.

Have we considered the truth, which says, [When God's people have] *"no prophetic vision [understanding, revelation] the people [of God] cast off restraint ..."* (Proverbs 29:18, ESV)? If we were to read that same verse from the positive side of it, it would tell us this: *When we as God's people* **do have** *a prophetic vision, understanding, and revelation, we* **will not** *cast off restraint.* I contend that today's Church, in general, is unrestrained. We have become so worldly in our lifestyle that surveys show that the way church goers live is no different than those who do not go to church. It makes sense. Many of us know too little of the kind of fear of God (driven by a passionate, reverential love), which causes us to live a restrained life. As the Lord opens our eyes to understand what is ahead of us in the Endtimes, we will want the Holy Spirit to live the life of Christ in and through us, which should be the only life we should desire for the world to see flowing through us to them.

When Jesus returns, He wants His Bride to be living a "cleansed," restrained, holy life, by and through His Spirit's power. If anything is needed in the Church today, it is a healthy dose of *restraint*. I understand something about that. I have failed the Lord and others in so many ways, but I do not want to be among those who fall down and stay down. I can testify that we should run the other direction to the arms of Jesus, as fast as possible! We need to be among those who cry out to God, receive forgiveness and cleansing, get up, wash our feet from the dust of living in this world, and press into Him more than ever! But without a growing, healthy, hungry-hearted understanding of what is ahead of us in the near future, we will do exactly what the Scripture says—we will tend toward casting off restraint!

Often, I engage Christians in conversations about the subject of the Endtimes, specifically because I am fully aware that there are many believers who are not urgently concerned about it; and because those who are not urgently concerned, should be. I have found that the vast majority of believers are discouraged and dismayed by the purveyors of outlandish, unbiblical ideas about the Endtimes in recent decades. Additionally, there are so many differing and opposing *opinions* in the Christian marketplace of Endtime ideas, which creates an incapacitating tsunami of confusion within the body of Christ about biblical prophecy.

Even among those folks who are interested, many tend to become severely distracted by everyday life, making a living, taking care of the children, concerns about political unrest, the news, increased violence at home and around the globe, disastrous world events, an unstable economy, job security, and more and more of the same!

Some suggest that they have enough to be concerned about without having to be worried about something they can't do anything about like Endtime prophecy. Granted we need to take care of our daily, God-given responsibilities. But this level of intense distraction is a sly, seditious, and seductive trap of Satan. Many believers are not well-read enough in the Bible to even realize that these things can be a trap.

Another common issue for many of us is the fact that the Book of Revelation and the Endtimes seem to be enigmas, far beyond our ability to make sense of it all. Some complain that it is as though the understanding of these things is locked away, and the key to unlocking them has gone missing. If any of that is how you have felt, rest assured you are not alone!

The good news is that God is **not** hiding Endtime truths from us while hoping we do not discover or understand them. The opposite is true. He wants to reveal His truths to us. God's prophetic truths are like any other jewels in God's Word. They are there to be understood. The *Incredible Key* to unlocking these truths is right in front of our eyes.

Surprising to some, it turns out that church attendees are not the only ones who might lack understanding of the Endtimes. Pastors and church leaders are hungry to understand the Endtimes, even though it is true that many of them are not well-versed in this crucial area of Bible study. In fact, it seems that one of the reasons that many pastors and Bible teachers do not wade into the waters of prophecy with their churches is because they honestly struggle to understand it. The problem with that dilemma is that church members rightly depend on their pastors to help them understand the Bible. This should be especially true concerning the study of prophetic truths. Therefore, if the pastor-shepherd of the flock fails to shine biblical light on prophetic truth, church members will be prone to read right past it; or they read it in an attempt to understand it, and become frustrated and discouraged. Satan uses this breakdown as a wedge to tempt believers to give up on prophecy. A Christian life without a true prophetic understanding is a Christian life without God's intended restraint.

> "Where there is no prophetic revelation [vision, understanding] *the people cast off restraint ...*" (the reader will notice that I quote this verse numerous times).
>
> Proverbs 29:18

Review, again, the following passage where the **Mystery of God** is highlighted, and ask yourself why it is that, until now, you have been completely unfamiliar with it. On the other hand if you are one of those who can recall having noticed this verse before, then ask yourself why it is that you may not have ever heard a sermon or read a book about it before.

> *"... in the days of the trumpet call to be sounded by the seventh angel, the mystery of God would be fulfilled [finished, completed], just as he announced to his servants the prophets."*
>
> Revelation 10:7

Most of us have been unfamiliar with the truths found in the *Mystery of God*. Granted, there are other *mysteries* in the Bible. But for our purposes, we are not addressing *mysteries*, as a general subject. Neither am I referring to the fact that God is *mysterious*. Rather, the particular mystery I am referring to is declared to be the *Mystery of God*, the *Great Mystery*; and it is that which is central to understanding the Endtimes. It is also central to how each of us will conclude the end of our walk with God in this life.

It is probably not a stretch to suggest that most of us learn about Endtime prophecy as we attend church regularly, listen to or watch Christian programming on radio, the internet or TV. Those avenues are most likely how we go about seeking answers about prophecy, right? With all of the exhaustive Bible study available to us, why is the *Mystery of God* rarely, if ever, mentioned? I use the words *"rarely, if ever, mentioned,"* because out of fifty years of having my ears attuned to prophetic study, I have only heard two Bible teachers mention it; one in passing in a debate on the rapture, and the other, one of my mentors. When did you last hear it taught, if ever? With so few teaching about the *Mystery of God*, it could be easy for us to brush this truth aside; after all, we might feel that, *if it were really important everyone would be talking about it, right?* That is absolutely not true. Life, itself, should teach us that is not necessarily the case.

How was it possible, during Jesus' ministry, for the greatest theologians of that day to be completely blind to the most important truth to ever be fulfilled? They were not only blind to the biblical truths surrounding His first coming; they were blind to Him who was, Himself, **The Truth**.

> *"… He began to teach them that the Son of Man must suffer many things, and be **rejected by the elders and chief priests and scribes**, and be killed, and after three days rise again."*
>
> Mark 8:31

Also, *"He came unto His own, and **His own did not receive Him**."*

John 1:11

Many things about Endtime prophecy are not yet as clear to us as they will soon become. But that is not the real cause for our inability to gain understanding. The greater problem is that some of what we have been taught, and are currently being taught, has been made unnecessarily complicated because speculations and opinions are pervasive, especially concerning prophetic Endtimes teaching. The cause of this problem is often relatively simple: *God's Word is simply not the **final** word*. Even though many Endtimes teachers claim that they are *not speculating or opinionating*, their adherents often remain confused. When Endtime prophecy teachers and writers traffic in unsubstantiated speculation it only muddies the waters for the average Christian, who may sincerely want to understand. Many such believers tend to give up on trying to understand prophecy as a result. They simply cannot reconcile what they "hear" in church or Christian media to what they read in the Bible! On the other hand, I would suggest that the vast majority of Christians are in another category concerning the Endtimes. These simply accept what their spiritual leaders teach, and they do so without a question or debate in their own minds, and they do not study the Bible allowing the Holy Spirit to teach them the facts. While we should thank God for preachers and teachers who alert believers to the importance of Endtime truths (I truly do!), we are still obligated, privileged and responsible for pursuing greater understanding on our own. We should not just *accept* what a teacher says by default. This includes what you are reading in this book. With your Bible in hand verify every bit of what you are reading in this book. Pray for His understanding. It matters for your own walk now, and it matters for the quality of your future Kingdom life during the Millennial Reign of Christ, and the *quality of your eternal life in the ages to come.*

In this book, I strive tenaciously to provide an in-depth, Bible-based approach to clarifying Endtime prophetic truth, allowing the Bible itself to bring us to conclusions, by the grace of God and to the best of my willing, but feeble, abilities. I hope you will recognize as you read along that we are building brick upon brick, truth verified by truth until the reader is able to reach a place of confidence that what is being said is, in fact, what God intended. It is intentional that this book does not read like Endtime fiction books, which are so prevalent in the Christian marketplace. Fiction has a place and value, if biblically based. However, the dots should be connected with specific biblical references in order to make a conclusive claim about each proposed idea.

Therefore, whatever the reader might find in this book, which can be shown not to be true to His Word, would be entirely my failure. On the other hand whatever is true in this book is to His glory alone. I realize that He alone can open the *eyes of our understanding* to receive anything from Him, and therefore, His truth is His truth, not mine. He is the Author and Finisher of our faith. And our heavenly Father has sent the Holy Spirit into our lives to guide and teach us. Any error presented here is just me getting in His way, even if unintentionally.

Writing this book has been a sobering experience. All the way through, there has been an intense prayerful desire to be true to the God's Word. I can honestly say that my writing has **not been driven** by what theologians think and teach, or what I had been taught as I grew up in a Bible-believing home. That is not to suggest that I have no regard for those things. I have the greatest appreciation and a grateful heart for my roots, and for those who have taught and guided me in the Word. The truth is that I owe so much to so many. All I am saying is that my greater respect is focused where it should be for any of us, as I am sure you will agree—on Christ and His Word, above all else and all others.

My sincere hope is that you will keep your Bible by your side, as you read this book. This is not a feather-weight book, not only because it discusses a truth with which many have been unfamiliar, but because the *Mystery of God* is a rich, eye-opening, eternally important subject, which cannot be separated from our Savior's own heart.

This book is set in **Five Parts.** These can be seen as being similar to the process of a building project. Each Part in the building process is planned in advance and has special and specific purpose.

Part by Part, *The Incredible Key,* the **Mystery of God,** is unveiled with the intent and desire that, as the reader grows in understanding of this truth, the Spirit of God will draw each of us into a more intimate relationship with Jesus, the Lamb of God, our Bridegroom. Jesus is looking forward to the *Marriage of the Lamb.*[4] Since the Church is His bride, we should have intimate knowledge and love for the *Marriage of the Lamb,* just as He does, along with other truths linked to it. It should be understood that since the *Mystery of God* reveals rich and deep truths about Christ's marriage to His Bride, it is inseparable from His heart's desire! Additionally, it is of great importance that the *Mystery* and the *Marriage* are obviously part of and cannot be separated from Endtimes prophecy; they, in fact, explain how and when the Endtimes events happen within the chronology of the Book of Revelation.

In **Part I, THE MYSTERY OF GOD UNLOCKS THE BOOK OF REVELATION,** we look at the End of this age as seen primarily in the Book of Revelation. There is a construction plan, the blueprint to the Endtimes. **Part I** is similar to an architect's rendering; in it, we will be able to see what the visible results of the construction will look like before we actually complete the building. Later on, we will learn what was in the *Master Planner's* heart and mind; what was behind this *Mystery* plan in the first place. We will better understand why He did things the way He did from Genesis to Revelation.

Most believers are aware that the rapture takes place at the sounding of the *"Last Trumpet,"* referred to by the Apostle Paul in 1 Corinthians 15:51-52. That *"last trumpet"* is the "seventh trumpet" found in Revelation 10 and 11. I am aware that some say those two references are not linked; the seventh trumpet, they say, is not the last trumpet. However, the inherent linkage between those two is the common denominator of the *"Mystery of God."* These two passages are the only two places in the Bible where the *Mystery, the last trumpet and the resurrection of the saints* are found together. The obvious reason for this is because both speak of the same events in the precise chronology as would be expected.

Chapter 1 details the fact that *The Mystery Begins to be Completed During the Days of the Last Trumpet!* The balance of the remaining three chapters of Part I substantiate the fact that **THE MYSTERY OF GOD UNLOCKS THE BOOK OF REVELATION.** This would include the other key details of the Endtimes, such as *the last trumpet, the resurrection and rapture, the judgment and rewarding of the saints, and the Marriage of the Lamb,* all of which are found in the same context of Revelation 10 and 11 (along with Revelation 19, for reasons explained throughout this book). A clear outline of the Book of Revelation will emerge in **Part I.** I explain what the concluding event of the *Mystery of God* is, in terms of how it plays out in Revelation, and then move into the other four *Parts* of the book to fully substantiate the truths behind the conclusions found in **Part I**. In other words, I explain Revelation, and then explain from Genesis to Revelation how and why the entire message of the Bible synchronizes and harmonizes so beautifully with the conclusions reached in **Part I**.

After having shown the clear chronological outline of the Book of Revelation in **Part I**, we will discover in **Part II, THE INCREDIBLE KEY—THE MYSTERY OF GOD**, those truths contained within the *Mystery of God*, which are found throughout the Bible. Beginning with **Part II**, the book will build one *Part* upon another, until we come to the *Marriage of the Lamb*, where we will see the Lamb in His marriage to the Church. By the time we get to that point, we will have made the connections of all of the primary Endtime events, demonstrating the clear outline of the Book of Revelation with the major events shown in their chronological order and location.

Anytime we are attempting to provide reasons why we should believe one thing as opposed to another in Scripture, we should be willing and able to affirm what we believe by means of many clear biblical evidences. By the time the reader has completed reading this book, the mountain of evidence will have been irresistibly compelling. We will have learned that this *Mystery* is actually described by name nearly 20 times in 13 different chapters in 7 of the New Testament books written by the apostles John and Paul. These are described in 10 major factors. The *Mystery* is further amplified in 35 distinctive details. When these are presented in our seminars, the typical response is something like: *Why haven't I ever noticed these connections before!"* Through those many evidential details, it will be seen that the truths which make up the substance of the *Mystery of God* were planned by God from before the foundation of the world. Not only did He plan it before the foundation of the world, just as Jesus and the Apostle Paul stated numerous times, He **CONCEALED** this *Mystery* in the Old Testament (actually made it "hidden" and "secret" for His reasons, about which we will learn); and then, He **REVEALED** this *Mystery* in the New Testament to the apostles, prophets, and saints; and finally, we will learn that this *Mystery* will be **FULFILLED** by Christ in the Endtimes with the last glorious detail: *The Marriage of the Lamb!*

Please keep in mind that we are not just learning cold, hard facts in all of this. We will see the essential facts converted into biblical realities that affect our day to day lives, right now. It's not just about ethereal by-and-by ideas without concrete meaning and value. The exact opposite is true. These truths should affect you in the deepest and most meaningful ways for your walk with Christ.

As explained in greater detail in Chapter 6, the Bible does not provide us with a one-sentence-definition of the *Mystery*. The *Mystery of God* encompasses the entire Bible, from Genesis to Revelation. Therefore, the definition is found in the description, rather than a classic definition as a term or phrase. For example, we will learn that understanding the *Mystery* is more like looking at the picture on the top of a jig-saw puzzle box, opening the box, and finding pieces of a puzzle. All of the pieces are there. The picture on the box tells you what it will look like once the pieces are solved. If we empty the pieces onto our work area, at first, it will seem a bit confusing. But in this case, we discover that there is good news about this puzzle! We have a lot of help, piece by piece, to determine what goes where.

As we pick up each piece of this *Mystery-puzzle*, we notice that each piece has a Bible verse referenced on it, specifically signifying which piece of the puzzle it is. Then additionally, that this same piece has additional Bible verse references written on each corner, which indicates that piece's relationship to other pieces. These references allow us to put the *Mystery-puzzle* together, as we move each piece into place with stronger and stronger assurance that we are on the right track. In light of this structure, guess work is not even a part of this puzzle. God intends for His Church to understand His puzzles, but only with His guidance, comparing spiritual things with spiritual! And that is the goal in this book. We intend to so thoroughly demonstrate the connections of the pieces of the *Mystery of God* that it becomes obvious as to God's prophetic meaning.

"These things we also speak, not in words which man's wisdom teaches but which the Holy Spirit teaches, comparing spiritual things with spiritual. But the natural man does not receive the things of the Spirit of God, for they are foolishness to him; nor can he know them, because they are spiritually discerned."

1 Corinthians 2:13–14

There are many pieces to this puzzle, and each one has its place in God's prophetic picture. Though we do not utilize this puzzle metaphor throughout this book, I use it here to provide the reader with an immediate idea of how we will approach the understanding of the *Mystery of God*.

Rather than a puzzle, beginning in **Chapter 5, WAITING**, the reader is introduced to the metaphorical cord we will actually utilize to help us maintain a mental picture of the *Mystery of God* throughout this book. We have all heard that a picture is worth a thousand words. This is certainly the case with this book. Our object, our mental picture, is a braided, multi-threaded, unbreakable, prophetic cord. Though introduced in **Part II**, the substance of this metaphorical cord is more thoroughly explained in **Part III, titled THE BRAIDED, MULTI-THREADED, UNBREAKABLE, PROPHETIC CORD**. Beginning in the Garden of Eden, the braiding of the multiple threads of the revelations of Christ and the *Mystery of God* intertwines the threads all the way through history to the *Marriage of the Lamb*. All of this as seen in Chapter 12 is, indeed, ***A GLORIOUS REVELATION*** of who Christ is!

Few seem to be aware that the *Mystery of God* was intentionally hidden by God Himself from the beginning until He revealed it to His apostles, prophets, and saints. This is stated in plain and unmistakable terms in the New Testament. We will see that the truths involved in the *Mystery of God* spanned human history all the way from the Garden to our own day, as a six-thousand-year old truth. But it was secret and hidden for four-thousand-years by God's own choosing. We will also learn why He did this.

In **Part III,** *THE BRAIDED, MULTI-THREADED, UNBREAKABLE, PROPHETIC CORD,* this cord is taken beyond a mere conceptual metaphor. It is explained by the application of multiple Scripture references. In this process, we learn that **Genesis is a Revelation of the Book of Revelation.** This takes us right into the Book of Genesis. There we will see Christ, **The Seed.** We will learn the beautiful meaning of Jesus' name found in Revelation, *"I am the Beginning and the End."* We will see with specific evidence that Christ, the Seed in the Garden, is precisely the Seed the Apostle Paul referred to, and the importance of this as it relates to the Endtimes. Paul connected Christ, who was Abraham's seed and was called the "son of promise," to the Seed (Christ) of the woman in the Garden. God said:

*"And I will put enmity between you and the woman, And between your seed and **her Seed;** He shall bruise your head, And you shall bruise His heel."*

Genesis 3:15

*"The promises were spoken to Abraham and to his seed. The Scripture does not say "and to seeds," meaning many people, but "and to **your Seed**," meaning one person, who is Christ."*

Galatians 3:16, NIV84

These are some of the fundamental truth-threads braided into the *multi-threaded, unbreakable, prophetic cord.*

There are many prophesied proofs and evidences of Christ, and therefore, the *Mystery of God,* throughout the Bible, of course. These proofs and evidences come in many forms, constantly affirming Him and His presence in the affairs of humanity and history.

- *He is seen in the form of a **type**, such as the Seed.*
- *He is seen in the various **covenants** He initiated with the saints of old, and eventually with the nation of Israel.*
- *His **shadow** is seen in many places, such as in the symbolisms found in the Law of Moses, and the system, furniture and instruments of worship in the Tabernacle and Temple. For instance: "So let no one judge you in food or drink, or regarding a festival or a new moon or sabbaths, which are a **shadow of things to come**, but the substance is of Christ"* (Colossians 2:16–17).
- *He was seen in the form of **epiphanies**. For example, He met with Abraham: "So he [Abraham] lifted his eyes and looked, and behold, three men were standing by him; and when he saw them, he ran from the tent door to meet them, and bowed himself to the ground, and said, "My Lord, if I have now found favor in Your sight, do not pass on by Your servant" (Genesis 18:2–3) Not only was this Abraham's "Lord" (which means lord or master), but we learn several verses later, this "Lord" called Himself "LORD," which is the word "YHWH," or "JEHOVAH." In other words, Christ as Jehovah, met with Abraham and Sarah, which is the occasion of God's promise that they would have a "son of promise."*

What I am demonstrating, above, is the fact that Christ is seen in one form or another throughout the Bible. In a graphic format, I provide an in-depth chart in Chapter 16, which is from the book *Interpreting the Symbols and Types*, by Kevin Conner. In that chart, he provides specific revelations of Christ in the Old Testament, book by book, from Genesis to Malachi. (I have named the title of this chart differently for my purposes. I call it *Christ the Mystery in the Old Testament*.) Those are some of the multiples of threads in the *Mystery of God*'s prophetic cord—*The Incredible Key that Unlocks the Book of Revelation and the Endtimes!* Christ's "prophetic threads" are throughout the Bible, which we will see. One of the subsections in **Chapter 16 is entitled, *A Thread is Worth More Than a Thousand Words!*** Concerning this word-picture of our prophetic cord, each thread is truly worth more than a thousand words.

Part III concludes with a subsection titled ***Indisputable***. The connection between Christ and His Bride, which is shown to be integral to the *Mystery of God* throughout the entirety of the Bible, is seen as indisputable through a myriad of biblical evidences. The importance of this cannot be overstated. ***Is it difficult*** for us to see Christ in every book of the Bible? Not if the eyes of our understanding are opened, of course. ***Is it difficult*** to understand that the blood that Jesus shed on His cross was shed for the Old Testament saints, just as it was for every believer from the cross onward in history? It is an undeniable truth that Christ's blood was shed for all saints, Old Testament and New Testament! Therefore, in **Part III**, the reader will discover that the subject of the *Mystery of God* and the subject of Christ Himself cannot be separated from the beginning of the Bible to the end. With a clearer understanding of that truth, we will discover God's plan and purpose from a different and exciting perspective.

The *Mystery of God* has always existed, even though God chose to unveil it only in the *"fullness of time,"* and according to *"His good pleasure!"* We may not be able to understand everything there is to know about the *Mystery of God*, but we can receive and accept what He has revealed to us, just as we receive and accept the truths regarding the Trinity without complete understanding. Faith is the key for what we do understand and for what we do not understand. *"Whatever is not of faith is sin"* (Romans 14:23).

Keeping in mind that the *Mystery of God* will culminate in the *Marriage of the Lamb*, **Part IV** is titled **THE LAMB AND HIS BRIDE**. As we continue braiding the *multi-threaded, unbreakable, prophetic cord* throughout this book, we will move toward that great day of the Lamb's marriage. At that time, all of heaven will break out in shouting and praise to God.

> *"And I heard, as it were, the voice of a great multitude, as the sound of many waters and as the sound of mighty thunderings, saying, 'Alleluia! For the Lord God Omnipotent reigns! Let us be glad and rejoice and give Him glory, for the marriage of the Lamb has come, and His wife has made herself ready.'"*
>
> Revelation 19:6–7

This is no minor event. This is the culmination of the Seed sown in Genesis, and it is the culmination of the announcement of the *Mystery of God* made in Revelation 10:7 to be completed during the days, or time period, of the sounding of the seventh trumpet:

"… in the days of the trumpet call to be sounded by the seventh angel, the mystery of God would be fulfilled [finished, completed], *just as he announced to his servants the prophets."*
Revelation 10:7

Part IV explains, from Genesis to Revelation, the marriage relationship between **The Lamb of God and His Bride.** The *Marriage of the Lamb* is reserved for the future, specifically after the resurrection, rapture, judgment and rewarding of the saints and prophets. While the *Marriage of the Lamb* occurs after the judgment and rewarding of the saints and prophets, the integral truths leading up to this marriage are initiated in Genesis, found to be typified throughout the Old Testament, directly stated in the New Testament, and then to complete fruition in the actual Endtime event itself in Revelation 19. The first marriage, that of Adam and Eve, provide the *first look* at Christ's marriage. Some may not have understood just how important that first marital picture is to Christ as the Church's Bridegroom. This may help us. What does it mean that there is a "first man, Adam" and a "last Adam, Christ," as the Apostle Paul stated? And furthermore, since there is a first Eve, whom God gave life by taking her out of Adam's side, is there a "last Eve," who comes from the "last Adam, Christ"? Who is this last Eve? Understanding the truths about the first and last Adam and the first and last Eve assists in explaining the *Marriage of the Lamb.*

We will also learn in **Part IV** the amazing connection between **The Last Eve and the Great Mystery.** In that context, we will see that God the Father is the *Perfect Wedding Planner.* We will come to understand more clearly, why Jesus explained to the Jews that there would be no marriage in heaven—except His own Marriage. We learn that **Betrothal in marriage** is not the same as our modern-day **engagement arrangement.** The difference is significant and relevant to the truths found in the *Mystery.*

There are important questions in **Part IV**, which plead for answers: *Does God have one Bride, or does God the Father and Christ, each, have a Bride? Of course the Trinity has to come into the mixture of these questions. Doesn't the Bible tell us that Jehovah had a wife named Israel? Doesn't the Bible tell us that Christ has a wife, the Church?* And those questions provoke, yet, other questions, such as, *Is our God a bigamist? Have we inadvertently suggested that He is a bigamist by an unsubstantiated theology; a theology which seems to indicate that both God the Father and Christ have or had separate wives?* Can it be denied that God's Word reveals **Only One Bridegroom and One Bride?** **Part IV** addresses the issue of **Old Testament Saints and the Bride of Christ.** Are Old Testament saints included in the Bride of Christ at the *Marriage of the Lamb?* In the conclusion of **Part IV**, we will make the connections between all of the questions, above, to Jesus' promise to His disciples, and us, when He said: *"I Go to Prepare a Place for You."* From the time that He came into this world as the Savior until the end of this present earth, He has been in the process of constructing that promised "place," which He calls the "whole building," "the household of God," "a holy temple" (Ephesians 2:19,21). And didn't He call the place He would prepare for His own, *The New Jerusalem* (Revelation 3:12; 21:2), which is the "city, whose builder and maker is God" (Hebrews 11:10)?

The basic concepts in **Parts II, III, IV**, and **V** are introduced in **Part I, THE MYSTERY OF GOD UNLOCKS THE BOOK OF REVELATION.** As we will see, those four *Parts* are loaded with the threads of which the prophetic cord consists.

This book begins with the *Mystery of God* as it begins to be fulfilled during the days of the sounding of the seventh and final trumpet just as 1 Corinthians 15:51-52 and Revelation 10 and 11 reveal. These specific Bible passages are significant. I want to see them with you now, even though we will review them in detail later on.

At the beginning of this Introduction, we saw Revelation 10:7, but let's see it again in the expanded context of Revelation 11, and that of 1 Corinthians 15:51-52. Please give special attention to the words I have emphasized:

> "Behold, I show you a **Mystery.** *We shall not all sleep* (die), *but we shall all be changed … at the last trumpet …* [which is when] *the dead will be raised …."*
> 1 Corinthians 15:51-52

> "… *in the days of the trumpet call to be sounded by the seventh angel, the mystery of God would be fulfilled* [finished, completed], *just as he announced to his servants the prophets."*
> Revelation 10:7, ESV

> "Then the seventh angel sounded: And there were loud voices in heaven, saying … You have taken Your great power and reigned. The nations were angry, and Your wrath has come, And **the time of the dead (resurrection and rapture)**, that they should be judged, And that You should reward Your servants the prophets and the saints …."
> Revelation 11:15–18

In the Book of Revelation many important events occur in succession: *The last trumpet sounds at which time the **Mystery of God** begins to be fulfilled, which includes the events of the resurrection, rapture, judgment of the saints and prophets, the rewarding of the same, and finally, the Marriage of the Lamb!*

On the surface, these events, sequentially, seem to be in the same chronological order of events as taught by many, who present the popularized pre-tribulation rapture concept of the Endtimes. That order of events is agreeable. But there are important differences worth noting. And it is those differences which provide the motivation for the reader to seriously consider the eternal impact of these truths regarding their own walk with Christ. The reader will see the Book of Revelation from a perspective that most who attend our seminars indicate something like this: *"Finally, I can understand the Book of Revelation for myself, instead of having just to accept and trust what you or anyone else tells me it says."*

However, the reader should be aware that this perspective, though it makes the Book of Revelation clearer, necessarily negates the currently popular concept by default. Differing perspectives cannot be true, simultaneously. But there is no reason for fear, when God opens our eyes to truth. Shouldn't we appreciate it when our understanding is made clearer regarding any subject of the Bible? Time and time again, I have experienced clarification through revelation. I have had those "ah-ha" moments when the Holy Spirit opened my eyes to understand things more clearly than ever. (Ephesians 1:18) And what a joy that is! Why wouldn't we gladly give up our own speculations in exchange for truth? Perhaps, this book will do the same for others. If so, I can only pray that it will bring you into a more intimate relationship with Christ, on a moment-by-moment basis!

Part V is titled **THE BRIDEGROOM IS COMING.** It is true that we cannot know the hour or the day, but we can know the times and seasons of His coming. That is an exciting revelation from the Word of God because it offers tremendous hope to many who have simply given up or experienced discouragement regarding their attempts to understand the Endtimes, only to hear someone suggest that it is impossible to do so.

Then the finale is found in **Part V**, where we reach the end of the *braided, multi-threaded, unbreakable, prophetic cord.* It is there that Jesus, our Bridegroom, in the most glorious of terms, finally sees the day arrive, which He has been looking forward to for thousands of years—the Marriage of the Lamb. In the last chapter of the book, **THE BRIDEGROOM TIES THE KNOT.** During the days of the final trumpet sounding, the *Mystery of God* will be completed [fulfilled, finished]. But it is when our Bridegroom *Ties the Knot at the Marriage of the Lamb* that the *Mystery of God* is finally, completely ***"finished!"***

The fulfillment of the *Mystery of God*, as seen in Revelation, is proven to be the **Key** that Unlocks the Book of Revelation and the Endtimes like no other biblical truth. Obviously, the *Marriage of the Lamb* is the **not end of the world.** Far from that being the case, it is at that moment that the *Millennial Reign of Christ*, as referred to earlier, is introduced as the next "age" that follows; and it is in that *"Reign"* in which Christ's Wife will rule with Him on the earth for one thousand years, before He makes a new heaven and new earth, as He promised. It is in that Millennial Kingdom age where the responsibilities of "priests and kings" come into the scenario. To the degree that we allow Christ's life to be lived in and through us in this life will determine our place and role in that Kingdom. Do you have that target, that goal, in your mind and heart, as you live out your life in the here and now?

If we do not have a clear biblical understanding of Endtime prophetic truths, we are warned that we will not live a pleasing life for Christ. Jesus' prophetic understanding was revealed to Him by His Father. To live like Him requires, among other things, a growing, and clearer, prophetic understanding. This is why we are told that *"Where there is no prophetic vision or understanding, the people cast off restraint."* This means we will be incapable of living by the restraining power of the Holy Spirit over the flesh, the world and the devil without a life-altering prophetic understanding. It is said of Jesus that He *"loved righteousness and hated iniquity,"* and therefore, He was *"anointed"* above others. This He accomplished through the anointed and restraining power of the Holy Spirit.

The *Mystery of God* is crucial for successful, day-to-day Christian living, and for preparation for what is ahead of us. This book concludes with the question: **Are We Really, Honestly, Getting Ready?** Or, are we "coasting toward the rapture"?

My passion is for God's family to be prepared, to be truly looking for His coming, to such a degree that it changes our priorities to His priorities. Prophetic understanding changes our love for Him to one of passion and commitment; we can become the *"ones who follow the Lamb, wherever He goes."* We can become those who *"…overcame … by the blood of the Lamb and by the word of their testimony …,"* and who do *"not love their lives to the death"* (Revelation 12:11). Is that the kind of love for Christ you have and I have?

To conclude this Introduction, I want to emphatically declare that the *Mystery of God* is inseparable from prophecy. Prophecy cannot be properly interpreted without it. Before we enter into the chapters of this book, I want to see with you just a few things which I trust will stir and fascinate the reader, and fuel a desire to know more.

Consider this! I hinted earlier that this *Great Mystery*, the *Mystery of God*, was hidden by God Himself before the world began and was not revealed until Christ and His apostles revealed it. Have you ever noticed the following references, which make that fact undeniable? Since it is undeniable, we should ask ourselves, why did God make the *Mystery of God* secret and hidden prior to Jesus' first coming? And furthermore, what difference does this make to learn the answer to the question of "why?"

Here's just a little bit of the Scripture about this:

- Romans 16:25-27 – "… the **Mystery kept secret** since the world began …."
- 1 Corinthians 2:6-8 – "… **Mystery**, the **hidden** wisdom which God ordained before the ages …."
- Ephesians 3:5 – "… the **Mystery** … in other ages **not made known** …."
- Ephesians 3:9 – "… the **Mystery**, from the beginning of the ages has been **hidden** in God …."
- Colossians 1:24-29 – "… the **Mystery** which has been **hidden** from ages and generations …."

To further fuel a desire to understand the Mystery of God, the following graphic snapshot is to be seen as a panoramic view of the *Mystery of God*.

It is very interesting to note that according to his own testimony, the Apostle Paul's preaching of this same Mystery was the specifically stated reason he was put into prison. The reason this is important is specifically because there is little to no importance being placed on the *Mystery of God* in today's teaching, preaching and writing. But how could it lack importance, when Paul put so much emphasis on it, even being willing to go to prison for teaching it?

The Mystery of God

**From the Garden of Eden
To the Marriage of the Lamb**

From Genesis to Jesus' First Coming

The Mystery of God **CONCEALED** in the Old Testament

- Romans 16:25-27
- 1 Corinthians 2:6-8
- Ephesians 3:3-5
- Ephesians 3:8-12
- Colossians 1:24-29

From Jesus' First Coming to Last Trumpet

The Mystery of God **REVEALED** in the New Testament

- Romans 9-11
- Romans 16:25-27
- 1 Corinthians 2:6-8
- 1 Corinthians 15:42-58
- Ephesians 1:1-22
- Ephesians 2:11-3:12
- Ephesians 6:14-20
- Colossians 1:24-29
- Colossians 2:1-2
- Colossians 4:2-4
- 1 Timothy 3:16
- Revelation 10-11

From Last Trumpet to the Marriage of the Lamb

The Mystery of God **FULFILLED** in the END

- 1 Corinthians 15:42-58
- Ephesians 5:22-33
- Revelation 10-11
- Revelation 19:6-9
- Revelation 21:2-3, 9-10

1. **Ephesians 6:19** – *"… that I may open my mouth boldly to make known* **THE MYSTERY** *… for which I am an ambassador* **IN CHAINS** *…."*
2. **Galatians 4:3** – *"… meanwhile praying also for us, that God would open to us a door for the word,* **to speak THE MYSTERY of Christ, for which I am also IN CHAINS** *…."*
3. **Ephesians 3:1-3** – *"For this reason I,* **Paul, the PRISONER of Christ Jesus** *for you Gentiles … how that* **by revelation He made known to me THE MYSTERY** *…."*

As I mentioned, it is my desire that, as a result of this Introduction, the reader would be at least intrigued by a few details, which may not have been noticed before. In the end, it is my hope and prayer that you will see why the *Mystery of God* is *The Incredible Key That Unlocks the Book of Revelation and the Endtimes!* On a more personal level, I pray that you will learn *How and Why the Mystery of God is the Key to Unlocking Your Own Ending Before Your Time Runs Out!*

That said, my goal is certainly **not** to highlight mere **knowledge** of the *Mystery* itself. Rather, it is that we should keep in mind that this book is not as much about the *Mystery*, as it is about the **Christ of the Mystery**, the very Lamb of God, who is our Bridegroom! At the end of the day, the *Mystery* is about Christ.

Now, let's turn our attention to learning how **THE MYSTERY OF GOD UNLOCKS THE BOOK OF REVELATION!**

Introduction Notes

[1] *English Standard Version*
[2] Billheimer, Paul E., *Destined for the Throne*, 1975, Revised Edition 1996, General Editor, Edwin Messerschmidt, Bethany House Publishers, Bloomington, MN, 16, 26, 27.
[3] "Coasting toward the rapture" was the very phrase used as a confession was made with tears by an attendee at the conclusion of the three days of teaching in one of my *Endlighten Ministries* seminars.
[4] *The Marriage of the Lamb* is found in Revelation 19:6-9. The *Mystery of God* and the Marriage of the Lamb are inseparable. Throughout this book, the phrase, "Marriage of the Lamb" is referred to over 200 times; and the phrase "Mystery of God" many more times. A primary conclusion presented in this book is that the connection between the *Mystery* and the *Marriage* plays a central role in determining the chronology of the Book of Revelation, and bringing greater insight to the key elements of the Endtimes, in general.

Part I

THE MYSTERY OF GOD UNLOCKS THE BOOK OF REVELATION

How *The Mystery of God Unlocks the Book of Revelation* is in view in **Part I**. The *Braided, Multi-Threaded, Unbreakable, Prophetic Cord*, to which I referred in the **Introduction**, reflects the *Mystery of God* throughout the Bible. Therefore, much hinges on it. It allows us to grasp the value of comparing Scripture with Scripture to interpret the Endtimes without having to engage in speculation. The process of comparing Scripture passages and truths, sets aside opinions, and allows God's own Word to speak for Him, which is the only confirmation of understanding we need. The *fulfillment of the Mystery of God* specifically provides the final facet of the key to unlocking and interpreting the Book of Revelation and the Endtimes. It provides the core truth that makes a clear outline of the chronology of Revelation possible. It stops the violence that is often done to the Book of Revelation, which results from frustrated efforts to unnecessarily force a square speculation into a round hole of prophetic interpretation.

The truth is that the Church's understanding of eschatology desperately needs to be updated. That is not a trite, trivial, or ill-advised remark. To some, the very proposal that our eschatology should be updated is perceived as near to being heretical. However, God's Word states that a day will come when our understanding of the Endtimes will be greater than it had been previously.

For those who feel that the ability to fully understand the Endtimes has always been the same down through history, there is a very important question that deserves an answer. Have we not realized, yet, that we are now in the *"time of the end,"*[5] as defined in the Book of Daniel by the angel Gabriel? Consider this: The Endtime prophecies of Daniel originally had been *"sealed"* by God Himself. God declared that they could not be unsealed until *the time of the end*. Furthermore, God defined the time of the end. According to God's definition (which is discussed in detail later), we are now in those days. Therefore, Daniel's prophecies are now "unsealed!" This being the case, additional insights are now available to us for understanding of the Endtimes (Daniel 12:4,9). This is not a little matter. The whole idea that more biblical knowledge and understanding will be opened to us in the Endtimes should not be a surprise. Jeremiah the prophet told us that in *"the latter days you will understand it perfectly"* (Jeremiah 23:20). And again, Daniel is told by the angel that there will be those in the "end" who will have "understanding." (Daniel 11:33,35; 12:10)

Are we going to be like some of the Jewish leaders, during Christ's ministry, who held to their traditions, rather than the revealed Word of God Himself, who was right in front of them? Wouldn't we be much better off to become like those noble Jews in Berea who were willing to study to see if what was being taught by Paul was, indeed, true?[6] May God help each one of us to not be so married to our own ideas and traditions that even the plain statements of Scripture will not be enough to cause us to consider fuller biblical insight and understanding.

How deep are we into the Endtimes? Does anyone really know? Well, of course, God knows. We would all agree, but has God revealed it to us in His Word, so that we can actually understand how deep we are into the Endtimes; that we are so very close to the Tribulation and the coming of Christ? Again, keep in mind I am **not referring** to the setting of **a specific day, hour, or date.**

Could I suggest that we should ask Him for whatever understanding He wants to give us, rather than limiting ourselves to our current perceptions? We should do what the prophets did, who *"… inquired and searched carefully"* [for understanding] (1 Peter 1:10). We should be like the Bereans, mentioned earlier. As we review the outline of the Book of Revelation together, we will be amazed at just how clearly we can understand the Endtimes.

Lastly, we will see the *Mystery of God* being fulfilled. It will be completely fulfilled at the *Marriage of the Lamb*. Jesus, the Bridegroom, will *Tie the Knot* in that *braided, multi-threaded, unbreakable, prophetic cord*, which begins in the Book of Genesis and continues all the way to the end of the Book of Revelation. At that point, the *"saints and prophets, and all of those who fear Your name"* will have already heard the last trumpet; they will have already been resurrected and raptured; they will have already faced the judgment and will have already received whatever rewards are due (Revelation 11:18), and then and only then, they will experience the glorious *Marriage of the Lamb!*

Chapter 1

THE MYSTERY WILL BE COMPLETED DURING THE DAYS OF THE LAST TRUMPET

"... in the days of the trumpet call to be sounded by the seventh angel, the mystery of God would be fulfilled [finished, completed], just as he announced to his servants the prophets."

Revelation 10:7, ESV

"Then the seventh angel blew his trumpet ... [this is] the time for the dead [resurrection of the saints] to be judged, and for rewarding your servants, the prophets and saints, and those who fear your name, both small and great, and for destroying the destroyers of the earth."

Revelation 11:15,18, ESV

"Behold! I tell you a **Mystery.** We shall not all sleep, but we shall all be changed, in a moment, in the twinkling of an eye, at the **last trumpet.** For the **trumpet** will sound, and the **dead will be raised** [the resurrection] imperishable, and we shall be changed."

1 Corinthians 15:51–52, ESV

"For the Lord, Himself will descend from heaven with a shout, with the voice of an archangel, and with the **trumpet of God.** And the **dead in Christ will rise** first [the resurrection]."

1 Thessalonians 4:16

The Scripture references listed above are fundamental to understanding this chapter, and they provide elements of the chronology of key events in the Book of Revelation and the Endtimes. Reading them as an introduction is very useful. Also, may I suggest that having a Bible available is an obvious tool. This is an examination of Scripture truth; therefore, may I ask you to join me in doing a little bit of *digging* as we roll along through this chapter. Bible study can require that we put our gloves on and dig a bit. But I promise we will not break out in a sweat!

There are disagreements among some as to whether the rapture takes place at the end of the Tribulation, or at the beginning of the Tribulation Period, or even at some other point prior to God pouring out His wrath on the earth. The current popularized concept is the "pre-tribulation rapture" concept. The proponents of that concept believe that the Church will be raptured (taken up to "meet the Lord in the air") *before the Tribulation begins on earth*. It is not within the scope of this book to review and study every "rapture" concept being taught today. However, since the "pre-tribulation rapture" concept is the most popularized, I have chosen to contrast what the Scriptures teach concerning the Endtimes compared to that concept. In the process of making that contrast, other Endtime perspectives will be addressed by default.

Although differences exist among most of us who teach and write about eschatology, there is almost universal agreement as to the list and sequence of Endtime events, as laid out in the Scriptures. Most believe the following to be the obvious and correct order:

1. *The sounding of the last trumpet;*
2. *the resurrection;*
3. *the rapture;*
4. *judgment of the saints;*
5. *the rewarding of the saints;*
6. *the Marriage of the Lamb and the Marriage Supper; and then*
7. *the Second Coming and the Reign of Christ for one thousand years on this earth,*
8. *Satan is bound and cast into the bottomless pit for one thousand years;*
9. *Satan is loosed at from his prison, only to be decimated, and cast into the lake of fire and brimstone, forever, along with the beast and the false prophet;*
10. *the final Great White Throne judgment of the unsaved, and*
11. *the making of a New Heaven and a New Earth.*

It should be fairly obvious that if we can learn where those events are found, in that order, within the Book of Revelation, we will have found the chronology, whatever it may be. That should make the chronological outline of the key events indisputable. Throughout this book, we demonstrate that the answer to all of this is found in *The Incredible Key That Unlocks the Book*

The Mystery Will Be Completed During the Days of the Last Trumpet

of *Revelation and the Endtimes*; that is, the *Mystery of God*. By allowing us to look at the events of the Endtimes through the lens of the *Mystery of God*, we discover that God has provided a clear picture of how these key prophetic Endtimes events will roll out, and thereby, the ability to understand the Book of Revelation more clearly. In this book, that clearer picture has been substantiated by a voluminous number of Scripture references intended to offer confidence to the believer, who may or may not have been through formal biblical training. This should demonstrate that Christians can actually understand the basics of the Book of Revelation without going to seminary or Bible college in order to grasp it.

It is our belief that the reason the body of Christ is so confused about the Endtimes, causing many to give up on understanding it at all, is fairly simple. Many sincere Christians have listened to, watched, and read about the Endtimes over the years, sometimes for decades, because they have sincerely wanted to know and understand. These are those who, in fact, care about the Endtimes, and they love God's Word. Yet, they are discouraged and confused because they sense the disconnect. We want to assist in changing discouragement into joy and excitement, and into a deep yearning to know and walk closely with Jesus more than ever before.

Many brothers and sisters in Christ, with whom I have personally spoken, have expressed their discouragement. I believe that many, if not most of them, have sincerely paid attention to what they have been taught, and they have taken it at face value, trusting their particular teachers. Most of them have continued to read the Bible for themselves, searching for answers. But when they attempt to reconcile what they read in the Bible with what they have heard from various sources, they find themselves, at best, still confused. I cannot guess how many times I have heard people tell me their stories of discouragement. Let's be clear. The pursuit of understanding by these folks is not because they have *itching ears*, or that they are those who just want to learn more for the sake of merely learning more. For them, what they have heard does not ring true to them, but they keep hoping and praying for answers.

Amazingly, a number of pastors have even confessed to me that they remain confused, even though they simultaneously confess that they can easily recite the list of the currently popular details they have learned over the years. Furthermore, **when** many of them teach on the Endtimes, that is, ***if*** they teach it at all, more often than not, they highlight the major points from among the current popularized ideas, and that's it! They don't go into much detail because many are sincerely unsure. On the one hand they are wise in their reservations to teach, in that they will not be guilty of teaching that which they have little to no confidence in the veracity of what they would be teaching. On the other hand each teacher is responsible to pursue God's Spirit to open their eyes so that they can feed the sheep with the enlightening work of the Spirit of God. This matter is so very serious! Pastors and teachers desperately need to have an awakening in the matter of the Endtimes, especially since we are drawing near to the end of this age.

One of the reasons for this general confusion and discouragement is that for decades, now, there has been a deluge of imagination-driven, speculative Endtime teaching flooding the Body of Christ. Having traveled to thirteen foreign countries, on several continents, I have found that the same problem exists where western eschatological influence has prevailed.

I don't know how to point out these things without someone suggesting that I am being unChristian in my criticism toward others who teach popular ideas. I do not have a lack of love for anyone who names the name of Christ. That love, however, does not and should not obligate me to agree. In fact, the same love, which requires me to disagree when necessary, also requires me not to denigrate. It seems to me that it should be easy to know whether or not someone is on a mission to attempt to be right for the sake of being right, rather than to earnestly and honestly seek to know the truth. If we are seeking just to be right, then there can be a tendency to crush others to reach the goal. But if we seek the truth, then there is a tendency to allow the fruit of the Spirit to prevail in that pursuit. That should be our modus operandi because it is His way. I sincerely trust you will sense our desire for His Spirit to shine through as you are reading.

So, in the spirit of agreeing to disagree, consider this. In some cases, prophecies fulfilled in the life, death, and resurrection of Christ were precursors of what He would finally and fully accomplish when the *Mystery of God* begins to be fulfilled. To explain, consider this, for instance. When Jesus arose from the dead, did that keep all saints afterward from dying? Of course not, but didn't He conquer death, as we claim so often in our teaching? Yes, He did! My point is that we will not yet experience the eternal impact of His conquest over death until the *Mystery of God* is completed, *as spoken by the prophets*. In 1 Corinthians 15:51-58, we are told that the last trumpet will sound and the dead in Christ will be raised incorruptible. When God's people receive their new-incorruptible bodies, they will have experienced victory over death, but not until then. Christ's conquering of death will have become our own experience, at that moment. Death on the earth will continue, but death will no longer have any effect on those who go in the rapture because their ***victory*** over death had just taken place for them.

Just to be clear, that doesn't mean that death will have been ***destroyed*** at that point. It only means that the Church will have had victory over death. The passage in 1 Corinthians 15:51-58, referring to the saints having ***victory*** over death, cannot mean that death is destroyed at that point. In fact, earlier in 1 Corinthians, we are told that *"the last enemy that will be destroyed is death ..."* (1 Corinthians 15:26). There is a biblical and common sense distinction between ***victory and destroyed.*** When then, does death get destroyed? That takes place just after Satan is cast into the lake of fire. The *last enemy*, death, is destroyed when it is cast into the lake of fire, as is seen in Revelation 20:14, where it says, *"Then Death and Hades were cast into the lake of fire ..."* (Revelation 20:14). After that, God's Word reveals that *"... there shall be no more death ..."* (Revelation 21:4). ***That*** is when death will have been destroyed.

The Mystery Will Be Completed During the Days of the Last Trumpet

Jesus conquered death, which was prophetic in one sense; because death, like Satan, though crushed and conquered by Christ, is yet to be destroyed until we see that the final destruction occurs in Revelation 20:10, 14 and 21:4.

Another tragic phenomenon taking place is that it seems as though many have come to rely on speculative fiction to connect the dots, rather than connecting the dots by means of biblical confirmation found in clear and verifiable terms. Fiction, though it can have a place in teaching or writing, is so popular and so pervasive within the Body of Christ that many Christians actually believe that the fiction novels are founded in sound, strong doctrine and that they represent a reasonably good portrayal of biblical reality. If an Endtimes fiction book is based on the truth of God, then great, but the reliance on fictitious ideas as primary approach to understanding the Endtimes may be a tragic admission of the fact that we are simply making up what we cannot prove in clear biblical truths.

Could it be possible that the lack of effectiveness in turning back the tide of wickedness, in our country and around the world could largely be because the Church has lost its way concerning the prophetic Word? To hear some tell it, prophecy is not central to the effectiveness of the Church in the world. But that's a far cry from what the Scriptures teach. Groaning in His spirit, as He looked at the day in which we live, Jesus said, *"When the son of man comes* [referring to His own return] *will He really find faith on the earth?* I found many examples of astoundingly misguided, and sometimes misleading, teaching about the Endtimes, as I was performing my ongoing research writing this book. I want to address some of the more important elements, which tend to keep believers either desensitized or inoculated from biblical Endtime truth.

The Mystery of God and the Sounding of the Last Trumpet

In the process of researching for this book, it was not difficult to find something written by a well-respected pre-tribulation-rapture proponent. Since I was focusing on the *last trumpet*, I was able to find good resources representative of their perspective. I wanted to document their opinion about that trumpet which the Apostle Paul said would signal the resurrection of the saints, and which would also enable the living saints to join those who were to be resurrected to meet the Lord in the air.

I feel that I am sufficiently qualified to discern whether or not someone represents the pre-tribulation rapture concept at a studied level. I formerly held to that teaching for some thirty years, so I have a very thorough understanding of it. Plus, I have been studying the Endtimes and prophecy for over fifty years.

In my research for this book, I came across a particular article that I felt was representative of the pre-tribulation concept; it was posted online. It was written by a well-known Endtime prophecy teacher.[7] I have footnoted the online link for the reader to be able to go there to confirm my notes. I have no desire to highlight personalities in this book. My purpose is to provide a typical pre-tribulation-rapture position regarding the *last trumpet* as found in 1 Corinthians 15 and the *seventh trumpet* as found in Revelation 10 and 11. Again, I love my brothers and sisters in Christ with whom I might disagree. My goal is to write what I believe the Scriptures teach. So, this is not about negatively criticizing him, or anyone else. I think it is, nevertheless, useful to provide readers with pertinent points from the pre-tribulation rapture perspective. This assists in bringing comparisons and distinctions of two views to the forefront. Besides, I assure you that this man is quite willing to defend his position. I do him no harm by directly referring you to his website. He, nor I, am hiding what we believe. Therefore, I believe my approach to be reasonable, both toward that writer, and for your sake, as a reader. And I hope you will receive it, accordingly.

Remember to put on your work gloves—a little bit of digging is required. Although I am typing vigorously, I'll gladly wait a moment, if you would be so kind to review those three passages found at the beginning of this chapter one more time before we dig in. Go ahead. I'll wait right here till you return!

Our brother in Christ stated that the "**SEVENTH** *trumpet and its adjoining resurrection*" in Revelation 10:1-7 and 11:15-18 is not the same "**LAST** *trumpet, and its adjoining resurrection*" referred to in 1 Corinthians 15:51-52, and in 1 Thessalonians 4:13-18 (emphases in his quotes are mine). Referencing J. Dwight Pentecost's book, *Things To Come*, he went on to explain that there are *"many trumpets"* in the Bible, and that the *"seventh trumpet"* in the *"series of trumpets"* found in Revelation 6 through 11, is not the *"last trumpet,"* referred to by the Apostle Paul in 1 Corinthians 15:51-58.

I found myself asking questions, such as: *When it comes to the use of the word **last** in the phrase "last trumpet" in 1 Corinthians 15, doesn't that imply that there is more than one trumpet somewhere in Scripture related to the "last trumpet?" Which trumpets are they and where are they found?* There are many trumpets in both the Old Testament and the New Testament, to be sure. However, since we are dealing with the Endtimes trumpets, and not symbolic types or shadows of trumpets, which are definitely seen in the Old Testament, let's narrow this down to the New Testament. Since there is no contradiction in Scripture, and since God's prophetic Word is *confirmed* and is *sure*, it would seem reasonable to look for and to find trumpets within the context of the Endtimes in the New Testament.

The Mystery Will Be Completed During the Days of the Last Trumpet

Since we are discussing a specific trumpet—the *"last trumpet,"* let's first establish where we find those specific words. They are found in one of our three introductory verses:

*"Behold, I tell you a **mystery**: We shall not all sleep [die], but we shall all be changed—in a moment, in the twinkling of an eye, **at the last trumpet**. For the trumpet will sound, and the **dead will be raised** incorruptible, and we shall be changed."*

1 Corinthians 15:51–52

Having established the fact that there will, indeed, be a *last trumpet*, this requires that there must be either one or more additional trumpets. Since we are discussing the Endtimes, it should be obvious that the one or more additional trumpets are Endtime trumpets. Whatever else this *last trumpet* is, it is **not** a trumpet being blown on a mountain somewhere in the Old Testament; and this would hold true, even if that Old Testament trumpet were *symbolic* of the *actual trumpet*, being referred to prophetically. The last trumpet is the actual last trumpet. In the Endtimes, if there is a *last*, there has to be a *first*. This trumpet would naturally be found in the New Testament, and that it would be found in Revelation hinges on the discussion about the Endtimes. And as is stated in 1 Corinthians 15, it would be found in the context of the **resurrection from the dead**. Now, let's pull together biblical facts to gain further understanding.

One of the key reasons for the failure to identify which trumpet in Revelation is the last trumpet referred to by the Apostle Paul, we must take into consideration the profoundly important fact that such identification does not singularly depend on locating the trumpet only. As we will see, to identify the last trumpet in Revelation hinges on the **conjunction of the seventh trumpet with the Mystery of God**, in the same, immediate context. By discovering those two key factors in the same, immediate context, we are safe to assure ourselves that God is referring to the same events, through the comparison of Scripture with Scripture to confirm the truth. To add further and greater evidence that those two factors, conjoined, present the clear truth, if we can find the "resurrection" of the saints in that same, immediate context, our assurance and confidence should increase, exponentially, to the point of being conclusive. This is, in fact, what we will see clearly.

The last of the trumpets in Revelation and the entire Bible, is seen precisely when the *Mystery of God* is being fulfilled during the "days" or time period of the sounding of the seventh trumpet. *This is important.* 1 Corinthians 15:51-52 teaches that the sounding of the "last trumpet," along with the rapture, takes place, conjunctively, as the *Mystery of God* is being "finished" or "fulfilled" (Revelation 10:7; 11:15-18). A vitally important fact is that the sound of the *seventh trumpet* is the initiator of the Endtimes fulfillment of the *Mystery of God*. By neglecting or disregarding the contextual combination of the *Mystery of God* and this *last trumpet*, many have stumbled past it, leading them to deny the connection between the trumpet in 1 Corinthians 15 and the trumpet in Revelation 10 and 11. This seems to be the case with our writer friend. Some are so singularly focused on the trumpet issue that they don't even see the consistent connection between the *Mystery* and the *trumpet*. Both passages of Scripture are referring to precisely the same trumpet. So, when we read Revelation 10 and 11, our focus should **include** the seventh trumpet as a common denominator for interpretation, but not singularly. If the reader misses this point, the Endtime train will go off the Endtime tracks. The other common denominator for interpretation is found on the track called the *Mystery of God!* That track, that *Mystery*, **includes** the last trumpet. Again, it should be noted that the initiation of the completion of the *Mystery of God* occurs within the "days" of the sounding of the seventh trumpet.

Since we are asking the reader to keep more than one thing in mind at a time, as we seek to connect the dots, let's read those key verses again, as a refresher.

"...in the days of the trumpet call to be sounded by the seventh angel, the mystery of God would be fulfilled [finished, completed], just as he announced to his servants the prophets."
Revelation 10:7, ESV

"Then the seventh angel blew his trumpet ... [this is] the time for the dead [resurrection] to be judged, and for rewarding your servants, the prophets and saints, and those who fear your name, both small and great, and for destroying the destroyers of the earth." (brackets are mine for easier reading).
Revelation 11:15,18, ESV

By taking the time to walk through the process of interpreting all three of our focus passages, we will be able to judge and discern the facts for ourselves, just as the Scripture reveals them. I am not asking you to simply disregard what you, or our writer-friend, or others say or believe about this important truth. I am asking you to consider what is being said by God Himself in His Word, as you study and compare Scripture passages. Notice the following highlighted details, because those are the keys to comparison in our study of the passages.

Three REPEATED Prophetic Factors

1 Corinthians 15	Revelation 10 and 11
(verse 51) MYSTERY	MYSTERY (10:7)
(verse 52) TRUMPET	TRUMPET (10:1,5,7; 11:15)
(verse 52) RESURRECTION	RESURRECTION (11:18)

The Mystery Will Be Completed During the Days of the Last Trumpet

1 Corinthians 15:51–52:

"Behold, I tell you a **MYSTERY**: *We shall not all sleep, but we shall all be changed—in a moment, in the twinkling of an eye, at the last* **TRUMPET**. *For the trumpet will sound, and the* **DEAD WILL BE RAISED** *incorruptible, and we shall be changed."*

In Revelation 10 and 11, just as is seen in 1 Corinthians 15:51-52, the same three common denominators are specifically and undeniably included here also in Revelation 10 and 11:

Revelation 10:7, 11:15, 18:

"… *in the days of the* **TRUMPET** *call to be sounded by the seventh angel, the* **MYSTERY OF GOD** *would be fulfilled, just as he announced to his servants the prophets … the seventh angel blew his TRUMPET …* [this is] *the* **TIME OF THE DEAD [RESURRECTION]** *to be judged, and for rewarding your servants, the prophets and saints, and those who fear your name, both small and great …" (brackets are mine for easier reading).*

Revelation 10:7; 11:15,18, ESV

It's important to point out that Revelation 10 and 11 are in precisely the same context regarding this seventh and last **TRUMPET**. In Revelation 10:1, 7 and in Revelation 11:15, we are able to quickly see that the last trumpet is being contextually referred to.

- **Revelation 10:1, 7:** "*I saw still **another mighty angel** (in addition to the previous six angels) coming down from heaven … in the days of the voice* [the trumpet voice] *of the seventh angel …."*

- **Revelation 11:15:** "Then *the seventh angel* blew his trumpet …."

There may be an explanation out there, somewhere, but I do not recall having read a pre-tribulation rapture proponent's explanation of these verses, in which they attempt to amplify, define, or highlight the phrase, the *"Mystery of God."* Why does the Spirit of God specifically highlight these undeniably vital Endtimes events in 1 Corinthians 15 and Revelation 10 and 11, by anchoring them with the truth called the *Mystery of God?* Furthermore, why would anyone cast it aside? What right does anyone have to do so?

But now, let's consider a few additional factors, all of which are among those events that are known to occur subsequent to the resurrection and rapture; that is, the judgment and rewarding of the saints and prophets. These, **unsurprisingly**, happen to be listed in chronological order, along with the *Mystery, the trumpet, and the resurrection*, just as they should be, when we read Revelation 10:7 and 11:15-18. Once your eyes are truly open to see this, the prophetic light begins to turn on and shine brighter. No one can honestly disregard these factors, nor should they; there is no need to do so.

There is no denying that the seventh trumpet in Revelation 10 and 11 is the last trumpet in the series of seven trumpets, all of which are *Endtime trumpets*. There is no denying that this particular trumpet is the last of all trumpets to be found in the Book of Revelation. It is this seventh and last trumpet, and it is found in Revelation 10 and 11. There is no denying that the **last trumpet referred to in the entire Bible** is the seventh trumpet in Revelation 10 and 11. All of these plain and simple facts are impossible to deny unless we violate the context through fictitious speculation. There is no justification for denying this fact.

Shouldn't these many biblical connections be enough to cause us to, at least, consider the possibility that we have misunderstood the chronology of Revelation? Aren't these clear facts, at least, enough to cause us to want to dig in to see if, in fact, there is something to all of this?

For most of us, what we have been taught would lead us to think that the list of events that we find in Revelation 10 and 11, should somehow also be found Revelation 4:1-2. After all, Revelation 4:1-2 is where the pre-tribulation proponents try to convince us that the resurrection and rapture are supposed to be taking place. You can read the commentaries of almost any pre-tribulation writer and you will see that they speculate that the rapture occurs in Revelation 4:1, where John is taken to heaven. They suggest John's experience of being taken to heaven is supposed to represent the Church being taken up to heaven. We are told that we should believe that this event is supposed to picture the rapture. But read it for yourself. John specifically confines this experience to himself, using the pronouns **"I"** and **"me."** *"After these things, I [the Apostle John] looked, and behold, a door standing open in heaven. And the first voice which I heard was like a trumpet speaking with me, saying, "Come up here, and I will show you things which must take place after this." Immediately I was in the Spirit; and behold, a throne set in heaven, and One sat on the throne"* (Revelation 4:1–2). It is poignant and significant that there is not the slightest hint of anything about any reference to the last trumpet in Revelation 4:1-2. The closest thing to the last trumpet is the *first* voice ... *like a trumpet*. I am not hinging my thoughts on this point, but a *first* is not a *last*; pure and simple. It seems that the Holy Spirit penned the specific use of the phrase, "*first* voice ... like a trumpet," rather than "*last* voice ... like a trumpet." One thing is quite certain, this "first" is not the "last" trumpet, no matter how one might look at it. It is, in fact, the antithesis of the last!

Look at the evidence in Revelation 4:1-2; not even one of the many key events we have reviewed, are found in, or near, or even in the entire section from Revelation 4-9.

The Mystery Will Be Completed During the Days of the Last Trumpet

You cannot find in that entire section anything about the *last trumpet*, the *resurrection and rapture*, the *judgment and rewarding of the saints*. It really does require a fiction book, filled with extraordinary speculation and conjecture, to squeeze any one of those events into Revelation 1 through 9. *That's because those events are simply not there. They are nowhere near that text; and they are not even close to that context.* Millions have allowed themselves to believe it. And why shouldn't they believe it? After all, their spiritual leaders have told them that this is what it **means**, even though it absolutely does not even begin to say it. Read it for yourself. Does it even hint at those key events in Revelation 4:1-2? The truth is that in order to hold to the pre-tribulation concept in Revelation, they have to somehow establish the rapture near the beginning of Revelation. They are *finding* something that is **not there** to be found! There may be other ideas on which to hang the pre-tribulation concept, but Revelation 4:1-2 is not one with an ounce of merit. (While I am using emphatic terms to make a strong declaration of the fact that there is not even "an ounce of merit," once again, I want to also say that I do not wish my intentions or spirit to be received as derogatory toward my brothers and sisters in Christ, who happen to hold to such ideas. I know they love the Lord and His Word, as do I.)

Here's the good news! We do find our list of key events in broad daylight, right under our noses, in Revelation 10:7 and Revelation 11:15-18. Again, this is not difficult, if we will simply read the plain language of the Word of God instead of opinions, speculations, and conjecture, whether it is our own or that of any others.

No matter what our current view of the Endtimes might be, why would anyone simply disregard the fact that the key events are clearly not found in 4:1-2? If these simple facts are disregarded, then we do violence to God's own method of showing us what He means by what He says: *We should all want to responsibly confirm any truth of the Word by the Word!*

The good news is that those are not the only connections or clarifications to consider. With the above facts stated, God, **unsurprisingly,** adds more proofs that the resurrection and rapture are not seen in the Book of Revelation until Revelation 10 and 11. This is what God *always* does for us. He makes specific connections so that we can be certain that He is referring to the same set of events.

Because 1 Thessalonians 4 is universally agreed to be linked to this same *last trumpet* and *resurrection*, let's bring it into the mix to further confirm and assure us that what we are concluding is, in fact, what God intends for us to understand and believe. After all, I would suggest that there are only a very few, if any, pre-tribulation rapture teachers in the world who would say that the trumpet, referred to in 1 Corinthians 15:51-58, and the trumpet referred to in 1 Thessalonians 4:13-18, are not the same trumpet. Our writer-friend certainly makes that connection boldly. I might add, so do I. If God's Word makes this connection, I certainly want to join hands with God, and any other believer.

This discussion about the *last trumpet* is no little matter, as all agree, regardless of our eschatological understanding. God's Word counts this truth as an essential factor for each of us in understanding the chronology of the Endtimes events. And how these Endtimes events are interpreted directly affect my life and yours. So, while we may have to take the time and energy to wrestle with details to make sure we understand God's meaning of these things, it is well worth that time and energy. It is important to the Lord Jesus, and therefore, it should be important to every one of us.

Strangely, our brother in Christ, who wrote the article, also theorizes that because Revelation 10 and 11 specifically does not use the words *last trumpet*, and instead it uses the words *seventh trumpet*, it seems that he has taken personal and arbitrary license to declare that it is **not the** *last trumpet*. There's only one little problem. He, nor I, nor you, has the last word on the last trumpet! God's Word does not offer wiggle room, here, and neither should we; as we will see!

Determining the truth about this last trumpet is very important for you, if you are one who has had the idea that you will be raptured out of this world before the Tribulation. This is important because if we breeze past this vital issue, we will likely fail to see the full picture. By default, this will be like putting blinders on to prevent additional light that we should be receiving.

It is critical that we understand the flaw, the inconsistency, in what is being said in the writer's article. He claims that the trumpet referred to in 1 Thessalonians 4 **IS the *last* trumpet.** Interestingly, neither 1 Thessalonians nor Revelation 10 and 11 call the trumpet, the *last* trumpet. But he claims that the reason the seventh trumpet in Revelation 10 and 11 is not the *last* trumpet is because it does not say *last*. Then it seems that without realizing it, he turns right around and claims that the trumpet in 1 Thessalonians 4 is the *last* trumpet, even though it doesn't use the word last, either. If he were not so obviously sincere, I would say that kind of reasoning is almost silly. It goes beyond silly; it is dangerous because it is so obviously erroneous. Every day, ordinary Christians read this, and are left with the expectation that they should believe it, simply because someone perceived to be an authority said it.

As he provides his opinion of the passage, he begins to list the key facts found in the text. But he clearly stops short. Blinders seem to block his ability to consider *the other essential facts,* **which are plainly stated, and which need no further interpretation.** He claims that the very words *last trumpet* would have been used in Revelation 10 and 11, if God had intended the *seventh trumpet* to be understood as the *last trumpet*. That conclusion does not satisfy simple rules of interpreting Scripture, no matter how sincere. His conclusion doesn't even satisfy his own rules of interpretation. In other words, if God **has to use** the word **"last"** in Revelation 10 and 11 in order for it to be the same *last* trumpet found in 1 Corinthians

The Mystery Will Be Completed During the Days of the Last Trumpet

15:51-58, then why doesn't God have to use the word *"last"* regarding the trumpet in 1 Thessalonians 4 in order to prove that it is the same trumpet?

The reader might wonder if I am trifling and bickering, making a mountain out of a molehill. This is *not a trifling matter*; it is a matter of the greatest magnitude for making clear God's order of things in the Endtimes, as seen in the Book of Revelation and everywhere else in Scripture.

When respected leaders make such contradictory claims, what are we to do? All we can do is to highlight the truth for those who are truly hungry for the truth, rather than seeking to merely be right when disagreeing with any brother or sister in Christ. God and His Word are not in the business of contradictions. Every one of us has failed to interpret and understand God's Word correctly, at some point in our growth in His truths. I certainly have. Our writer-friend, doubtless, has no desire or intention of contradicting God's Word. I would hope that each of us would want to receive help from others when we lack in any points of Scripture. In this case, this brother seems to reach his conclusion based on a preconception, rather than allowing the Word of God to be the *only judge and jury, "comparing spiritual things with spiritual things,"* as the Apostle Paul stated.[8] The fact is that when we anchor the Endtimes in the truth of *The Key* of the *Mystery*, confusion will vanish, as we will see with even greater clarity as we move forward.

Please don't misunderstand. To be sure, I know that 1 Thessalonians 4: 13-18 refers to the *last trumpet* and *rapture*, even though the word *last* is not used there. I am merely comparing his statements because of their inconsistency regarding the references to the Scripture he uses. The trumpet referred to in 1 Thessalonians 4:13-18 is clearly the last trumpet, as he and I would both agree! We see the details in context, including the key connected factors of the resurrection of the saints, who will have already died, and the catching up of the saints to be with the Lord at the rapture. 1 Thessalonians 4:16–17 says:

> *"For the Lord, Himself will descend from heaven with a shout, with the voice of an archangel, and with **the trumpet** of God. And the **dead in Christ will rise** first …."*

What more do we need to see in order to agree that this is absolute proof that the trumpet of God in 1 Thessalonians 4 is precisely the last trumpet of 1 Corinthians 15:51-52? Almost every evangelical prophecy teacher, including our friend who wrote the article, will tell you that these verses in 1 Thessalonians refer to the time of the rapture, as signified by the *trumpet* and the *resurrection from the dead*. Therefore, they also believe that this is the same trumpet and resurrection as is found in 1 Corinthians 15:51-52. I completely agree. Why would anyone **not agree?**

That is precisely the point. We all agree on the passages in 1 Corinthians 15 and 1 Thessalonians 4, but proponents of the pre-tribulation concept fail to include the same trumpet of Revelation 10 and 11. Isn't there just as much, even more, clear evidence of the detailed connections between 1 Corinthians 15 and Revelation 10 and 11, as there is between 1 Corinthians 15 and 1 Thessalonians 4? How many ways can it be said? The key details of the trumpet and resurrection are seen in all three; I Corinthians 15, 1 Thessalonians 4, and Revelation 10 and 11. So, we must review and compare them in specifics.

The *Mystery of God* enables even greater affirmation of the last trumpet in both passages. *By adding the Mystery of God into the comparisons and connections, we are simply adding greater evidence that all of these Scripture passages are referring to the same trumpet and resurrection, etc.*

We all have our "theories". However, I think it is fair to say that as we grow in our understanding of God's Word, we tend to grow from having our own perceptions and theories about truth into a better understanding, as we confirm truths by comparing Scripture with Scripture. I want my theories to be dashed to pieces. *Do you?* An important and honest question is this: Why would anyone be afraid of our own theories falling apart? **We should want our own theories to fall apart!** If in the face of the clear statements of the Word of God, our theories do not hold up, then we should praise God that our theories have been dashed to pieces, and this should give us reason to rejoice. Every time that happens to our theories, our doctrines are further purified, and our understanding is free to become clearer. That is precisely what I am seeking to point out. Simply read those very references we have been discussing. The simple process of reading through them is all that is necessary to see that they have a strong connection, not only in the fact that they are referring to the Endtimes, but because they are the same factors, textually and contextually. The Holy Spirit is connecting **all** of them, not *some* of them.

At the beginning of this chapter, I asked you to join me by putting on your spiritual work gloves and to grab your spiritual shovel so that we could dig a bit. The time has come, as we dig just a bit deeper. Due to our familiarity with these key verses, let's please not skip past them. Let's prayerfully read for clear comprehension. For emphasis, I will embolden and capitalize specific words or phrases to assist us in getting the picture.

> *"Behold, I tell you a* **MYSTERY**: *We shall not all sleep, but we shall all be changed—in a moment, in the twinkling of an eye, at the* **LAST TRUMPET**. *For the trumpet will sound, and* **THE DEAD WILL BE RAISED** *incorruptible, and we shall be changed. For this corruptible must put on incorruption, and this mortal must put on immortality. So when this corruptible has put on incorruption, and this mortal has put on immortality, then shall be brought to pass the saying that is written: "Death is swallowed up in victory."*
>
> 1 Corinthians 15:51–54

The Mystery Will Be Completed During the Days of the Last Trumpet

*"... in the days of the **TRUMPET** call to be sounded by the **SEVENTH ANGEL**, the **MYSTERY OF GOD** would be fulfilled [finished, completed], just as he announced to his servants the prophets"* [Emphasis and insertions mine].

Revelation 10:7

*"Then the **SEVENTH ANGEL SOUNDED**: And there were loud voices in heaven, saying, "The kingdoms of this world have become the kingdoms of our Lord and of His Christ, and He shall reign forever and ever!" "... the **TIME OF THE DEAD**, that they should be judged, And that You should reward Your servants the prophets and the saints, And those who fear Your name, small and great."*

Revelation 11:15–18

*"For this we say to you by the word of the Lord, that we who are alive and remain until the coming of the Lord will by no means precede those who are asleep [those who have already died] For the Lord Himself will descend from heaven with a shout, with the voice of an archangel, and **AND WITH THE TRUMPET OF GOD. And the DEAD IN CHRIST WILL RISE** [in resurrection, in the rapture] first. Then we who are alive and remain shall be caught up together [in the rapture] with them in the clouds to meet the Lord in the air. And thus we shall always be with the Lord."*

1 Thessalonians 4:15–17

Can you see the connections? Is it a mere coincidence that these passages provide us with the only places in Scripture that make all of these connections; and that these are all pertaining to the Endtimes events? With this simple reading, how can this be unclear? Where is the confusion? The sounding of the trumpet and the resurrection of the saints have a primary connection. Then when we add the *Mystery of God* to these comparisons, they become inextricable. But that's not all. There are additional key linking factors in these passages, which provide greater assurance that these are all referring to the same thing.

I want to see with you the key linking factors in all of these Scripture references (1 Corinthians 15, 1 Thessalonians 4, and Revelation 10 and 11) merged into one short list. It paints a clear picture for key Endtimes events:

The primary issue of the *Mystery* (Revelation 10:7; 1 Corinthians 15:51) spans all of Scripture (as we will see throughout this book). Because these verses are thoroughly connected with the other key Endtimes passages, the *Mystery* becomes the glue that binds them together.[9]

1) The Lord descends with a shout (1 Thessalonians 4:16);
2) With the voice of the archangel (1 Thessalonians 4:16);
3) With the trumpet of God (1 Thessalonians 4:16);
4) The seventh and last trumpet is to sound;
5) We are told in Revelation 10:7 that the *Mystery of God* will be finished [fulfilled, completed] during the "days" or time period of the seventh (which is the last trumpet);[10]
6) Both the resurrected saints (Revelation 11:15-18), and the living saints, are caught up together in the clouds to meet the Lord in the air (1 Thessalonians 4:17);
7) The judgment of the saints takes place (Revelation 11:15-18). Obviously, in order for the saints to be judged, the saints have to be *caught up* [raptured] *to meet the Lord.* The fact of being *caught up* links this directly with (1 Thessalonians 4:17, 1 Corinthians 15:51-57);
8) The rewarding of the saints takes place (Revelation 11:15-18). In order for the saints to be rewarded, the saints have to be judged, first, which once again links Revelation 11:15-18, 1 Thessalonians 4:17, and 1 Corinthians 15:51-57.

Where does all of this leave us? A useful question to ask is this: *If the rapture of the Church takes place in Revelation 10 and 11,* why do so many say that the rapture of the Church takes place in Revelation 4:1-2? That is a reasonable question. It is a *make it or break it* question for pre-tribulation proponents. Since, in Revelation 4:1-2, there are **no connections** to the last trumpet, the resurrection, or judgment, or rewarding of the saints, that fact alone, at minimum, reduces the possibility that the rapture is found there? Only through the most speculative approach to Revelation 4:1-2 could someone even suggest that the rapture is found there.

Most evangelical believers have been taught that the rapture will occur before the Tribulation. Friend, if you are one who hopes in that idea, just imagine your confusion when the Tribulation begins without the rapture taking you out of here first. You will suffer great confusion and disorientation, as the "birth pangs" intensify just prior to the beginning of the Great Tribulation. (see Matthew 24:1-14) This should be sobering to anyone who has been relying on that escape route.

As I mentioned earlier, a fundamentally significant reason for much confusion in the Church about the Endtimes is the misguided belief that Revelation 4:1-2 is where the rapture occurs chronologically in the Book of Revelation. In the next chapter, we will seek to alleviate some of that confusion, by taking a look at **The Big Picture in Revelation.**

Chapter One Notes

[5] Daniel 8:17; 11:35, 40; 12:4, 9.

[6] "These (Jews) were more fair-minded than those in Thessalonica, in that they received the word with all readiness, and searched the Scriptures daily to find out whether these things were so" (Acts 17:11).

[7] http://www.bibleprophecyblog.com/2013/07/the-last-trumpet.html (All quotes regarding this subject and referred to herein, are cited from the article found at the link).

[8] I confess that I have done the same thing before, and it is likely that I have blind spots in my own understanding. We all do. That's the beauty of the body of Christ; we can help one another to more clearly understand God's Word.

[9] The reader will find it useful to take a moment to become familiar with the *Mystery of God* Chart on page xxxviii. Additionally, there is a very different and more in depth chart in Appendix A on page 379, to understand just how interconnected and interrelated all of the *Mystery* factors and *Mystery* Scripture references really are, especially concerning their linkages to the Endtimes.

[10] Several times in this book, I reference this same Greek language concept, as it relates to the *Mystery of God*, because of its importance: The Greek "proleptic aorist" grammatical structure provides that the *Mystery of God* will be fulfilled during the "days" of the seventh trumpet. During those same "days" more fulfillment-events will occur, namely, the resurrection, rapture, judgment, rewards, and the *Marriage of the Lamb*!

Chapter 2

THE BIG PICTURE IN REVELATION

"…Come up here, and I will show you things which must take place after this."
Revelation 4:1

"…You must prophesy again concerning many peoples, nations, tongues, and kings."
Revelation 10:11

"Let us be glad and rejoice and give Him glory, for the Marriage of the Lamb has come, and His wife has made herself ready." And to her, it was granted to be arrayed in fine linen, clean and bright, for the fine linen is the righteous acts of the saints. Then he said to me, "Write: 'Blessed are those who are called to the marriage supper of the Lamb ….'"
Revelation 19:7–9

The Big Picture:
1 Corinthians 15, Ephesians 5, 1 Thessalonians 4, Revelation 10-11, Revelation 19

As we compare spiritual truth with spiritual truth in the Bible, whether Endtime prophecy or any other truth, receiving guidance and understanding from the Holy Spirit is God's prescribed means of conforming our understanding to God's meaning. This is true individually and in our study fellowship with other believers. The Holy Spirit is the one who has instructed us to *"Study to show ourselves to be approved by God as workmen who do not need to be ashamed, thereby rightly dividing or discerning the Word of God …."* When it comes to studying the Book of Revelation to *"show ourselves approved by God,"* a dependable outline can be a useful study tool.

Some tasks in Bible study, though important, might feel tedious, even boring for some, as far as the process is concerned. I was often impatient with the tediousness of my high school

English grammar classes. Among the many facets of my English classes that bored me to tears was that of having to develop outlines. Admittedly, most of my tears were more as a result of mediocre grades in English grammar than boredom, if the two could be distinguished. Outlining was particularly bothersome. Having been out of high school for five decades, my perspective on these things has changed quite a bit. Outlining has strangely become a precious commodity; one which has dramatically increased in value.

Am I boring you? Please don't be bored! As you will see, this little bit of tedium has intentional value. So, you might ask, what is so good about an outline? To bring credibility to the description of an outline, I have borrowed from Indiana University. No, that's not my alma mater; and no, I was not born there. Okay, here's the confession: Their definition popped up first in my online search. Here it is: *"An outline is a kind of graphic scheme of the organization of your paper. It indicates the main arguments for your thesis as well as the subtopics under each main point."*[11] Is that not as clear as you would like it to be? I will now attempt to translate for the rest of us: *About that which you are writing, an outline demonstrates a more simple, organized perspective of the main points, along with sub-points.* How did I do? OK? That's great! Please send a note of commendation to my high school English teacher. Trust me, she will know me by name. These teachers never forget star students. And as a matter of another personal confession, I can assure you; neither do they forget those on the other end of the stardom spectrum!

I have found that outlining can be indispensable regarding the Book of Revelation. Properly outlining the Book of Revelation is like the value of mining for diamonds. If Revelation is a diamond mine (and it is!), then in practical terms, extracting and utilizing an outline of God's intended message is indispensable for clarity. Later, in this chapter, I have not only provided a line-by-line outline in a typical textual format, but I have also provided a more graphic layout of the Book of Revelation. I do not believe that I am promising too much to say that once you grasp the outline and the graphic layout, much of what may be, to some, a muddied understanding of Revelation will begin to become clear.

However, an outline is merely the skeleton. The internal parts, and the muscular system, and the flesh have to be put onto the bones. In this and the two following chapters, we will watch the dry bones outline come to life. I can promise this will be anything but boring. **Seeing**, and being able to **understand what you see**, in Revelation is quite exciting and spiritually awe inspiring.

In addition to an indispensable outline, as we review passages that are referring to the same truths in comparison with other prophetic passages, the biblical requirement will be met, *"By the mouth of two or three witnesses shall a thing be established.* That is a basic requirement for correctly interpreting passages. Additionally, it is required in the Lord's instruction through the Apostle Peter that we are to exclude *private or personal interpretations*[12] in the important work of *rightly dividing or rightly handling* the Scriptures. In other words, the Holy Spirit has provided God's Word, the Bible itself, as the singular means of confirming God's Word. Personal opinions are inadequate, even dangerous if we conclude an interpretation based on our opinions to the exclusion of a preponderance of the *clear biblical evidence*. By following those simple guidelines from Scripture, as to how God requires that we interpret His prophetic Word, we can find assurance and confidence that we have gained the understanding God intended us to receive. Yet, the greatest privilege we have in gaining understanding is through the work of the Holy Spirit. The Holy Spirit is the One who brings truth to life through His enlightenment in our spirit!

The key words or phrases I want to review with you initially are the *last trumpet*, the *resurrection*, and the *Mystery*. As we have seen, each of those key truths and events are found in 1 Corinthians 15:51-52, and in Revelation 10-11 (highlighted in 10:7 and 11:15-18).

This has to do with the precise wording of God's own statements; not opinions. Whatever happened to the Bible being dependable? I thought we believe that the Bible is **God's declared truth**, which is the only conclusive truth that we should follow. When we find precise statements from God, we must happily discard our ideas, and restructure them to match His statements. Of course this will require that we set aside preconceived notions and speculations, and seek to make sure that all of it flows without contradiction from within the whole counsel of God's Word.

If we are to ever get a clear understanding of the Book of Revelation, we must be willing to enter into the book with a love of the truth that is greater than the desire for being right for the sake of being right.

Back to the Future

Earlier, we briefly mentioned the connection between the last Adam, Christ, and the last Eve, Christ's own special Eve, His Bride. That connection has been given to us by the Holy Spirit to help us understand the chronological timing of key Endtime events in the Book of Revelation. The Great Mystery (relating to the marriage of Christ to His Church found in Ephesians 5) is the same Mystery which will be fulfilled (completed, finished) during the "days" of the sounding of the last trumpet in the entire Bible, the seventh trumpet.[13]

So, we are still in the process of fully discovering the most complete biblical answers possible for some very important Endtimes questions. Furthermore, we are about to embark on an awesome journey into understanding the Book of Revelation. For some, even many, this will be the first time the Book of Revelation becomes understandable, just as it was for me when I first learned these truths.

To assist in this journey, I want to raise some questions:

How can the resurrection and the rapture take place in Revelation 10 and 11? Isn't that in the middle of the Book of Revelation? Haven't we been taught that the rapture takes place before the Tribulation begins?

Comment: When anyone can find the last trumpet, the resurrection, and the rapture in Revelation 4, or anywhere in the larger context of Revelation 4 (which is where the popular pre-tribulation proponents attempt to fit the rapture into to the Book of Revelation), please call, text or write me. I say with all sincerity, feel free to contact me. I only ask that those who choose to respond, please do not write or call to share your thoughts in terms of opinion or preconceived speculation, based on what someone has taught you. Just provide the very words from clear biblical quotes, using the plain words and statements that God uses, and that any reasonable person using common sense can read and understand for themselves.

- **Since these key rapture-related events, seen in Revelation 10 and 11 are approximately in the middle of the Book of Revelation, does that indicate that there is a "mid-tribulation rapture"?**

Simply put: No, it doesn't mean that at all. We will answer that question in upcoming chapters. It would be premature to enter into in-depth discussion at this point. But it's important to pose the question here.

- Since the trumpet, the resurrection, the judgment and rewarding of the saints are all shown in the plain text of Revelation 10 and 11, then another reasonable question to be answered is this: **Why is the Marriage of the Lamb shown to happen in Revelation 19 at the end of the book, instead of in Revelation 10 and 11, in conjunction with other events in our list of Endtime events stated above? After all, doesn't the Marriage of the Lamb take place in sequence after the last trumpet, the resurrection, rapture, judgment and rewarding of the saints and prophets?**

Comment: The answer to this question is one of the key reasons for this chapter. In this chapter, the reader will find what might be one of the simplest, yet most surprising, truths in this book. It was for me when I first learned it. I was so surprised that I found myself reading and re-reading Revelation. I wasn't trying to re-read so I could understand it. I was re-reading, over and again, out of complete amazement. The bottom line answer to the question is this; that is, this is what we must understand about Revelation's structure. The main events of the Book of Revelation are "repeated" within Revelation. Because of this, each of the two comparative parts (chapters 4-13 and 14-19) each show the same events in chronological order. Each of the two parts provides details not specifically seen in the other. This is much like the four Gospels of Matthew, Mark, Luke and John. Each Gospel tells the life and ministry of Jesus. But each adds insights to the other, which when all are combined into a "harmony of the Gospels," a more complete and clear picture emerges. The two comparative parts of Revelation do the same thing, giving us a more complete picture of the Endtimes as seen in Revelation. Therefore, when we superimpose the first part onto the second part, the details involved in the Mystery of God come together like hand in glove. Only then does the Marriage of the Lamb take its rightful place in the chronology of Endtime events, as seen in Revelation. Suddenly, the chronology of Revelation comes into focus. All of the events included in the Mystery of God fit, just as God designed, as we will see together.

Diamonds

The Crater of Diamonds State Park in Arkansas is the only place in the world where you can pay a small $8 fee to hunt for diamonds. Any diamond found is theirs to keep. In 2015, someone from Colorado found an 8.52 karat diamond, which was the 5th largest diamond ever found there. Their website says, *"Most visitors like to dig in the soil and screen for diamonds. This usually involves searching through the first six inches to one foot of soil. Visitors can turn the soil over with a small hand tool while looking in the loose soil. Some visitors like to use a screen to sift the soil."*[14] They advertise that you can even rent an Advanced Diamond Hunting Kit for $13 a day. (No, they are not paying me to advertise this!) Less than two weeks ago, now, I drove past the freeway exit for the diamond park. I simply didn't have the time for it, and I'm the kind of guy who could zone out, and dig relentlessly from morning to night, not stopping for lunch, coming up with nothing, and walking away having had a great time of relaxation. Of course finding a diamond would be a blast too, even a small one, for extra satisfaction.

Imagine that! Advanced level diamond hunting for a total of $21 plus tax per day, including the $8.00 entrance fee. Such a deal!

Wow! What if you were given private access to the entire 37-acre diamond field to work it all by yourself. The Park Rangers then told you that the rules are that you have only so much time, then it's over … period, no further opportunity to dig. Keep in mind that in 2015, 468 diamonds were found, weighing nearly 100 karats, and over 13 of those were above one karat in weight. And don't forget about the 8.52 karat diamond found in the same year.

What if the Park Rangers, to your amazement, told you that you are guaranteed to find diamonds and that the whole idea of the Park being made available was specifically for you to find them. How would you go about digging for those diamonds since 37-acres is a rather vast area? Since you are not here with me as I am typing away, could I make a suggestion? *Wouldn't it be a good idea to hunt for those diamonds little by little? Wouldn't you want to set up a precise marking system to know where you have been, so you can be certain you have covered every square inch? Would I need to tell you that it would be a good idea to* **put your back, as well as your heart, into this process?**

The truths in the prophetic Word of God are infinitely more valuable than every diamond in that field, and for that matter, all of the diamonds in the world. So, if you will remember, I requested that you keep your gloves and shovel handy. We are about to dig for some of the most precious diamonds in the Book of Revelation, and for that matter, some of the most precious diamonds to be found in the entire Bible.

Joy in Digging!

It is my desire and goal in **Part I** to remove many of the difficulties concerning the general structure of the outline of the Book of Revelation. By doing so, we should be able to more readily understand the substance revealed in it.

In the chapters included in Part I, we will see things that are breathtaking. The greatest and most precious of which is *The Diamond*, Himself; that is, *The Revelation of **Jesus Christ*** in glorious terms as only could be expressed by the Holy Spirit.

I sincerely appeal to the reader to ***not skip*** past the following litany of verses. Take the time to read word for word and relish the glory of our Lord Jesus in the selection of a few verses from the beginning of Revelation to the end of it. These give us a little taste of His glory, wetting our spiritual appetite before we see the graph and outline of the book. In our Endtime seminars, I almost always will make this statement: *What many believers see in the Book of Revelation is the revelation of the Antichrist. But the Book of Revelation is not about the revelation of the Antichrist; it is about the revelation of Jesus Christ.* After all, isn't that precisely what the first words of the Book of Revelation states? It plainly says, "*The revelation of Jesus Christ ….*"

This Book of Revelation is ultimately, verifiably, and justifiably about our Lord, Savior, and Bridegroom … Jesus Christ! Let's read and take in His glory. Please note that the following verses are pulled out of the text from different parts of the Book of Revelation to allow us to see just those parts which speak specifically to His glory.

THE BIG PICTURE IN REVELATION

[The Apostle John said]: *"Then I turned to see the voice that spoke with me. And having turned I saw seven golden lampstands, and in the midst of the seven lampstands One like the Son of Man, clothed with a garment down to the feet and girded about the chest with a golden band. His head and hair were white like wool, as white as snow, and His eyes like a flame of fire; His feet were like fine brass, as if refined in a furnace, and His voice as the sound of many waters; He had in His right hand seven stars, out of His mouth went a sharp two-edged sword, and His countenance was like the sun shining in its strength.* **And when I saw Him, I fell at His feet as dead ...."**

Revelation 1:12–17

"You are worthy, O Lord, To receive glory and honor and power; For You created all things, And by Your will, they exist and were created."

Revelation 4:11

"And I looked, and behold, in the midst of the throne and of the four living creatures, and in the midst of the elders, stood a Lamb as though it had been slain, having seven horns and seven eyes, which are the seven Spirits of God sent out into all the earth."

Revelation 5:6

"And they sang a new song, saying: 'You are worthy to take the scroll, And to open its seals; For You were slain, And have redeemed us to God by Your blood out of every tribe and tongue and people and nation' … saying with a loud voice: 'Worthy is the Lamb who was slain To receive power and riches and wisdom, And strength and honor and glory and blessing!'"

Revelation 5:9–10, 12

"And every creature which is in heaven and on the earth and under the earth and such as are in the sea, and all that are in them, I heard saying: 'Blessing and honor and glory and power Be to Him who sits on the throne, And to the Lamb, forever and ever!'"

Revelation 5:13

"… [they] fell on their faces and worshiped God, saying: 'We give You thanks, O Lord God Almighty, The One who is and who was and who is to come, Because You have taken Your great power and reigned. The nations were angry, and Your wrath has come, And the time of the dead, that they should be judged, And that You should reward Your servants the prophets and the saints, And those who fear Your name, small and great, And should destroy those who destroy the earth.'"

Revelation 11:16–18

The Incredible Key

"They sing the song of Moses, the servant of God, and the song of the Lamb, saying: 'Great and marvelous are Your works, Lord God Almighty! Just and true are Your ways, O King of the saints! Who shall not fear You, O Lord, and glorify Your name? For You alone are holy. For all nations shall come and worship before You, For Your judgments have been manifested.'"

Revelation 15:3–4

"And I heard the angel of the waters saying: 'You are righteous, O Lord, The One who is and who was and who is to be, Because You have judged these things. For they have shed the blood of saints and prophets, And You have given them blood to drink. For it is their just due.' And I heard another from the altar saying, 'Even so, Lord God Almighty, true and righteous are Your judgments.'"

Revelation 16:5–7

"Then a voice came from the throne, saying, 'Praise our God, all you His servants and those who fear Him, both small and great!' And I heard, as it were, the voice of a great multitude, as the sound of many waters and as the sound of mighty thunderings, saying, '**Alleluia! For the Lord God Omnipotent reigns! Let us be glad and rejoice and give Him glory, for the Marriage of the Lamb has come, and His wife has made herself ready.**' And to her it was granted to be arrayed in fine linen, clean and bright, for the fine linen is the righteous acts of the saints. Then he said to me, 'Write: Blessed are those who are called to the marriage supper of the Lamb!' And he said to me, 'These are the true sayings of God.'"

Revelation 19:5–9

"Now I saw heaven opened, and behold, a white horse. And He who sat on him was called Faithful and True, and in righteousness He judges and makes war. His eyes were like a flame of fire, and on His head were many crowns. He had a name written that no one knew except Himself. He was clothed with a robe dipped in blood, and **His name is called The Word of God.** And the armies in heaven, clothed in fine linen, white and clean, followed Him on white horses. Now out of His mouth goes a sharp sword, that with it He should strike the nations. And He Himself will rule them with a rod of iron. He Himself treads the wine press of the fierceness and wrath of Almighty God. **And He has on His robe and on His thigh a name written: KING OF KINGS AND LORD OF LORDS.**"

Revelation 19:11–16

"Then I saw a great white throne and Him who sat on it, from whose face the earth and the heaven fled away. And there was found no place for them. And I saw the dead, small and great, standing before God, and books were opened. And another book was opened, which is the Book of Life. And the dead were judged according to their works, by the things which were written in the books. The sea gave up the dead who were in it, and Death and Hades delivered up the dead who were in them. And they were judged, each one according to his works. Then Death and Hades were cast into the lake of fire. This is the second death. And anyone not found written in the Book of Life was cast into the lake of fire."

Revelation 20:11–15

"Then He who sat on the throne said, 'Behold, I make all things new.' And He said to me, 'Write, for these words are true and faithful.' And He said to me, 'It is done! I am the Alpha and the Omega, the Beginning and the End. I will give of the fountain of the water of life freely to him who thirsts. He who overcomes shall inherit all things, and I will be his God and he shall be My son. But the cowardly, unbelieving, abominable, murderers, sexually immoral, sorcerers, idolaters, and all liars shall have their part in the lake which burns with fire and brimstone, which is the second death.'"

Revelation 21:5–8

"'Behold, I am coming quickly! Blessed is he who keeps the words of the prophecy of this book.' Now I, John, saw and heard these things. And when I heard and saw, I fell down to worship before the feet of the angel who showed me these things. Then he said to me, 'See that you do not do that. For I am your fellow servant, and of your brethren the prophets, and of those who keep the words of this book. Worship God.' And he said to me, 'Do not seal the words of the prophecy of this book, for the time is at hand. He who is unjust, let him be unjust still; he who is filthy, let him be filthy still; he who is righteous, let him be righteous still; he who is holy, let him be holy still. And behold, I am coming quickly, and My reward is with Me, to give to every one according to his work. I am the Alpha and the Omega, the Beginning and the End, the First and the Last.' Blessed are those who do His commandments, that they may have the right to the tree of life, and may enter through the gates into the city. But outside are dogs and sorcerers and sexually immoral and murderers and idolaters, and whoever loves and practices a lie. I, Jesus, have sent My angel to testify to you these things in the Churches. I am the Root and the Offspring of David, the Bright and Morning Star.'"

Revelation 22:7–16

"And the Spirit and the bride say, 'Come!' And let him who hears say, 'Come!' And let him who thirsts come. Whoever desires, let him take the water of life freely."

Revelation 22:17

The Incredible Key

Glorious!

By merely reading the Word of God, above, we can gain a sense of the glory of Christ. Those passages, indeed, present **The Big Picture in Revelation!** His omnipotence, omniscience, sovereignty, and His majesty, and so much more, are witnessed. He is to be reverentially feared with a holy fear; the kind of fear that humbly and lovingly responds to His invitation to come to drink of the water of life freely. He, as seen in the Book of Revelation, is personally like a great diamond field. This is the *true field of dreams*—the field of "true riches."[15]

There are many testimonies throughout Scripture, which add witness to the glory of our great God and Savior, Jesus. Isaiah, the prophet, tells his experience of the glory of the LORD:

> "... *I saw the Lord sitting upon a throne, high and lifted up; and the train of his robe filled the temple ... And I said: "Woe is me! For I am lost; for I am a man of unclean lips, and I dwell in the midst of a people of unclean lips; for my eyes have seen the King, the Lord of hosts!"*
>
> Isaiah 6:1 and 5, ESV

The Apostle Paul went into the third heaven and saw this same glory with his own eyes. This was his attempt to express what he saw and felt: Paul said that he "... *heard things that cannot be told, which man may not utter*" (2 Corinthians 12:4, ESV). Paul was a man who did not lack for words. In this case, however, it is no wonder that he could not utter what he had seen?

On the Mount of Transfiguration, Peter, James, and John saw Jesus transformed right before their very eyes.

> "*And he was transfigured before them, and* **his face shone like the sun, and his clothes became white as light.** *[Then while] He was still speaking ... behold, a bright cloud overshadowed them, and a voice from the cloud said, "This is my beloved Son, with whom I am well pleased; listen to him." When the disciples heard this, they fell on their faces and were terrified."*
>
> Matthew 17:2, 5–6, ESV

In the Book of Revelation, is it any wonder that when John saw Jesus in His heavenly glory, he said this: "*And when I saw Him, I fell at His feet as dead*" (Revelation 1:17)?

Oh, that we might see Him and know Him in His glory! But dear friend, has He not given us His Word and His Spirit, by which and by Whom we are promised great and precious promises?

Through His Word, we are to be transformed: "*...do not be conformed to this world, but be transformed by the renewing of your mind ...*" (Romans 12:2). Isn't that what Jesus does for and in His Bride, the Church, by the power of the Holy Spirit, through His mighty Word? He washes our lives with His Word, so as to renew our minds. *"... Christ ... loved the Church and gave Himself for her, that He might sanctify and cleanse her with the washing of water by the word ..."* (Ephesians 5:25–27).

In addition to becoming transformed by His Word, we are also transformed by His Spirit as we gaze into His mighty Word:

> *"Now the Lord is the Spirit; and where the Spirit of the Lord is, there is liberty. But we all, with unveiled face, beholding as in a mirror the glory of the Lord, are being transformed into the same image from glory to glory, just as by the Spirit of the Lord."*
>
> 2 Corinthians 3:17–18

His Plan is for us to be transformed into His image by the Word and by the Spirit on a moment-by-moment and day-by-day basis!

All of the testimonies and truths we have just reviewed draw us to Him if we have ears and eyes to hear and see. He knows that our *hope of glory* is found in allowing the Holy Spirit to live Jesus' life through us during this life so that we will be privileged to have the greatest glory possible with Him during the Millennial Reign of Christ on earth and in eternity. He loves us and wants this for us. This is His intention, His Plan. Jesus, our Lord, Savior, and Bridegroom, bled, died and rose from the dead, and thereby overcame. Through His having overcome, He is able to offer us the grace and power to overcome the world, the lust of the flesh, the lust of the eyes, the pride of life, the Devil, and that final enemy called Death, so that He can bring us into His glory. *"... that the genuineness of your faith, being much more precious than gold that perishes, though it is tested by fire, may be found to praise, honor, and* **glory at the revelation of Jesus Christ ...*"* (1 Peter 1:6-9).

Our ultimate experience of glory will be when the Church, His assembly, His own, His Bride, is taken in the rapture and is glorified with Him at the *Marriage of the Lamb*. He desires and deserves for us to conform to His image in our outward lives by becoming transformed to His image in our inner life, by His Spirit and Word. The overcoming is not about a change someday in heaven. This is about right now, while we have breath in our bodies.

How can this happen in and for us, to the degree He desires? As is repeated several times throughout this book, the Apostle John, when writing about the coming of Christ, says this:

> *"And everyone who has this hope in Him [concerning His coming], purifies himself, just as He is pure."*
>
> 1 John 3:3

And this: The writer of Proverbs 29:18 gives us a strong admonition about the power of having a clear prophetic understanding when he writes that "*Where there is **no prophetic vision**, the people [God's people] cast off restraint ….*" This means then, that *Where there **IS** a prophetic vision, one that aligns with God's own, having set aside speculation and opinion, we will **NOT** cast off restraint…we will be restrained from the world, the flesh and the devil, as we walk with Him.*

It's not that any one of us has perfect understanding. As for me, I don't. I have yet to find any Christian writer who makes the claim that they do. Nevertheless, in this book, I seek to provide a clearer understanding of God's prophetic Word, which as stated in the verses above, will allow us to glorify Jesus, our Bridegroom, in and through our daily lives, as we become overcomers through His grace and power. This will allow us to experience His glory, both now and in eternity! Is that what you want? Hungry-hearted believers are those who passionately want to know Him and who passionately want to walk with Him being led by the Spirit. We have the joy and privilege of increasingly growing in our desire to overcome in this life for the glory of the One who purchased us with His blood.

In order to gain that clearer prophetic vision, I want to first see with you a graphic layout, and then the simple outline of the Book of Revelation. This will enable us to fill in the blanks as we go along, making sense of Revelation overall.

The Book of Revelation: The 'Unveiling' of Jesus Christ

Chapter 1 — Revelation of the Son of man and the Son of God

Chapters 2-3 — Jesus' Messages to the Churches

Chapters 4-5 — John in Heaven ~ Jesus Unseals LITTLE BOOK; Little Book Shows Details of Great Tribulation

Chapters 6 through 13

The TRIBULATION TOLD and SHOWN to John
7 SEALS and 7 TRUMPETS / Revelation 6 – 11

Revelation 10:6-7; 11:15-18
"DELAY NO LONGER"
MYSTERY of GOD BEGINS to be FULFILLED

SEVENTH (LAST) TRUMPET, Resurrection, Rapture, Judgment & Rewards

11 - 13: Amplification of details of 3 1/2 years Great Tribulation pertaining to a "Woman", Dragon, Beast, False Prophet; and beginning of fulfillment of the Mystery of God. [Chapters 11-13 each show 3-1/2 year Tribulation from three perspectives:
Chapter 11 ~ The Two Witnesses'; Chapter 12 ~ The Church's; Chapter 13 ~ The World's]

JOHN is told in 10:8-11 that he MUST EAT the LITTLE BOOK and then REPEAT the Prophecy Again
~~~
There are 42 repeated details.
Similarities are mirrored
Comparing chapters 4-13 and 14-19

Chapters 14 through 19:10

The TRIBULATION REPEATED by John
7 ANGELS and 7 BOWLS / Revelation 14 – 16

Revelation 19:1-10
MYSTERY of GOD FINISHED / FULFILLED at the MARRIAGE OF THE LAMB
Ephesians 5:22-32

17 - 19: Amplification of details of 3-1/2 years pertaining to a "Woman", the Dragon, the Beast, the False Prophet; and the Bridegroom and Bride completing the fulfillment of the Mystery of God at the Marriage of the Lamb

---

Chapter 19:11-16 — Second Coming

Chapters 19:17-20:15 — Armageddon Begins, Millennial Reign of Christ, Final Judgment

Chapters 21-22 — New Heaven and New Earth, New Jerusalem Comes Down out of Heaven

The Kingdom of God

Outline of the Book of Revelation

Chapter 1: A revelation of the Son of man and the Son of God.

Chapters 2-3: Jesus' messages to the Churches.

Chapters 4 and 5: While in the spirit on the Lord's Day, John is called to heaven; John sees Jesus, the Lamb, loosen the seals of the "little book (scroll)"; that little book is then shown to reveal what is in the 7 Seals, and subsequently, the 7 Trumpets (chapters 6-11).

Chapters 6-13: The revelation of the end is given to John by the messenger. The judgments and wraths of the Great Tribulation are seen in the 7 Seals and the 7 Trumpets (6-11).

Chapters 11-13 Involve:
- Three different perspectives on the 3 ½-year Great Tribulation Period;
- Details about the dragon (Satan), 10-horned-beast (antichrist), and the false prophet;
- Additionally, a "Woman" is seen—the Church, the Saints;
- A 7-year Tribulation Period is never mentioned in Revelation. The number seven (7) is used 54 times, but not once in reference to a 7-year Tribulation. The Great Tribulation of 3 ½ years is mentioned five times[16] in chapters 11-13, from those three perspectives mentioned above;
- During the "days" of the sounding of the seventh and last trumpet, the *Mystery of God* is to be fulfilled (completed, finished). Revelation 10:7 specifically refers to the *Mystery of God* (See 1 Corinthians 15:51-58 also). The *Mystery of God* involves the sounding of the last trumpet, the resurrection (and rapture), the judgment and rewarding of the saints, as witnessed in Revelation 10 and 11, and of course the ultimate reward to the saint is that of being a part of the Marriage of the Lamb. The *Marriage of the Lamb* is brought into the picture in Revelation 14-19, which is the repeat, or the "prophesy again," of what John had already seen in Revelation 4-13. We will identify 42 direct similarities within chapters 14-19, which are "repetitions" of what are seen in Revelation 4-13.

Chapters 14-19: The revelation of the end is given by John. John is told that he must "prophesy again," mirroring the events seen in Chapters 6-13. Then he begins to repeat the prophecies found in the "little book," which he had just "eaten," as he was instructed to do in 10:8-11. Forty-two (42) details are repeated as John follows through to "prophesy again."

— *Chapters 14-16 Involve Seven Angels and Seven Bowls*

— *Chapters 17-19 Parallel details from chapters 11-13 are repeated in chapters 17-19, with clear comparative distinctions made between the two women mentioned.*
- Details of the dragon (Satan), 10-horned-beast (antichrist), the false prophet;
- Additionally, a "Woman" – the Harlot is seen;

THE BIG PICTURE IN REVELATION

- The *Mystery of God* culminates in the *Marriage of the Lamb* (Revelation 19:1-16.) This is tied-in with Ephesians 5:22-32, where Christ and His bride are in view in the context of the "Great Mystery."
- Followed by the Second Coming (Revelation 19:1-16)

Chapters 19:17-20:15: Second coming of Christ; Armageddon begins; Satan, the Beast and the False Prophet are cast into the lake of fire; Millennial Reign of Christ; Satan is loosed for a short period, defeated and cast into the lake of fire; and the Final Great White Throne Judgment of the Unsaved.

Chapters 20-22: The Kingdom of God.

Having seen **The Big Picture in Revelation,** including the graphic and textual outlines, which are now in place for your review, I want to see with you the profound and stunning insight found in **The Revelation Divide.**

Chapter Two Notes

[11] Using Outlines, http://www.indiana.edu/~wts/pamphlets/outlines.shtml.

[12] 2 Peter 1:20 "knowing this first of all, that no prophecy of Scripture comes from someone's own interpretation" (2 Peter 1:20, ESV).

[13] Revelation 10 and 11 (The context of both chapters is the seventh trumpet).

[14] http://www.craterofdiamondsstatepark.com/digging-for-diamonds/how-do-i-search-for.aspx

[15] Luke 16:11.

[16] Explanatory note: There are actually five mentions of 3 ½ years of Great Tribulation, in three different phraseological configurations: A) one-thousand-two-hundred-and-sixty days—Revelation 11:3 and 12:6; B) forty-two months—Revelation 11:2 and 13:5; C) time, times, and half a time—Revelation 12:14. Again, a Tribulation period of seven years is never mentioned in the Book of Revelation. In each mention of the 3 ½ years it refers to the same Great Tribulation. There are no other mentions of the 3 ½ years in any other chapters in Revelation, or anywhere else in the Bible, with the exception of Daniel 9:27. However, Daniel 9:27, though it is an important passage for Endtime prophecy study, is outside of the scope of this book. If the Lord permits, our next book will address the prophecies of Daniel.

Chapter 3

THE REVELATION DIVIDE

"… You must prophesy again concerning many peoples, nations, tongues, and kings."
Revelation 10:11

"'Let us be glad and rejoice and give Him glory, for the Marriage of the Lamb has come, and His wife has made herself ready.' And to her it was granted to be arrayed in fine linen, clean and bright, for the fine linen is the righteous acts of the saints. Then he said to me, 'Write: Blessed are those who are called to the marriage supper of the Lamb ….'"
Revelation 19:7–9

In the graphic layout in the previous chapter, we could readily see it is announced in Revelation 10:7 that the *Mystery of God* will be fulfilled during the "days" of the seventh trumpet. When the last trumpet sounds in Revelation 11:15-18, other Mystery-events subsequently begin to be *fulfilled*. Notice the *trumpet sounds, the resurrection, the judgment of the saints, and the rewarding.*

"Then the seventh angel blew his **trumpet** … [next, we see] … **the time of the dead** [resurrection] *that they should be* **judged**, AND *that You should* **reward** *Your servants the prophets and the saints ….*"
Revelation 11:15-18

And all of those listed events happen within the specifically stated context of the *Mystery of God*, and the last trumpet—that is, the seventh and *last trumpet!*

"… *in the days of the trumpet call to be sounded by the seventh angel* [the last trumpet in Revelation and in the entire Bible] *the* **MYSTERY OF GOD** *would be fulfilled* [finished, completed], *just as he announced to his servants the prophets*" (Emphasis and insertions mine).

Revelation 10:7, ESV

A Little Bit of Greek

"A Little Bit of Greek" is necessary for our study of the *Mystery of God*. You will notice that several times in this book I provide a footnoted explanation regarding the Greek "proleptic aorist"[17] usage in Revelation 10:7. The original Greek language in this verse shows us that everything attached to or resulting from the sounding of this seventh trumpet is to be basically seen as a package deal, as a *whole*. That is to say, everything from the time the seventh trumpet sounds and all the way through to the Second Coming of Christ is to be seen as inclusive in the seventh trumpet's effect or results.

Before I explain the Greek structure, however, I want us to be reminded of our objective. This short exercise regarding Greek is to shine God's floodlight onto the completion of the *Mystery of God*, which occurs "in the days of", or in the time period of, the sounding of the seventh trumpet, as seen in Revelation 10:7 and 11:15-18; and then, eventually, the tie-in to the *Marriage of the Lamb* in Revelation 19:7.

When in the fullness of time God brings the *Mystery of God* to a completion at the *Marriage of the Lamb*, it will be a dramatic and climactic moment in the plan of God; and rightly so. It will be the glorious, long-planned marriage of His Son. The *Marriage* has always been and will be known as the heart of God's plan throughout history. It is, therefore, imperative that our growing understanding of the *Mystery of God* become all the more clear and complete. The following explanation will help us get there.

At issue is the fact that the *Mystery of God* involves the list of events God had declared to the prophets, and which the prophets foretold (see Revelation 10:7: "*as He declared to His servants the prophets*"). That same list of events, which were "*declared to the ... prophets,*" is detailed in Revelation 11:15-18: The list is the same list being addressed throughout this book: *The sounding of the seventh [and last] trumpet, the resurrection [and therefore the rapture], the judgment of the saints and prophets, and the rewarding of the saints and prophets*. All of these events occur in the "days" or during the "time period" of the sounding of the seventh trumpet. Each of the listed events is not necessarily completed instantly when the seventh trumpet sounds. There are "days", or a period of time, involved in the events included in the resulting effects of the sounding of the seventh trumpet. The number of days is irrelevant for our purposes, and the Bible doesn't tell us that number, even though we can know that it is a relatively short period. The previous six trumpets, which will have already sounded, involved days, or a period of time, during which many events are listed as occurring during each individual trumpet's sounding. The same is equally true with the seventh trumpet.

To be very clear, the last event in the series of events will be the *Marriage and Marriage Supper of the Lamb* [the marriage of Christ to His bride]. All of the list of events in this Seventh Trumpet occur prior to the Second Coming of Christ. At the Second Coming of Christ, He will set up His Millennial Kingdom on earth, as stated in Revelation 19:5-15.

At this juncture, we can be well served by calling on a number of scholars for their insights about Revelation 10:7 and 11:15-18. For many students of the Bible, the commentary on these passages in Revelation by Dr. John Walvoord and Dr. Roy Zuck in their *The Bible Knowledge Commentary* carries much credibility. I want to highlight the fact that Dr. Walvoord is revered among those who teach that the rapture of the Church will occur prior to the Tribulation Period. The fact that they are proponents of the "pre-tribulation rapture" concept does not mean that differing proponents cannot or do not agree on many details within the Endtimes details. We do; just not on where the rapture takes place within the Book of Revelation, along with a few other key elements. Nevertheless, I refer to them here because of the acceptance of their commentary.

Drs. Walvoord and Zuck acknowledge that the results of the sounding of the seventh trumpet in Revelation 10 and 11 extend from the sounding of the seventh trumpet all the way through to the Second Coming of Christ. They make some profound and succinct points regarding these passages, which are certainly worthy of noting here. They write:

> "[Revelation] 11:15 … the full results from the sounding of the seventh … trumpet are only introduced here and not brought to finality [here] … The fact that this [the announcement of the kingdom in Revelation 11:15] will be fulfilled at the Second Coming **_makes it clear that the period of the seventh trumpet chronologically reaches to Christ's return_** …"[18] (bracketed text and emphases are mine).

I completely agree! The *"period of the seventh trumpet"* (which is stated in terms of "days" or a period of "time") extends, or *"reaches to Christ's return"* (which means that this, of necessity, therefore includes the *Marriage of the Lamb*). We will see more about this later.

The bottom line result in the text of Revelation 10:7 and 11:15-18 is this:

1. The scene in Revelation 10:7 reveals only the "announcement" of the fact that the *"Mystery of God will be completed"* during the *"days,"* or period of *"time"* of the sounding of the seventh trumpet. The grammatical purpose of Revelation 10:7's announcement of the fact that the *Mystery of God* will be completed is not intended to state that it **begins** in Revelation 10:7. It does not **begin** to be completed at this announcement. This is because

the coming completion of the *Mystery of God* is **recognized** or **acknowledged** as a reality in Revelation 10:7, but not **realized** or **initiated** until Revelation 11:15-18.

2. The initiation or beginning of the completion of the *Mystery of God* is not prophetically **realized** until the Revelation 11:15, where we are plainly told that the seventh trumpet is blown or sounded.

So, what's so important about all of that? Perhaps, to some Christians, such Greek technicalities may not bear a lot of weight, at first. But, we must gladly remember that "every word of God is pure"; and we should gladly ascend to a clear and pure understanding of the Word of God!

I want us to look at it this way: Revelation 11:15-18 not only reveals the "sounding" of the seventh trumpet, but those few verses also reveal that the list of events in our discussion actually **begin** to be completed as part of what Dr. Walvoord describes as the "results" of the sounding of the seventh trumpet. And that is a major part of what I am highlighting. In essence, therefore, the *Mystery of God* does **"begin"** to be **"completed,"** but only as the seventh trumpet actually begins to sound in Revelation 11:15, and it is completed during those "days" of the sounding of the Seventh Trumpet.

This is the seventh and last trumpet, and it is directly tied to 1 Corinthians 15:51-52. We will see that connection in just a moment.

If you are not familiar with the idea of digging into the original Greek language of the New Testament, I can only imagine that you are reading this hoping that we will get past all of this soon. I understand. But, may I appeal to you to keep your digging shovel in hand for just a few more moments, and to give this part of our foundational information the attention it truly deserves? Putting it another way, without it you will be partially blind for the remainder of the book. So, thank you for digging with me just a bit more.

I want to us to read the actual text of our two passages, so that we grasp the important context.

*"... <u>**in the days**</u> [or period of "time"] <u>**of the trumpet call to be sounded**</u> by the seventh angel, [during those days] <u>**the mystery of God will be completed**</u> [finished, fulfilled], just as he announced to his servants the prophets."* (brackets and emphases are mine).

Revelation 10:7

*"<u>**Then the seventh angel blew his trumpet**</u>, and there were loud voices in heaven, saying, 'The kingdom of the world has become the kingdom of our Lord and of his Christ, and he shall reign forever and ever.' And the twenty-four elders who sit on their thrones before God fell on their faces and worshiped God, saying, 'We give thanks to you, Lord God*

*Almighty, who is and who was, for you have taken your great power and begun to reign. The nations raged, but your wrath came, and **the time for the dead to be judged, and for rewarding your servants, the prophets and saints, and those who fear your name, both small and great**, and for destroying the destroyers of the earth.'" (emphases are mine).*

Revelation 11:15–18, ESV

I want to assure you that it is not essential that you wrap your mind around every detail of the "proleptic aorist" of the Greek language in order to understand what the Scripture is saying. In my case, I have had the privilege of reaching out to Greek scholars for verification and clarification. In the process, they have graciously tweaked my understanding, for which I am grateful. The technicalities of whether or not the verb in Revelation 10:7 is ingressive aorist or proleptic aorist is of little importance, as it relates to the objectives of this book. Nevertheless, I feel it is important to offer sufficient clarification, so as to avoid a stumbling block or confusion for some.

Part of our objective is to learn what God has included in the "results" of the sounding of the seventh trumpet, and the list of events involved in the *Mystery of God* in the Book of Revelation. And the determination of the "aorist" usage in these verses can be seen as *distinctions without much, if any, impactful difference* as it relates to the message of the Mystery of God. Nevertheless, because this book is intended to be a foundational handbook for the truths pertaining to the *Mystery of God*, I have gladly provided added clarification, as a matter of published record.

So, we see that a series of events occur during the "days" of the sounding of the seventh trumpet, and some of those are listed in Revelation 11:15-18. This connected structure was made clear through an excellent discussion with a highly respected Greek scholar, Dr. Buist Fanning. He has graciously given me permission to quote his expertise and insights,[19] translating Revelation 10:7 from Greek to English. He states:

"I think it's correct to see the verb at the end of Revelation 10:7 as a futuristic aorist, since the temporal clauses that precede it set the temporal frame in the future: 'but in the days of the sound of the seventh angel, when he will sound his trumpet, then the mystery of God will be completed as he announced to his own servants the prophets.'

The proleptic aorist in Revelation 10:7 '... looks at the entire action as a whole that will be accomplished in the future. **This will not happen in a single instant, of course**, but the completion is seen in its entirety and its time frame is connected to the seventh trumpet ...'"

Amen! I agree that the Greek verb used in Revelation 10:7 does not indicate the "start of a process", as it relates to the "announcement" of the fact that the *Mystery of God* **will be completed.** But he is **not suggesting that there is not a series or list of events involved** in the completion of the *Mystery of God.* He is only addressing the actual Greek language used in Revelation 10:7. Obviously, then, Revelation 10:7 merely **announces** the sounding of the seventh trumpet. Revelation 11:15-18 specifically shows us the actual sounding of the seventh trumpet, and the initiation and results of the sounding of that trumpet. As the list of events begin to unfold, we can then see that they are inextricably part of the "whole" to which Dr. Fanning refers.

It is equally true that within the meaning of what he calls the "entire action **as a whole,**" it must be understood that the *whole* is made up of *parts.* In this case, the parts are the series of events affected by or resulting from the sounding of the Seventh Trumpet; that is, *the resurrection, the judgment of the saints and prophets, and the rewarding of the saints and prophets.* I should add that those very events are precisely what is referred to, when we read: "… the *Mystery of God will be completed …*" In other words, the *Mystery of God* will be completed during the "days," or "time period," of the Seventh Trumpet.

Let's recall that the Apostle Paul makes it explicitly clear that the *Marriage of the Lamb* to His bride, the Church, is the "Mega-Mystery."[20] With that in mind, we can unequivocally state that the *Mystery of God* will find its ultimate conclusion at the actual event of that *Marriage.* Of necessity, from the moment of the sounding of the seventh trumpet until the *Marriage of the Lamb,* all of the listed events are **part** of the **"whole."** How true, and how wonderful this is, just as Drs. Fanning, Walvoord, and Zuck have indicated.

Furthermore, it must be understood that when the last trumpet actually sounds (Revelation 11:15) there are certain things within the series of events which will occur in a split second, and others will not occur in such an instantaneous way. The Apostle Paul explained this in 1 Corinthians 15:51-52:

> *"Behold, I tell you a <u>**MYSTERY**</u>: We shall not all sleep, but we shall all be changed—<u>in a moment, in the twinkling of an eye, at the **LAST TRUMPET**</u>. For <u>the trumpet will sound, and the **DEAD WILL BE RAISED**</u> [RESURRECTION] incorruptible, and we shall be changed."*

Because of the series of events laid out for us in Revelation 11:15-18, we know that once that Seventh Trumpet sounds and the resurrection occurs in a "moment, in the twinkling of an eye," the remaining series of events also definitely occur during "the days [or time period] of the sounding" of the seventh and last trumpet.

The proleptic aorist verb, therefore, allows for the inclusion of the series of events, which occur within the "days" of the seventh trumpet. In the chronology of events, this takes us all the way through to the Second Coming, just after the *Marriage of the Lamb*, just as Drs. Walvoord, Zuck, and Fanning indicate.

During the time period of the sounding of the seventh trumpet, those climactic listed events in Revelation 11:15-18 ***begin*** to occur. The **resurrection** (and thereby, the **rapture**), the **judgment** and the **rewarding** of the saints and the prophets, happen in sequential order, one after the other. Yet something else remains to be included and will be seen in the parallel, repeated passage found in Revelation 19:7. That remaining, crowning event, which is the climactic event of the *Mystery of God*, is the *Marriage of the Lamb* itself! The unequivocal connection between the climactic events in Revelation 10 and 11 (the seventh and last trumpet sounding, resurrection, rapture, judgment and rewarding of saints) and the final climactic event in Revelation 19 (the *Marriage of the Lamb*) make up the highlighted list of contextual events. According to Revelation 11:15-18, they **begin to be completed** when the trumpet is sounded. Then, immediately after that trumpet sounds, "loud voices" are heard in heaven announcing and exclaiming the fact that at that juncture "the Lord and His Christ" are laying claim to the "kingdoms of this world." In other words, the events which follow the sounding of the seventh trumpet lead into the Second Coming and the Millennial Reign of Christ. So, here, the Seventh Trumpet sounds, and those key events begin to occur in sequential order:

"Then the seventh angel sounded: And there were loud voices in heaven, saying, 'The kingdoms of this world have become the kingdoms of our Lord and of His Christ, and He shall reign forever and ever!'"

Revelation 11:15, NKJV

"And the twenty-four elders who sit on their thrones before God fell on their faces and worshiped God, saying, 'We give thanks to you, Lord God Almighty, who is and who was, for you have taken your great power and begun to reign. The nations raged, but your wrath came, and the time for the dead to be judged, and for rewarding your servants, the prophets and saints, and those who fear your name, both small and great, and for destroying the destroyers of the earth.'"

Revelation 11:16–18, ESV

The loud voices and the twenty-four elders' worshipful declarations have just given us the complete layout of events from the point of the sounding of the last trumpet (as referred to in Revelation 10:7 and 11:15-18; 1 Corinthians 15:51-52; and 1 Thessalonians 4:13-17), all the way through the proclamation of the "reign" of Christ, and then the actual physical reign of Christ. He returns with His bride to the earth to set up His kingdom.

Concerning His reign on earth; first, it is announced in heaven with the emphatic statement that He has assumed His kingship over the kingdoms on earth. That declaration is made **BEFORE** He is seen as physically returning to the earth (Revelation 11:15-17; 19:6; and 19:11-20:6. (We encourage the reader to pause and review those few verses of Scripture to see the actual statements of God on this matter.

This brings up a most beautiful prophetic fact. It should be no surprise to us that we find this same exact scene found in Revelation as being formerly prophesied in Daniel 7:9-10, 13-14! In Daniel, we first see the **proclamation of Christ being given the kingdoms of this world, first in heaven**. And then He is seen physically taking dominion of the kingdoms on the earth. Both are prophesied in Daniel:

> *"As I looked, thrones were placed, and the Ancient of Days took his seat; his clothing was white as snow, and the hair of his head like pure wool; his throne was fiery flames; its wheels were burning fire. A stream of fire issued and came out from before him; a thousand thousands served him, and ten thousand times ten thousand stood before him; the court sat in judgment, and the books were opened."*

> *"I saw in the night visions, and behold, with the clouds of heaven there came one like a son of man, and he came to the Ancient of Days and was presented before him. And to him was given dominion and glory and a kingdom, that all peoples, nations, and languages should serve him; his dominion is an everlasting dominion, which shall not pass away, and his kingdom one that shall not be destroyed."*
> Daniel 7:9–10, 13-14, ESV

We read this incredibly important statement in Amos 3:7: *"For the Lord GOD does nothing without revealing his secret to his servants the prophets"* (ESV). How glorious is God's prophetic Word! Surely, we can plainly see that He does nothing without first showing it to His servants the prophets, as seen here in Daniel and again in Revelation.

This chapter is about the Revelation Divide. What does this mean? Understanding how the outline of Revelation is laid out is not as difficult as some suggest. Nevertheless, one of the more confusing tasks for many in interpreting Revelation 6-19 begins when they come to Revelation 11-13. In chapters 6-11, it is very clear what is happening: *The Seven Seals and the Seven Trumpets* are detailed. When we arrive at Revelation 11-13, the key to understanding is to realize that there are three distinct perspectives being given to us concerning the three-and-one-half years of the Great Tribulation. Those three chapters show the Great Tribulation from the perspectives of the *two witnesses, then the Church, and then, the world*.

THE REVELATION DIVIDE

Then, in Revelation 14-19:16, another section if seen, which reveals familiar themes and events. In these chapters an interesting phenomenon seems to be occurring. It seems as though these chapters are found to refer to the same set of factors as were found in Revelation 6-13. What's going on here? This can be confusing for many. One of the reasons for the potential for confusion is because most of us have been taught that this section, chapters 14-19:16, is a continuation of judgments which began in Revelation 6-11.[21] So, to those who find themselves confused, a primary reason for the confusion is that they have been taught that the the major events of Revelation chapters 6-19 should be viewed like this:

- *First, the Seven Seals;*
- *Then the Seven Trumpets;*
- *Then the continuation of the wrath of God picks back up with the Seven Bowls (Vials).*

They correctly say that the *Seven Trumpets are clearly shown to be directly connected to and extend like a telescope from the Seventh Seal (see Revelation 8:1-2).*

Their error is made when they make the **claim** that the continuation of that prophetic telescope picks back up later in Revelation 15 and 16 with the *Seven Bowls* [or *Vials*]. They interpret this to mean that the *Seven Bowls* are a continuation of the telescoping from the seventh Trumpet seen in Revelation 10 and 11. There is only one little problem with that idea. It's not so! That is merely a speculation or opinion, rather than a biblical fact proven in the text.

We will show that rather than a telescope connecting the *seventh Trumpet to the Seven Bowls*, John is actually "repeating" or "prophesying again" what he had seen earlier. This he was told to do by the might angel in Revelation 10:8-11. (Take a moment to review those verses in your Bible. It's very clearly stated what John must do!) And that is what we see happening from Revelation 14-19. He is telling again what he had seen in the form of the *Seven Seals* and the *Seven Trumpets*.

Interestingly, even Dr. Walvoord points to this in *The Bible Knowledge Commentary* (at Revelation 16:1-2, Volume 2, page 966):

> "The question has been raised as to whether the bowls of the wrath of God are chronologically subsequent to or identical with the seven trumpets of the angels. There is clearly much similarity between the trumpet judgments and the bowl judgments."

He goes on to explain why, in his opinion, why they are not the same. I agree that they are not stated in the same words. These are merely repeated from John's perspective and words as he "prophesies again," as he was told to do. There are differences in these repeated portrayals of what he had seen in Revelation 4-13, in a very similar fashion as that of the Gospel writers. The Gospel writers told about the ministry of Christ, but each did so from their own perspective, led by the Holy Spirit. This is not difficult. And, furthermore, whatever differences there are in the comparative similarities, those few differences are "additions" to the narrative, not contradictions. To pick at those differences is to disregard the impact of the preponderance of clear evidence. Nevertheless, it is only fair to point to the fact that Dr. Walvoord has a different perspective on the point. We disagree, and demonstrate why the Book of Revelation clearly has this "repeated" ("prophesy again") structure.

At this juncture, if the reader is not intimately familiar with the Book of Revelation, it can be relatively easy to fall into greater confusion. If we allow ourselves to be confined to someone else's opinions (including mine), rather than the actual passages of Scripture, we will most likely completely overlook details God has given us. But as will be demonstrated, the approach often presented by proponents of a pre-tribulation rapture, and who see the Book of Revelation through the perspective of their three-point layout of the *Seven Seals, Seven Trumpets, Seven Bowls* (Vials), noted above, disregards the profoundly important *Seven Angels* nestled in Revelation 14.

Do you remember the story about the field of diamonds in Arkansas on page 65? God conceals many secrets in the Bible. He wants us to search for them. He wants us to want His truths so much that we are willing to "dig" for them. In this case, we need to realize that the Seven Angels in Revelation 14 are precious diamonds in the Book of Revelation. When they are disregarded or overlooked, Revelation cannot be understood, since these *Seven Angels* reflect the "repeat" of the *Seven Seals* found in the first half of Revelation. Once we include those *Seven Angels* as major elements or players in the outline of Revelation, our understanding will become clearer. (NOTE: I want to encourage the reader to hang in there, as you begin to grasp the big picture. Utilizing the graphics and the coming chapters, things will become more and more clear.)

There is a good reason why so many of the events detailed in chapters 14-19 are strikingly similar to the same events found in Revelation 4-13. Pre-tribulation proponents, and those of other perspectives, often teach that the activities and events in chapters 14-19 are to be seen as the **continuation** of wrath and judgment, which began in Revelation 6. But that presents numerous problems; such as, *Who are those saints and prophets being raised from the dead, judged and rewarded, back in Revelation 11?* To them, Revelation 10 and 11 cannot reflect the actual timing of the sounding of the last trumpet, the resurrection, the judgment of the saints and the rewarding of the saints. To allow that, would, of necessity, unravel the pre-tribulation approach. Furthermore, why does it say in Revelation 11:15 that *"… The kingdoms of this world have become the kingdoms of our Lord and of His Christ, and He shall reign forever and ever!"* (Revelation 11:15)? Doesn't the Lord Jesus lay claim to the kingdoms of this world, by His power and authority, as He is about to embark upon His second coming? (See Revelation 11:15 and Revelation 19:3-6) So, how is it that the *"kingdoms of this world"* are shown as becoming the *"kingdoms of our Lord ..."* right in the middle of the Book of Revelation? It is those kinds of things that are confusing to many. It should be confusing, if there is an attempt to fit this declaration into the idea of a pre-tribulation rapture. These two conflicting ideas are like water and oil, which do not mix. I want to be quick to state that I am in no way suggesting that there is a *Mid-tribulation Rapture*, either.

So, what is going on here? According to our pre-tribulation proponent-friends, the Tribulation, which began in Revelation 6, simply continues, they say, without missing a beat through Revelation 16, with the exceptional parenthetical sections in Revelation 11-13, or some other explanation (too many variations to explain here). To them, it is all a continuous series of events. Therefore, some of them would say, the judgments seen in the *Seven Bowls (or Vials)* are the concluding judgments that began with the Seven Seals being opened in judgment in Revelation 6, continuing on through the Seven Trumpets, and then continuing on through the next set of judgments, which they say is the *Seven Vials or Bowls*.

The problem is that once we allow for the understanding of the *Mystery of God*, and its role in the Endtimes, along with a clearer outline of Revelation derived by that understanding, the pre-tribulation concept is shown to be incorrect. The reason for this is that the events of Revelation 4-13 are mirrored in Revelation 14-19; and the clear, chronological similarities are more than stunning! It's vitally important that a certain potential confusion is removed right here and now! And, that is this: **There is something that I am NOT saying by this explanation.** I am <u>**NOT saying**</u> that the same events occur twice as though God's judgments are poured out on the earth twice. That is absolutely NOT what God's Word is telling us. <u>*I AM saying*</u> that the same events are told twice within Revelation; that is, the first section Revelation 4-13 is "re-told" in the subsequent section in Revelation 14-19. John is told to repeat them (to tell them again), which is precisely what John does.

This is precisely why there are forty-two (42) specific, chronological similarities in each of those two comparative parts within Revelation, which are detailed in a more graphic form in the next chapter, **42 Unmistakable Similarities: Comparing Revelation 4-13 With 14-19.**

The *Seven Angels and Seven Vials/Bowls* in 14-19 are a mirror image of the *Seven Seals and Seven Trumpets* in 4-13. The forty-two (42) specific, chronological details deserve explanation. Why would anyone simply choose to ignore these unmistakable evidences of a "repeat" within the Book of Revelation? We will get to that in just a few minutes! But first ...

OK, But What About the *Marriage of the Lamb?*

Almost all who teach on the Endtimes (whether we teach a pre-tribulation rapture, mid-tribulation rapture, pre-wrath rapture, or post-tribulation rapture) teach that the *Marriage of the Lamb* sequentially follows the rewarding of the saints, which is referred to in Revelation 11:15-18. Yet the Marriage of the Lamb doesn't show up until Revelation 19:1-16. And that **seems** to be far removed from the **Mystery of God**, *the sounding of the last trumpet, the resurrection, and the judgment and* **rewarding of the saints and prophets.** However, in the sequence of events in Revelation 10 and 11, when the seventh and last trumpet in Revelation sounds (Revelation 11:15), "loud voices in heaven" are shouting something very important:

> *"Then the seventh angel sounded:* **And there were loud voices in heaven, saying, 'The kingdoms of this world have become the kingdoms of our Lord and of His Christ, and He shall reign forever and ever!' And the twenty-four elders who sat before God on their thrones fell on their faces and worshiped God, saying: 'We give You thanks, O Lord God Almighty, The One who is and who was and who is to come, Because You have taken Your great power and reigned.** *The nations were angry, and Your wrath has come, And the time of the dead, that they should be judged, And that You should reward Your servants the prophets and the saints, And those who fear Your name, small and great, And should destroy those who destroy the earth.'"*
>
> Revelation 11:15–18

What's that all about? In this scene, throngs in heaven, along with the *twenty-four elders*, recognize that the time has now arrived for the King of kings and LORD of lords to declare His claim to the *"kingdoms of this world."*

For good reason, it should peak our interest to know that this same event is revealed twice in Revelation! Each time we see this scene revealed (Revelation 11:15-18 and 19:1, 4-6), it is at the end of the Great Tribulation, and is in the context of the *Mystery of God* and the *Marriage of the Lamb* being finished (completed, fulfilled). Having seen this scene the first time in Revelation 11:15-18, now we see it the second time, in Revelation 19:1, 4-6.

> *"After these things I heard a* **loud voice of a great multitude** *in heaven, saying, 'Alleluia! Salvation and glory and honor and power belong to the Lord our God!' ... And the* **twenty-four elders and the four living creatures fell down and worshiped God** *who sat on the throne, saying, 'Amen! Alleluia!' Then a voice came from the throne, saying, 'Praise our God, all you* **His servants and those who fear Him, both small and great!'**

*And I heard, as it were, the voice of a great multitude, as the sound of many waters and as the sound of mighty thunderings, saying, 'Alleluia! For **the Lord God Omnipotent reigns!**'*

As previously stated, repetition occurs throughout the vast majority of Revelation. There is a profoundly simple reason. The overall events of the Great Tribulation are told in Revelation, first by God's messenger to John, and then re-told by the Apostle John. John is shown these events, and then he is told that he must tell them again, which is precisely what he does. He repeats the events from his own perspective. Once we have a clear understanding of what the *Mystery of God* entails, it is not difficult to put the pieces of this *Great Mystery* puzzle together. In fact, if we were watching a video, instead of reading, we could animate the first section of Revelation, as told to John, then digitally superimpose the first section over the second section in which John is now re-telling the same events. By so doing we would see how the first and second are the same sets of events, from two perspectives. And I emphasize that this is especially important, as it relates to the details of the *Mystery of God* and the *Marriage of the Lamb*.

The *Marriage of the Lamb*, according to the Apostle Paul, is declared to be basic, or integral, to the Mystery of God, which he also calls the *Great Mystery*. Paul left no doubts, when he wrote that **this great Mystery speaks of the marriage of Christ and His Church.**[21] There is only one *Marriage for Christ*. Some might say, *Okay, I can see the listed details involved in the Mystery in Revelation 10 and 11, the trumpet sounding, the resurrection, etc. And I see that the Marriage of the Lamb is the Great Mystery, according to the Apostle Paul. But I need to see the reconciliation of the first section (4-13) with the repeated prophecy in the second section (14-19).*

The Divide in Revelation Actually Reveals the Connection

What could possibly create a direct connection between Revelation 10-11 (where we see the *Mystery of God* beginning to be fulfilled) and Revelation 19:1-16 (where we see the *Marriage of the Lamb*)? I want to see with you the astounding answer. If you are like I was when I was puzzled by that question, I believe you will be amazed to see what God uses to make simple the complexities most of us have imposed upon the Book of Revelation. I openly confess that I had been confused about this for years ... until the *Mystery of God* cleared things up, as we are about to see together. May I ask the reader to mark your place here for a moment, and take another glimpse at the graphic layout and outline of Revelation just a few pages back on page 73-75.

The Incredible Key

It is essential that we understand the chronological outline within the Book of Revelation in order to gain greater understanding of the content and message. Having the wrong chronological outline has and will guarantee confusion. To a very large degree, this is what many in the Church experience as they read Revelation. Most Christians who might read the Book of Revelation during their routine Bible reading, will confess that while it is mesmerizing, it remains an enigma; very confusing and hard to understand. There are nationwide Bible study groups that have extensive sessions studying the Book of Revelation. On the one hand thank God for all of the Bible study going on in such groups. I've been marginally involved in them. I've witnessed the good, and I rejoice in and with them in honoring the Lord in such studies. But when it comes to the Book of Revelation, one of the common remarks of those who have attended and who are sincerely looking for answers is that they remain confused after the completion of the course. It's not that they don't receive a lot of material, or that they don't cover the entire book. It's just that many sincere believers finish a Revelation study course, and still find it near to impossible to really understand for themselves or to explain Revelation to someone else.

The truths in the Book of Revelation are vital for the spiritual health of individual believers and local churches alike, and the body of Christ as a whole, and even more so than many presently seem to believe. The current lack of understanding is affirmed by the way we choose to prioritize our lives, even though we claim that the "signs of the times" are everywhere. I am not judging anyone, please believe that. My thoughts on this are not intended that way; rather, I am attempting to point to the problems in our understanding. Nevertheless, someday, sooner than later, every believer is going to face the issue of what our priorities for life and eternity really are. Is there any doubt that the heat is being turned up in this world? Staggering world events continue to increase, and those events are becoming more personally impactful on us and our loved ones --- they are getting closer to home!

Things will change! For some, it will be a change for the better; for others, it will spell tragedy. Some will have failed to have received a love of the truth, and as a direct result, they will be unable to understand what is happening around them, as trauma unfolds and multiplies. Jesus described this, when He said, *"Then you will be handed over to be persecuted and put to death, and you will be hated by all nations because of me.* **AT THAT TIME many will turn away from the faith and will betray and hate each other**, *and many false prophets will appear and deceive many people. Because of the increase of wickedness, the love of most will grow cold, but he who stands firm to the end will be saved"* (Matthew 24:9–13, NIV84, emphasis mine).

Some will be like Lot's wife, who from her heart looked back toward Sodom and Gomorrah though she and Lot had been specifically instructed by God's warning: "Do not look behind you." She had been taken out of Sodom and Gomorrah by God's mercy, yet she had some kind of longing in her heart; a longing that was greater than her love and longing for God and His Word to them. This same type of longing will cause many to fail God and fail themselves and their loved ones in these Endtimes. If we do not make the right choices now, then when the harder times come—and rest assured those days have already begun, we will be like the children of Israel, after they left Egypt. They became hungry and longed for the food of Egypt to which they were accustomed. Rather than choosing God's way, in the middle of their hunger, they chose to serve their own appetites. We can either choose to satisfy our hunger by choosing the Bread of Life,[22] or we will choose the meager crumbs of this world and Satan. God's people are to learn, along the way of life, that we cannot have it both ways. *"Man shall not live by bread alone, but by every word that proceeds out of the mouth of God …."* Many do not want to hear it. But for those who have a hungry heart for the truths of God, please be reminded that very few from that initial *Egypt-Exodus-Generation* made it into the Promised Land. And as it was then for those few who do, they will have great blessing in the Kingdom and God will have been honored.

Like the watchmen on the wall in the days of the kings of Israel and Judah, there are those who are now sounding the alarm with great urgency. Those who heed will have the opportunity to be spiritually prepared and will literally be looking for Jesus' return for the rapture. Those, who do not, will pay a tragic price. Even that last sentence is hard for many in the Church to relate to. The reason is that they have believed an Endtime teaching that advances an inadequate motivation for the preparation[23] of our souls for Jesus' coming! The truth is that among many there is no real urgency about the Endtimes. I am not referring to anxiety about the Endtimes. Rather, *passion* is the operative word, along with pursuit, dedication, yieldedness, love, conscious awareness of the brevity of life and time, fulness of the Spirit, and a ready heart to *follow the Lamb wherever He might* lead us by His Spirit. Imagine that you are among Noah's acquaintances on the day before the rain began to fall. Noah believed God; the others did not. Noah truly **believed** to the point of **action**; his acquaintances **disbelieved** to the point of **inaction**. This is the Church today! If you believe, you will take action turning your heart humbly to Him, asking for His mercies, so that your eyes, ears and heart will be open to His voice and Word. If you do not believe you will not take action. Again, Jesus posed that question to which I referred earlier: *When the Son of man comes will He really find faith on the earth?* Where are you in this?

"Seek the Lord, all you meek of the earth, Who have upheld His justice. Seek righteousness, seek humility. It may be that you will be hidden in the day of the Lord's anger."

Zephaniah 2:3

Receiving from Him a **love of the truth** is an essential key to receiving an **understanding of the truth**. Too often, our perspective on the Book of Revelation is clouded by an outline that misguides and blinds us, guaranteeing we will not understand. The minutia, the complex details, can overwhelm us, if we do not have a correct outline. As we read and study Revelation, we can become so focused on the traumatic and seemingly relentless series of events that our sight becomes blurred by the coming stormy seas. That's enough to discourage anyone! Surely, we want to be among those whose eyes are fixed on the Captain of our ship.

Sailing in the Book of Revelation

I once heard the story of a well-known baseball player whose life had gotten off course. He went through rehab. Then the day came when he declared that his life had changed. He was glad to finally have a media interview about his change. In that interview, he was asked how things were going for him, now that he had made a change. His answer was: *"Well, my life was off course, going the wrong direction. Then I turned 360 degrees, and now my life is going in the right direction!"* Even though we can easily understand what his meaning was, he was nevertheless obviously mistaken in the way he had said it. By saying that he had turned *360 degrees*, this would indicate that he would still be going in the exact same direction as he had been going before "the change." Direction matters! And having solid evidence that we are going in the right direction is what gives us confidence in our travels.

In the midst of confusing storms in our pursuit of understanding of Revelation and the Endtimes, it can be easy to get off course. The good news is that our Captain has an inherent compass. He will make sure we are going in the right direction, as long as we stay in His ship, and don't take the helm, speculating on the direction to go.

Imagine that we are on this great sailing ship and we are going to travel through a sea called the Book of Revelation. Ours is an amazing ship, and seems sufficient for any sea she might traverse. There are many important things to know about the ship, but there are even more things to know about this sea called the Book of Revelation. It is common knowledge that it takes time and effort to study the operations of the ship, and to learn the ropes. If we fail to learn the ropes, we will invariably crash on the rocks of speculation and opinion, and end in shipwreck in our understanding. It is, therefore, incumbent upon any student, while endeavoring to sail on the turbulent sea of Revelation, that we should be careful to avoid our own, or anyone else's, speculations and opinions. We must follow directions by confirming, with many evidences, that we are going the right direction. But once we have familiarized ourselves with the ship and the critical basics about the sea; and once we have tested the waters, we can begin our journey. If we are guided by our Captain's eye, we will have safe and successful travels.

THE REVELATION DIVIDE

"Nothing in all creation is hidden from God's sight. Everything is uncovered and laid bare before the eyes of him to whom we must give account."

Hebrews 4:13 NIV84

Thankfully, He tells us:

"I will instruct you and teach you in the way you should go; I will guide you with My eye."

Psalm 32:8

Much comfort can be gained by the Captain's ancient declaration:

"Surely the Lord God does nothing, Unless He reveals His secret to His servants the prophets."

Amos 3:7

We can have great confidence in what He has revealed. And of course we have the promise of our heavenly Father that He has given us the Holy Spirit to *"teach us all things"* and to *"show us things to come."* (John 16:13).

We are in the best hands for this journey on the seas of Revelation. We know that we must seek His guidance, His direction, and His knowledge. He knows the ropes. He *made* the ropes. He is the one who built the ship and He made the sea, and He is the only one who has the ability to get us safely through our journey to safe harbor. By many evidences, our Captain repeatedly offers assurance of safety and peace, not only because He is at the helm guiding the ship, but because He gives us the grace to set aside speculations and opinions,[24] and to learn to rely upon His confirmed Word; His *"sure word of prophecy"* (2 Peter 1:19).

Once we have left the harbor, which is found in Revelation chapters 1 through 5, the Captain orders the opening of full sails, while maintaining close watch on the weather and piloting the ship by His inherent compass. Order must be maintained on any ship, but on this ship, it is the only way it will get to its destination. The strong hand and heart of the Captain is more than sufficient for the task. The Captain assures us that He has the *little book*; an important *little book*, which contains the map of the remainder of the journey, and the course coordinates that we must take. His *little book* is first mentioned in Revelation 5, where Jesus is seen opening the seals of this *little book*.

At this point, the Captain suggests that we get out our video camera and take video of the entire trip, and to capture the details from His viewpoint on the bridge.

Almost immediately after having gotten onto the high seas, the turbulence begins to buffet the ship. No worries, though. Our ship is mighty in the truth and our Captain is at the helm. From the vantage point of our Captain, things are under complete control, and our trust is in Him.

What a journey it is; a long journey over a period of several years—three-and-one-half years to be precise. Our eyes are opened to see things happening on the earth; such things never known to mankind. They will be so traumatic that we wonder how some, who will learn about this journey, will believe it. The Captain has given names and numbers of each and every event. His steady hand at the helm begins to take us through what can be called the raging waters of the Seven Seals and Seven Trumpets. He keeps reminding us that what we are seeing are the many events of the Great Tribulation Period.

What we witness as we travel on the tempestuous sea of Revelation are some things so horrific that it is difficult to comprehend the impact on those who rebel against God. This is truly a long and arduous journey. Event after event has taken their toll on the world. We are seeing man's wrath, Satan's wrath, and God's wrath, all of which are devastating.

After having traveled for what has now been almost *"1,260 days,"* or *"time, times and half-a-time,"* or what is commonly referred to as the *"three-and-one-half years"* of the *Great Tribulation*,[25] we are finally coming to the end of our journey.

It is at this point that we hear the Captain's helper call for the Apostle John, the Captain's chief journey recorder. John has been witnessing all of these events, just as the Captain had told him that he would. The helper tells John that the *Mystery of God* is about to begin to be fulfilled, because the seventh and last trumpet is about to sound. He tells him that even though he will now witness the sounding of the last trumpet, the resurrection, and the judgment and rewarding of the saints, there is still one more event that must be accounted for, and thereby, the complete fulfillment of *Mystery of God* as was shown to God's prophets; and that one more event is the *Marriage of the Lamb*. He then shows John all of the events he had just mentioned, and only then does he show him the *Marriage of the Lamb*, the capstone of the *Mystery of God*.

Not leaving any event out, he tells him that he will also show him those things that follow. Those are the things that pertain to the second coming of our Captain—the King of kings and Lord of lords, and the battle of Armageddon, the Millennial reign of Christ, the eventual Great White Throne Judgment of the unsaved, the creation of the new heaven and the new earth, and the great city the New Jerusalem, which will come down out of heaven to the earth.

The Captain preempts all of those scenes, when His helper tells John that he must prophesy, once again, those things that he has been seeing. He explains to John that by repeating what he is seeing, this will add greater clarity to the outline of the whole Book of Revelation. The helper explains that *"… in the mouth of two or three witnesses, shall a thing be established. As you prophesy again, by re-telling the key elements of the Book of Revelation, you are supplying another witness to these truths to establish it according to God's Word and ways. This is the prophetic Word being confirmed, making it sure, just as was written by the Apostle Peter.*[26]

The Revelation Divide

In closing, he says to him: *"But John, for now, there is something you must do. The video recording is complete, and I have special instructions from the Captain for you."*

At this moment, we notice that the Captain has brought us to a safe harbor, and docked the ship. From above, we hear loud singing, praising, and shouts of tremendous adoration, as loud voices in heaven declare that the *"kingdoms of this world have become the kingdoms of our Lord and of His Christ!"* What a moment this is!

Then in a flash the last trumpet begins to sound; dead saints and prophets are resurrected; the living saints join them in the rapture, which happens in the twinkling of an eye; the Judgment Seat of Christ is seen; rewards are meted out; and then these are ushered into a place of singing and rejoicing, as the announcement is made for the Marriage of the Lamb and His bride.

Suddenly, the scene changes. The Captain's key helper tells us that He wants the Captain's journey-recorder, the Apostle John, to take the time to replay the video, and restate what he has been seeing. The Captain does not want John to take the helm. All He wants John to do is to "prophesy again," giving commentary on what John had witnessed as we had traveled for the past three-and-one-half years. The Captain tells His helper to give His little book to John. It is obvious that this is the same little book, the sealed book, which the Captain had unsealed in order for us to take this trip. And now, John is commanded to eat that same little book. We are all a bit surprised at what seemed to be a strange command. But the helper explains that we are to keep in mind that the little book contains the map and details of the journey. This repeat of the details will further explain how the Endtimes takes place. It becomes clear that there would be no way for John to re-tell the details without having eaten the little book. We learn that this clearly indicates that John has been commanded to digest and assimilate the truths in the little book, which he had already witnessed, and to prophesy again those same things with the guidance of the Holy Spirit.

There we are sitting close by and watching this entire scene, and suddenly the Book of Revelation begins to become clearer. For years, each of us had wondered and discussed what this section of the Book of Revelation meant.

> *"Then the voice which I heard from heaven spoke to me again and said, 'Go, take the little book which is open in the hand of the angel who stands on the sea and on the earth.' So I went to the angel and said to him, 'Give me the little book.' And he said to me, 'Take and eat it; and it will make your stomach bitter, but it will be as sweet as honey in your mouth.' Then I took the little book out of the angel's hand and ate it, and it was as sweet as honey in my mouth. But when I had eaten it, my stomach became bitter. And he said to me, '**you must prophesy again** about many peoples, nations, tongues, and kings.'"*
>
> Revelation 10:8–11

The compassionate and wise heart of the Captain causes us to understand some of the details of this moment of transition concerning the Book of Revelation. As if it were a classroom lesson in translating to English from the original Greek New Testament, the Captain quotes the English version: "*You must prophesy **again** about many peoples, nations, tongues, and kings.* He goes on to explain. "The Greek word for *"again"* is (παλιν, **pálin**). It is translated *"once more,"* or a *"repeated action."*[27] He tells us that this would mean that this verse could be translated like this: "*You must prophesy once more, you must repeat what was prophesied about many peoples, nations, tongues, and kings. The events that affected "many peoples, nations, tongues, and kings" must be re-told.* He continues, *One more important word must be understood more fully.* Because it is the Captain who is teaching us, we are all ears. *The Greek meaning of the word "**about**" is* επι, *epí, which can simply mean "about" or "concerning."*[28] So, this is why my helper has told John that he must repeat this prophecy. "*You must prophesy once more, you must repeat this prophecy, that same prophecy **concerning** many peoples, nations, tongues, and kings.*" That is, he must prophesy again about the same peoples, nations, tongues, and kings, whom he had seen during the events of Revelation 4-13.

The *Instant Replay* in Revelation

Our video camera has recorded not only the events of the journey, but our Captain speaks up and explains. *John, you have witnessed My prophetic Word and the events are recorded. You have eaten the "little book" containing those things, and you have digested it. I know that it turned bitter in your stomach, because this trip has been nothing short of Great Tribulation; in fact, it is like no other time in history, and there never will be another time like it, until the day when all is finished in this present creation. This is why I have called it the "time of Jacob's trouble."*[29] *You have witnessed the recording of relentless wrath—My wrath, the wrath of humanity on the earth and on one another, along with Satan's wrath. It is a bitter thing to see. But now, I want you to repeat what you have seen. I want you to take that video footage and review it. I want you to show and explain what you saw. But before you begin to prophesy again, I want to remind you that as soon as those events were completed, I allowed you to see this same journey from three perspectives, which were intended to help you to make known these things. From Revelation 6, and on through much of Revelation 11, you saw events in the form of the Seven Seals and the Seven Trumpets. But there were other details you saw taking place during that same Great Tribulation.*

Our Captain then explains that the Great Tribulation Period of three-and-one-half years is to be viewed from three different perspectives beginning in Revelation chapter 11 and continuing on through chapter 13. To make sure we understood, he highlighted them.

- *The first perspective is that of the "two witnesses". Their roles will play out for "one thousand two hundred and sixty days" in Revelation 11:3 (that would be three-and-one-half years; that is the Great Tribulation);*
- *The second perspective is that of the "saints" (the Church), as they go through this same period of "one thousand two hundred and sixty days", as stated in Revelation 12:6, or as it is also referred to as "time and times and half a time" (that is, three-and-one-half years), as mentioned in Revelation 12:14;*
- *And the third is from the unsaved world's perspective, as the antichrist, beast, and the false prophet are revealed in this same Great Tribulation. Again, this is seen during the three-and-one-half years, or as a "forty-two month" time period, as it is referred to in Revelation 13:5.*

He continues with a couple of concluding remarks, all of which are surprising to the guests on the ship. He says that *the five times, in which the three-and-one-half years are mentioned in Revelation 11, 12 and 13, are the* **only** *places in Revelation in which the Great Tribulation time period is mentioned. This is because these all reflect the same time period, each of which has its own emphases. Also, out of the fifty-four (54) times the number seven (7) is used in the Book of Revelation,* **not once** *is the number seven used in reference to the period of Tribulation. It's not there. The reason for this is because only three-and-one-half years of Great Tribulation are referred to in the Book of Revelation. There is nothing there about a Tribulation period of seven years, as many claim. This is explained by Daniel the Prophet in Daniel 9:24-27. But we can talk about that on another occasion.*

The Captain ends His clarifications by telling John, and us, that by seeing the Great Tribulation from all three perspectives we will be able to understand more clearly what is happening, overall.

John takes it all in, recording every detail. Then wasting no time, he begins to follow the Captain's order, just as he was commanded to do. The video recording is now seen on a big screen right in front of us, and we find ourselves watching an **"instant replay."**

You Must Prophesy Again

The instant replay is just that; a repeat. Now, as John proceeds from Revelation 14 and going forward into Revelation 19, we become completely convinced that we are watching **a play back, an instant replay** of Revelation 4-13, the very journey we had just taken. But in this case, our Captain has turned off the sound from the video, and we are hearing the Apostle John "repeat," giving his own commentary on what he had seen and heard—and by this repeat, **John prophesies again.** It is made unequivocally clear that the pivotal turning point in the layout of the Book of Revelation is stated in Revelation 10:8-11.

The evidence of the *repeat* begins to mount, as the *instant replay* of the prophecy rolls on. We learn that there are 42 specific similarities that demonstrate that we are seeing the same events of Revelation 4-13 restated, leaving us with no doubt. John refers to the Seven Angels in Revelation 14, which are the re-telling of the Seven Seals. He goes on to refer to the Seven Bowls or Vials, which are the re-telling of the Seven Trumpets.

As John is about to begin to share the specifics of the 42 similarities in the repeat of the prophecy, a discussion breaks out on our ship. All agree that the *Mystery of God* is announced in Revelation 10:7, and is seen as beginning to be completed in Revelation 11:15-18 according to the events that had been videoed, including the trumpet, the resurrection, the judgment and the rewarding of the saints and prophets; and that all of these things had been foretold by the prophets. But the question has come up again about the *Marriage of the Lamb*, with some of us wanting to know when, where and how it fits into the scenario they had just witnessed in the first section, Revelation 4-13.

Our Captain steps in and says,

"I am so glad that you want to know the answer to that question. It exposes hungry hearts and a love of the truth. After all, the Marriage of the Lamb is obviously part of My Journey, My Mystery. All of the details about the Mystery of God are not found in the Book of Revelation. In fact, most of the supporting details are not found there. Vitally important details were given to the Apostle Paul, and it is critical that you study and understand those details. But rest assured, all of you will see how the Mystery will play out, once John tells you about the Marriage of the Lamb. He will tell you about this at the point at which he is finishing his task of 'prophesying again.' That is where you will be able to make the connection between the Mystery and the Marriage of the Lamb. I will, through John's testimony, reveal even more details of what he received by eating the 'little book.' So, sit back and watch the review of the journey of the three-and-one-half years of the Great Tribulation. You are going to see that there are 42 specific details from Revelation 4-13 repeated in chronological order in 14-19, providing another witness of these same truths. I don't want to leave you, or those who come after you, with any doubts. This repeated prophecy is specifically provided to help all to understand Revelation. Your hungry hearts for the truth will find favor and grace in what you are learning."

And with that said, John begins sharing the **42 Unmistakable Similarities: Comparing Revelation 4-13 With 14-19.**

Chapter Three Notes

[17] The Greek "proleptic aorist" grammatical structure signifies that the *Mystery of God* will be completed during the "days", or period of "time", of the seventh trumpet. During those "days", or period of "time" of this seventh and last trumpet Revelation 11:15-18 details the completeion of the resurrection, rapture, judgment, rewards, and then Revelation 19:7-9 details the inclusion and completion of the Marriage of the Lamb!

[18] John F. Walvoord, "Revelation," in *The Bible Knowledge Commentary: An Exposition of the Scriptures*, ed. J. F. Walvoord and R. B. Zuck, vol. 2 (Wheaton, IL: Victor Books, 1985), 956–957.

[19] Dr. Buist Fanning is the Senior Professor Emeritus of New Testament Studies at Dallas Theological Seminary in Dallas, Texas (retired after 42 years as a professor!) Furthermore, I agree with the accolades given online by many as to the gracious gentleman Buist is. My interactions with him regarding Greek research have proven to be very insightful and a real personal joy.

[20] These chapter divisions are not intended as a precise representation of all varieties of pre-tribulationist perspectives. There are several differing approaches. Rather, it is a generalization, due to variations of ideas among THEM.

[21] Ephesians 5:22-32

[22] "And you shall remember the whole way that the Lord your God has led you these forty years in the wilderness, that he might humble you, testing you to know what was in your heart, whether you would keep his commandments or not. And he humbled you and let you hunger and fed you with manna, which you did not know, nor did your fathers know, that he might make you know that man does not live by bread alone, but man lives by every word that comes from the mouth of the Lord." (Deuteronomy 8:2–3, ESV) Also, see Matthew 4:4, Luke 4:4, and "And Jesus said to them, "I am the bread of life. He who comes to Me shall never hunger, and he who believes in Me shall never thirst" (John 6:35).

[23] I want to be clear that when I refer to "preparation," I am not advocating that we go out to a mountain and put on white robes and wait for Jesus. Furthermore, it seems to me that any physical preparation for hard times should be done with helping others in mind, rather than merely protecting ourselves.

[24] 2 Peter 1:19-21.

[25] Revelation 11:2,3; 12:6, 14; 13:5.

[26] 2 Peter 1:19-21.

[27] Greek: PALIN (παλιν, (3825)), the regular word for "again," is used chiefly in two senses, (a) with reference to repeated action; (b) rhetorically, in the sense of "moreover" or "further," indicating a statement to be added in the course of an argument. (Vine, W. E., & Bruce, F. F. (1981). Vine's Expository dictionary of Old and New Testament words. Old Tappan NJ: Revell).

[28] Zodhiates, S. (2000). *The Complete Word Study Dictionary: New Testament* (electronic ed.). Chattanooga, TN: AMG Publishers.

[29] Jeremiah 30:4-7.

CHAPTER 4

42 UNMISTAKABLE SIMILARITIES: COMPARING REVELATION 4-13 WITH 14-19

"Surely the Lord God does nothing, Unless He reveals His secret to His servants the prophets."
Amos 3:7

"By the mouth of two or three witnesses every word shall be established."
2 Corinthians 13:1

"Be diligent to present yourself approved to God, a worker who does not need to be ashamed, rightly dividing [handling] the word of truth."
2 Timothy 2:15

"… not in words which man's wisdom teaches but which the Holy Spirit teaches, comparing spiritual things with spiritual."
1 Corinthians 2:13

There are 42 Unmistakable Similarities[30] in chronological order. These profound similarities found in Revelation 4-13 are mirrored in Revelation 14-19. Why did God do this? By comparing these two sections in Revelation, we will begin to understand Revelation. If we love truth, confirmed truth, we should want to ascend the mountain of evidence, appreciating God' incredible confirmations of His prophetic Word, and agree with God, while setting aside our own speculative ideas.

In this comparison of the 42 similarities, we will realize there is, indeed, a "repeat" of truths within the Book of Revelation. The Apostle John was commanded to "prophesy again," that is, to "*write*" the prophecy again, which had just been revealed to him. We want to compare what he had seen with what he subsequently had written, just as he had been commanded. We will compare the details one by one, chronologically, and the reader can decide.

By this simple, straightforward process, we should be able to confidently conclude several things: 1) *The decisive role of the Mystery of God in understanding the outline of the Book of Revelation;* 2) *That this comparison will, once and for all, affirm the fact that the latter half of Revelation is a "repeat" of the first half;* 3) *That the last half section of the Book of Revelation is not the continuation of the first half section, as is commonly supposed;* and, 4) *By the confirmation of all of the facts, mentioned above, we can determine the actual and verifiable outline of the Book of Revelation.*

I want the reader to understand, as we move into the heart of this chapter, that this comparison is essential for removing the plague of confusion that typically accompanies understanding the Book of Revelation. Therefore, this chapter is an "eye-opener", to say the least!

1. **Revelation 14:1** ~ He "looked" and saw Mount Zion. Not only is a mountain a "high place," but Hebrews 12:22 also tells us that Zion is a heavenly place.
   Revelation 4:1 ~ He "looked" and received a revelation of Heaven or a high place.

2. **Revelation 14:1** ~ There is a revelation of the Lamb in this vision.
   Revelation 5:6 ~ There is a revelation of the Lamb in this vision.

3. **Revelation 14:1** ~ There is a revelation of 144,000 sealed ones in this vision.
   Revelation 7:1-8 ~ There is a revelation of 144,000 sealed ones in this vision also.

4. **Revelation 14:1** ~ They are sealed in their foreheads.
   Revelation 7:3 ~ They are sealed in their foreheads.

5. **Revelation 14:2** ~ A voice is heard from Heaven.
   Revelation 4:1 ~ A voice is heard from Heaven.

6. **Revelation 14:2** ~ Thunder is heard.
   Revelation 4:5 ~ Thunder is heard.

7. **Revelation 14:3** ~ A new song is heard.
   Revelation 5:9 ~ A new song is heard.

8. **Revelation 14:3** ~ There is a revelation of the throne of God.
   Revelation 4:2-3 ~ There is a revelation of the throne of God.

42 Unmistakable Similarities: Comparing Revelation 4-14 with 14-19

9. **Revelation 14:3** ~ Four "beasts," or four living creatures, are seen.
   Revelation 4:6 ~ Four "beasts," or four living creatures, are seen.

10. **Revelation 14:3** ~ The elders are seen.
    Revelation 4:4 ~ The elders are seen.

11. **Revelation 14:4** ~ Purity is seen (typified by the word "virgins").
    Revelation 4:4 ~ Purity is seen (typified by white robes).

12. **Revelation 14:4** ~ They are with, and like, the Lamb (because if they follow His footsteps and life, then they end up where He is --- in the throne).
    Revelation 3:21 ~ Those who live as He lived, and fully follow Him, will end up where He is—in the throne (Revelation 4-5 mention that throne 17 times).

13. **Revelation 14:5** ~ They have no guile; they are faultless.
    Revelation 4:5-6 ~ This is the nature of the Lamb.

At this point, in the Apostle John's "repeat," *something should become very evident.* And that something is that this is indeed John, "prophesying again." For further astounding evidence of this, let's make further comparisons.

Now We Come to Seven Seals and Seven Angels

The key to the following comparison between the Seven Seals and the Seven Angels is this: The end of a thing is revealed, and declared from the very beginning of that thing (Isaiah 46:9-10). The application of this Isaiah truth is utilized here in the Book of Revelation. The messenger shows John the beginning of each seal. That is to say, when the messenger is showing John about the each seal, he is doing so from the perspective of what will happen in each seal, futuristically. But John, in his message, is looking back and refers to the result of each seal; or we could say that John revealed the consequence of each seal after it happened.[31] Once we understand his perspective, we will more clearly see the similarity between the Seven Angels and the Seven Seals. Perhaps, the reason these Seven Angels are overlooked with such ease is because of our own expectations. Some "expect" John to say things from one perspective, when he is stating things from the different perspective. Again, understanding these angels requires we understand that John's declarations about the Seven Angels in Revelation 14 deal primarily with the *end result* of the events taking place in each Seal, whereas Revelation 6-8 deals with the *beginning* or *foretelling* of each of the Seven Seals.

14. **Revelation 6:1-2 ~ Seal One ~** For the meaning of this seal see the astounding comparison of Ezekiel with the seals of Revelation. There, as Ezekiel prophesies the events of the Endtimes, especially reflected in the Book of Revelation, he provides clear scriptural reasons why the first seal is the preaching of the gospel and is not the Antichrist, as some claim. God always provides two or more witnesses. In this case, there are two witnesses of this in Revelation (Seal One and Angel One), and another witness in Ezekiel, demonstrating an unequivocal conclusion as to what this Seal and Angel refer to.
Revelation 14:6-7 ~ Angel One ~ The Gospel is preached.

15. **Revelation 6:3-4 ~ Seal Two ~** The red horse holds the potential of being interpreted as either Islam or Communism or some unity of both, in part or whole. It should be noted that we are told that Daniel's prophecy was given by God specifically for Daniel's people, which would mean that the book's focus is specifically on Israel and the Jews. Revelation, however, seems to be much broader in scope, covering not only Israel but the entire world. Even though Revelation is broader in scope, it is clear that Israel remains the centerpiece of God's prophetic picture because of the "remnant," the "lost sheep of the house of Israel," in the land of Israel at the time of Christ's return.

Due to Daniel's geographical description of the 10-horned beast (and the little horn; one of the horns on that beast), there is reason to believe that Seal Two includes Islam, if it doesn't specifically refer to it. Nevertheless, because we do not yet see or understand these events clearly, the second Seal's fiery-red horse could also reveal Communism because of what it has done in the earth, taking peace from the earth with their "sword." Communism has done this throughout the world, as Islam currently does. Wherever Communism and Islam have engaged in the world[32], eventually if not immediately, terrorism and destruction have been their inherent hallmarks and bywords. This seal is associated with a "great sword," which again, gives reason for consideration of both Islam and Communism, which if combined, holds the potential of being the greatest army ever known to mankind, as we are seeing evolve today.

Note in Revelation 13:2 that the feet of the beast are the feet of a *bear*. The feet uphold or provide the foundation for the beast. In the secular context, the bear is a sign of Russian Communism today. Interestingly, in Daniel's prophecy (7:5), the "Medo-Persian" empire is in view, as seen in the second beast listed by Daniel. That geographical territory, today, is completely governed by Islam. Removing all doubt about "who" or "what" that second beast is in Daniel, the angel Gabriel, specifically revealed that empire/beast in Daniel 8:20. That reference to modern day Iran (Persia) and its relationship to Russia is intriguing and worthy of strong consideration in the interpretation of this second seal. Therefore, because of the breadth of the antichrist-beast's control in the world in the Endtimes, this red horse could very well be the combination and unity (if only temporarily) of both of them. The red horse could represent both the spirit of Communism and Islam, which could be the root of the world system of the Antichrist.

The goal in these remarks is not an effort to be "right," rather it is to offer helpful, though admittedly speculative suggestions, which seem to be reasonable; but they are just that, suggestions and speculations. Whatever the precise interpretation may be, one thing is very certain: *This seal speaks of the great destructive nature of this beast, and its effect on the whole earth.*

> **Revelation 14:8 ~ Angel Two ~** As John sees the beginning of seal two and the world system it brings, he sees at the same time the end of that system. Here judgment is pronounced on "Babylon."

16. **Revelation 6:5-6 ~ Seal Three ~** Here we find tremendous economic upheaval in the earth. The final result of this chaos will be the Antichrist imposing his world economic system on the nations. Those who choose to participate in that system will have to accept the mark of the beast. Economic upheaval will be a primary reason why otherwise sane people will accept a "mark." May God help anyone who cannot see this prospect coming on the world, even as I type this note.

    Revelation 14:9-12 ~ Angel Three ~ John specifies "the third angel" in verse 9, so angels one and two are in verses 6 and 8. Angel three gives a warning about accepting the mark of the beast related to the economics of buying and selling. As John sees seal three, he is *also seeing the end result of that seal,* which is revealed in the third angel.

17. **Revelation 6:7-8 ~ Seal Four ~** This seal brings death to one fourth of the earth.

    Revelation 14:13 ~ Angel Four ~ No wonder the voice of this fourth angel reveals death. Note that those who "die in the Lord" will be blessed. This reference may give the idea that some who die will not be "in the Lord." Regardless, we see death in this fourth messenger or voice in Revelation 14.

18. **Revelation 6:9-11 ~ Seal Five ~** Here the martyrs are crying out to be avenged. But the Lord says that others of their brethren must yet die as they did, as martyrs. When a saint is martyred, it is like planting a seed in the ground that will later give a wonderful harvest of souls and blessing. Jesus, referring to His death, says, *"Except a corn of wheat fall into the ground and die, it abideth alone: but if it die, it bringeth forth much fruit"* (John 12:24). No wonder the Psalmist says, "Precious in the sight of the Lord is the death of his saints" (Psa. 116:15). Imagine how precious Stephen's death was to the Lord (Acts 7). Saul was never the same after witnessing the glory that was upon that first martyr. Stephen's death was undoubtedly a key influence in Paul's life and ultimately in his

conversion. Therefore, since Paul took the message of the Gospel and the *Mystery of God* to the Gentiles, we can say that Stephen's death also became a major factor in the conversion of the Gentiles! If many saints are dying during the fifth seal, as Revelation 6:9-11 indicates, then the obvious fruit of this seal will be a great harvest!

Revelation 14:14-16 ~ Angel Five ~ Here we find that there will be a great harvest on the earth. (Christ's life and Stephen's life, as well as that of the Apostles and many other saints, brought forth a great harvest for the same reason ~ the "seed" died, and life came to the world through what was planted.)

19. **Revelation 6:12-17 ~ Seal Six ~** This is simply an announcement of the wrath of God.

    Revelation 14:17-20 ~ Angel Six ~ Here the "vine of the earth" is cast into the "great wine press of the wrath of God. So, the message of this angel is synonymous with the message of the sixth seal, which is God's wrath. Note that in verses 17 and 18 we find the sixth and seventh angels. One announces the coming of wrath, which is the same announcement that is made when the sixth seal is opened. The other angel, the seventh, seems to bring that wrath upon men as he casts the vine of the earth into the wine press of the wrath of God.

20. **Revelation 8:1-2 ~ Seal Seven ~** When the seventh seal is opened there is a revelation of seven angels with seven trumpets. The trumpets are seven plagues.

    Revelation 15:1 ~ Angel Seven ~ After the sixth angel announces that wrath is coming, the seventh angel brings that wrath (Rev. 14:19). One verse later, in Revelation 15:1, we are told what that wrath is. It is seven angels with seven vials. The vials are seven plagues.

21. **Revelation 7:9-17 ~** Note that after the announcement of wrath at the sixth seal in Revelation 6:12,17, but before the seven angels with the seven trumpets in Revelation 8:1-2 actually bring that wrath on the earth; we are given a revelation of a great multitude that comes out of the Great Tribulation in Revelation 7:9,14. They are standing before the presence of God.

    Revelation 15:2 ~ Exactly the same thing happens here. After the wrath is announced in chapter 14 and before the seven angels actually pour out that wrath on the earth, we see a great multitude here who have clearly come out of the Great Tribulation because they have gotten the victory over the beast, his image, his mark, and over the number of his name. They, too, are standing before the presence of God.

22. **Revelation 7:10-12 ~** This multitude is worshiping the Lord.

    Revelation 15:3-4 ~ This multitude is also worshiping the Lord.

23. **Revelation 8:4** ~ In this context smoke fills the Temple.
    Revelation 15:8 ~ In this context smoke fills the Temple.

Now We Come to the Seven Trumpets and the Seven Vials

24. **Revelation 8:7** ~ TRUMPET One deals with the earth.
    Revelation 16:2 ~ VIAL One deals with the earth.

25. **Revelation 8:8** ~ TRUMPET Two deals with the sea.
    Revelation 16:3 ~ VIAL Two deals with the sea.

26. **Revelation 8:10** ~ TRUMPET Three deals with rivers.
    Revelation 16:4 ~ VIAL Three deals with rivers.

27. **Revelation 8:12** ~ TRUMPET Four deals with the sun.
    Revelation 16:8 ~ VIAL Four deals with the sun.

28. **Revelation 9:1-3, 5** ~ TRUMPET Five deals with darkness and pain.
    Revelation 16:10 ~ VIAL Five deals with darkness and pain.

29. **Revelation 9:14** ~ TRUMPET Six deals with the Euphrates River.
    Revelation 16:12 ~ VIAL Six deals with the Euphrates River.

30. **Revelation 10:7; 11:15-19** ~ TRUMPET Seven ~ There are ten details given below that are related to this seventh trumpet:

The Ten Details Given Concerning the SEVENTH TRUMPET, Repeated in the SEVENTH VIAL (Bowl)

31. Revelation 10:7 and 11:15 ~ The seventh angel is involved.
32. Revelation 11:15 ~ There were great voices in Heaven.
33. Revelation 11:15 ~ The kingdoms of the world are taken.
34. Revelation 11:18 ~ Man's anger is seen.
35. Revelation 11:18 ~ God's wrath comes upon man.
36. Revelation 11:19 ~ There is a revelation of the Temple.

37. Revelation 11:19 ~ Lightning accompanies the seventh trumpet.
38. Revelation 11:19 ~ Thunder accompanies the seventh trumpet.
39. Revelation 11:19 ~ An earthquake accompanies the seventh trumpet.
40. Revelation 11:19 ~ A great hail accompanies the seventh trumpet.

Revelation 16:17-21 ~ VIAL Seven ~ There are ten details given below that are related to this seventh vial. If exactly the same ten details are given for the seventh vial as were given in the seventh trumpet, then we can conclude that they are the same event. (Please note that the ten items, below, relating to the seventh vial corresponds to the 31-40, above, relating to the ten items which relate to the seventh trumpet. I count these comparisons as each being items numbered 31-40.)

The Ten Details Given Concerning the SEVENTH VIAL (Bowl), A Repeat in the SEVENTH TRUMPET

31. Revelation 16:17 ~ The seventh angel is involved.
32. Revelation 16:17-18 ~ There is a great voice and voices are in Heaven.
33. Revelation 16:19 ~ The kingdoms of the world are taken (as seen by the fall of the city, the capital city, Babylon, and the cities, which are governmental centers).
34. Revelation 16:21 ~ Man's anger is seen.
35. Revelation 16:19 ~ God's wrath comes upon man.
36. Revelation 16:17 ~ There is a revelation of the Temple.
37. Revelation 16:18 ~ Lightning accompanies the seventh vial.
38. Revelation 16:18 ~ Thunder accompanies the seventh vial.
39. Revelation 16:18 ~ An earthquake accompanies the seventh vial.
40. Revelation 16:21 ~ A great hail accompanies the seventh vial.

If we add these ten details to our comparison between Revelation 4-10 and Revelation 14-19, we arrive at a total of forty similarities. We continue then, with the last two, numbers forty-one and forty-two:

41. **Revelation 12:1 ~** Immediately after the seventh trumpet, and the ten things that are related to that trumpet, there is a revelation of a woman.
    Revelation 17:1 ~ Immediately after the seventh vial, and the ten things that are related to that vial, there is a revelation of a woman. The Holy Spirit makes twelve very clear contrasts between these two women. We will not go into the discussion of the meaning

of these "two," here. The essential point at this juncture is to simply point out that this assists in the comparison, but that the "two women" are distinctively different women, and though fascinating to discuss, this is too broad for inclusion in this book.

Note: I want to at least point out a helpful statement concerning these two women, in order to leave the reader something to begin further study on this subject. Notice that plagues are sent in the Book of Revelation because of these two women. Plagues are sent to *deliver* the first woman, found in Revelation 12. Plagues are sent to *judge* the second woman, found in Revelation 17.

42. **Revelation 10:7** and **11:15-18** ~ In the days (or time period) of the seventh trumpet, the Church, His Bride, is resurrected and, along with the saints who are alive at that time, raptured. She is carried to the judgment and the ensuing rewards. While the Marriage and Supper, are not named events, just yet, we have unequivocal confirmation that the *Marriage of the Lamb* is the next major event in this specific sequence of events, because of the very fact that the *Great Mystery*, according to Ephesians 5:22-32, irrefutably connects the two.

Revelation 19:7-9 ~ We find that after the Seventh Vial the Bride is taken to the *Marriage of the Lamb* and the Marriage Supper.

In all of the forty-two (42) details, above, we are seeing Revelation 4-13 being repeated in 14-19. The ten (10) details associated with the Seventh Trumpet are the same ten (10) associated with the Seventh Seal (Bowl). I want to add emphasis to this. I have included an additional graphic, below, demonstrating the comparative details of the Seventh Trumpet and the Seventh Vial (Bowl). Once again, these details assure us of the fact that John has "prophesied again."

Is There Any Doubt?

While some readers may not be familiar with all of the details in Revelation, rest assured that having a Ph.D. is not required to recognize that two things have just been demonstrated. First, the Apostle John was told that *he must prophesy again*. Second, *he did just that*. John's "repeat prophecy" was God-breathed inspiration, as the Holy Spirit guided John to write from his own perspective, just as it was with the writers of every other book in the Bible. God used each of them, as holy men, to write His Word, using their own personality and verbal abilities, as they were led and carried along by the Holy Spirit.

"For prophecy never had its origin in the will of man, but men spoke from God as they were carried along by the Holy Spirit."

2 Peter 1:21, NIV84

I want to see with you in the chart, below, some of the most fundamental parts of what we have just learned, above. This small chart shows the first prophecy, then the repeated prophecy of John. They mirror one another. Each of these conclude with different and additional parts of the Mystery of God in view; the sum of which make up the whole of the *Mystery of God* essential factors.

John **RECEIVES** the Prophecy of the Great Tribulation Revelation 5 - 11	John **REPEATS** the Prophecy of the Great Tribulation Revelation 14 - 19
The 3-1/2 year Great Tribulation as seen in the **7 Seals and 7 Trumpets** (Revelation 6-11); Ending with the Announcement of How and When The *Mystery of God* **will be Finished** (*Fulfilled*) Revelation 10:7	The 3-1/2 year Great Tribulation repeated in the **7 Angels and 7 Vials** (Revelation 14-19); Ending with the *Mystery of God* being concluded and **Completely Finished** (*Fulfilled*) in the *Marriage of the Lamb* Revelation 19:7-9
The *Mystery of God* includes the sounding of the *Last Trumpet, the Resurrection, the Judgment and Rewarding of the Saints and Prophets* Revelation 11:15-18	The *Mystery of God* includes the events listed in Revelation 11:15-18 and concludes with the *Marriage of the Lamb* Ephesians 5:22-32 (key verse 5:32); Revelation 19:7-9

What does this comparison show us?

When we merge those two, Revelation 4-13 and Revelation 14-19 (as seen in the graph above), we find the clearest possible understanding of these two sections of the Book of Revelation. You would also understand by combining the events at the end of each of these two sections, or by superimposing one on the other, something quite amazing comes into view:

1. The 7 Seals are seen in the 7 Angels.
2. The 7 Trumpets are seen in the 7 Bowls (Vials).
3. Two women are seen: A godly woman, and harlot woman.
4. The dragon, the beast, and the false prophet are seen in both sections.
5. The Mystery of God is seen in Revelation 10:7 and Revelation 11:15-18 (at the end of the Tribulation Period), which reveals and includes the sounding last trumpet, the resurrection, the judgment and rewarding of the saints. But with the combining of the two sections, we can now see in John's repeated prophecy that the conclusion also includes the ultimate fulfillment

of the **Mystery of God;** that is, *The Marriage of the Lamb*. And all of that is in perfect order, when these two combined sections are merged in the *Marriage*.

In my original draft of this book, the chapters of Part I (now) were the last Part at the end of the book. However, it became obvious that these first four chapters simply had to be inserted into the beginning of the book, even though the reader might not yet have a strong familiarity with the powerful truths found in a deeper understanding of the *Mystery of God*. With those first four chapters showing us the conclusions of the *Mystery of God*, especially regarding the ultimate fulfillment in the *Marriage of the Lamb*, let's see **PART II, THE MYSTERY OF GOD: THE INCREDIBLE KEY.** This PART II should cause any sincere believer to rejoice and praise God in the same spirit in which the Apostle Paul exclaimed, "*Oh, the depth of the riches both of the wisdom and knowledge of God!*" (Romans 11:33). In PART II, we will broaden and deepen our understanding of the *Mega-Mystery* in the Bible. It is actually the very heartbeat of Jesus our Bridegroom, for the Church, His Bride!

Chapter Four Notes

[30] Byers, Marvin, *The Final Victory: The Year 2000?*, 1998, 3rd Edition (Shippensburg, PA, Treasure House). These basic forty-two (42) similarities are used with permission from Pastor Marvin Byers, who first published them. Please note that I have made additions and changes in several items to assist in my use in this chapter. Therefore, it should be noted that if the reader should be willing to take the time to read Pastor Byers' book, please keep in mind that I am responsible for the additions and changes herein, and they do not necessarily reflect Pastor Byers' perspective.

[31] Although we cannot embark on a broad study of the seals here, it may help to understand that once a seal is opened, it continues to operate on the earth until the end. For example, when the sixth seal is opened, the consequences of all the first five will still be in effect on the earth. (Byers, *The Final Victory*).

[32] Furthermore, it is fast becoming obvious that the collaboration and synchronization of activities between Islam, Communists, Socialists, Progressives and others are taking their negative toll on the United States and the world.

PART II

THE MYSTERY OF GOD: THE INCREDIBLE KEY

We have the joy and privilege as Bible-believing Christians of looking into and learning the prophesied Endtimes. Urgently, we need to understand that the Endtimes is impacting our day-to-day lives, and the heat is turning up! There are many *endings* we could consider, when we talk about the Endtimes. We could consider *the end* that comes at the resurrection and rapture; or *the end* at the judgment of the saints; or at the rewards event; or the Millennial Reign of Christ on earth; or perhaps *the end* of Satan, the antichrist, and the false prophet; or even *the end* of this earth as we now know it, since the day will come when God creates a new heaven and a new earth.

The specific *end* I want to see with you begins when the last trumpet sounds. It is at that moment that the *Mystery of God* will *begin to be completed*. When the trumpet sounds, those who had already died *in Christ* will be resurrected, and both the dead and the living will be gathered together to meet the Lord in the air. Those who meet Him in the air will go to the judgment, and experience the rewarding (or lack thereof) of His saints.

This is that same End, which the Apostle Paul also was referring to when he called it the *Great Mystery*. That *Mystery* was identified by the Apostle John as the *Mystery of God*. The Apostles John and Paul reveal to us that the final element of the fulfillment of that *Mystery* will be the *Marriage of the Lamb*. In Part II, we begin to view all of the aforementioned events through the lens of the *Mystery of God*.

The *Mystery of God*, and the *Marriage of the Lamb* as a part of the fulfillment of that *Mystery*, are at the heart of what drives this book, because Christ's *Marriage* is in the heart of Christ!

Ironically, even though the *Mystery of God* is an intriguing, biblical phrase, most Christians I speak with are, at best, vaguely familiar with the phrase, but completely unaware of its meaning. Why and how can that be? It was given to us by God Himself, conspicuously declared in bright flashing lights so it would stand out in His Word. For the first thirty years of my Christian life, I failed to stop long enough to learn about it in more detail.

In the Old Testament, this Mystery was concealed; but in the New Testament it was revealed. It was a *Mystery* hidden and not understood in the Old Testament, even though the prophets prophesied it, and every book in the Old Testament conveyed it, in one way or another. Beginning with Jesus' declarations in the New Testament, it was a Mystery that was then revealed to the apostles, prophets and saints. Now, all of us can see and understand this *Mystery* in order to live out our present lives, and to demonstrate our love for Christ. This demonstration results in rewards in the next age. According to Jesus and the Apostle Paul this *Mystery* began before the foundation of the world. If the *"eyes of our understanding"* (Ephesians 1:18) are opened by the Spirit of God to receive and understand this *Mystery*, we can begin to live in the light of it. I have found that by doing so, we open up a whole new facet of the abundant life Jesus promised. With a true and clear prophetic understanding, we are empowered by the Holy Spirit to live a "restrained" life (See Proverbs 29:18 and 1 John 3:3).

Now that this *Mystery* has been revealed in the New Testament, we can look back and find it throughout the Scriptures, beginning in the Garden of Eden. Then tracing it all the way to the end of the Bible, we will learn together that this *Mystery* is the *Key* for unlocking the understanding of the events of the Endtimes in the Book of Revelation.

What you and I know about the *Mystery of God*, and how we live in the light of it matters—seriously matters. Let's face it! The Endtimes matters; and our own personal end matters. The swift approach of eternity, whether at the hands of the undertaker or Upper-Taker demands passionate urgency about the things of God in our daily lives. Are you one who wants to know Christ intimately, and to grow in the knowledge of Him, day by day and moment by moment? Are you one who is hungry for understanding the Endtimes? The *Mystery of God* is essential for gaining a biblical understanding of the prophetic Endtimes. Many are only now learning that their own personal end will be greatly affected by whether or not they receive, believe and live in the light of the revelation of the *Mystery of God*.

In one important sense, we are so deep into the Endtimes, and so close to the fulfillment of God's prophetic Endtimes events (already in progress) that it can be rightly said that some are *already behind the curve*. But God is able to give each of us grace to know and follow His Word and His will for our lives. Cheer up! Soon, what is now a mystery, will soon be no longer mysterious. It is the heart of God for you and I to know and understand the *Mystery of God*.

Before we enter into the chapters included in **Part II**, I want to offer encouragement to those readers who do not view themselves as seasoned Bible students. It may be true that there are those who know more than others about the Scriptures. I certainly know many whom I look to as elders in the Word, some of which I consider to be mentors in my life, even though some of them may not even know it.

The truths we are about to delve into are in many ways deep and rich with meaning. You may come to certain thoughts that leave you scratching your head a bit, when you first read about them. Don't be too bothered by it. Just read on. Things will begin to clear up as you continue on through the book.

When I was first introduced to these truths about the *Mystery of God*, I already had a degree in theology. Yet, I had to spend time meditating on the facts of these truth in order to thoroughly *understand it*! I assure you. You are not alone. The Holy Spirit is your teacher; the very best of all teachers! This is not to say that you should disregard those who look after your soul, such as your pastor. But each of us will have to answer to God for himself or herself, without regard to anyone else. God loves us. He is the greatest Father, and He has fulfilled His promise to send His Spirit into your life, if you are His own. So, ask Him. Ask, Abba, Father, who wants to hear from you, to teach you. If you hear someone knocking, that would be Him already knocking at your heart's door, desiring to come in to dine with you. Those disciples on the road to Emmaus, on the day of Jesus' resurrection could not see Him, until they broke bread with Him. Let's break bread together with Him, and allow Him to open the *eyes of our understanding of the Mystery of God!*

Chapter 5

WAITING!

"Beloved, now we are children of God; and it has not yet been revealed what we shall be, but we know that when He is revealed, we shall be like Him, for we shall see Him as He is."

1 John 3:2

"... eagerly waiting for the revelation of Jesus Christ ...."

1 Corinthians 1:7

Good things come to those who wait. In certain scenarios, waiting is an understandable necessity, such as when we are in the surgery waiting room. In other scenarios, it is a privilege and joy, such as when we are waiting to see a newborn child or grandchild, or during the graduation of a kindergartner, high schooler or university graduate. It seems, however, that in many scenarios, waiting is often misunderstood, especially when we consider the historical and biblical meaning behind the word wait or waiting. Spiritually speaking, *waiting* is rooted in patience; one of the fruit of the Spirit.[33]

Knowing that some of us don't spend a lot of time looking up the meanings of words in the original languages of the Scriptures, Hebrew, Aramaic, or Greek (although, it is recommended), may I ask you to bear with me for three short paragraphs for a foundational concept? This concept is found in the Hebrew language.

The Hebrew word *qavah* (קָוָה) is translated in the King James Version of the Bible as the word, "wait," 29 times.[34] It is further defined as *"to wait for, look for, i.e., look forward with confidence to that which is good and beneficial, often with a focus of anticipation in a future event."*[35] A derivative of *qavah* is the word, תִּקְוָה *tiqvah*, which means to *"cord or tie several strands of flexible material made into one length of thick string."*[36]

The combined ideas involved in those words can be illustrated by picturing someone "braiding strands of threads together into a thick string or cord." Waiting can be seen as both the time involved and the process and activity involved.

To help us see the picture, imagine Sarah at her tent door *waiting* for Abraham to come home from a day trip to Shechem. There she sits, working away. In her lap are numerous threads. She is busy braiding threads into a thick multi-threaded cord. What is she doing? Well, she is **waiting**—AND she is also ***braiding a multi-threaded cord***, right? She is doing both because that is what we can see in the broader meaning of **waiting**. She is waiting/braiding until her husband arrives home. Upon Abraham's return, he greets Sarah at the tent door: *"Honey, I can see that you have been waiting!"* By using that word, would he be referring to Sarah's *"time spent expecting, hoping and looking forward"* to his return, or would he be referring to the *activity* Sarah was doing while he had been gone? The answer is yes, and yes.

This is the precise picture I want you to see concerning our approach to explaining the *Mystery of God* in the Scriptures. Thread-by-thread, we will be braiding the cord!

The entire process, from Genesis all the way through to the first coming of Christ in the Gospels, can be seen as a *"waiting"* period. The Old Testament saints were NOT just sitting on their hands, doing nothing. They were busy waiting, while God was braiding the prophetic threads. Those threads were those things God spoke through the prophets[37] concerning Messiah's coming.[38]

That was the Old Testament scenario. We will see, looking from our New Testament perspective back into the Old Testament, that God was, in fact, braiding the threads. God is never anxious and never hurries. He has always waited until the *"fullness of time"* to accomplish His purposes. *"But when the fullness of the time had come, God sent forth His Son ..."* (Galatians 4:4). The Old Testament saints waited for the revelation of Christ, the Messiah, who to them was expected and hoped for, yet not fully understood.

Then at the beginning of the New Testament age, the *Mystery of God* was revealed to the apostles and saints.[39] Of course, it was the Holy Spirit who revealed and explained it to them. Once it was revealed to them, it is significant that we are told that its fulfillment would take place at the end of the Church-age. That is why we find that the final phase of the ***fulfillment*** of the *Mystery of God* in the Book of Revelation.[40]

Back then, the early Church was waiting. And we are doing some *waiting of our own.*[41] We are waiting for the beginning of the fulfillment of the *Mystery of God*. That fulfillment will begin when the last trumpet sounds, and the resurrection and rapture take us to the judgment, rewards, and on to the *Marriage of the Lamb*. The historical threads of the Old Testament, the revealing of the *Mystery of God* to the apostles and saints, and the final fulfillment of that *Mystery* are precisely those things which will be enlarged upon throughout this book.

The Scriptures teach that Paul and the saints of his day were living at the ***beginning*** *of the last days*. The generation alive when Jesus returns will be at the ***end*** *of the last days*, or the *"latter days" of the last days*.[42]

Peter made things clear when he said that there will be a generation which experiences the very last days. Think about it! The logic is obvious. In 1 Peter 1:5, he used specific phraseology to describe the time in which the final day of our salvation comes;[43] that is, that day when Jesus comes again. Peter wrote that we are *"kept by the power of God through faith unto **salvation ready to be revealed in the last time.**"* The Greek words that make up the phrase, "the last time," are translated as "the very last opportunity,"[44] "the uttermost opportunity," or "the ends of opportunity." The last opportunity is fast approaching!

We should understand that there is more to this picture than our natural eyes see and our natural ears hear. After all, it is a mystery, God's *Mystery*! We should expect there to be more. This is why Jesus said over and again, both in the Gospels and in Revelation: *"He who has an ear to hear, let him hear ...."*[45] With our spiritual eyes and ears, we want to see and hear from Him about His *Mystery*, from beginning of Scripture to the end of Scripture. So, let's **wait** together! Let's witness the braiding of the multi-threaded, unbreakable, prophetic cord—The *Mystery of God*!

Chapter Five Notes

[33] Galatians 5:22-23.
[34] Strong, J. (1995). *Enhanced Strong's Lexicon.* Woodside Bible Fellowship.
[35] Swanson, J. (1997). *Dictionary of Biblical Languages with Semantic Domains: Hebrew (Old Testament)* (electronic ed.). Oak Harbor: Logos Research Systems, Inc.
[36] Ibid.
[37] *"Of this salvation the prophets have inquired and searched carefully, who prophesied of the grace that would come to you, searching what, or what manner of time, the Spirit of Christ who was in them was indicating when He testified beforehand the sufferings of Christ and the glories that would follow. To them it was revealed that, not to themselves, but to us they were ministering the things which now have been reported to you through those who have preached the gospel to you by the Holy Spirit sent from heaven—things which angels desire to look into"* (1 Peter 1:10–12, emphasis mine).
[38] *"Surely the Lord GOD does nothing, unless He reveals His secret to His servants the prophets"* (Amos 3:7).
[39] See Ephesians 3:3-14; Colossians 1:24-29, and 4:2-4.
[40] The Greek "proleptic aorist" grammatical structure makes it clear that the *Mystery of God* will be fulfilled during the "days" of the seventh trumpet. During those same "days" more fulfillment-events will also occur, namely, the resurrection, rapture, judgment, rewards, and the Marriage of the Lamb!
[41] 1 Corinthians 10:1-11, with emphasis on verse 11:*"Now all these things happened to them as examples, and they were written for our admonition, **upon whom the ends of the ages have come ....**"*
[42] 1 Timothy 4:1; James 5:7.
[43] We must keep in mind that the word "salvation" doesn't only refer to being justified, "born again," or saved from hell. As the old timers used to say: "***I have been saved*** from the penalty of my sin. ***I am being saved*** from the power of sin. ***I will be saved*** from the very presence of sin."
[44] (Byers, *The Final Victory*, 1998), 280. The Greek word "time" here is translated as "opportunity" in Galatians 6:10 and Hebrews 11:15. The Greek word "last" here is translated as "ends of" in Acts 13:47, and as "uttermost" in Acts 1:8 and Matthew 5:26. It means the extreme limit of time or place.
[45] Matthew 11:15.

Chapter 6

THE SCOPE OF THE MYSTERY

Direct references to the Mystery of God:

Romans 16:25-26; I Corinthians 2:7 and 15:51-56; Galatians 3:8;
Ephesians 1:9-10, 18; Ephesians 3:1-9; Ephesians 5:31-32; Ephesians 6:19;
Colossians 1:26-27; Colossians 2:2; Colossians 4:3; 1 Timothy 3:9, 16;
Revelation 10:7; Revelation 11:15-18

The *Mystery of God* encapsulates God's overall message to humanity. Yet, the scope of it is more than just a *general message in general terms to people in general*. The *Mystery of God* specifically explains so many things that would otherwise be unclear. This is especially true regarding how important the *Mystery* is for understanding the Endtimes.

The Incredible Key, the *Mystery of God*, is the driving force in this book to bring us to an understanding of the Book of Revelation and the Endtimes. However, without wrapping our minds and hearts around, at least, some of the details of the truths of the *Mystery of God* throughout the overall message of the Bible, we will not fully understand the impact of the *Mystery of God* on the details of the Endtimes. Understanding the Book of Revelation and the Endtimes is inherently dependent on understanding the *Mystery of God*, even though the scope of the *Mystery* is much greater than the narrower subject of the Endtimes.

Many of us would be so glad if we could actually make sense of the Book of Revelation. I do not overstate the promise when I say that **we should, and we can understand** Revelation much more clearly than we do.

I certainly don't want to assume too much. Perhaps, you are one who has already spent a lot of time praying, searching and studying for understanding of the Endtimes, and this book is just another in a long line of books you are reading as you seek to gain further insight. Either way, if you have yet to include *The Incredible Key*, the *Mystery of God*, in your studies, this chapter will be of special value.

In this chapter, the scope of the *Mystery of God* is described. I use the word "describe," because it is not my intention to define the *Mystery of God* like a dictionary defines a specific word or phrase. It is important for the reader to understand that the *Mystery* is more like taking a journey than a word to be defined. The benefits derived from such understanding will become very practical for daily life in Christ. This is because God has given us an equation to work with, and it looks like this: The greater our understanding of Endtime prophecy, then the greater the grace and strength we will receive from the Spirit to be *restrained*[46] from the wiles of the devil, the world, and our own fleshly ways. In support of that claim, we can refer to Proverbs 29:18, *"Where there is no prophetic vision* [understanding or revelation] *the people* [God's people] *cast off restraint ...."* God also spoke to this matter through the Apostle John, *"And everyone who has this hope in Him* [of His coming] *purifies himself, just as He is pure"* (1 John 3:3, ESV).

We can see then, that it is His desire and plan to bring us to a sound, biblical understanding and a clearer *prophetic vision* of the Endtimes; and that He equates having such clarity as one of His means of bringing us into living a godly and righteous life; a life that honors Him in and through the power of the Spirit. Let's remember that it is His will, as our Bridegroom, to *"... sanctify and cleanse her [His Bride] with the washing of water by the word, that He might present her to Himself ..."* (Ephesians 5:26–27). This begs the question: *When does He present His Bride to Himself?* He presents her to Himself at the *Marriage of the Lamb*.

The *Scope of the Mystery* begins in Genesis and ends in Revelation. All the way through the Bible God braids His prophetic cord. At the end of that prophetic cord is the *Marriage of the Lamb*, where Jesus *ties the knot* at His own marriage. It was His *"good pleasure"* to patiently work with His Bride down through history until she has been made ready for Him to present her to Himself. The Bridegroom, Jesus, deserves to be honored by the Bride! She should be humble, submissive, obedient, respectful and loving with and toward Him. We should want to put to death the works and lusts of our fleshly way.

> *"... the fruit of the Spirit is love, joy, peace, longsuffering, kindness, goodness, faithfulness, gentleness, self-control. Against such there is no law. And those who are Christ's have crucified the flesh with its passions and desires."*
>
> Galatians 5:22–24

If we say that we love Christ, our Bridegroom, then we have the privilege of pursuing purity, by Him, through Him, and for Him. By having a vibrant, even passionate love for Him, rooted in a lively hope of His return, our lives will inherently be more aligned with His will? And shouldn't that hope of His return affect us so deeply that it creates a yearning and hunger to allow the Holy Spirit to live Christ's life through us, demonstrating our faith and sincerity toward our Bridegroom? Try to imagine a bride, any bride, who says that she truly loves her bridegroom, while demonstrating no passion toward him, by word or acts of kindness and love.

THE SCOPE OF THE MYSTERY

*"And now, little children, abide in him, so that when he appears we may have confidence and not **shrink from him in shame at his coming.**"*

1 John 2:28, ESV

Equally true is the fact that a bridegroom, any bridegroom, should show the same toward his bride. But concerning our Bridegroom's passionate love toward us, we have no such worry or concern. He lacks nothing in His demonstration of love toward His Bride! He laid down His life for her, suffering death as the price to purchase her with His demonstration of love. He lives to love, for which He deserves and will receive ultimate glory!

Strangely, many Christians actually believe that when He comes in the rapture, we will immediately enter into a rosy and blissful existence in heaven for eternity. We imagine that we will go into heaven to nothing less than an ethereal glory, without regard to how we have treated the Lord of Glory, who paid an unspeakable price to redeem us. Given the price He paid, and given the lack in each one of our lives, we should at least ask ourselves whether or not our lives reflect His life. Or, do we have a careless, cavalier heart attitude that says that *nothing about the way I have lived will matter because I am saved and on my way to heaven. He paid it all, and I am going to be with Him forever; so, what could possibly be a problem?*

His Bride should seek humility with a yielded attitude of heart, demonstrated in *"reverence and awe"* (Hebrews 12:25–29) and *"fear and trembling"* (Philippians 2:12). He is wholly deserving of such *"respect"* from each of us (Ephesians 5).

The Apostle Paul yearned to bring the bride of Christ, His body, into a life of purity. He expressed it this way:

*"For I am jealous for you with godly jealousy. For I have **betrothed you to one husband** that I may **present you as a chaste virgin to Christ**. But I fear, lest somehow, as the serpent deceived Eve by his craftiness, so your minds may be corrupted from the simplicity that is in Christ."*

2 Corinthians 11:2–3

After His resurrection, our Bridegroom, Jesus Christ, went back to His Father to "prepare a place"[47] for us. In the *fullness of time* He will come again and receive us to Himself. But until then, the Apostle Paul's passion about our future was driven by his desire to present believers to Christ *"as a chaste, pure virgin."* Tragically, some assume that because they have been born again, redeemed by His blood for salvation, they are, therefore, automatically chaste or pure for eternity. This is simply not true, practically nor eternally!

The Bible teaches, and common sense demands that by simply looking inward for a mere moment, we will declare that any purity or holiness in us or about us is nothing more and nothing less than *Christ's own purity* being lived in us and through us by the Spirit of Christ, who dwells in us. And yes, because He is in us, along with His purity and holiness, we are indeed pure and holy in the eyes of the Father, as it relates to our salvation in Christ. But that specifically pertains to being born again, salvation. His righteousness, purity and holiness is imputed to us, so that He can have a bride, who is accepted in Christ before the heavenly Father. That demonstrates His love toward us.

Sanctified living, which demonstrates our love toward and for Him and His Body is something very different. These two—salvation and sanctification—are not different in quality. They both originate by and through Him. We willfully choose to respond to Him in each case. They are different in their effect. In the first case, He has demonstrated His love for us by giving His life for us. In the second case, we are demonstrating our love for Him by giving our lives to and for Him, which happens on a moment-by-moment basis. By the grace and the power of the Spirit, believers have the privilege of choosing, on this moment-by-moment basis, to allow His life to fill and flow through us, as pure water, cleansing us and thereby demonstrating our love and yieldedness to Him.[48]

We are told,

"Husbands, love your wives, just as Christ also loved the church and gave Himself for her, **that He might sanctify and cleanse her with the washing of water by the word**, *that He might present her to Himself a glorious church, not having spot or wrinkle or any such thing, but that she should be holy and without blemish."*

Ephesians 5:25–27, NKJV

We, His church, have a problem; one which is every believer's circumstance. That problem is our fleshly, self-life. Can it be denied by any one of us that this is a problem? It is not the kind of problem that has no solution; but still, it is a problem, which He wants to resolve with and for us.

In our flesh, "*dwells* **no good thing**," as the Apostle Paul said in Romans 6 and 7. The only good thing in us, when God looks into our lives, is His Own Son's life dwelling in us by and through His Spirit. If we believe, or if we have been taught, that there is no relevant consequence resulting from how we treat our Bridegroom before the *Marriage*, we are utterly mistaken. If we interpret our new birth, our salvation, to mean that we can now coast toward the rapture, as we wait to get out of this messy world, then we are either deceived, or greatly lacking in the doctrines of Christ. I am not advocating the erroneous idea that we are to work to obtain salvation. But what I am saying is that many of us treat the Lord Jesus, our Bridegroom, with an unaffectionate attitude of heart and life. There is only one little problem. Jesus gives us His understanding of the relationship: "*If you love me, you will keep*

THE SCOPE OF THE MYSTERY

my commandments" (John 14:15, ESV). And of course, that cannot be accomplished, except by the power of the Holy Spirit, as we grow in the grace and knowledge of Jesus!

If we as believers are praying and seeking to know Him, then we know that our hearts want a more intimate relationship with Him. We are not satisfied. Isn't it good news to know that He is pursuing us more than we are pursuing Him? The true Christian life and walk doesn't end with salvation. That is as ridiculous as giving birth to a baby and then expecting that baby to grow up on its own, turning out to be right, do right, take care of himself, feed himself, clean himself, clothe himself, and so forth. Obviously, there is much more to our relationship with Him than being born. Let's allow Him to draw us to Himself, more and more with the attitude of heart that cries out: *He must increase, but I must decrease!*

It is not about me becoming better. It's not about me doing more. The Christian life is about Him increasing and me decreasing. He is 100% in us! The problem is that once His 100% begins to filter through my life, or yours, often, others can hardly see Him, unless we are truly learning what it really means to decrease. If we do not learn to humble ourselves, dying to our own will, then by the time His life shows up on the outside, He might not be seen by others, at all. But don't be too discouraged. In Christ's eyes, He needs and wants His Bride to become blameless in this life. He wants His Bride's life to become sanctified and cleansed by the washing of the water of the Word. That washing is only accomplished by the Holy Spirit in and through us, as we learn through trials He allows, teaching us to allow Him to live His life through us. This is how the fruit of the Spirit flows through, and shows through our lives to others. Therefore, He is the one who is glorified and who affects the lives of others. It is by His power, and not by our own.[49] Thank God! He is ready to help us and He understands that we are dust!

What does all of that have to do with *The Scope of the Mystery of God*? First, it has to do with our own personal end. Is my life pure and presentable to Him, so that I would not be ashamed if He were to come today, or if my life ended today? Am I living as an "overcomer" in this life? Is my love for Him growing; is it maturing, and more intimate than ever before? Is He truly honored in and through my life? Do others see Jesus' life in and through me? The *Mystery of God* addresses my own end but it also addresses the *Endtimes*!

As I stated up front in this chapter, the scope of the *Mystery* is from beginning to end of the Bible. Since all of this relates to us as His Bride, and to Him as our Bridegroom, it most definitely relates to prophecy in the Endtimes. Here's what I mean. The *Marriage of the Lamb* is, undeniably, an Endtime event. I dare not say that is merely an "event;" rather, it is the culmination of all other events up to that point. His eternally planned *Marriage* represents His love and joy in the light of all that He will have done on our behalf from before the foundation of the world up to that very moment. Our relationship with Him deserves to be saturated with affection during our lifetime, so that when we see Him face to face, He will be pleased with us, as His Bride.

> *"... it was granted her to clothe herself with fine linen, bright and pure—for the fine linen is the righteous deeds of the saints."*
>
> Revelation 19:8, ESV

I am aware that we are granted the "righteousness of Christ"[50] for salvation. Of course, to this the Scriptures completely agree. But when it comes to the Bride in Revelation 19:8, the Word of God is specifically referring to *the righteous deeds of the saints*. Those *righteous deeds* are specifically our responsibility and privilege. In this, we choose to allow the Holy Spirit to do those righteous deeds in and through us in His will and for His glory. The last time I checked, we rightly teach that we are not justified by the *"righteous deeds of the saints."* To suggest that the *"fine linen, bright and pure"* found at the *Marriage of the Lamb* refers to justification, would contradict the truth of salvation by grace as a gift of God. This *gift* cannot be gained by our deeds; it is a free gift!

The *"righteous deeds"* referred to at the Marriage of the Lamb is precisely what it says and means: *"the righteous deeds of the saints."*

Furthermore, the Bride is to clothe herself in her righteous deeds. This is **not** the same as justification regarding salvation. This can easily be illustrated. Let's remember the Last Supper in the upper room, where Jesus and His disciples ate together, just before the time of His crucifixion. At the end of the supper, Jesus began washing the disciples' feet. Peter challenged Jesus, basically telling Him that He should not be washing his feet. Peter didn't want His Lord to do that, implying that he and the others should be washing Jesus' feet.

> *"Peter said to Him, 'You shall never wash my feet!' Jesus answered him, 'If I do not wash you, you have no part with Me.' Simon Peter said to Him, 'Lord, not my feet only, but also my hands and my head!' Jesus said to him, 'He who is bathed needs only to wash his feet, but is completely clean; and you are clean, but not all of you.'"*
>
> John 13:8–10

Jesus knew that Judas was not *"completely clean."* But the rest of the disciples were. Why did Jesus wash their feet? It seems that there were, at minimum, two reasons:

1) Jesus told them that His action was for an example. What He did to them, they were to do for one another. That symbolism tells us to help each other, love one another, provoke one another in love and good works, so that Christ's Body, the Saints are able to endure our walk in this world, as we wait.

THE SCOPE OF THE MYSTERY

2) Secondly, Jesus makes it clear that they, as His children, and now we, as His children, are *completely clean*, just as every soul who has been justified before God through His cleansing blood for salvation. But what about the feet? As Jesus was careful to make it clear, the feet are symbolic of our walk in this world; and our feet, therefore, get the daily dirt of life on them. To that extent, Jesus was telling Peter, the other disciples, and us, that we must get our walking (our feet) washed by Christ and by one another.

Our moment-by-moment walk—how we live in this body in this life in this world—is where the *righteous deeds of the saints* come into the picture at the *Marriage of the Lamb*. The Judgment Seat of Christ and the rewards or lack of rewards of the saints will have already occurred by the time of the event of the *Marriage of the Lamb*. It is not our righteousness that gets us to the *Marriage*. But whatever we will be clothed with at that *Marriage*, will have already been determined by the righteous deeds we allowed Him to do through us by His Spirit during this lifetime.

Friend, our walk with Christ is not that of merely being born again. Please don't misunderstand. Being born again, or justified, is the beginning point, which we must have. But we need to grow beyond the beginning. We are given the opportunity and privilege of allowing the work of the Holy Spirit and His Word to be accomplished in us. This is not a burden to bear. His *"yoke is easy and His burden is light"* (Matthew 11:30). That yoke involves a moment-by-moment volitional choice we make, so as to either walk in the Spirit or to walk in our fleshly thinking. When we are in that yoke with Him, peace and rest rule our lives.

Like a good father and mother training their children, so is God's relationship with us. As a result of us choosing to yield to His work in and through us, He will bring His life through us in the form of the fruit of the Spirit through the grace and power of the Spirit. And it is His fruit in and through us that becomes those righteous deeds of the saints.

> *"For the moment all discipline seems painful rather than pleasant, but later it yields the* **peaceful fruit of righteousness to those who have been trained by it.**"
> Hebrews 12:11, ESV

Many Christians simply do not realize that we are responsible for how we will be clothed at the *Marriage of the Lamb*. I do not mean to suggest that we use our own power to gain our spiritual clothing for the *Marriage*. Any good and righteous deed requires that the only One who is good and righteous does that deed by His power in and through us. In that, He is glorified. I, for one, do not want to have a skimpy robe in His presence. It is not that I am worried about salvation; not at all. Rather, we are to be learning that Jesus, on the cross, looked forward with the **joy set before Him of having purchased His Bride for His marriage at the**

Marriage of the Lamb. He was, at that very moment by His suffering and death, purchasing that Bride, with the *joy of His marriage to His Bride set before Him*! (refer to Hebrews 12:1-2; John 16:22).

He wants us to live a life that demonstrates that we, as His Bride, honor Him with our lives. When we enter into the heavenly marriage ceremony room, nothing will please Him more that for each of us to be clothed in a robe of righteousness, which will demonstrate the quality of having had a great love for Him during our lifetime on earth. *Does that have any personal meaning to you? As for me, anytime I meet someone who has a kindred spirit about these things, it is always like a mini-revival meeting.* As we draw near to Him looking forward to the Marriage of the Lamb, we enter into His joy now, in this life! Those who have that understanding seem always to be those who love His appearing and who are allowing His coming to affect their lives, not only day by day, but their heart's desire is that this affects them *moment-by-moment*, in the most practical of terms.

In John 14-17, Jesus is nearing the time of His crucifixion. He spends much time giving very important instructions and teachings to His disciples. He spends much time with His Father, also. Within those chapters, He reveals many stunning things. He comforts them with the fact that they are His Bride, and He is going to go away, and while gone He is going to prepare a place for them. (Revelation reveals that place is the New Jerusalem.) He explains to them that His life will be in them, through the Spirit. He illustrates this by a metaphor. He tells them that He is *The True Vine* and that we are the *Branches on the Vine*. His life-giving sap will flow through and from Him into us. From that life will come fruit. He even gives them the downside of failing to bear fruit. He will prune that part which hinders the growth of fruit—painful, but absolutely necessary! Perhaps, you are in pain; physical, mental, emotional or spiritual pain; none of us is exempt from such. We are to humble ourselves, yielding to His pruning. The point I am making is that no matter the reasons for our pains or troubles, as we yield to the pruning in our hearts, He will cause "all things" to work together for our good and His glory. He, alone, knows what you need. While He permits that which He could prevent in our lives, He never gives us more than He knows we can bear. This is because He is there to bear it with us, until we are finished being exercised by it, and become matured enough at that moment for Him to begin to add the next elements of growth; or perhaps, to even take us to heaven to be with Him. No matter what we go through, we learn to see just how great our God is!

Once He had given His disciples all the comfort possible, as He was to soon face the crucifixion, Jesus turned to prayer with His Father. And what do we find in His prayer? Joy! While this is, without a doubt, an intense moment for Jesus, as He was facing the cross shortly, still His heart's focus was on His Father and His branches, His own disciples. He had already told them, "*These things I have spoken to you, that my joy may be in you, and that your joy may be full*" (John 15:11, ESV). But then He goes deeper, explaining that "*… you have sorrow now,* *but I will see you again, and your hearts will rejoice, and **no one will take your joy from you***" (John 16:22, ESV). As Jesus was closing His prayer, He makes a wonderful prayer request of His Father: *"But now I am coming to you, and these things I speak in the world, that they may have my joy fulfilled in themselves"* (John 17:13, ESV). This is precisely why the Bible and Church history tell us about the joyful approach the apostles and early saints had toward their deaths, though most were brutally martyred for Christ. They laid down their lives, breathing their last breath with joy in their hearts, witnessing to Jesus' promises!

How did he indicate that this joy would be fulfilled? *"I have said these things to you [disciples], that in me you may have peace. **In the world you will have tribulation. But take heart; I have overcome the world***" (John 16:33, ESV). Joy, His joy, will be fulfilled in us as we learn to take up our cross and follow Him. We know that in this life we will have tribulation, but we also know that He has already overcome the world. We find our joy in Him, not in this world. Did He not plainly tell us that the world will hate us? He further instructs us through the Apostle Paul, *"All that desire to live godly in Christ Jesus will suffer persecution"* (2 Timothy 3:12). That is the Christian life, the abundant Christian life; the Spirit of grace and joy He brings to us, whether through the good times or during times of what often seems to be impossible trials and trauma!

I was talking with a brother in Christ, a genuine lover of the Lamb of God, who happens to be in ministry. He told me that his entire Christian life had been consumed in knowing all that he could in God's Word about the Bride of Christ, and the *Marriage of the Lamb*, and to learn to live in the light of those truths. In a saddened tone of voice, he regretfully shared that many of his best friends in ministry have little to no real passion or interest in the subject of the Bride of Christ. Is there any wonder that we, the Church, His Bride, lack in understanding the authority behind our mission, and His willingness to provide His grace, power, and joy in the face of this wicked world?

Earlier, I quoted Proverbs 29:18. It's a regular staple of mine; because I need it, and I know we all do. Let's see it again: *"Where there is no prophetic vision* (understanding, revelation) *the people cast off restraint ..."* (Proverbs 29:18, ESV). Sadly, this is the condition of much of Christ's Bride, today. Most of us, it seems, have been guilty of casting off restraint, which means that our robes are lacking in righteous deeds; we are not becoming blameless, or chaste virgins, as we ought. But, we can—starting at this very moment!

A zealousness for righteous living, teaching, and preaching has been to a regrettable and tragic degree on the back burner in America for a long time, even though there is probably more religious noise-making going on. Instead, we have chased every imaginable method to draw people into the Church building. Without a fresh outpouring of the Holy Spirit and without a clearer "prophetic vision or understanding" of the Endtimes, we **will not**, and we **cannot** be satisfactorily restrained from our own ways to the glory of God. Without a fresh anointing of His Spirit, why would we think the unsaved would want to join in with us? Because the unsaved world sees the Church's obvious lack of love for one another in the most practical of terms, why would they want to join in with us? What do we have to offer them that would be any different than the life they now live?

If we turn that coin over to the opposite side and look at it from the perspective of *What would Jesus do?* Surely, each of us has been taught that we must conform to Christ; but what does that look like? Let's pose another question. Do you believe that the best life you could ever experience would be to allow the Holy Spirit to live the life of Jesus through you?[51] I trust you can answer that question with a resounding—Yes! Why do so many of us not even realize that the Holy Spirit was given to us to *teach us all things,* and also *show us things to come.* Furthermore, John wrote in Revelation 19:10 that the *"testimony of Jesus is the spirit of prophecy."* All I am saying is that God's Word tells us that if we are to allow the Holy Spirit to live the life of Jesus through us, then His life, Spirit, and testimony include prophecy. A short-sighted neglect of prophecy can only result in our own harm, shame, and lack of faith and faithfulness.

How faithful is our God! He has made a way for us to come to Him, confess our sins, turn from our wicked ways, and He will forgive our sins and cleanse us from all **unrighteousness.** In other words, He will give us righteousness, in exchange for unrighteousness. He will give us beauty *for ashes!* And that is no little matter.

One of the most precious God-given privileges we have is to draw near to God for understanding the Endtimes, and our own ending. He promises to speak life and power into such a hungry, contrite heart, as His Spirit brings a growing urgency into our spirit about the use of our time and resources for His glory, rather than for ourselves. I am absolutely **not** talking about going up into a mountain cave and getting away from the world. The opposite is true. Jesus said, *"Occupy until I come"* (Luke 19:12-13, KJV). That word, occupy simply means to continue "doing business." We are to be in the world, but **not of** the world!

Ah! The great equipping of His prophetic Word is for our lives in the *here and now!* There is a fire that can burn in our souls, which can keep us growing in love for one another as believers, while we are also allowing Christ's life to flow through us into the lives of others, including the unsaved, and even those who would persecute us. That fire will burn in us as we begin to see the Endtimes from God's perspective, and begin to understand in a deeper, richer way, just how much our Bridegroom, Jesus, loves His Bride, God's assembly of saints!

The **Mystery of God** is *The Incredible Key* that unlocks the *Endtimes,* just as the title of this book declares. On a more personal level, the *Mystery of God* is *The Incredible Key* to our own ending, as we live life with our Bridegroom with the *Marriage of the Lamb* in view.

The scope of the Mystery

Removing Mysteriousness from the Mystery of God

I will be using a primary metaphor to assist the reader in picturing the process, the events, the people, and the details, which God uses to reveal the *Mystery of God*. In Chapter 5, **WAITING**, the reader was introduced to a braided, multi-threaded, unbreakable, prophetic cord, in which each thread continues to be braided into the cord to make the truths of the *Mystery of God* clearer.

That cord will begin, and then extend throughout the book as a metaphorical means of seeing the *Mystery of God* throughout the Bible; and what it means. Once we come to the end of the cord, we will see a completed picture, a completed cord, the *Mystery of God*. We will understand the Book of Revelation and the Endtimes with excitement and a sense of relief, engendered by that greater understanding. The Book of Revelation will finally make sense to many who have struggled with it. What a relief and blessing that will be for those who have had hungry hearts to understand and to know Christ and His prophetic Word more intimately. This is precisely what happened to me. The truths in the *Mystery of God* changed my walk with Christ in a dynamic way. This began for me over two decades ago, now. Until then, I had no understanding of this *Mystery*, but there it was—the *Mystery of God*— hiding in plain sight. I had read Revelation 10:7 many times over the years during my times of Bible reading. But I had not recognized the importance of it.

> "… *in the days of the trumpet call to be sounded by the seventh angel, the* **Mystery of God** *would be fulfilled* [finished, completed], *just as he announced to his servants the prophets"* (emphasis and insertions mine).
>
> Revelation 10:7

For many years, I had asked the Lord for a clearer understanding of many facets of the Endtimes. I had spent many hours in seemingly insatiable study. But for years, clearer understanding had been, for the most part, elusive. I was extremely well versed in the standard, currently popular teaching about the Endtimes, which I had learned growing up. But I could not fully reconcile many of those ideas with Scripture. To me, there wasn't an abundance of Scripture to support the major tenets of what I had been taught. Many of the things I had known from my youth seemed, at best, to be speculative. Nevertheless, God used even the Scriptures supporting those ideas to keep my heart drawn to Him long enough to gain further understanding, for which I am grateful.

Then He was gracious to allow me to be introduced to the *Mystery of God*. My understanding of the Endtimes began to change fundamentally. And I am not alone. Others testify to the same affect. My testimony is that after having gained a clearer understanding of the Endtimes, my walk in the Spirit and the Word began to take on greater and greater grace and strength in the most practical of terms. To repeat the point: *"And everyone who has **this hope in Him** [in Christ's return] purifies himself, just as He is pure"* (1 John 3:3). It is difficult to fully explain just how much God has done in my heart and life since He allowed me to know and understand the truths of the *Mystery of God*. In no way am I suggesting that knowledge of the *Mystery of God* had been the instrument of change. Rather, it is the **God of the Mystery**, through the work of the Holy Spirit, who makes the changes. And those changes are not me getting better. The change is what I quoted from John the Baptist earlier when he said. *"He must increase, but I must decrease"* (John 3:30). That is to say that the change coming through my life is nothing more and nothing less than Christ's own life, demonstrated in the fruit of His Spirit filling and overflowing. How great, kind, loving and merciful is our God to allow any of us to receive His great grace, so that we can, in turn, allow Him to have His way in our lives! Isn't this what we are supposed to want—the person of Christ flowing and overflowing in and through us, in and by the Holy Spirit? Are we not supposed to want Him to *teach us all things*, and to *show us things to come?*

Friend, the *Mystery of God* certainly qualifies as part and parcel of "things to come." If you have been unfamiliar with the truths of the *Mystery of God*, you are not alone. After having often discussed the *Mystery of God* with Church leaders, theologians, and many other Christians who have studied the Endtimes, I can assure you that you are in good company.

Each of us has much to learn. Thankfully, God continues teaching us. When it comes to the *Mystery of God*, my hope is that you will not attempt to *discover* this truth only by intellectually grasping it; rather, as you seek Him for understanding, by His mercy, you will ask Him to *reveal* this truth to you by His Spirit. It seems obvious that He offers us the opportunity to humbly depend on Him to show us the truth, rather than Him depending on us to analyze and discover it. His revelation is the only way truth will ever come alive in our hearts, anyway!

Still, as mysterious as the *Mystery of God* may seem for some, at this juncture, let's not unwittingly make it altogether mysterious, as though it is something inordinate or weird. The word *mystery* for some believers may conjure up unintended, even silly, notions. Not only are silly notions unnecessary, but it is also important to see that the *Mystery of God* is more than just a biblical phrase. It is an essential doctrine, the scope of which covers the entire Bible. More than that, this truth is essential for greater grace for each of us, as we seek victory in Christ during these last days. Furthermore, since Jesus Christ is the central theme of the whole Bible, and since the *Mystery of God* reveals Jesus Christ in a vitally important way, we should hunger to understand thoroughly what He has revealed about Himself in this *Mystery*.

As we drill deeper in the next chapter, **The Overview of the Mystery,** I want to see with you the details of the *Mystery of God*.

Chapter Six Notes

[46] Proverbs 29:18: "*Where there is no prophetic vision [understanding] the people cast off restraint ....*"

[47] John 14:2.

[48] Romans 12:1,2; Ephesians 5:25-27; John 17:17.

[49] Zechariah 4:6 "*So he answered and said to me: 'This is the word of the LORD to Zerubbabel: Not by might nor by power, but by My Spirit, Says the LORD of hosts.'*" (Zechariah 4:6, NKJV).

[50] Romans 3:22.

[51] Well do I remember when one of my dearest friends posed that question to me the first time. That question, and my answer to it (yes!), has left an indelible impact on my life.

Chapter 7

OVERVIEW OF THE MYSTERY

SPECIAL NOTE OF EXPLANATION

In this chapter there are descriptions detailing the truths found in the Mystery of God. I have provided two very beneficial charts.

1) The first one is at the end of this chapter (page 140) which provides a quick reference snapshot of the Mystery's Bible verse locations, and how they are inseparably linked to one another, guaranteeing that all of these refer to the same Mystery.

2) The second chart is found in Appendix A. This chart is the most critical chart in the entire book for truly gaining the fastest, clearest understanding of the key factors of the Mystery of God. This asset is my "go to" chart for teaching or simply sharing with others about the Mystery of God. Every New Testament reference specifically referring to the Mystery is made clear in that chart. (When you review Appendix A, you will realize that many of the Bible verse references are used more than once. This is because within a given Bible verse more than one Mystery factor is found, and therefore, the verse is assigned to each separate factor. Once you review the chart, it will become obvious.

The Overview

The key elements of the truths found in the *Mystery of God*[52] are repeated numerous times in numerous ways in the New Testament. Strangely, it is completely passed over by many of us. God kept this **"Great Mystery"**[53] as a secret,[54] hidden in God[55] from before the foundation of the world,[56] until the time of His choosing. The time of His choosing began when Jesus revealed that there are *"mysteries of the kingdom,"* as was reported by Matthew, Mark, and Luke.[57] Continuing in the time of His choosing, the Holy Spirit later revealed the details of this "Great Mystery," the *Mystery of God*, to the Apostles Paul[58] and John,[59] who, in turn, revealed and taught its truths to His Church.

The Holy Spirit, through the apostles Paul and John, unveiled the final threads in this multi-threaded, unbreakable, prophetic cord; the cord which began with the first thread in the Garden of Eden and which ends in Revelation. And it is there in Revelation that the spectacular concentration of Endtime events is found; those which directly pertain to the *Mystery of God*. Those events are concentrated in Revelation 10, 11, and 19. It will be at the *Marriage of the Lamb* in Revelation 19, that grand occasion of His Wedding, during which Jesus will, indeed, **tie the knot**!

What If's

The *Mystery of God* is critical for knowing and walking with God, as we are preparing for the traumatic and dramatic days just ahead of us in this world, and for His coming. To propel us, I want to provide a few **what if** questions.

What if, by gaining a biblical understanding of the Mystery of God, you were to experience the following benefits—and much more?

1. *What if* you could finally make sense of the Book of Revelation?
2. *What if* you could gain a better understanding of the role of Israel and the role of the Church in the Endtimes?
3. *What if* you could gain an understanding of the *Marriage of the Lamb*, and why it should matter to you, right now, in this life?
4. *What if* the *Millennial Reign of Christ* were to become a great motivation for how you live your life because you want to honor Him by qualifying to rule with Him in His Millennial Kingdom?
5. *What-If*, as a result of understanding the *Mystery* and seeking to live in the light of it, you could receive added grace for living in holiness and purity of heart?
6. *What if* you could gain a constantly increasing desire to please your Bridegroom, Jesus Christ?
7. *What if* praise and worship were to become a spirit-filled celebration of your love for Him, like never before, especially in your private time of worship?
8. *What if* you discovered a profound urgency in your heart to yield to His will in moment-by-moment walk with Christ?
9. *What if* you could receive a new level of passionate urgency to become an overcomer in Christ, as you see the Day approaching?

There is so much more, but through these few questions, I trust the reader can begin to get a feel for the value of the *Mystery of God*!

OVERVIEW OF THE MYSTERY

Note

Regarding the *Mystery of God* details, which began above, you will note that I do not expanded on them in this chapter more than is absolutely necessary. At this juncture, I am merely seeking to assist the reader in gaining a basic familiarity with the *Mystery of God* by means of an overview. Further exploration and expansion will make up the balance of the book.

From the vantage point of the New Testament, we learn that the many details of the *Mystery of God* in the Old Testament will be found all the way back into the Book of Genesis. There, the first bridegroom and bride, Adam and Eve, provide a prophetic reference to the *Marriage of the Lamb*, as is eventually detailed in the Book of Revelation. (This fact is verified in other Scripture passages, which we will review later.) Although God's Word states that the *Mystery of God* was hidden and secret in the Old Testament, the *Mystery* was only hidden just beneath the surface; it was always there by God's own design, only for Him to "uncover" in the fullness of time. To state these things concisely, we learn that the *Mystery* was **concealed** in the Old Testament, **revealed** in the New Testament, and will be *fulfilled* in Revelation.

The completion of the fulfillment of the *Mystery of God* will come at the event of the *Marriage of the Lamb*. Why would God choose to bring the events of the ages to a culmination in the form of the event of the marriage of His Son? Throughout Scripture there is a continuous revelation of the marriage and the marriage covenant, beginning with Adam and Eve. It is true that the events of the entire Bible can be seen as reflecting God's Wedding Plan for His Son. Is it merely a "little" coincidence that in the context of the beginning and the end, in Genesis and Revelation, God brings marriage to the front and center? In the beginning, it was the marriage of Adam and Eve. In the end, it is the *Marriage of the Lamb*, Christ Himself, who is the last Adam, to His own *Eve*, the Church. Going beyond all of those events, when God creates the "new heaven and a new earth," He reveals that future creation in terms pertaining to Christ's marriage relationship and the oneness of it all.

> "Now I saw a new heaven and a new earth, for the first heaven and the first earth had passed away. Also, there was no more sea. Then I, John, saw the **holy city, New Jerusalem, coming down out of heaven from God, prepared as a bride adorned for her husband.** And I heard a loud voice from heaven saying, 'Behold, the tabernacle of God is with men, and He will dwell with them, and they shall be His people. **God Himself will be with them and be their God.**'"
>
> Revelation 21:1–3

Among other important truths, these verses pertain to the marriage covenant relationship of Christ, as the Bridegroom, with His Wife-Bride, to whom at this juncture, He is married.

This is significant because this takes place subsequent to all things pertaining to this present earth-order; that is, the Second Coming, the reign of Christ on earth, the final judgment, etc. Furthermore, this reveals the ultimate results of the fulfillment of the "New Covenant," prophesied by Jeremiah the prophet. This is obviously referred to throughout the New Testament.[60] And do we not know that the very words, *New Testament*, mean *New Covenant*? The *New Covenant* is, among other things, a marital covenant. Revelation 21, *"a bride adorned for her husband"* is clearly seen as evidence of the covenant promises having been fulfilled at that point. Our Lord is faithful to fulfill every covenant He makes.

Without seeing this marital covenant connection, to which the entire Bible speaks, it would be nearly impossible to fully grasp God's overall plan and His purpose for the *Mystery of God*. We must keep in mind, at all times, that a fundamental fact about the *Mystery of God* is the coming together in Christ of all saints, Jews and Gentiles, from both the Old and the New Testament.

God made covenantal promises to the Old Testament saints. But those promises **could not nor would not have been received** by them without Christ having first paid the purchase price to obtain His Bride. It was God's sovereign plan to bring all together to be one in Him. Christ paid with the shedding of His own blood for the destruction of the wall of separation. *"For He Himself is our peace, who has made both one, and has broken down the middle wall of separation,"* (Ephesians 2:14). Because He destroyed that wall by His death on the cross, the Old Testament saints are now made to be complete together with us and us with them. Therefore, we can now receive the promises together. Can we be sure of this, and that it is a correct understanding of God's designed will? It is specifically because of this truth that I want to repeatedly see with the reader the importance of Hebrews 11 and 12, in relation to the *Mystery*. In particular, let's see Hebrews 11:39-40:

> *"And all these* [the saints before Christ's death] *having obtained a good testimony through faith, did not receive the promise, God having provided something better for us, that they* [the saints before Christ's death] *should not be made perfect* [complete] *apart from us* [the New Testament saints].*"*

I would ask that we take note that the list in Hebrews doesn't begin with the nation of Israel. It goes back further than the nation of Israel, all the way back to the beginning. The point I am making by highlighting this is that Hebrews 11:39 and 40 melds together the saints from the beginning to the end, as "one body." And that "one body" is Christ's body. Christ's body is His bride. The *Marriage of the Lamb* to His bride will bring to a conclusion, finish, the *Mystery of God*.

OVERVIEW OF THE MYSTERY

The Descriptive Details of the Mystery

If you are willing to take the time to open your Bible, and turn to each of the numbered references, found in the CHAPTER NOTES at the end of the chapter, you will gain the fuller understanding. Obviously, reading the actual Scripture passage is much better and deeper than only reading my connections and commentary. So, for the truest connection with the heart of Christ in this truth of the Mystery of God, consider grabbing your Bible and read along.

Now, let's pick back up where we left off on page 133 in the **Overview** of the Mystery's Descriptive Details. Each Detail is reference-numbered to the CHAPTER NOTES, which provides the Bible verses for that numbered detail.

It is so beautiful and telling that the *Mystery of God* has been expressed throughout the Bible by God's use of the intimate language of love in *Marriage*. When God repeatedly and consistently foretells there is coming a day when *"I will be their God, and they shall be My people,"* He is referring to the New Covenant relationship—His eternal relationship with all of those who are His people. He is describing Jews and Gentiles alike, who by His grace believe and are one in Christ. First, He expressed this concept in the differing covenants in Old Testament prophecies,[61] all of which were part of this same revelation concerning the *Mystery of God*. Then in the New Testament God made it unequivocally clear that all of His covenantal promises were to be ultimately and completely fulfilled in the New Covenant.[62]

This *Mystery* is interchangeably called the *mystery of God*[63] and the *mystery of Christ*.[64] Though previously secret and hidden (by God Himself), it was revealed, first to the apostles, then by the apostles for all saints of God to know and understand.[65] This *Mystery* was related to preaching to the Gentiles.[66] The Gentiles were told that this *Mystery* is related to the spiritual riches offered to them in Christ.[67] It could not be detached from the preaching of the Gospel. Paul even tied the two together, when he called it the *Mystery* of the Gospel,[68] which inherently means that it was and is the *Mystery* concerning our faith.

It is certainly worth noting that there is a tendency for Bible students to conclude that the reason Paul was put in prison was because he *preached the Gospel*. While that is part of the picture, it is not the complete picture. Leaving no doubt as to what the complete picture was, Paul outright declared that the reason he had been put into prison in chains was because he preached this *Mystery*,[69] which is clearly seen in the following verses:

> *"And pray for us, too, that God may open a door for our message, so that we may proclaim the **mystery of Christ, for which I am in chains**. Pray that I may proclaim it clearly, as I should."*
>
> Colossians 4:3–4, NIV84

*"For this reason I, Paul, **the prisoner of Christ Jesus for the sake of you Gentiles**— Surely you have heard about the administration of **God's grace that was given to me for you, that is, the mystery** made known to me by revelation, as I have already written briefly."*

Ephesians 3:1–3, NIV84

*"Pray also for me, that whenever I open my mouth, words may be given me so that I will fearlessly make known the **mystery of the gospel, for which I am an ambassador in chains**. Pray that I may declare it fearlessly, as I should."*

Ephesians 6:19–20, NIV84

What was it about Paul's testimony to the religious, but unconverted, Jews that enraged them. They not only wanted him put in prison, they wanted to murder him? The claim of the Gospel in the death, burial and resurrection of Christ, in and of itself, was disturbing enough to the Jewish leaders of Israel. But as mentioned above, what put Paul in prison, and which also enraged the Jews to the point of killing him,[70] was the inclusion of *one little extra claim* in his preaching. He preached that the *believing Gentiles became citizens of the commonwealth of Israel immediately upon salvation.* They interpreted his preaching to mean that Gentiles would somehow become actual physical citizens, rather than *spiritual citizens of a spiritual city and country,* "*whose builder and maker is God,*"[71] of which they had no understanding.

When Paul was testifying before the Jews, they listened to everything Paul said, right up to the point at which he openly declared that God had sent him to preach to the Gentiles also. Keep in mind that what he preached to the Gentiles was the Gospel. Yet, as Paul explained in numerous Scripture references, preaching the good news of the Gospel to the Gentiles included preaching the good news that the believing Jews **and** believing Gentiles are to be "*one new man*"[72] in Christ. Jews and Gentiles are "*fellow citizens of* [spiritual] *Israel,*"[73] and of the same "*household of God,*"[74] the "*Israel of God!*"[75] Far from diminishing or superseding the Gospel itself, the preaching of the *Mystery* magnifies the Gospel, the good news of Christ. This is especially the case when referring to the Gospel's benefits to the Gentiles; especially when a Jews/Israelite realized that this was a revelation of what was promised to Abraham. Paul plainly taught this: "*And the Scripture, foreseeing that God would justify the Gentiles by faith, preached the Gospel to Abraham beforehand saying, 'In you all the nations shall be blessed.'*" (Galatians 3:8). The phrase, "*… God would justify the Gentiles* [all nations]" specifically and unequivocally refers precisely to the *Mystery of God*. It is the making of the two to be one that is plainly in view in God's promise to Abraham.

Paul preached that Christ had broken down the middle wall of separation between the two,[76] abolishing the enmity between the two.[77] Therefore, those two—believing Jews and believing Gentiles—had become *one in Christ, spiritually*.[78] The fact that the *two* (Jews and

Overview of the Mystery

Gentiles) would become *one in Christ* was prophesied and promised to Abraham. That was and is a critical anchor of what must be understood about the *Mystery of God*. This is essential, not only for understanding God's *Mystery*, as a concept, but to also understand its relevance to the Endtimes, especially in Revelation, as we will see more and more clearly, going forward.

Because the *Mystery of God* is unveiled from the beginning of the Bible to the end, it is good to be reminded that we are headed toward that very destination, *the Endtimes*. The Book of Revelation is of course essential in matters of the Endtimes.

I have found over the years that most believers simply do not have a grasp of a clear outline of the Book of Revelation as they begin to review that incredibly important book. Not having a clear outline perplexes many as they seek to understand the content, truths and chronological order of the Book of Revelation. Thankfully, we have already seen an outline and layout of Revelation showing a concentration of key Endtime events pertaining directly to the *Mystery of God*.[79] Once we have a correct paradigm regarding the *Mystery of God*, most of the chronology of the Endtime events are more plainly set in place. It is much like a camera lens being maneuvered until the picture comes into focus.

The strategic point at which those key events come into focus is also found in what Paul taught when he wrote 1 Corinthians 15: *"... in a moment, in the twinkling of an eye, **at the last trumpet.**"*[80] The concentration of key events, with which many are familiar, are these: 1) the sounding of the last trumpet,[81] 2) the resurrection,[82] 3) the rapture,[83] 4) the judgment,[84] 5) and the rewarding of God's people.[85] Finally and significantly, another even greater promised event is included and highlighted in this Mystery. Paul and John emphatically indicate that believing Jews and Gentiles—the two having been made to be one body, would finally be *joined with Christ as His Bride at the Marriage of the Lamb*.[86] The few paragraphs above do not tell the narrative; they tell the facts, item by item. They are the interconnected details, the backbone in the skeletal structure of the outcome of the *Mystery of God*, which will allow the narrative to come alive.

To further assist in understanding how this *Mystery* is revealed and linked together throughout the New Testament, a graph is included on the next page.[87] It is not my intention that we take the time to work through the graph at this point. My intention for this graphic, at this juncture, is to simply provide a quick snapshot to demonstrate just how tightly interconnected the *Mystery* factors are. They are inseparable. They feed off of each other because they are linked together, as you will notice in a glance. The layout of this graphic is not the graphic I would ask the reader to use for study. I have provided a graphic in Appendix A, which is much easier for that purpose. Please take a passing glance at the following **Mystery Facts** graphic in order to gain a *feel* for the interconnectivity of the Facts, and then refer to Appendix A for the most important explanatory and comparative graphic. I cannot emphasize enough just how important the graphic in Appendix A is for gaining a solid understanding of the *Mystery of God*.

"MYSTERY FACTS"

1. The MYSTERY was hidden in God from the beginning
2. It is the MYSTERY of God and of Christ
3. We are called to be ministers of this MYSTERY
4. This MYSTERY has been revealed to the saints, apostles, and prophets
5. The MYSTERY is related to preaching to the Gentiles
6. The MYSTERY is related to spiritual "riches" among the Gentiles
7. It is the MYSTERY of the gospel and, therefore, it is the MYSTERY of our faith
8. It is a MYSTERY for which Paul was in prison
9. It is the MYSTERY that is completed (finished, fulfilled) at the last trumpet, the resurrection, at the rapture, judgment of saints, the rewards, and the Marriage of the Lamb.
10. This MYSTERY Reveals Israel and the Gentiles Become One In Christ

Rom. 16:25-26
Rom. 11:13,17,25-26
I Cor. 2:7
Gal. 3:8
Eph. 1:9-10,18
Eph. 2:11-22
Eph. 3:1-9
Eph. 6:19
Col. 1:26-27
Col. 2:2
Col. 4:3
I Tim. 3:9
I Tim. 3:16
I Cor. 15:51-56
Rev.10:7; 11:15-18; 19:6-9; 21:9-22:5
Eph. 5:31-32

Overview of the Mystery

When we compare the references in the chart above, we learn rather quickly that they do not point to several different mysteries. Rather, one factor about this *Mystery of God* leads to another, and to another; they are interrelated to one another with specific terms, phrases, and concepts from within their biblical text ... and all within the boundaries of the same *Mystery*! The *Mystery of God* is truly a *braided, unbreakable, multi-threaded, prophetic cord.*

In the following chapter, I want to see with you that this *Mystery* has been in play since before the world began, and that it is anything but a new idea! The only time it **seemed** like a new idea was at the point at which it was revealed to the apostles, prophets, and saints at the beginning of the New Testament. It was new to their understanding, but not new to God or His eternal plan for the marriage of His Son at the *Marriage of the Lamb*. We will learn the profound reason for that in the next chapter titled, ***Six-Thousand-Year-Old Truth***.

Chapter Seven Notes

[52] Revelation 10:7
[53] Ephesians 5:32 – In the Introduction, I mentioned that the word in the original Greek language for "Great Mystery" is "Mega Mystery." This is because it is just that; the "mega" mystery of the Bible!
[54] Romans 16:25.
[55] 1 Corinthians 2:7; Ephesians 3:5 ,9; Colossians 1:26.
[56] Ephesians 1:3-11; Matthew 13:10, 11, 34, 35.
[57] Matthew 13; Mark 4; Luke 8.
[58] 1 Corinthians 2:3-8; Ephesians 3:1-9; Ephesians 6:19; Colossians 4:3.
[59] Revelation 10:1, 5-11.
[60] Matthew 26:28; Mark 14:24; Luke 22:20; 1 Corinthians 11:25; Hebrews 9:18, 20; 10:29; 12:24; 13:20; and others.
[61] Genesis 17:7, 8; Jeremiah 24:7; 31:33; 32:38; Ezekiel 11:20; 36:28; 37:26,27; Hosea 2:23; Zechariah 8:8; 13:9; Romans 9:26; 2 Corinthians 6:16; Hebrews 8:10; Revelation 21:7 (along with many other indirect references to the same covenantal idea).
[62] 2 Corinthians 6:16; Hebrews 8:10; Hebrews 11:39-40; Revelation 21:3.
[63] Colossians 2:2; Revelation 10:7.
[64] Colossians 2:2; Colossians 4:3.
[65] Ephesians 1:9; Ephesians 3:3-5; Colossians 1:26; Romans 16:25-26.
[66] Ephesians 3:4-8; I Timothy 3:16.
[67] Colossians 1:26-27; Ephesians 3:4-8; Ephesians 1:9-10, 18.
[68] Ephesians 6:19,20; 1 Timothy 3:9.
[69] Colossians 4:3; Ephesians 3:1-3; Ephesians 6:19, 20.
[70] Acts 9:22 23; 13:50; 14:2, 19; 17:5, 13; 18:12; 20:3; 21:11, 25 28a; 25:10; 26:7.
[71] Hebrews 11:10.
[72] Ephesians 2:15.
[73] Ephesians 2:19.
[74] Ephesians 2:19.
[75] Galatians 6:16.

[76] Ephesians 2:11-22 through 3:1-9.
[77] Ephesians 2:15.
[78] Ephesians 2:11-22 through 3:1-9.
[79] Revelation 10:1-7 and 11:15-18; Revelation 19:6-9.
[80] 1 Corinthians 15:52.
[81] 1 Corinthians 15:52; 1 Thessalonians 4:15-17; Revelation 10:1, 7 and 11:15-18.
[82] 1 Corinthians 15:52; 1 Thessalonians 4:15-17; Revelation 10:1, 7 and 11:15-18.
[83] 1 Corinthians 15:52; 1 Thessalonians 4:15-17; Revelation 10:1, 7 and 11:15-18.
[84] 1 Corinthians 15:52; 1 Thessalonians 4:15-17; Revelation 10:1, 7 and 11:15-18.
[85] Revelation 11:15-18; 1 Corinthians 3:12–15; Revelation 22:12; 1 Corinthians 9:24-25; Romans 2:6; Galatians 6:9; 2 Tim. 4:6-8; Matthew 16:27.
[86] Ephesians 5:25-32; Revelation 19:7-9.
[87] Byers, Marvin, 2000, *The Mystery: A Lost Key*. Hebron Press, Miami, FL., 146. The graphic is used with permission from Pastor Byers. I have revised and added to it, to include several passages, most of which he addresses, but which he chose for his stated reasons to not include in his original graphic. Any such changes I have made do *not* suggest that he is in agreement or disagreement as to my revised graphic. I have added them to assist me in explaining my objectives in this book.

Chapter 8

SIX-THOUSAND-YEAR-OLD TRUTH

Concealed for Four-Thousand Years
Revealed for Two-Thousand Years

The Apostle Paul made it clear that, up until the time of the apostles, the *Mystery of God* had been **concealed** (hidden and secret). At the time of Paul's writing, it had been concealed for approximately four-thousand-years, that is, since the creation of Adam. Then Christ and the Apostles **revealed** the *Mystery of God*, and from that time, until now, approximately two-thousand-years have passed. The span of time of these periods of concealment and revelation has covered a total of approximately six-thousand-years.

It is **correct** to say that the *Mystery of God* was not known and understood during the four-thousand-years of Old Testament history. As the Bible states, God had a purpose in making it a secret until the New Covenant had come in the *fullness of time.* However, if someone were to suggest that the *Mystery* didn't exist, due to its secreted and hidden position prior to the New Covenant, that would be absolutely **incorrect**. Furthermore, the fact that current Church leadership has failed to understand and teach the *Mystery of God* to God's people does not negate the plain, biblically-stated reality of the *Mystery of God*. When biblical doctrine is **not** handed down to the next generation, a certain level of blindness enters into the Church by default. No condemnation is intended concerning this failure. Until twenty-plus years ago, I too, had failed to understand and teach this *Mystery*. Pastors and teachers must begin to share with others the truths of the *Mystery of God*. It is part of the godly traditions (as opposed to traditions of mere men) to be handed down to others in the body of Christ.

"And the things that you have heard from me among many witnesses, commit these to faithful men who will be able to teach others also."

2 Timothy 2:2

"So then, brothers, stand firm and hold to the traditions [of God] that you were taught by us, either by our spoken word or by our letter."

2 Thessalonians 2:15, ESV

We have an obligation and privilege to hold to these traditions [or doctrines] of God. These traditions are not like those Jesus referred to when He condemned the hypocrisy of some of the Pharisees. Jesus said, *"For laying aside the commandment of God, you hold the tradition of men ..."* (Mark 7:8). The traditions to which I am referring are, very specifically, the traditions or doctrines of God, including the *Mystery of God*. The Church has failed to *"stand firm and hold to"* this specific doctrinal truth of the *Mystery of God*, and this failure is to our own harm and profound disadvantage.

True, Pure, Uncorrupted Doctrine

There is coming a day in which many of us will have run out of time.

"For it is time for judgment to begin at the household of God; and if it begins with us, what will be the outcome for those who do not obey [adhere to] the gospel of God?"

1 Peter 4:17, ESV

There is a day approaching fast when all of the **talk** about the return of Christ will have become a **reality**. Or, do we even believe that? We are told that in the last days *"scoffers"* will question the coming of Jesus.[88] Many in the Church do not realize they are already scoffing. No, they don't open their mouth and let out a string of scoffing remarks, which would prove they are scoffers. Rather, the Church has many scoffers, as revealed by their choice to say they are looking for Christ's coming, while utterly neglecting the pursuit of knowing our coming Bridegroom more intimately, and neglecting the pursuit of greater understanding of His coming. Simply put, they do not "love His appearing"; they just say they are looking forward to the return of Christ. There is no bite in their spiritual bark. These are those who might say something like this: *I believe Jesus might come within a hundred years or so.* Yet, it's not so much what they are saying, as much as it is the heart attitude, shown in their lack of pursuit of an intimate relationship with Christ in the light of a true heartfelt belief that He is coming soon.

Do we believe in His coming to such a degree that it fuels the passion for following the Spirit of God as He leads us on a moment-by-moment, and day-by-day basis? It will be a time of regret for many who have failed to receive a love, a passionate hunger, for the truth.

For those who do not gain such a passion, can it be otherwise? It would seem that those who say that they will be glad to just have a "little cabin" in the Kingdom, as long as they get there, are likely confessing their lack of passionate love for Christ. It is disturbing how lightly we speak of eternal matters. Are we merely "mouthing" the words without the substance of heart behind the words? Why are there going to be believers in the *Millennial Kingdom of Christ*, who will experience "weeping and gnashing of teeth?"[89] How tragic that will be!

Many of us have become, or will become so passive and complacent in our spiritual walk that our spiritual senses will have become dull, causing us to run out of spiritual strength—*just when we need it most in the face of great trauma*. It's a strange fact, but many of us will be in that condition, even though we have heard excellent Bible preaching and teaching. This will be true even while we are attending Church faithfully, reading our Bibles, and even praying.

Consider looking at it this way. Perhaps, you have seen a stream of clear water in the mountains, where the water is rushing over the rock bed. Amazingly, when you focus on the top of the rocks, you notice moss growing. How can that happen with all of that pure, cold water pouring over them year after year? Having been raised in a Christian home, I heard, early on, about what some called moss-back Christians. Those are the ones who say they are following God, but what they are really doing is going to Church, hearing preaching of the pure Word of God, and not taking it to heart, allowing it to eventually, if not immediately, roll right off of their backs. These are *"hearers of the Word, but not doers."*[90]

No one is pointing fingers or casting stones in this. We have all been guilty of this to one degree or another. I am ***not*** addressing "to one degree or another." What is being addressed is a tragic lifestyle with no change in sight, and seemingly, no desire for it. Some may have even been that way for quite a while. For others, once God's Spirit finally got their attention, and they cried out to God to help them, things began to change. There is a difference between someone who hears what God says, cries out to God for His mercies and grace, though feeling they are failing miserably, as opposed to the "believer" who simply chooses to allow all of that pure spiritual water to continue flowing right over them, without a hint of desire to yield to the work of the Spirit of God in their lives. Warning: *These are not the days to be playing religious games.* We should pray for God's mercy and grace to be awake and receive sound teaching from Him and His Word during this critical time in history—the Endtimes!

Friend, God knows your heart, and His Spirit is within you, if you are His. The truth is that if we are Christians, then *"The Spirit Himself bears witness with our spirit that we are children of God ..."* (Romans 8:16). Knowing that He knows us as His own,[91] and that He knows "those who are His,"[92] we can "know that we have eternal life."[93] Perhaps, there is an eternally personal reason the Spirit of God has led you to read this book. You have a drawing from Him to come to Him, to know Him. Don't allow Satan to steal that from you through His lying and deceitful whispers in your ear. Even if Satan points out some fault of yours, know this: *If the Spirit of Christ dwells in you, then Satan is not the important one who will point out your faults; the Spirit of Christ will also point out your sins, your faults, and failures. The differences between Christ's voice and Satan's are many.* One difference we must believe is that Satan's "words" condemn; Christ's "heart" draws you to Himself for forgiveness, grace, growth and greater yielding to His Spirit and righteousness, all without condemnation.

One of the problems is that there may be an ongoing tendency for many to be "coasting toward the rapture." This will tend to be more prevalent among those who do not have a "prophetic understanding." Why is it that so many of us, claiming that we believe in the soon coming of Christ, also readily testify at the same time that we have a minimally motivating vision concerning the Endtimes! Some even openly testify that they simply don't care about it very much, or at all. They tend to say things like, *What will be, will be! What's going to happen is going to happen, and I'm not going to spend my time on those kinds of things.* That is tragic and it demonstrates woeful ignorance of the heart of Christ, who passionately wants those who claim to be His bride to have the same testimony He has, as found in Revelation 19:10: *"... the testimony of Jesus is the spirit of prophecy."*

With that problem in mind, let's recall what Jesus taught about the kingdom of heaven and the ten virgins. All ten of them had prepared for the coming of the Bridegroom by buying oil. The problem was that five of them didn't buy "enough." So, when the "Bridegroom" finally came, those five were not allowed into the wedding party. Whatever else you and I might believe that Jesus' story of these virgins represents, one thing is certain: *Five didn't make it inside to the wedding.* I want to go into the wedding, don't you?

God gives strong warnings about those who think they are "prepared," but who are not. Perhaps, the greatest lack in today's modern, feel-good, everything-is-going-to-be-alright, prosperity-driven, carnal, worldly, and earth-bound churches (too many such churches, certainly not all) is that the "sheep" have been miserably failed concerning their training in the Word of God, and in the walk in the Spirit. What is missing, and what has played a huge role in this failure, can be largely summed up in four words two sets of two. Ironically, each set of two seems to be a turn-off for a large portion of those of us who claim the name of Christ, even those who attend Church regularly. The first set of two words are **"sound teaching"** (solid, Bible teaching, and not just opinions and feel good thoughts). The second set is the name of the very One who is to "teach us all things" and to "show us things to come:" The **Holy Spirit**. This second set should speak for itself. He is the One who will teach us sound doctrine. So, I want to focus on the first set: **Sound doctrine**.

THE SIX-THOUSAND-YEAR-OLD TRUTH

I am aware that some will be offended at my remarks describing too many of today's Christians in our evangelical churches. If you feel I am offensive, please read the rest of the book, and then ask the Holy Spirit if that feeling is correct and true.

The reality that someone feels they are already receiving sound teaching, but have not so much as even heard of the biblical phrase "the Mystery of God," should give pause. This is surely a reasonable statement, right? Furthermore, to put even more weight to the point, consider the fact that it was the Apostle Paul who said that one of the key reasons he was given an apostleship by Christ was specifically to teach about this *Mystery of God*. How, then could someone be receiving sound teaching of the *"whole counsel of God"* when the *Mystery of God* is completely left out?

Beware, dear friend! The failure to obtain sound teaching spells disaster for your future. It is heartbreaking to talk with so many believers, who will not take the time to know God and His Word. They claim God, but there are those who don't give Him their heart's attention, which He wants and deserves. They go to church, they sit for sermons, and maybe even attend a study class or small group, and they "learn" things, but they have no passionate "vision," more often than not, because of the very fact that they have not gained sound teaching. Sound teaching has a way of waking up one's soul, especially when that teaching is about the "last days." When sound teaching is believed, and then lived out in the power of the Holy Spirit, He always gives us grace for our growth and strength for a moment by moment walk with Him. And this is essential for persevering in these "last days."

The Apostle Paul warned with the strongest of terms, foretelling of this very time in which we live and warning that it will get even worse, just as Jesus also prophesied. In Paul's letter, in which he passionately instructed his young protégé, Timothy, he made the case for just how important sound doctrine, "sound teaching," is.

*"For the time will come when **they will not endure sound doctrine**, but according to their own desires, because they have itching ears, they will heap up for themselves teachers; and **they will turn their ears away from the truth, and be turned aside to fables."***
2 Timothy 4:3–4

Let's repeat what Paul just told us in a paraphrased form. It might help.

"For the time will come when men [and women] will not put up with sound teaching. Instead, to suit their own desires, they will gather around them a great number of teachers to say what their itching ears want to hear. They will turn their ears away from the truth and turn aside to myths."
2 Timothy 4:3–4, NIV84

Hopefully, that is not you, since you are likely in pursuit of truth. Then again, some readers may be asking the same question that every one of the disciples, one by one, asked Jesus at the "last supper" before His crucifixion, after He had indicated that there would be someone who would turn their back on Him (speaking of Judas). Each disciple asked, "*Is it I?*" If you feel concerned that you could be like that, then I would suggest that it is probably not you, at all. If our hearts are tender enough to respond asking, "*Is it I?*" Then while there may be truth to the fact that we do lack certain things in our Christian life, it is likely that it is also true that we don't want to continue to lack. That's a good place to be, as we continue to grow in Him—humble, weak and aware that we are in need of His presence and power. As the Apostle Paul testified about himself, "*… when I am weak, then am I strong.*"[94] As the Apostle Peter testified from his own life experience, "*God resists the proud, but gives grace to the humble.*"[95]

In Paul's instruction, above, he used the word "*sound*" to describe the spiritual quality of the doctrine or teaching we should obtain, to enable us to avoid the problem he referred to. He used the word "*αγιαινω, hugiainō*" (Greek for "sound"). That word is defined as "true, pure, uncorrupted." The Holy Spirit, alone, can give us true, pure, uncorrupted doctrine.[96] It's not that our pastors and teachers cannot teach us; they can, and they should. But that is not what I am talking about here. What I am talking about is an experiential truth, having to do with the Holy Spirit living out the life of Christ in and through us as the written Word of God is "made alive" in us by Him. That kind of truth can only come from Him. No human can provide it to us. That kind comes by God's mercy, as He gives us an "ear to hear" Him and gives us enabling grace to follow Him. For that kind of "spiritual quality," we should be willing to "cry out to God" to receive it from His hand and heart. As for me, as God has opened my eyes to see myself in the mirror of His Word, I find myself completely undone before Him, so often crying out to Him for His life to flow through me, which is the only way we can "truly live" as Christians!

This is especially applicable in the last days. One of the ways the Holy Spirit guides us to sound teaching is by warning us against the opposite of sound teaching. Paul told Timothy to teach the Churches this disturbing truth.

> "*Now the Spirit expressly says that in latter times some will **depart from the faith**, giving heed to deceiving **spirits and doctrines** of demons, speaking **lies** in hypocrisy, having their own conscience seared with a hot iron ….*"
>
> 1 Timothy 4:1–2

Some may say, "That's not me, because I would never listen to deceiving spirits and doctrines of demons. But is that really the case? It is quite possible for any one of us to be deceived. Jesus warned us concerning the last days to "not be deceived." He was careful to add this forewarning: *"See, I have told you beforehand"* (Matthew 24:25).

Far from being impossible to be deceived, *many will be deceived.* And the deception is getting stronger and stronger in this world. Are we not constantly amazed at the saturation of lying and deception in this generation? Lying spirits are pervasive in government, business, media, social media, families, education, and even in church life. Unless we are constantly drawing near to Him in worship and prayer, individually, putting on the armor of God, we emphatically will not be able to "stand" in the days of trauma and evil we now face, and with the coming increases in intensity.

It may be hard to imagine, but many Christians I encounter are *untaught* in "sound teaching." I am not condemning them. Far from it. I am appealing to each of us to pursue the Lord with all of our hearts to know Him, because it is through Him we can know sound teaching. Wake up, Church! Study the Word, personally. Pray, like Paul prayed in Ephesians 1:17-19:

> *"… that the God of our Lord Jesus Christ, the Father of glory,* **may give to you the spirit of wisdom and revelation in the knowledge of Him, the eyes of your understanding being enlightened; that you may know …."*
>
> Ephesians 1:17–18

Sound doctrine involves the Spirit of God teaching us how to compare spiritual truths with spiritual truths rightly, so we can be certain that what we think is the truth is, in fact, God's truth. Sound teaching requires study of the Word of God. In our current world of blazing technology, and the distractions and short attention spans that come as a result, we have to purpose in our hearts, and in prayer, to dig into the Word of God, so that our spiritual ears are open and ready for the Holy Spirit to teach us what He wants us to know.

> *"All Scripture is given by inspiration of God, and is profitable for doctrine, for reproof, for correction, for instruction in righteousness "*
>
> 2 Timothy 3:16

As good and useful as technology can be, we would be well served to understand that we, as individual members of the body of Jesus Christ, should sincerely question whether or not we are allowing ourselves to be trapped in the web of technology, including cell phones, video games, TV, radio, and the internet, to such a degree that quality time spent alone with God, His Word, in prayer and worship are almost non-existent, or perhaps diminished, except for the safety net of Church life.

For those who want to *"follow the Lamb wherever He goes,"*[97] it is time to unplug some things, and return to our *"first Love."*[98] What hope does sound teaching have in the face of the attractive entertainment that is capturing our minds and hearts in the ways of the world, unless we choose to make the sacrifice? Is it really a sacrifice? After all, the joy of allowing the Holy Spirit to live the life of Christ through us, which is the best life that anyone can live, should out-weigh the carnal trappings of this world. It's a choice. Choices have consequences, both in this life, during the *Millennial Kingdom of Christ,* and on into eternity.

Here's a wonderful fact: When we choose to place worldly desires and distraction on the altar of sacrifice and allow His fire to burn those things to ashes, He has promised to take those ashes and make something beautiful and pleasing in His eyes. We become a servant to God's will instead of our own will and the ways of the world. Much is said in the Bible about this. That is precisely what Jesus did, and it is what He wants for us. It is Jesus Himself who will …

"… provide [us with] ***a crown of beauty instead of ashes, the oil of gladness instead of mourning, and a garment of praise instead of a spirit of despair.*** *They will be called oaks of righteousness, a planting of the Lord* ***for the display of his splendor*** [glory]*"*

Isaiah 61:3, NIV84

"Let this mind be in you which was also in Christ Jesus, who … coming in the likeness of men… He humbled Himself and became obedient to the point of death, even the death of the cross. Therefore, God also has highly exalted Him and given Him the name which is above every name …."

Philippians 2:5

And this:

"Behold, I am coming quickly! Hold fast what you have, that no one may take your crown. ***He who overcomes****, I will make him a pillar in the temple of My God, and he shall go out no more. I will write on him the name of My God and the name of the city of My God, the New Jerusalem, which comes down out of heaven from My God. And I will write on him My new name. He who has an ear, let him hear what the Spirit says to the Churches."*

Revelation 3:11-13

To be sure, when God says that something is a mystery, we would do well to respond in our spirit with a desire to know and understand it. Isn't it wise to pursue such things to determine what this sound teaching might be? But how can it ever become sound for us, if we do not understand it? The *Mystery of God* is profoundly sound! Understanding the *Mystery*, and how it enables us to understand the Book of Revelation and the Endtimes, requires your mind and heart's purposed attention; and of course, it requires His grace and Spirit. So, I encourage us to set aside the attractions and distractions swirling around us, and turn up our spiritual hearing aid, and be prepared to check out each point, comparing Scripture with Scripture, asking the Holy Spirit to be your Teacher, so that you have confidence in the truths presented. With that in mind, let's verify in terms of human history that the *Mystery of God* is a *six-thousand-year-old truth*, which means that it was **Planned from Before the Beginning**.

Chapter Eight Notes

[88] 2 Peter 3:3.
[89] Luke 13:28.
[90] James 1:23.
[91] John 10:27.
[92] 2 Timothy 2:19.
[93] 1 John 5:11-13.
[94] 2 Corinthians 12:10.
[95] 1 Peter 5:5.
[96] John 16:13: It is the Holy Spirit who is given to us to "teach us all things," including "things to come."
[97] Revelation 14:4.
[98] Revelation 2:4.

Chapter 9

THE MYSTERY OF GOD: PLANNED FROM BEFORE THE BEGINNING

*"... to make all see what is the fellowship of **the Mystery, which from the beginning of the ages has been hidden in God** ..."* (emphasis mine).

Ephesians 3:9

*"... the preaching of Jesus Christ, according to the revelation of the **mystery kept secret since the world began** but now made manifest, and by the prophetic Scriptures made known ...."*

Romans 16:25–26

"Jesus Christ is the same yesterday, today, and forever."

Hebrews 13:8

"For I am the Lord, I do not change ...."

Malachi 3:6

When we see the Lord face to face, if He chooses to show us how and why all things played out the way they did in human history, there is something I would very much want to understand. I would like to ask Him what the process looked like as He caused all things to work together for His glory and our good—that would be trillions of trillions of things working together at the same time! How did He work it all out with every little detail coming together from beginning to end? How did His miraculous plan for human history, from Adam and Eve until He made a new heaven and a new earth, work out to precisely seven-thousand years?

The Incredible Key

Some Christians believe that the earth is thousands of years old. Others believe that the earth is millions of years old. There are extremely knowledgeable theologians and believing scientists on each side of that debate. I have a specific opinion as to which is correct, but this book is not the forum for debating that point. However, I am referring to *how long* humanity has been on the earth, not *how old* the earth itself is. For the purpose of this chapter, neither of those age-of-the-earth concepts affects the answer to the question of how long God will have dealt with humanity on this earth before He makes a new heaven and a new earth.

God's dealings with humanity on this earth will soon reach six-thousand years. Then after the resurrection, rapture, the judgment and rewarding of the saints, and of course, the *Marriage of the Lamb*, He will set up His one-thousand-year (millennial) reign on earth. That, then, will conclude precisely seven-thousand-years.[99] That idea may be new to some of us, but the prophets proclaimed it, and the apostles and early church leaders referred to that seven-thousand-years.

We know that the God who made the heavens and the earth has absolutely no problem keeping up with everything. Prideful humanity portrays an attitude that suggests we know a lot about what all exists within creation. The truth is that the more we learn about creation, the more we realize how little we know, whether it is here on earth or in the universe. Go online sometime and just look at NASA's space pictures; or, walk outside on a clear night and look at the stars and the planets. With the naked eye, on a pitch-black night with no light-noise, we can see approximately nine-thousand stars; a minute fraction of what is actually there.[100] According to astronomers' latest calculations, there are approximately 170 billion galaxies in the observable universe. The complexity of all of that is beyond our human ability to take it in.

Yet God's will and plan has always taken *everything* into consideration. He numbers the hairs of our heads. He takes notice when a sparrow falls to the ground. He keeps an account of the each tear we shed. And He takes into consideration man's free will.

> *"Nothing in all creation is hidden from God's sight. Everything is uncovered and laid bare before the eyes of him to whom we must give account."*
>
> Hebrews 4:13, NIV84

Concerning believers, He works all things for good for those who love Him and who are called according to His purpose, as Paul stated in Romans 8:28. He went on to give us one of the key reasons for this kind of beneficence.

> *"… in order to make known the riches of his glory for vessels of mercy, which he has prepared beforehand for glory—even us whom he has called, not from the Jews only but also from the Gentiles …."*
>
> Romans 9:23–24, ESV

THE MYSTERY OF GOD: PLANNED FROM BEFORE THE BEGINNING

Whatever happens in this world or our own lives, it will ultimately accrue to His glory, for our ultimate good, and eventually as a witness against the ungodly, who in their lifetimes refused to bow their knee to the Lord of glory! How great is our sovereign God!

God's sovereign will and plan have not been derailed or diminished. Everything that might seem to be out of order, from the human perspective, does not and cannot move outside of God's ultimate purposes. While taking every iota of everything and everyone into consideration, God, who *inhabits eternity*, and who gave humanity free will, is still accomplishing His plan, while simultaneously taking into consideration man's free will. That concept is definitely a "God-thing." It is one of those things much like the doctrine of the *Trinity*; it's true but difficult, if not impossible, to fully understand or explain.

While I cannot explain how it all works (which is why I would enjoy hearing Him explain it someday, if He would so choose), I am thankful and satisfied with the message of the Bible; that we are not mere robots. We can choose to love Him or not; we will make that choice. This is the way it has been from the beginning. From the very beginning in the Garden of Eden, He has had a plan. Christ's plan was to gather to Himself a bride. Throughout the Old Testament, we read of covenant after covenant, all the way to the New Testament (Covenant). The initiation of that New Covenant began to be realized through Christ at His first coming.

But some Christians are confused because they have unwittingly swallowed a theological error that has become entrenched in many, if not most, churches and seminary circles throughout the world. Some of the theologians teach that God had to change His plan when some, from among the physical family of Israel, rejected Jesus as their Messiah and King at His first coming. There is only one little problem with that idea. Israel was "blind" only "in part!" Some Bible teachers have gone so far as to teach that the Kingdom did not come during Christ's ministry. They claim the Kingdom could not come, because of the rebellious ones among the children of Israel, who rejected Him at that time. This erroneous idea is similar to and part of the reason behind the development of what is called Replacement Theology.[101] Replacement Theology is the erroneous belief that the Church has replaced Israel as God's chosen people. To suggest that God's purpose for His own people somehow changed because *"he came to His own and His own did not receive Him,"* lacks substantiation in Scripture. That kind of reasoning is similar to the erroneous idea that Adam and Eve's sin somehow surprised God. Therefore, some might imply, God had to scurry around and figure out what to do, since sin had entered into the human race, implying that He had not foreseen the Garden of Eden event. The idea of God being surprised, daunted, befuddled or having to change His Plan demonstrates a great lack of understanding of the *Mystery of God*, which had been planned since *before the world began*.

Another reason these erroneous ideas exist is because of a misunderstanding of the meaning of that passage in John 1:11-13, referred to above.

*"He came to His own, and **His own did not receive Him**. But as many as received Him, to them He gave the right to become children of God, to those who believe in His name: who were born, not of blood, nor of the will of the flesh, nor of the will of man, but of God."*

In this case, **"His own"** to whom John referred, were divided into two groups: *Those from among **His own** chosen nation who **did not receive Him**, and those from among **His own** chosen nation who **did receive Him**.* Both groups—those who ***did receive Him*** and those who ***did not receive Him*** were the Apostle Paul's *"brethren according to the flesh,"* which he referred to in Romans 9:1-5. Whether they were saved or unsaved, Paul's *physical Israelite brethren* were those through whom *according to the flesh, Christ came* into the world:

*"I tell the truth in Christ, I am not lying, my conscience also bearing me witness in the Holy Spirit, that I have great sorrow and continual grief in my heart. For I could wish that I myself were accursed from Christ **for my brethren, my countrymen according to the flesh, who are Israelites**, to whom pertain the adoption, the glory, the covenants, the giving of the law, the service of God, and the promises; of whom are the fathers and from whom, **according to the flesh, Christ came**, who is over all, the eternally blessed God. Amen"*

Romans 9:1–5

All Israelites were and are His "chosen people" for the purposes Paul stated, with the ultimate objective found in this: *"... **from whom, according to the flesh, Christ came ....**"*

Furthermore, when John wrote, in the Gospel of John 1:11, that Christ's *"own did not receive Him,"* those were the very same ones, whom Paul called His *"brethren,"* His *"countrymen according to the flesh, who are Israelites ...."* Neither John nor Paul was claiming that these *"according to the flesh"* were believers. These were his physical *"brethren...countrymen according to the flesh, who are Israelites ...."* Paul made a clear distinction between *flesh* and *spirit*, just as Jesus had done previously. Regarding this, Jesus was unequivocal. In John 3, He told Nicodemus, a ruler of the Jews, unless you are *"born again"* you *"cannot see the kingdom of God."* He went on to tell Nicodemus: *"... that which is born of the flesh is flesh; that which is born of the Spirit is spirit."* Nicodemus' nationality had provided exposure to him of God's Word but otherwise did nothing for him concerning the matter of salvation.

Later on, in speaking to religious, but unbelieving Jewish leaders, Jesus said: *"You are of your father, the Devil,"* in John 8:44. Can it be denied, whether we refer to Nicodemus or any other physical Israelite, that their reliance on ancestry (or our own), instead of faith in Jesus the Messiah, was a self-constructed stumbling block? Later on, Jesus described some who would be in the Church who *"say they are Jews, and they are not. They are the synagogue*

THE MYSTERY OF GOD: PLANNED FROM BEFORE THE BEGINNING

of Satan" (Revelation 2:9 and 3:9). Both Jesus, John, and Paul make the distinction between the believing and unbelieving, which is the way it has always been.

We already read, "*He came unto His own, and His own did not receive Him.*" Many will recall the remainder of this well-known passage:

"*But as many as did receive Him, to them He gave the right to become children of God, to those who believe in His name: who were born, not of blood, nor of the will of the flesh, nor of the will of man, but of God.*"

John 1:12–13

Those who did receive Him were Israelites in the flesh also. The difference was and is that these particular ones "received Him."

If you have your Bible nearby, let's take the time to look at Romans 9:1-8 and 11:1–5. We will begin at Romans 11:1, for reasons that will become obvious. Without reading along in the Bible, however, I can assure you that it can be somewhat more difficult to "see" what all Paul tenaciously and fervently wants to make clear about the *Mystery*. The apostle is insatiable in that desire. He is regularly addressing this issue in many of his letters. In some ways, he seems to be so determined that some might suggest that he is obsessed with it. But if he is obsessed, let's remember that since these truths came from the Holy Spirit, then it must be the Holy Spirit who is the one who is *obsessed*.

There is a good reason for Paul's extensive effort to make these things clear. These concepts are fundamental for understanding the complete transition into the New Covenant, in which Christ brings together both Jew and Gentile into one people, having torn down the wall of separation through His own sacrifice on the cross. In other words, this is about the *Mystery of God*.

It is in these passages that the teaching of the Apostle Paul ties back to the same concept about which John wrote concerning the Jews, who had received Jesus when He came, and those who had not received Him. Let's review some of the segments about which Paul writes to gain greater clarity.

"I say then, has God cast away **His people?**" (Romans 11:1). Who are **His people?** Without very careful reading, it is easy to pass over what Paul is saying here. Many can find this passage a bit confusing. The main reason for their confusion is a lack of understanding of the truths found in what Paul says is the "*Mystery of God.*" What Paul is now referring to in these passages is too important of a concept to pass over lightly. He is taking on the task of defining "His people," that is, God's people. Paul makes a distinction between **Physical Israel**, that is, the physical people God chose "according to the flesh," through whom Christ would come into the world in a physical body. (Romans 9:3-5); and **Spiritual Israel**, those from among **physical Israel**, who became believers (plus, the Gentiles who did or who would become part of Spiritual Israel in the future).

He refers to those within physical Israel, who are children of Abraham in the flesh, but who are not spiritual seed (children) of Abraham. He says that they are ***"not all Israel who are of Israel, nor are they all children*** [simply] *because* [of the fact that] ***they are the seed of Abraham."*** In other words, they are not spiritual Israel or spiritual children of Abraham in God's eyes, just because they are Israelites and are simply of the physical seed (lineage) of Abraham. Those physical relationships do not make them children of God. (9:6-7) Paul makes that fact unequivocally clear.

"His [physical] people" who are stated by Paul to be unbelieving, in Romans chapters 9 and 11, are the very same ones from within the people of physical Israel about whom John said that they **"DID NOT** *receive Him."* God did not *"cast them away."* They were the ones who cast God away. ***They "did not receive Him."*** So, did God cast them away or not? Paul immediately follows this up with an exclamation. *"Certainly not! For I also am an Israelite, of the seed of Abraham, of the tribe of Benjamin"* (Romans 11:1).

Without taking a breath, after having referred to this matter of "His people," the chosen people, physical Israel, Paul immediately makes it clear that God continues His covenantal relationship with physical Israel, the physical children of Abraham regarding those promises He made to Abraham and his physical lineage. But those things are on the physical level, and as had always been, that relationship could not become a spiritual relationship, until they *"believe."* This is true for everyone and not just the physical children of Abraham.

Simultaneously, Paul goes on to say that he has, himself, now become part of spiritual, believing Israel. Concerning an eternal-life-relationship through Christ, **eternal life is only for those who believe, like Paul, and like Abraham.** This blessing is in a clear contradistinction to those who are Israel, *only* in the flesh, but not in the spirit; and who are children of Abraham, *only* in the flesh, but not in the spirit.

Paul's eternal-life-relationship is stated only as he lays claim to being part of the believing *"remnant."*[102] His proof is that God has always had *"a remnant"* from within and from among physical Israel, the physical children of Abraham. That *"remnant"* is a remnant because of nothing but God's grace, and certainly not because of any physical factor. That was, is, and always will be the case: *Grace is God's only way of salvation*—and certainly not using a physical heritage or lineage. Again, please know that I am not belittling the physical relationship with Jews or Israel and God. God's plan will yet be fulfilled concerning them, just as He promised.

Paul goes on to say, *"God has not cast away His people whom He **foreknew** ..."* This is made clearer, when he states, *"... at this present time there is* [still] ***a remnant*** *according to the election of grace"* (Romans 11:2, 5, brackets inserted for clarity are mine).

Therefore, those who were physically born into the physical family and nation of Israel, but who also by grace and faith alone had trusted in the God of Abraham, Isaac, and Jacob; they, like any other person, transitioned from death to life into the spiritual *family of God.*

THE MYSTERY OF GOD: PLANNED FROM BEFORE THE BEGINNING

With this saving faith, they become what Paul later called the "Israel of God," the spiritual "commonwealth of Israel." Today, those in physical Israel who believe are *"grafted back into"* their *"natural olive tree"* of Christ. They, then, become identified in Scripture as being part of the *remnant*.

Who is this ***"remnant"*** Paul has just referred to? As stated, they are physical *"Israelites,"* who *"believed"* and had *"become children of God"* by grace through faith. They were, indeed, of the faith of Abraham. No matter which of God's covenants **this believing remnant** happened to have lived in, there had been and continued to be a **believing remnant** on the earth since the Creation. The examples again include Adam and Eve, Abel, Enoch, Noah, Shem, Abraham, Isaac, Jacob, the nation of believing Israel, and New Covenant believers, all of which are part of God's continuously growing family down through history. (Again, I refer the reader to Hebrews 11 and 12.)

Parenthetically and very importantly, I want to be very careful concerning this matter, so as to not be misunderstood about the promises made to Abraham and his physical children. God made the promises to Abraham ***before*** the law of Moses. Therefore, as we are told in Galatians 3:17-18, neither the law, nor the fulfillment of the law by Christ, negated the promises to Abraham. A tangible and key example of how all of this works out in the end, is regarding the "promised land" Israel. To whom did God promise the "promised land" that is the physical land of Israel? God made that promise to Abraham and his descendants. This is where the two factors (physical and spiritual) meet in sweet accord. Abraham and his descendants, but only those who come to God in faith, believing God, and who are redeemed by the blood of Christ (which includes all Old Testament saints) will inherit that land just as it was promised. This is referred to when Jesus mentioned this little fact: "And I say unto you, that many shall come from the east and west, and shall sit down with Abraham and Isaac and Jacob in the Kingdom of Heaven …." This Kingdom of Heaven will be occupying the earth during the Millennial Reign of Christ. Abraham, Isaac, and Jacob (and their seed who are redeemed) will be occupying the "promised land." This promise is confirmed over and over in the Scriptures. (Here are a few references: Genesis 15:18; 17:7-8,19; Hebrews 6:13-18, etc.) Furthermore, Gentiles who desire to live in the promised land will also have the ability to choose to live there. This is a direct result of having been included in the "inheritance" in Christ. There is much more that could be said about this parenthetical point, but I will not be able to expand on it in this book.

Later on, I address the above passages once again from a somewhat different perspective. I want us to read some of this text together, in concluding this chapter, because it is clarifying, and affirms the essence of what Paul has been saying.

The Incredible Key

"... For they are not all Israel who are of Israel, nor are they all children [just] because they are the seed of Abraham ... That is, those who are the children of the flesh, these are not the children of God; but the children of the promise are counted as the seed."

Romans 9:6–8

All of these things are involved in the *Mystery of God*. And all of them have been *Planned From Before The Beginning*. Turning back to John:

"He came to His own, and His own did not receive Him. But as many as received Him, to them He gave the right to become children of God, to those who believe in His name: **who were born, not of blood, nor of the will of the flesh, nor of the will of man, but of God.**"

John 1:11–13

That is it in a nutshell! All of heaven did not go into shock, when *"...* **His own** *did not receive Him."* God *foreknew* these things. It is impossible for Him to be caught off guard. Throughout human history, God has always operated on the basis of **His own** time table. He wasn't sitting in heaven, watching Adam and Eve fall, only to find Himself scrambling for a Plan B, scratching His head trying to figure out what to do next, now that there were problems with those humans He had created. No, His Plan has always been in place, including delays or shortening of times—from beginning to end.[103]

So, when we consider this matter in the context of *prophecy*, it is ludicrous to suggest that God took some risk as He crawled out on a limb called prophecy. Did He foretell the future, and then sit down on His sovereign, eternal throne, biting His fingernails in fear, wondering if it would work out—somehow? No! There was zero risk in that sense! It's hardly worth talking about. His prophetic Word is a *"confirmed [sure] Word of prophecy."*[104] That is not to say that those prophets, who did the prophesying for God, bringing the message to us, understood all that they prophesied. Some prophecies were sovereignly kept hidden for God's reasons, for God's timing for those things to be revealed within His Plan. That is why we learn that this or that event in the Old or New Testament took place in the *fullness of time* or some similar wording. God provided whatever enlightenment of truth He knew was needed under the banner of each of the covenants. Sometimes, He did this through individuals, and sometimes through His chosen nation, Israel, or even the angels or an appearance of Himself. But he did so, all the way down through history, and always in conjunction with His covenants, to which He has been, and always will be, faithful.

For instance, the Bible reveals that God always had a plan in mind for salvation. He knew before He created Adam[105] that in order for Adam and Eve and the rest of humanity to love Him, this would require free will; the ability to choose freely. God, of course, knew that Adam would sin. Adam sinned, and so have we. God sent His Son, Jesus, to offer His body on the cross and to shed His blood to pay the price for satisfying God's righteous justice and judgment against sin. Through His supreme sacrifice, Christ makes redemption available to lost souls. He counted, and still counts those who choose to believe Him by faith to be His purchased possession and people.

Furthermore, it has always been Christ's plan that the redeemed ones would be betrothed to Him with the view of the eventual *Marriage of the Lamb* in mind. Not only was this typified in the first marriage on earth (Adam and Eve), but the marriage relationship itself is specifically used numerous times[106] in Scripture as a foreshadow of Christ's marriage to His Bride. This is not only seen through *types*; it is most clearly understood in the declarations of the apostles Paul and John. The marriage, to which the apostles often referred, is called the *Marriage of the Lamb* in the Book of Revelation. As previously discussed, the *Mystery of God* and the *Great Mystery* are the same *Mystery*. It cannot be overemphasized that the *Marriage of the Lamb* is revealed as an intrinsic and inseparable concluding event in this *Great Mystery*. It is specifically the *Great-Mystery-truth*, the *Mystery-of-God-truth*, which God uses in His Word to help us understand His unchanging plan.

In the balance of all things, there is more than just this *Mystery*-truth that we should want to know in these last days. However, with the understanding of this *Mystery* in hand and heart, we will clear up a vast portion of the confusion about the Endtimes, and begin to see it more clearly than before. **Part IV** of this book gathers the key events of the Endtimes together to enable us to see how it all fits together. Please keep in mind that everything from Genesis to Revelation was in God's Sovereign Plan from before the beginning. For now, we will continue to lay an even stronger foundation of essentials found in this *Mystery*.

The Mystery Is Not Some "New-Fangled" Idea

The *Mystery of God* is not some new-fangled idea. As we expand on nearly twenty (20) key *Mystery* Scripture references to this *Mystery* in seven (7) New Testament books, we will realize that it cannot be central to Paul's teaching and simultaneously be a "new-fangled" idea. It may be new to the reader and rarely spoken of by our Church leaders, but it is far from new.

I want us to keep in mind then, that each of the nearly twenty references should be pictured as the threads braided together as part of His strong, prophetic cord. All of these many details have a common denominator by context in the actual word, *mystery*. Each reference is shown to be the very same mystery. Of course the strength of this truth is not the mere use of the word *mystery*. After all, there are several mysteries as Jesus said. Rather, the strength is found in the combined truths detailed in the nearly twenty Scripture references, as we compare Scripture with Scripture confirming the veracity of the direct linkages. In each reference one or more specific ***factors*** about the *Mystery* is mentioned, and each is interconnected with the others by specific words and phrases, which the Holy Spirit was careful to provide as linkage. The overwhelming evidence of those key factors being braided together into a multi-threaded cord offers us confidence that God is referring to one and the same *Mystery of God* in each and all references. That kind of solid biblical confirmation cannot be disregarded without doing violence to God's Word.

A study of the *Mystery of God* may be new information to those who have not yet seen Christ and His saints in this light, but it is **not new.** In human history terms, a six-thousand-year-old truth is not exactly new! But beware! Soon, His six-thousand-year progression will come to a sudden end, as prophesied. It will be finished with great fanfare, to God's glory, beginning at the *last trumpet, resurrection, judgment and rewarding of saints,* and then the culminating glory shortly after that at the *Marriage of the Lamb*! It will happen in a *"moment, in the twinkling of an eye."*

The Apostle Paul wrote:

"Behold, I tell you a **mystery***: We shall not all sleep, but* **we shall all be changed—in a moment, in the twinkling of an eye, at the last trumpet***. For the trumpet will sound, and the dead will be raised incorruptible, and we shall be changed"* (emphases mine).

1 Corinthians 15:51–52

"[so that] when you read, you may understand my knowledge in the **mystery** *of Christ,* **which in other ages was not made known to the sons of men***, as it has now been revealed by the Spirit to His holy apostles and prophets:"* (insertions and emphases mine).

Ephesians 3:4–5

"… I became a minister according to the stewardship from God which was given to me for you [Gentiles], to fulfill the word of God, the **mystery** **which has been hidden from ages and from generations, but now has been revealed to His saints***"* (insertions and emphases mine).

Colossians 1:25–26

"… in the days of the trumpet call to be sounded by the seventh angel, the **Mystery of God** **would be fulfilled [finished, completed]***, just as he announced to his servants the prophets"* (emphasis and insertions mine).

Revelation 10:7

When the *Mystery of God* was given to us in Scripture by the Holy Spirit, it was obviously not new to God. It had been planned in His heart since **before** the world began.

THE MYSTERY OF GOD: PLANNED FROM BEFORE THE BEGINNING

Interestingly, God established specific prophetic markers (threads) about this *Mystery* in the Old Testament, so that in the fullness of time—the time at which God intended for it to become known, His people would then be able to look back and understand more clearly His Plan from the beginning. With that understanding, given by the Holy Spirit, New Testament saints are now able to learn even greater truths from the Old Testament. These *Mystery-truths* are no longer in the shadows; they are in plain view. The *Mystery of God* was revealed by the apostles, and they explained its truths.

In the Old Testament, the saints and prophets, through whom those prophetic markers were given, could not understand the meaning of everything they prophesied. This is because the ultimate substance and meaning of the *Mystery of God* were incomprehensible in their mind, though spoken through them. It was hidden from them by God Himself until His perfect time for revealing them would come. These truths, and the additional examples of those to whom it was foretold as prophetic lessons were kept for us *"upon whom the ends of the ages would come."*[107] They could not be fulfilled without Jesus destroying, through His cross, the middle wall of separation between the Jews and Gentiles, making the two to be one, which includes those who had been in His family since the Garden of Eden! Neither we, as New Testament believers, nor they, as Old Testament believers, could be complete without one another—in Christ!

Hebrews 11, the chapter which highlights the Old Testament men and women of faith, ends with a very important truth, as it segues into Hebrews 12. This truth is often neglected, but it should be seen as one of the hinge pins on which the door of the *Mystery of God* swings. The following verse is profound in its scope, and without using the actual word, *Mystery*, it is a fascinating verification of the *Mystery*:

*"And all these [saints before Christ's death] having obtained a good testimony through faith, **did not receive the promise**, God having provided something better for us, that they [saints before Christ's death] **should not be made perfect** [perfect means "complete"] **apart from us** [the New Testament saints]."*

Hebrews 11:39–40

Paraphrasing and interpreting those verses could read something like this:

All of the believers in the Old Testament who had obtained a good testimony through faith did not receive the promise, at that time; and therefore, were not yet made complete in and through Christ. The reason they could not be made complete, apart from New Testament saints, was because Christ had not yet died and risen from the dead. But then, once Christ had died and risen, the redemptive work of Christ was completed, which destroyed the middle wall of separation between the Old and New Testament saints. We are now completed together, as one in Christ, and we will all receive the promises together as one in Him.

Jesus made Old and New Testament saints to be "completed together" as one, as we saw above, and He made Jews and Gentiles to be one!

*"For He Himself ... has **made both one, and has broken down the middle wall of separation** ... so as to create in Himself one **new man from the two**, thus making peace, and that He might **reconcile them both to God in one body through the cross** ... For through Him **we both have access by one Spirit to the Father.**"*

Ephesians 2:14–18

He brought the two—Old Testament saints (those before Israel, and those within Israel; all of the Old Testament saints) and New Testament saints—together as one in Him. Concerning this truth, we need to be careful to see the difference between **ALL Old Testament saints** and the narrower group of saints called Israel. There is a distinction to be made, but as we will see together, this is, ultimately, a distinction without a difference. There is a critical reason this is so important to understand which I want to see with you.

All-in-One

By the subtitle to this section, I am saying that all the *covenants of the Old Testament find their ultimate conclusion in one covenant—the New Covenant*. The New Covenant was prophesied by Jeremiah,

"Behold, the days are coming, says the Lord, when I will make a new covenant with the house of Israel and with the house of Judah ...."

Jeremiah 31:31

As we will see, this New Covenant included believing Gentiles, as part of the promises to Abraham.

The word *"testament"* can mean *"covenant."* The New *Testament* refers to the New **Covenant**. The New Covenant is not only new in the sense of something newer, as compared to something older, it is new in its quality.[108]

However, when it comes to using the term **Old Testament**, that is, **Old Covenant**, there is a difference to be made. The *Old Testament* contains a plurality of covenants. The *Old Testament* spanned the period from the creation until Jesus came. That involved several covenants, and not just one. So, if God made several different covenants, at different periods, then why do we call it the Old Testament (singular) or the Old Covenant (singular); why don't we call it the Old Testaments (plural) or Old Covenants (plural)?

THE MYSTERY OF GOD: PLANNED FROM BEFORE THE BEGINNING

The acknowledgment of the plurality of covenants was affirmed by the Apostle Paul. He referred to the covenantal responsibilities given by God to the Israelites when he said that the Israelites were those *"to whom pertain…the **covenants** [plural] … and the **promises** [plural] …"* (Romans 9:4). Paul uses the plural term "covenants," purposefully and legitimately.

Think of the Old Testament like a crescendo in music. A good example is a mighty song of praise that begins with a soft, low tone and volume, but which ends on a high, glorious and thunderous note with high and glorious words of praise. You can just feel it, as you glorify God, joining your voice with many others in four-part harmony along with multiple instruments, as you are singing with all of your heart! This is the kind of music that builds up and builds up and builds up—it crescendos—to the big finish, the finale.

Regarding the "crescendo" in the Old Testament, we start with the simpler, softer and lower tone. The covenants in the Old Testament build up and build up, as God's newer covenants crescendo, until Jesus comes, at which time the higher and more glorious, and "better" New Testament (Covenant) is experienced. It's a beautiful symphony of the Truth.

- God's covenant and promise, which He made with and to Adam and Eve, obviously preceded the covenant God made with Noah. In the Adamic covenant, we are introduced to the woman's Seed, which we learn in the New Testament is the promise of Christ Himself. That covenant, though big in meaning, was a small seed. The significance is not diminished by its size. How can one diminish the significance of Christ Himself? Nevertheless, the revelation of this Seed is minimal, as the crescendo begins to build.

- On to the next covenant: God's covenant and promises that He made with and to Noah did not remove or negate the blessings of His covenant with Adam and Eve. Far from it, by saving only Noah and his family, God made sure that the Seed-line was carried on, both regarding the fleshly family-line, and the spiritual family-line. The blessings and promises of the Adamic covenant, therefore, merged with the newer Noahic covenant. That newer covenant provided greater revelation, which we are now able to see more clearly, as we look back to that time in Scripture.

- God's covenant with Abraham, though a profound covenant with great and precious promises, did not negate or remove the blessings of His covenant with Noah, nor those which came from the Adamic covenant. The newer Abrahamic covenant added to that of the Adamic and Noahic covenants. We can hear the music building and building in a biblical crescendo! The instruments and the voices are growing stronger and louder; so much so, that they will be heard forever, as God promised.

- The same held true with Isaac, Jacob, and eventually the nation of Israel, including the Mosaic Covenant. I'm quite certain that most of us are aware that the covenant that God made with the nation of Israel is that covenant which Christians view as the "Old Covenant." That is true, as long as we keep in mind that all of the blessings and promises of all of the previous covenants from the very beginning have accrued and remain in place, encapsulated within and/or running along side of the covenant God made with the nation of Israel. All of the previous covenants were not superseded; they were included in God's covenant with Israel. There is much more to this part of the covenants, but those things are outside of the scope of this discussion, and this book as a whole.

- Each newer covenant was given to that generation and to those generations which followed. All of them were in preparation for Christ's first coming. God was calling-out a people to Himself in each covenant, all along the way through history. Paul explained in His letter to the Galatian church that the law, which came <u>430 years after God's covenantal promises to Abraham, did not set aside the Abrahamic covenant</u>. He wrote: "*What I mean is this: The law, introduced 430 years later, **does not set aside the covenant previously established by God and thus do away with the promise** [to Abraham]*" (Galatians 3:17, NIV84). This is an enormously important statement for our understanding.

Each of the covenants was a covenant of God's mercy and grace. Each revealed more and more about God Himself, His desires, His will, and His plan. This was true and established in His Word, even if all of the revelation given to His people back then was not made clear to them at that moment. Those who lived under each of those covenants received grace from God to trust in Him during that particular covenant period, and grace was afforded to them for what was delineated in that particular covenant in conjunction with the previous covenants. However, more than just grace, each received the mercy of God; mercy because God was the faithful one to hold to the requirements of the covenant. Those who were believing saints had faith, but not necessarily faithfulness; therefore, it was God's mercy which carried them through. It might be said that some saints in history have been found *faultless* in the eyes of man. Still, we know that no one, since Adam and Eve's sin in the Garden, has ever kept covenant perfectly, being *faultless in the eyes of God*, except Jesus Christ Himself!

One last, fundamental thought about the above discussion regarding covenants is this. When Jesus came into this world, bringing with Him the New Covenant in His blood and cross, that New Covenant fulfilled many previous covenantal requirements, which had begun in the previous covenants. This is affirmed as Jesus opened the eyes of the understanding of the two disciples on the road to Emmaus, after His resurrection.

THE MYSTERY OF GOD: PLANNED FROM BEFORE THE BEGINNING

"And beginning at Moses and all the prophets, He expounded to them in all the Scriptures the things concerning Himself."

Luke 24:27

In that conversation, Jesus spoke of those things referring to Himself in the Old Testament; that is, He expounded to those two men of the references to Himself in each of the covenantal periods found in the Old Testament. For instance, Jesus explained the **Adamic covenant**, in which He was revealed as the prophesied Seed, who would someday come as the Redeemer. By Christ's coming in to the world, He revealed Himself as the Seed referred to in the Adamic Covenant. However, in the **New Covenant**, because Jesus had now come, we are no longer talking about **the FACT of the Seed**; rather, we see the **PERSON of the Seed, which is Christ Himself**. Still, the Adamic Covenant is not yet completely fulfilled; only in part. Why? Because Satan has not yet been completely and fully "crushed" as was prophesied in Genesis 3:15. That will finally and completely take place in Revelation 20:10. In that verse, we have a prime example demonstrating this simple truth: *Until a specific promise or element of previous covenants (throughout history) is completely fulfilled or superseded by subsequent covenants that specific promise or element remains in force, until all is ultimately fulfilled.*

That may sound strange to some, initially. However, we must take into consideration that Paul gave us a certain insight into this "Seed," which links directly to the "two becoming one." That "two becoming one" is ultimately fulfilled in the *Marriage of the Lamb*. I will not expand on this, except to say that Christ is "the Seed" referred to in the Garden of Eden. We are told over and again that we are "in Christ". Though we are "spiritually" or "positionally" in Christ now, at the *Marriage of the Lamb* there will be the most real marriage ever known—Jesus marriage to His Bride, the Church. The two are made to be one, just as the Apostle Paul states in no uncertain terms in Ephesians 5:22-32! There is so much more to this, but that's as far as we will go for now.

Furthermore, concerning the covenant God made with the nation of Israel, it is important to realize that those things which are not superseded in the New Covenant remain intact for Israel. Those things which remain intact are for Israel, the Jews, and they are free before God to continue in them. However, none of those things are intended for the salvation of their souls, and they are ceremonial. For instance, whether a particular Jew is saved or unsaved they are free before God to commemorate the Feast Days, which the Lord gave to them in everlasting covenant. No one has the right to tell them they should not celebrate them. But, whether you are a Jew or Gentile, regarding the requirements of the law which were "against us, which was contrary to us ... He has taken it out of the way, having nailed it to the cross;" He has wiped out those things by His cross.

"... having wiped out the handwriting of requirements that was against us, which was contrary to us. And He has taken it out of the way, having nailed it to the cross."

Colossians 2:13–14

From that point forward, the only elements of all of the previous covenants in the Old Testament, which would remain effective in the New Covenant (Testament), were those which were not explicitly removed, replaced, or superseded through clear evidence within the New Testament. If they were not removed, replaced, or superseded in the New Covenant, then they remain to this day and are relevant to every believer. This does not speak to a greater burden to bear under the Law. Rather, it speaks to things being "better"[109] in the New Covenant, including the incredible gift of the Holy Spirit, who now lives within believers to fulfill the covenant in our daily lives by His power and not our own!

Understanding the covenants, as explained above, is important because this leads us into greater understanding of the *Mystery of God*. There has been a great lack of teaching in the Church about the *Mystery of God*, while at the same time there has been much teaching about the covenants. It should make sense that when the *Mystery* and the covenants are brought into view together, there must be a clear explanation as to how they function together. This was and is a critical point at which many derail in their understanding as they attempt to reconcile the *Mystery of God* and the covenants throughout the Bible. Few seem to have been taught that the truths involved in the *Mystery of God* are central to the idea that both the Old and New Testament saints are now "completed" together as "one new man." This new revelation of the *Mystery* was a huge surprise to the many believing Jews, who had come to Christ in salvation back in the early days of the Church. That *Mystery* (how the two, Jews and Gentiles, are made to be one) was not *made known* until Jesus had come. I cannot impress on the reader, enough, just how important that fact is. This was massive—a monumental point in the history of Israel, and in the history of the Church. This was foundational, fundamental to **THE TRANSITION OF THE JEWISH-ONLY EARLY CHURCH.**

Chapter Nine Notes

[99] A fascinating study on this subject is Tim Warner's book, *The Time of the End*, published in 2012.

[100] According to http://www.universetoday.com/100/how-many-stars-are-there-in-the-universe/ (accessed November, 2016): "If you had perfect eyesight and traveled to completely dark skies in both the Northern and Southern Hemispheres, and there was no Moon, you might be able to count almost 9,000 stars with the naked eye. With a good pair of binoculars, that number jumps to about 200,000, since you can observe stars down to magnitude 9. A small telescope, capable of resolving magnitude 13 stars will let you count up to 15 million stars. Large observatories could resolve billions of stars... According to astronomers, there are probably more than 170 billion galaxies in the observable Universe, stretching out into a region of space 13.8 billion light-years away from us in all directions. And so, if you multiply the number of stars in our galaxy by the number of galaxies in the Universe, you get approximately 10^{24} stars. That's a 1 followed by twenty-four zeros.

[101] The mistaken belief that the Church has replaced Israel as God's chosen people. As will be demonstrated in this book, God's people, on a spiritual relationship level, have *never been merely a physical people*. Even within the physical nation of Israel, only those who believed God, were part of His *spiritual family*. None of the unbelieving were part of God's remnant of true believers.

[102] Genesis 46:27; 1 Kings 19:18; Romans 11:4.

[103] Matthew 24:22; Matthew 21:5; Revelation 10:6.

[104] 2 Peter 1:19: "*And we have the prophetic word more fully confirmed, to which you will do well to pay attention as to a lamp shining in a dark place, until the day dawns and the morning star rises in your hearts*" (2 Peter 1:19, ESV).

[105] 1 Peter 1:18-21.

[106] Genesis 2:24-25 (Chapter 17, *The Last Eve and The Great Mystery* addresses this in more detail).

[107] 1 Corinthians 10:11: "*Now these things happened to them as an example, but they were written down for our instruction, on whom the end of the ages has come.* (1 Corinthians 10:11, ESV).

[108] Zodhiates, S. (2000), This testament is called "new [καινα {2537}, qualitatively new]" (Heb. 9:15), equivalent to "the second" (Heb. 8:7), or "the better one" (Heb. 7:22). The same meaning would pertain to the blood of His covenant which would be the blood of His promise, the blood of Christ (i.e., His sacrificial death) (Heb. 9:20; 10:29).

[109] Hebrews 7:22, 8:6.

Chapter 10

THE TRANSITION OF THE JEWISH-ONLY EARLY CHURCH

In the initial days of the Church during this New Covenant period, the understanding of the *Mystery of God* was **definitely new** to the Jewish-only apostles, the Jewish-only leadership, and the Jewish-only saints throughout the Church. During the time of transition from the Old Covenant into the New, the *Mystery of God* was revealed to the apostles and saints. The embryonic elements of the *Mystery* were new and counter to what they had known under the Old Testament. One good evidence of that fact was the event in which there was one variance from their standard, Old Testament system; it caused a major uproar within the Church.[110] The raging issue was whether or not God required circumcision for the new Gentiles believers. Initially, dispute and debate in Antioch became contentious and held forth the possibility of serious division in the Church. Paul and Barnabas challenged the Jewish believers, who had come to Antioch from Judea claiming that the Gentiles were required to be circumcised according to the Law of Moses. The basic issue in all of this was *how the Gentiles were going to fit in* with the previously all-Jewish Church; what was or was not to be required of the Gentiles. Finally, it was determined by the Church in Antioch that Paul and Barnabas, along with other brothers, should go up to Jerusalem to see the apostles and elders about this contentious question.

Before we go further, we should ask a question. Weren't the people of Israel already required to receive Gentiles into citizenship prior to this period, if they met God's stipulated requirements? According to what God had instructed Moses, Gentiles were to be welcomed to become part of Israel, God's physical, chosen people.[111] They were to be received and counted as integral to the nation, and not a half-citizen.[112] It should be noted that if those Gentiles believed in the God of Israel in their hearts, like Ruth and Rahab did, then they also became part of God's *spiritual family*. The physical assimilation of Gentiles into the nation of physical Israel was an important *type*, or *shadow*, of things to come. Let's keep in mind that any time either an Israelite or a Gentile believed and trusted in God, they were to become part of the true *Israel of God*. When the Apostle Paul said that *"they are not all Israel, who are of Israel,"* he was, at minimum, referring to the fact that they were not all part of the *Israel of God*. Just because they were a natural-born Israelite did not make them part of the spiritual family of God, the *Israel of God*. That is why many Christians are confused about the meaning of the phrase *the chosen people*. More about that later.

The rich truths contained in what would become known and understood as the *Mystery of God* opened up the understanding of the early all-Jewish Church to a revelation that was initially shocking and confusing for them. They had always only been told that their mission was to go the *"lost sheep of the house of Israel,"*[113] just as Jesus had instructed. Yet, after Jesus had returned to the Father in heaven, and as the Church was looking back on that historical Day of Pentecost, during the time when only Jews were coming into the Church, something happened that jolted that all-Jewish Church.

We learn in the New Testament writings, as God's revelation in the New Covenant became clearer, that the transition from the Old Covenant to the New Covenant would require of the Jewish leaders to reconfigure their understanding of God's perspective about the Gentiles. This did not change God's gathering of a Bride. Christ's gathering of His Bride remained on track, just as it had been since the Garden. But at this early New Testament (Covenant) juncture, their Jewish understanding had to be radically changed.

The Church Door Began To Swing Wide Open

Before those aforementioned events took place, a new day had already begun to dawn on the previously only-Jewish Church. One day, while in a trance, Peter was shown the same vision three times.

> *"[Peter] saw heaven opened and an object like a great sheet bound at the four corners, descending to him and let down to the earth. In it were all kinds of four-footed animals of the earth, wild beasts, creeping things, and birds of the air. And a voice came to him, 'Rise, Peter; kill and eat.' But Peter said, 'Not so, Lord!* **For I have never eaten anything common or unclean.'** *And a voice spoke to him again the second time,* **'What God has cleansed you must not call common.'** *This was done three times. And the object was taken up into heaven again."*
>
> Acts 10:11–16

Someone has said in jest that this was probably more like a nightmare for Peter, rather than just a trance. I guess so! Even his answer to the voice he had heard during the trance tells of his determination to follow the rules God had given to Israel. If Peter was nothing else, he was a truly committed Jew. *"For I have **never** eaten anything common or unclean,"* he said. That's

The Transition of the Jewish-Only Early Church

pretty committed. Many of us struggle just to do without chocolate for more than a month! OK, how about for even a day? To keep the rules, Peter was completely committed to not even enter into the home of a Gentile. Peter had known, believed, and lived according to the law; therefore, he knew that if he had entered into the home of a Gentile he would have been ceremonially "unclean." Understandably, this trance shook Peter to his core.

God knew that it would take a miracle to cause Peter to eat anything that was common or unclean for the Jews. God graciously, made it abundantly and miraculously clear to Peter what he was to do. We should understand that this issue was much bigger than one man's beliefs and lifestyle; much bigger! This was about God gathering a Bride for His Son. This situation may have been a mystery to Peter, but that which had been a mystery was about to become a revelation to the Church.

When Peter came out of the trance, while he was still thinking about it and what it might mean, he was told by the Spirit of God that three men were coming to meet with him. He was told that he was to go with those men, doubting nothing. Sure enough, when they had arrived, and he had greeted them, he inquired as to why the men had come.

> *"And they said, "Cornelius the centurion, a just man, one who fears God and has a good reputation among all the nation of the Jews, was divinely instructed by a holy angel to summon you to his house, and to hear words from you." Then he invited them in and lodged them …."*
>
> Acts 10:22–23

It is an interesting side note that Peter did something that must have shocked his family and every Jew around him. Questioning nothing, he invited Cornelius' Gentile representatives *into his home for the night*. That alone was enough to cause any Jew to think that Peter had strayed from the path of purity in his beliefs!

The next morning, Peter, along with some other Jewish brothers from the Joppa Church, traveled to Caesarea to Cornelius' house. One can only imagine what Peter had to go through to explain and convince His Jewish brethren from the Joppa Church to go with him, along with the Gentile representatives, to Cornelius—yet another Gentile!

When Peter arrived, he went in and found that Cornelius had called together his relatives and close friends. Then Peter made it clear that only God could have made this meeting possible, because, he said:

> *"… You know how unlawful it is for a Jewish man to keep company with or go to one of another nation. But God has shown me that I should not call any man common or unclean. Therefore, I came without objection as soon as I was sent for …."*
>
> Acts 10:28–29

In today's church many Gentile believers may not have taken the time to try to understand the radical change Peter went through in all this. In fact, some have even suggested that Peter had lacked spirituality because of his initial hesitation. That is not even close to being true. This was asking a lot of a Jew, like Peter. But he followed the Spirit and stepped outside of his Jewish comfort zone and went in obedience, without objection, to what the Spirit of God had shown him. Through the Spirit's leading, and Peter's obedience to that leading, the first Gentiles were grafted into the spiritual commonwealth of Israel, the natural olive tree. These Gentiles were grafted into that tree and were made part of the spiritual remnant gathered into the people of Israel. It was during that very meeting in Cornelius' home that the all-Jewish Church doors *began to swing wide open to the Gentiles!*

God in His wisdom made sure that we have the opportunity to understand what happened at that moment with Peter and Cornelius. When we continue reading the follow up to the conversion of Cornelius and his relatives and friends, further evidence is given of just how exclusively-Jewish the early Church had been until then.

And Now—Peter Was On the Hot Seat

When the Jewish brothers-in-Christ in Jerusalem heard about the Cornelius event, Peter had some serious explaining to do. In everyday English, it might read like this: *The news about Peter's meeting with the Gentiles got back to the other apostles and Jewish believers in Jerusalem and Judea. So, when Peter arrived back in Jerusalem, the Jewish believers quizzed him with shock and criticism. "You entered into and ate in the home of Gentiles!"* (Acts 11:1–3). They truly did believe that Peter had failed God.

After Peter explained how the Holy Spirit had fallen upon the Gentiles, just as He had fallen on the Jews at the beginning, the apostles and the other Jewish believers were so dumbfounded that "*… they became silent ….*" Once the truth concerning the Gentiles had sunk in, and they assimilated their shock and awe, then "*… they glorified God, saying, 'Then **God has also granted to the Gentiles repentance to life**.*'" (Acts 11:18). Again, it was at that point that the Church doors truly began to open to the Gentiles.

Remember that while this was a total shock to all of the Jews, it had been God's sovereign plan all along. The reader will notice that I regularly refer to the fact of God's foreknowledge of all of this had been in place since before the world began. None of this was a surprise to God, nor was it new to Him. Let's remember that God included this very moment among the promises He made to Abraham:

The Transition of the Jewish-Only Early Church

"And the Scripture, foreseeing that God would justify the Gentiles by faith, preached the gospel to Abraham beforehand, saying, "In you all the nations shall be blessed." So then those who are of faith are blessed with believing Abraham."

Galatians 3:8–9

Still, the complexities involved weren't over yet. Now that the Jews and Gentiles were becoming one in Christ, there were many details to work out. God began to reconcile the impact of the New Covenant upon the Old Covenant era, both for Jews and Gentiles. Once the impact of the inclusion of the Gentiles into the Church began to take root, both the Jews and the Gentiles had to reconcile their misconceptions in very practical terms, especially those pertaining to the promises, blessings, and cursings given to Israel. God had given certain promises and obligations to those who were the physical children of Abraham, Isaac, and Jacob. This was, in part, what had caused Peter's dilemma regarding going into Cornelius' house in the first place. But now, it was important for the once all-Jewish Church to fully understand that in Christ there are *"better things;"* better in every way. After all, this is the New Covenant, the New Testament! The Book of Hebrews was written to make this point unequivocally and emphatically clear. It's a wonderful study, but an enlargement on this subject is outside the scope of this book. Nevertheless, Hebrews refers to the matter of "better" thirteen (13) times in Hebrews 1:4; 6:9; 7:7, 19, 22; 8:6 (twice); 9:23; 10:34; 11:16, 35, 40; 12:24.

Better Things

The New Covenant consists of "better things" than those found in the Old Covenant.[114] A good example is when Jesus summed up "all of the Law and Prophets," in the two commandments, on which they all hang:

*"Jesus said to him, 'You shall **love the Lord your God** with all your heart, with all your soul, and with all your mind. This is the first and great commandment. And the second is like it: You shall **love your neighbor as yourself**. On these two commandments hang all the Law and the Prophets.'"*

Matthew 22:37–40

Additionally, Jesus gave a "new commandment:"

*"A new commandment I give to you, that you **love one another; as I have loved you,** that you also love one another."*

John 13:34

Those three commandments are nothing short of privileges and opportunities offered to us as his disciples, which can only be lived out through the grace and power of the Holy Spirit in our lives. Does what Jesus said about these commandments remove, negate, disallow or neglect God's moral commands? Or is there something else at work in this? The Apostle Paul helped us when he wrote:

*"For what the law [of Moses] could not do in that it was weak through the flesh, God did by sending His own Son in the likeness of sinful flesh, on account of sin: He condemned sin in the flesh, that **the righteous requirement of the law might be fulfilled in us who do not walk according to the flesh but according to the Spirit."***

Romans 8:3-4

Paul makes it explicitly clear that the only way that the "righteous requirement of the law" can be fulfilled in us is by our walking according to (or in and through) the Spirit.

Under the New (Covenant) Testament, anything found in *any and all other biblical covenants*, which are **not specifically shown to have been superseded** by God's New (Covenant) Testament, remained in force. How these things remained in force is important.

Another point of clarity is that Jesus' death removed those ordinances from off the back of Jews who come to Christ for salvation. Spiritual, or born again, Jews/Israel were no longer under that heavy yoke. There is much New Testament evidence of this. (Please refer to Acts 15:10-11; Galatians 2:11-21 through 4:6.) That is not to suggest that born again Jews are permitted to abide by any custom or ceremony which was prohibited by the New Covenant. Certainly, not! For example, after Christ's sacrifice on the cross, there remains no more sacrifice for sin. Therefore, for any person, Jew or not, to offer animal sacrifice is prohibited and unnecessary. On the other hand there are many covenantal matters, which are not removed from the Jews; celebrating biblical, Jewish feast days is permitted, and not negated by the New Covenant, as far as Jewish believers are concerned. While there may be some debate about some of these issues among Gentiles, the fact remains that everything "Jewish" was not negated by the New Covenant. (Please refer to Romans 9, Acts 15, and associated references.)

Nevertheless, it is useful for Gentile Christians to realize that it was the Gentiles who were relieved from certain Jewish customs, etc., but which remained for the Jews as part of the everlasting covenant God had made with Abraham and his physical descendants. Our ignorance of this is, perhaps, a key reason why Jews may not accept the Gentilized Church message. On the one hand God had given them those commands in an everlasting covenant, which they were told by God that they were to abide forever. Then on the other hand Gentile Christians came along late to the game, in a manner of speaking. Once the numbers of the

Gentile believers grew and overwhelmed the number of Jewish believers, things began to change for the worse. The Gentilized Church has *required* born-again Jews to disobey what had been commanded by God Himself in order to come into the *"kingdom."* Which should they adhere to? Gentile believers often don't know, or often don't respect, physical Israel's covenantal relationship given to them by God.

These things can be confusing. But there is hope. When confusion is in the New Testament Church regarding this matter, we can rest assured that the Holy Spirit has given us the answer in His Word. In this case, a clearer understanding is found in Paul's powerful writings. Next we will see that something extremely important happened, which brought understanding and stability within the Church. I want to see this with you in the next chapter: *The Apostle Paul Brings Clarity!*

Chapter Ten Notes

[110]"Now the apostles and elders came together to consider this matter. And when **there had been much dispute**, Peter rose up and said to them: "Men and brethren, you know that a good while ago God chose among us, that by my mouth the Gentiles should hear the word of the gospel and believe. So, God, who knows the heart, acknowledged them [the born-again Gentiles] *by giving them the Holy Spirit, just as He did to us* [Jewish believers], and **made no distinction between us and them**, purifying their hearts by faith" (Acts 15:6–9).

[111]Exodus 12:48; Deuteronomy 4:5-7; Leviticus 17:8.

[112]i.e., Ruth and Rahab, both of which are in the lineage of Jesus.

[113]Matthew 10:5-7; Matthew 15:24.

[114]In describing the ways in which the New Covenant is better than that which preceded it, The Book of Hebrews uses the word "better" thirteen (13) times—better sacrifice, better covenant, better priesthood, better hope, better promises, etc. (Hebrews 1:4; 6:9; 7:7, 19, 22; 8:6 (twice); 9:23; 10:34; 11:16, 35, 40; 12:24).

Chapter 11

THE APOSTLE PAUL BRINGS CLARITY

*"... by revelation **He made known to me the mystery** ... by which, when you read, you may understand **my knowledge in the mystery of Christ** ...."*

Ephesians 3:2-4

*"**But we speak the wisdom of God in a mystery**, the hidden wisdom which God ordained before the ages for our glory ...."*

1 Corinthians 2:7

Most of us are likely familiar with the instruction to children, when taking a trip in a car, that goes something like this. *Please get in, sit down, and buckle your seatbelts.* As we enter into this chapter, we could repeat that same idea. As J. Vernon McGee was so fond of saying on the Through the Bible Program, *"Let's get on the Bible bus!"* So, may I encourage you to please grab your Bible for easy referencing; it's an excellent GPS—take a seat, and buckle your seatbelt! This will be a great trip!

Anyone who has spent time reading the New Testament realizes that the Apostle Paul was a man mightily used of God to explain the New Covenant. It would not be an overstatement to say that Paul was called by God to give doctrinal understanding and stability within God's family. By explaining the New Covenant and the *Mystery of God*, he simultaneously brought understanding, first to the Jews, and then to the Gentiles. Eventually, he became accustomed to providing understanding to the new Gentile believers, as to the relationship between Jews and Gentiles in Christ.

Saul of Tarsus (later called Paul) was struck blind by the light of Jesus on the road to Damascus, as he was on his way to zealously persecute the Church. This was his encounter with Jesus which may have blinded him, but in his blindness, he saw the light of God in his soul. While Saul was still in his blinded condition, Jesus met elsewhere with another of His disciples, Ananias, whom he commanded to go to meet Saul and to lay hands on him and heal him from his blindness. Ananias questioned the Lord, telling him that this is the man who had been terrorizing believers. But Jesus had a plan, and no amount of fear was to keep that plan from going forward. So "… the Lord said to him (Ananias):

> *"Go, for he is a chosen vessel of Mine* **to bear My name before Gentiles, kings, and the children of Israel.** *For I will show him how many things he must suffer for My name's sake"*
>
> Acts 9:15–16

God had been long preparing Paul as a chosen vessel. His calling was not only to the children of Israel, but he was also a chosen vessel to **"bear My name before Gentiles!"** His conversion was both traumatic and dramatic. In light of the fact that he had not been one of the original disciples and apostles, his testimony had been different than theirs. He was careful to point out that all of the other apostles had been known by Jesus during Jesus' ministry, but then *"… **last of all** He was seen by me also,* **as by one born out of due time. For I am the least of the apostles,** *who am not worthy to be called an apostle, because I persecuted the Church of God"* (1 Corinthians 15:8–9).

Paul sincerely must have felt he was the *"least of the apostles."* Yet, he was anything but that. Perhaps, in the context of having persecuted the Church of God, his feelings were warranted. However, his calling and usefulness in God's New Covenant were anything but the least. He was special in his calling for many reasons. His early encounters with the other apostles and leadership in the Church in Jerusalem could not have come at a better time or for a better reason. God had called him to bring further reconciliation between the past and the future of God's chosen ones, His family, His Church, both Jews, and Gentiles.

This was the situation in Antioch:

> *"And certain men came down from Judea and taught the brethren, 'Unless you are circumcised according to the custom of Moses, you cannot be saved.' Therefore, when Paul and Barnabas had no small dissension and dispute with them, they determined that Paul and Barnabas and certain others of them should go up to Jerusalem, to the apostles and elders, about this question."*
>
> Acts 15:1–2

I confess that I love that scenario. I don't love the dissension and dispute. What I love is the fact that they were willing to come together with other mature believers, including the apostles and the leadership in the Church in Jerusalem. They gathered for prayer and discussion, being careful to listen for the Holy Spirit to speak to them to bring unity in understanding and direction. Since they weren't able to reach a unified conclusion in Antioch on the issues, they agreed to seek resolution by traveling to Jerusalem to meet with the apostles and other leaders there. How great is that! Parenthetically, the day is soon coming when such gatherings, even though they will be very private and personal, even under duress, will happen more and more often among hungry-hearted believers because of the increased persecution.[115]

The Jerusalem Council

What a monumental event in the life and growth of the body of Christ occurred in Acts 15! When Paul and Barnabas, and the other brothers arrived at Jerusalem, *"the apostles, the elders, and the whole Church"* (Acts 15:22) came together in a major council meeting to deal with the complex and confusing issues confronting the Church. Obviously, since the time of Cornelius' conversion (previously, an unsaved Gentile), Gentiles had begun to become part of the Church. But now, specific problems were arising because of the requirements being imposed on the Gentile converts, as it related to the Law of Moses.

At the Jerusalem council, Paul and the others reported what *"... God had done with them. But some of the sect of the Pharisees who believed rose up, saying, "It is necessary to circumcise them, and to command them to keep the law of Moses"* (Acts 15:4–5). What? Why would they say such a thing? After all, some would say they should have known better, if they were believers in Christ. These particular Pharisees were saved ("who believed"), and yet, here they were claiming that these Gentiles needed to *keep the Law of Moses?* How strange is that?

Well, maybe not so strange after all. About this time during the council, Peter stood up and gave testimony again of what had happened back when he had gone to Cornelius' home. He calmed the crowd down by his testimony, so the meeting was then open for Barnabas and Paul to speak. *"Then all the multitude kept silent and listened to Barnabas and Paul declaring how many miracles and wonders God had worked through them among the Gentiles"* (Acts 15:12).

Their testimonies were now given. Then after Barnabas and Paul had spoken, it was James' turn, as a key apostle and pastor of the Jerusalem Church.

> *"Men and brethren, listen to me: Simon [Peter] has declared how **God at the first visited the Gentiles to take out of them a people for His name. And with this the prophets agree** ...."*
>
> Acts 15:13–14

What did he mean by that? What is this about the *"prophets"* agreeing to the fact that God would *"take out of"* the Gentiles *"a people for His name?"* Hold that thought, please.

James continued, giving a prophetic illustration, as an example among many in the Old Testament, to show how the prophets agreed. He referred to Amos 9:11, 12:

"After this I will return and will rebuild the tabernacle of David, which has fallen down; I will rebuild its ruins, And I will set it up; **So that the rest of mankind may seek the Lord, even all the Gentiles who are called by My name, Says the Lord** WHO DOES ALL THESE THINGS."

He then finished by saying that the believers from among the Gentiles are not required to do all that the believers from among the Jews would do. He wasn't wrong, or out of the will of God, in his declaration. He was following the Holy Spirit, which should be no real surprise to anyone who understands the *Mystery of God*!

With the agreement of all of the apostles and elders of the Church, including those Pharisees who had originally objected, James wrote a letter to the Churches, which was taken by the hand of Paul and Barnabas and others as a resolution which had been received from the Holy Spirit. After all, it was the Holy Spirit who had led in the council in Jerusalem, as was stated in James' letter.

"Therefore I judge that we should not trouble those from among the Gentiles who are turning to God ... For it seemed good to the Holy Spirit, and to us, to lay upon you no greater burden than these necessary things: that you abstain from things offered to idols, from blood, from things strangled, and from sexual immorality. If you keep yourselves from these, you will do well. Farewell."

Acts 15:19, 28–29

The content of that letter was agreed to by the *"apostles, elders and brethren"* in Jerusalem and it was to be read to the believing Gentiles, telling them that the leadership was aware that they had been told that they *"must be circumcised and keep the law,"* but they were relieved of this requirement. The letter encouraged them not to be *"troubled"* with such words. With the letter in hand everyone departed from the council **in** *"one accord."*

Was that everything? Was that all there was to the issues concerning Jews and Gentiles reconciling within the Body of Christ? No! There was much more, yet to be processed in the Church, but that particular fundamental resolution was dynamic and powerful. Their instructions, affirmed by the Holy Spirit, gave the basics for a better understanding of how God intended to meld the Jews and the Gentiles into *"one body,"* later reiterated by Paul ten times.[116] It was the Apostle Paul, who would expand on these things to fully clarify the Holy Spirit's message. And the message that the Apostle Paul would expand on would be revealed little by little, as being those truths inherent in the *Mystery of God*. This is reminiscent of what Joshua commanded the Israelites as they were about to enter into the Promised Land finally:

THE APOSTLE PAUL BRINGS CLARITY

*"And the Lord your God will drive out those nations before you **little by little**; you will be unable to destroy them at once, lest the beasts of the field become too numerous for you."*

Deuteronomy 7:22

Clearly God's ways are His ways. Our proclivity is to get ahead of Him.

We have read of Peter's trance and the council in Jerusalem. So what do these things add up to? What do they have to do with the *Mystery of God*? Many in today's Church have missed the target on this subject. It's important to understand the background concerning the inclusion of Gentiles into the previously, all-Jewish assembly of believers. Through the death and shedding of Jesus' blood, it had been made clear that the *"middle wall of separation"* between the two had been destroyed by Him. But what Jesus accomplished was more than just tearing down the wall that separated the two. Those two, who had been separated by that wall, were now made to become one by and in Christ Himself. That is a fundamental underpinning of the *Mystery of God*.

Some contend that when the two became one in Christ there remained, therefore, neither Jew, nor Israel, nor Gentile. They say that none of that is pertinent any longer. Therefore, they would say, when we are *"in Christ,"* no distinctions between Jews and Israel and Gentiles can be made in the Church. Strangely, many of those who say those things, also make a *division* between the Church and *"the Israel of God."* But there is one little problem with that. The *"Israel of God"* is, in fact, the Church, the Body of Christ, as Paul made clear.

"Neither circumcision nor uncircumcision means anything; what counts is a new creation. Peace and mercy to all who follow this rule, even to the Israel of God."

Galatians 6:15–16, NIV84

Let's not allow any confusion to muddy this critical topic. Let's see that in the most emphatic of terms Paul's connected references and terminology in describing the Church deserves special attention. We should understand that there is a very real difference between physical Israel and the spiritual remnant who are believers and who are gathered from among the children of Abraham/Israel—as that remnant.[117] There is no difference—zero, zip, nada—between those from within the people of Israel, who are believers, and those who are Gentiles, who are believers. Now they are BOTH the "Israel of God" in one family in Christ! From the Garden to the *Marriage of the Lamb*, God has always only had one family, one assembly, one Bride. Christ's Plan had always been to gather a Bride for Himself, including those before there ever was a *nation of Israel*. Was God **NOT** the Father, spiritually, of all those who had trusted in Him, before there was a called-out Nation of Israel? All of them were His "chosen ones;" in relationship with Him by His gracious covenants with them before there was a "chosen nation." Those who were believers before the time of Abraham, Isaac, and Jacob were in covenant, and were part of God's ongoing remnant!

Bringing All Together Under One Head

Consider the Apostle Paul's statements in addressing this very point in Ephesians 1:4-5, 9-10 (key phases only, for clarity):

> *"For he chose us **in him before the creation of the world** ... in accordance with his pleasure and will ... And he made known to us the Mystery of his will according to his good pleasure, **which he purposed in Christ, to be put into effect when the times will have reached their fulfillment**—to bring **ALL THINGS IN HEAVEN AND ON EARTH TOGETHER UNDER ONE HEAD, EVEN CHRIST."***
>
> Ephesians 1:9–10, NIV84

What an amazing and revealing statement! When did all of that begin? Paul states that all believers were *"chosen in Him **before the creation of the world.**"* After He had created the world, He waited until *"the times will have reached their fulfillment,"* then He brought **"all things in heaven and on earth together under one head;"** and that Head was and is Christ! What then is this saying? Notice that all of this is within the context of the *Mystery*. As an intrinsic part of the *Mystery*, Christ *"tears down of the middle wall of separation,"* and brings **"ALL THINGS IN HEAVEN AND ON EARTH TOGETHER UNDER ONE HEAD, CHRIST."**

Who are all of these who are in heaven and on earth? After the New Testament covenant was ushered in, the Old Testament saints are seen to be with the Lord in heaven, along with New Testament saints who had also died in Christ.[118]

> *"Therefore it says, 'When he ascended on high he led a host of captives, and he gave gifts to men" (In saying, He ascended, what does it mean but that he had also descended into the lower regions, the earth? He who descended is the one who also ascended far above all the heavens, that he might fill all things).'"*
>
> Ephesians 4:8–10, ESV

> *"We are confident, yes, well pleased rather to be absent from the body and to be present with the Lord."*
>
> 2 Corinthians 5:8

THE APOSTLE PAUL BRINGS CLARITY

These "TOGETHER"-ones to which Paul is referring, include all who were chosen *"in Him before the creation of the world,"* both Old and New Testament saints. Yes, it is true that I am repeating this several times. At the risk of beating this drum too much, I deeply desire that this repetition is a good teacher. When it comes to the *Mystery of God*, I trust that, due to the lack of our exposure to this critical teaching in the past, such repetition can be beneficial to us.

Is the Church so given over to Division Theology, which makes a difference between saints in the Old and New Testaments, that they cannot see this? (Please refer to Appendix C, *Division Theology*) Truly, there had been a middle wall of separation. But that wall has been obliterated by the mighty Jesus by His own suffering on the cross, bringing in the New Covenant, of which the Prophet Jeremiah spoke in Jeremiah 31:31-37. How blind, how erroneous, is the Gentilized Church if Gentiles attempt to segregate the Old Testament saints from being UNDER ONE HEAD, CHRIST! Again, we read that vitally important statement of the great reconciliation in Hebrews 11:39-40 (NIV84):

> *"These* [including Old Testament saints listed in Hebrews 11] *were all commended for their faith, yet none of them received what had been promised. God had planned something better for us so that* **ONLY TOGETHER** *with us would they be made perfect* [**complete**]*."*

That was God's design; His will and plan. This had been planned before the world began! Covenant by covenant God made promises, all of which were to be brought to fulfillment in Christ and through His Body, either at the His first coming, or His second coming, or the eternal Kingdom.

Each covenant from the Garden forward, especially the crowning *New Covenant*, received promises. Each of the covenants foretold of Him who was to come: *Christ, the Head*. Each of the covenants accrued, one upon another, with a common denominator: *The gathering of His Bride into one, under one Head, Christ*. Nevertheless, in the fullness of time, when Christ came, He confirmed the covenant with His blood, dying and thereby making the covenant strong and effective before God.

Here, again, the Mystery of God is front and center, just as the Apostle Paul explained:

> *"For this reason I, Paul, the prisoner of Christ Jesus for the sake of you Gentiles— Surely you have heard about the administration of God's grace that was given to me for you, that is,* **the Mystery** *made known to me by revelation, as I have already written briefly. In reading this, then, you will be able to understand* **my insight into the mystery of Christ**, *which was not made known to men in other generations as it has now been revealed by the Spirit to God's holy apostles and prophets.* **This mystery is that through the gospel the**

THE INCREDIBLE KEY

*Gentiles are **HEIRS TOGETHER WITH ISRAEL, MEMBERS TOGETHER OF ONE BODY**, and **SHARERS TOGETHER** in the **PROMISE** in Christ Jesus."*

Ephesians 3:1–6, NIV84

Ephesians 3:1-6 is another vitally important revelation for understanding the *Mystery of God*. It is this very revelation that desperately needs to be shouted from the rooftops in our churches, once again—right now! We need to ascend to it, for exactly what it is: *The Incredible Key: The Mystery of God*, and all of the truths that come with it.

Consider that Christ is the Head of the Church, which is His Body. When we consider Christ as a Person, we see that we are one with and in Him, spiritually. But if we step back, and ask the question: *How does the Lord identify His Body?* The answer is that He identifies His Body in numerous ways. We, His Body, are called *a Bride, a family, a temple, the Church, a house, the Israel of God, the commonwealth of Israel, an olive tree, a country, a city, the New Jerusalem,* and so forth. The point is that none of these identifications segregates the Body of Christ from the Head—Christ Himself! His Body is one with the Head, of course. He chooses to use many ways to show us truths about Himself, about His desire, will and plan, about ourselves, about the way we are to live in relationship with one another, and about the future in light of our oneness with our Head, Christ.

These things could not be clearer than the picture given to us by the Apostle Paul in Romans 11. He identified Gentiles as *"wild olive branches."* Those in Israel, who actually had the faith of their father, Abraham, were the ones Paul called the *"natural olive tree."* He said that these were, and are, those who are physical Israel, but who also became children of God by faith, like Abraham. They believe. Paul went on to say that the *"wild olive branches"* (Gentiles) are **grafted into** that *"natural olive tree"* (spiritual Israel). Gentiles, as grafted-in branches, are identified with that spiritual remnant of Israel, the *"natural olive tree."* So then, we see that all who have true faith, like the faith of Abraham, are in Christ, spiritually, from Genesis to Revelation.

Let's understand that Abraham, Isaac, Jacob, and the nation of Israel were not the chosen people because they were intrinsically good, or that they were better than others. They were chosen because of the Sovereign Chooser—God Himself—was merciful and good.[119] God had a plan to bring His Son into the world through the means of a specially chosen people, beginning with Adam and Eve, to whom was promised the *Seed*, Christ Himself, in Genesis 3. There is a reason the Gospel of Matthew gives us the genealogy of Jesus beginning with Abraham through the generations to His birth. But have we noticed that Luke's genealogy begins with Christ's birth and follows it back all of the way to *"Adam, the son of God?"*[120] Is God telling us something here that we may have overlooked? It's true that Jesus was from the *"seed of Abraham."* It is equally true that Jesus was of the *Seed*, prophesied in the Garden

The Apostle Paul Brings Clarity

of Eden. Think about it: Jesus was born of the fleshly seed of the first couple. Spiritually speaking, Jesus was also born of the *seed of the woman,* meaning, that it would take God Himself to make it possible for a virgin to give birth. This is why Luke wrote:

> *"... The Holy Spirit will come upon you [Mary], and the power of the Highest will overshadow you; therefore, also, that Holy One who is to be born will be called the Son of God."*
>
> Luke 1:35

All of the *chosen* people in the Bible are identified as those who down through history were willing to receive His Word, as revealed by God in Person, or in His *covenants* and *promises.* They trusted Him by grace through faith for His redemption, as was symbolized through the shedding of the blood of animal sacrifices. These sacrifices represented types and shadows of "better things" to come; and then, ultimately realized in the Person of Jesus, the Lamb of God who shed His blood, as the only means of eternal redemption.

All the while those with whom He made covenant are those whom Christ was gathering as His Bride, bringing each of them *"under the Head, Christ."* Then when the pages of Scripture highlighted Abraham, we see that God found a friend in Abraham. He made a covenant with Abraham. Was Abraham, or any other believer, faithful *to the fullest extent* concerning their covenant responsibilities?[121] I would say, no. As it always has been and is now, only God could keep the covenant, which is precisely what God did, and what God does. (We can pause and praise God for that!)

Every covenant and promise God made throughout human history were essential. His covenants had one primary goal in mind: bringing Jesus into the world. All along the way, the Father was gathering a Bride for Jesus, based on the purchase price He paid for all saints of all time. The Son fulfilled all covenants. So much so did He fulfill the covenants that God proclaimed His Son, Jesus, actually to be the Covenant. (Isaiah 42:6). The best news of all is that we are in Him, who is our Covenant!

As it is with so many things that happened through this reconciliation and transition into practical application of the New Covenant, we can picture this as a many faceted diamond. There is beauty no matter how you look at it. One of the flashes of light, from just one of the facets we see in this diamond, is given to us by the Holy Spirit through the Apostle Paul's writings. This flash of light is found in Romans, chapters 9 and 11—and a very brilliantly shining flash of light it is!

They Are Not All Israel
They Are Not All Children of Abraham

Previously, in Chapter 9, *The Mystery of God: Planned From Before The Beginning*, I had drawn our attention to Romans 9 and 11. I had mentioned that we would look at those passages again from a different perspective. I now want to see with you that additional perspective. The message in this chapter is to see how the Apostle Paul clarifies and applied the *Mystery of God* during the time of transition in the Church, as it specifically relates to moving from the Old into the New Covenant. Let's keep in mind that in Romans 9, Paul makes a clear distinction between those who are **physical Israel**, born as Israelites, but who were **NOT** *part of the spiritual remnant from within Israel.*

> "... For they are not all Israel who are of Israel, nor are they all children because they are the seed of Abraham ... those who are the children of the flesh, these are not the children of God; but the children of the promise are counted as the seed."[122]
>
> Romans 9:6–8

Paul further explains it this way, when describing physical Israel. He said of his own flesh-and-blood countrymen that they are:

> "... **my countrymen <u>according to the flesh</u>, who are Israelites** [<u>**physical Israelites**</u>], *to whom pertain the adoption, the glory, the covenants, the giving of the law, the service of God, and the promises;* **of whom are the fathers and from whom, <u>according to the flesh, Christ came</u>**."
>
> Romans 9:3–5

In other words, the nation of physical Israel was called by God to receive the privilege of certain responsibilities, which God had given to them through covenant, including Christ being born into this world through the line of Israel, *"according to the flesh."* Even though they were given these privileges and responsibilities, which Paul listed above, the truth is that only a "remnant" from among them truly believed.

The faith of Abraham did not automatically exist in the hearts of Abraham's fleshly descendants just because they were able to claim that Abraham was their father. The same is true, not only regarding the lineage of Abraham, but also concerning the nation of Israel. Not everyone who was a part of the nation of Israel could claim that they had faith in the God of Abraham, Isaac, and Jacob in their hearts, just because they were Israelites. Paul could not have made this more emphatically clear when he preached to the Jews in Antioch in Acts 13.

THE APOSTLE PAUL BRINGS CLARITY

*"Men and brethren, sons of the [physical] family of Abraham, and those among you who fear God, to you the word of this salvation has been sent. For those who dwell in Jerusalem, and their rulers, **because they did not know Him, nor even the voices of the Prophets which are read every Sabbath**, have fulfilled them in condemning Him"* (bracket mine).

Acts 13:26–27

In that passage, we plainly see that Paul, in explaining the Word of God to his *"own countrymen,"* face to face, made the distinction between those who were children of God and those who were not, even though they were all children of Abraham, physically. He made that distinction loudly, clearly, and of great necessity!

John made this distinction in John 1, as we said. *"He [Jesus] came unto His **own (countrymen, according to the flesh)**, but His own did not receive Him."* That famous verse suddenly carries more meaning. Then we read this:

*"But as many as received Him, to them [**His own countrymen, according to the flesh**] He gave the right to **become children of God**, to those who believe in His name: who **were born, not of blood, nor of the will of the flesh, nor of the will of man, but of God.**"*

John 1:12–13

That's it! It's not about the flesh or the physical. It's about the spiritual. There are two families in this world. There have only always been two families in this world! Those who are born of the flesh ***only***; they are born *"of blood … they are born of the will of the flesh … they are born of the will of man"*—**but NOT of God**! And the second family is made up of those who are ***"born of God"***—they are the spiritual children of God, whether in the Old or the New Testament. These are those who have faith, as exemplified in Hebrews 11. They are those who *"are looking for that city, whose builder and maker is God,"*[123] and both Old and New Testament saints are included.

It's important that we see Jesus in the light of all of that. As Paul said in Philippians 2:5-8, Jesus came *"in the likeness of men,"* and was *"found in the appearance of man."* That likeness and appearance were a natural thing resulting from having been *"born of a virgin,"* who was a human being, and through the ancestral physical line, which meant that Jesus was in that line of the *"fathers … according to the flesh …,"* just as Paul had stated! But that was the physical line. What about the *spiritual line?* First of all, Jesus' spiritual line was direct: God! He *"was God,"*[124] and He was *"from"* God.[125] This is why Jesus told Nicodemus that he must be *"born again."*[126] Obviously, Nicodemus had already been born of the physical flesh. Nicodemus was already in Abraham's physical line, according to the flesh. But then he was told that he needed to be born again, into the spiritual family of God. For those who say that Old Testament saints are not part of God's *"called-out assembly,"* which is what the word *"Church"* means,[127] Nicodemus is a good example of a so-called *pre-Church, Old Testament person*, who came into the family of God the same way we do in the New Testament. Nicodemus was invited to be born again even though his conversion is seen taking place under the law during the Old Testament era before Christ died and rose again. Do we not know that until Jesus' sacrifice and atonement were complete, His blood was not yet applied? Did that keep Jesus from offering Nicodemus the *new birth*, right then and there, while still operating under the Law of the Old Covenant? We tend to put God in our "doctrine box," and limit Him and His purposes.

To confirm this point fully, we are told that Jesus Himself was *"born under the law;"*[128] He was born in the Old Testament period. This had to be true, because Jesus was the one who fulfilled all the law, and brought in the New Covenant. No surprise there! The Covenant of Grace has always been by grace alone, through faith alone, in Christ alone!

Some theologians have gotten things messed up by attempting to *compartmentalize* and *dispensationalize* the Bible to such a degree that it seems their efforts at systematizing the Bible tend to distort the overarching grace of God—or, what has been called His covenant of Grace. I want to be careful to say that those same theologians, more often than not, absolutely believe in the operations of the grace of God in the Old Testament. That's not the problem. The complications come into the picture as a result of how they compartmentalize the saints in both Testaments; the segregation of the saints in the Old from the New. That error taints and confuses the truths of the covenant of God's grace, which stretches from the Garden of Eden to the End of God's dealings with humanity prior to the making of a new heaven and a new earth. In doing so, they have created a division between God's Old Testament saints and the Church, which leads to many tragic complications generally, but especially regarding Endtime prophecy. But those two—the Old Testament saints and the Church—are part of the same family and kingdom. They are the same and always have been, no matter the titles God has used from covenant to covenant.

The word "dispensation" (Greek: oikonomia; οικονομια) is often inaccurately defined and applied in theological teaching. Dispensation is sometimes referred to as a *period of time* or as an *age* or *era*. The biblical word "dispensation" actually pertains to management. The Apostle Paul stated that he had been given the "oikonomia" or "management" or "stewardship" of the *Mystery of Christ*. And that *Mystery* is precisely the very *Mystery* we are focused on in this book. It is that same *Mystery* to which he referred five times as having been *hidden, secret or not known* until it was revealed to the apostles in the New Testament. While Paul was given a role in this *management*, the ultimate "steward" and "dispensation" of the *Mystery* was Christ Himself in His own "management" of the timing of events in accordance with the *Mystery* of His will, divine pleasure and purpose. The Greek construction in Ephesians 1:9-10 (ESV) reveals that this *Mystery* of His will is specifically "set forth in Christ"; in other words, God's purpose from beginning to end is known in Christ, how Christ was made known to the world, and how this was His will concerning the *Mystery*. That purpose was hidden until the "fullness of the times." Not only did Christ come in the fullness of the times, but He will come again in the fullness of the times and gather His own to Himself, as He promised.

> *"Having made known to us the **mystery** of His [Christ's own] will, according to His good pleasure which He purposed in Himself [Christ], that in the dispensation [His own management] of the fullness of the times He might gather together in one all things in Christ, both which are in heaven and which are on earth [from beginning to end]—in Him."*
>
> Ephesians 1:9–10

The importance of this insight is to say that the most profound factor in biblically defined dispensationalism is that God has been managing (*dispensationalizing*) history all along. That management specifically and directly pertains to the Mystery, which is why Paul made this declaration: "*To me ... his grace was given, that I should preach among the Gentiles the unsearchable riches of Christ, and to make all see what is the **fellowship** [Greek: oikonomia, dispensation, management] of the **mystery, which from the beginning of the ages has been hidden in God** who created all things through Jesus Christ ....*" (Ephesians 3:8-9) What was going on "*from the beginning of the ages which was hidden?*" Why did God "hide" the *Mystery*? Paul tells us that God "*made known to us the **mystery** of His will, **according to His good pleasure which He purposed in Himself** ....*" (Ephesians 1:9) In other words, He did this as part of His management of His will. He has the right to do so and He did so "*according to His good pleasure which He purposed in Himself ....*" He is sovereign; He is the Sovereign Manager and Dispensationalizer! This *Mystery* is about Christ and His gathering together all into one body, His body to bring us to the *Marriage of the Lamb* and everything that follows in the Kingdom of Christ on earth!

Spiritual Israel: One in Christ

From time to time, I am asked if Israel and the Church are the same thing. This question is most often answered with a question to qualify what the questioner means. *Do you mean physical Israel or spiritual Israel?* After all, there is a clear distinction to be made between *physical Israel* (God's covenant-bearing people, through whom Jesus was physically born into the world), and the *spiritual Israel, the called-out ones* (God's spiritual assembly throughout the ages.) Of course we must keep in mind, as we define *spiritual Israel*, that all of those from within *physical Israel*, who became part of God's *spiritual family* by grace through faith like their father, Abraham, are obviously both; *physical Israel* and *spiritual Israel*. Jesus' disciples are perfect examples of this, while most of the leaders in Israel (during Jesus' ministry) *"did not receive Him."* Therefore, those who did not receive Him were physical Israel, but they did not become part of *spiritual Israel*. And what about those saints who lived before Abraham and the formation of the nation of Israel? All believers, whether in the Old Testament or the New Testament are part of the *spiritual family of God*, which in the New Covenant, are still called the "spiritual" *Commonwealth of Israel* (Ephesians 2:12-13) and *His body the Church* (Ephesians 2 and 3, etc.).

God takes from among all of mankind, throughout all history, a people for His own possession—including from among those who are of *physical Israel*, and from among those who are *physical Gentiles*, worldwide. Those who receive Him by grace through faith, whatever their physical tag, become spiritual children of God. That concept is easy to grasp. But tragically, many who believe and teach this easy-to-grasp truth, also, erroneously disregard, neglect, or even deny, that all of those spiritual children of God are also now called *"citizens of the commonwealth of Israel,"* the *"Israel of God."*[129]

> *"Therefore remember that you, [who had] once [been] Gentiles in the flesh...that at that time you were without Christ, being aliens from the commonwealth of Israel and strangers from the covenants of promise, having no hope and without God in the world. BUT **NOW in Christ Jesus** you [Gentiles] who once were far off have been brought near by the blood of Christ ...."* (emphasis mine).
>
> Ephesians 2:11–13

All of these are the Church. In the face of Romans 9 and 11, and Ephesians 2 and 3,[130] this truth can only be denied to our own hurt. Concerning the degree of this hurt, the Gentilized Church of today is hurting greatly.[131] We need an error-shattering, paradigm shift in this area of Bible teaching.

I find Zodhiates' explanation of *"Commonwealth of Israel"* defines this truth in exquisitely succinct and accurate terms. He states that the Apostle Paul:

> *"... speaks of a "commonwealth of Israel" (Eph. 2:12) or "Israel of God" (Gal. 6:16) from which many, even Jews by birth, are aliens, and into which the Ephesians [Gentiles] had been admitted (Eph. 2:13). By this "commonwealth of Israel" or "Israel of God" the apostle means a true spiritual Israel, practically equivalent to all the faithful. It might be defined as the whole number of the elect, who have been, are, or shall be gathered into one under Christ. In other words, all the believers of all time constituting the Church universal [the Body of Christ].*[132]

THE APOSTLE PAUL BRINGS CLARITY

To that, I say, Amen! And Amen! In gathering a people for His own possession, did God cease calling His family *Israel*? Did He not combine both Jew and Gentile into "*one new man,*" seen as God's "*olive tree?*" That olive tree had previously been composed of the believers, the spiritual remnant, from among the physical people of Israel. But now the olive tree includes that remnant, spiritual Israel, and believing Gentiles, whom Paul said are grafted into the "natural" olive tree of spiritual Israel, the Israel of God. We will expand on the discussion of Romans 11 in the next chapter, *The Mystery of God: A Glorious Revelation*.

At the conclusion of the Jerusalem council in Acts 15 to which we previously referred, the apostles stated in a letter that was circulated to the churches, that it was, in fact, the Holy Spirit[133] who had emphatically affirmed the truths that they were writing about. And it was those truths, in part, that the Apostle Paul later identified as some of the elements of this *Mystery of God*.

Jesus preempted covenantal transition, the Old to the New Covenant, which was to be soon taught by the apostles when He opened up the understanding of the saints to the fact that there are many mysteries.[134] Clarification regarding the *Mystery of God* began in the Book of Acts with Peter's experience with God giving him a vision in a trance, which led to Peter going to Cornelius' Gentile house. From Acts 10 and onward through to the end of this age, the substance of *Mystery of God* was to be received, preached, and explained to the Jew first, and then to the Gentile world also. This was called the **Good News** for good reasons. For those who were physical children of Abraham, who had trusted in Jesus as their Lord and Savior, the *Mystery of God* was *Good News*. In these last days, part of the Church's commission is to be an instrument of God in making unsaved Jews "jealous" of the Church's relationship with the God of Abraham, Isaac, and Jacob.

> *"For I speak to you Gentiles; inasmuch as I am an apostle to the Gentiles, I magnify my ministry, if by any means I may **provoke to jealousy** those who are my flesh and save some of them. **For if their being cast away is the reconciling of the world** [to God], **what will their acceptance be but life from the dead?"***
>
> Romans 11:13–15

The grafted-in Gentiles were to live in such a loving relationship with God and with one another that unsaved, physical Israel (those who were not yet *spiritual children of God*) would be drawn into jealousy of that relationship, provoking them through the Holy Spirit to be drawn to their Messiah for salvation. They were to be re-grafted into their "natural olive tree!"

> *"And they also, if they [unsaved Jews/Israel] do not continue in unbelief, will be grafted in, for God is able to graft them in again."*
>
> Romans 11:2

The *chosen people* of Israel had been given a responsibility by God to exemplify the truth of His kingdom to the world, telling Gentiles that they could become a citizen of the nation of Israel. They would need to believe in and accept the God of Israel in order to become a citizen with God's chosen people. The Good News for the *chosen people* is that this *Mystery of God* would ultimately bring about the fulfillment of those responsibilities, about which God had covenanted with them. This was **Good News**, indeed! Additionally, they never could keep all of the laws given to Israel by God, but now, in the New Covenant, through Christ's finished work on the cross —He caused the requirements for such *shadows* to cease because He had provided something much better; namely, His Spirit. The Holy Spirit was sent to live within them, and us, which allowed Him to fulfill the righteousness of the Law in and through our lives by His power. This went beyond good news. This could easily be called **Great News** for physical Israel, as well as for those in Israel who believed in the Messiah, Jesus! And so it was and is!

Then on the other hand for the Gentiles, the *Mystery of God* through the preaching of the Gospel, was and is this **Good News**! It was good news because Gentiles could now become children of God by grace through faith, part of the *Israel of God*, and not have the burden of those things in the Law of Moses, which Peter declared that *"neither our fathers nor we were able to bear,"* as stated in Acts 15:10.[135]

Now, Gentiles anywhere in the world can become "citizens of the commonwealth of Israel"— the "Israel of God"—through and in Christ. Gentiles are "grafted in." Furthermore, being "in Christ," Gentiles also become joint-heirs, who will inherit the Land just as God had promised Abraham and his descendants. That's **Good News**! We can now be called "children of Abraham" in faith. We are in "the Seed," Christ, and Christ, the *Seed*, is in us.[136] All of this is part of the *Mystery of God*, as defined by the Apostle Paul and the Apostle John. This naturally accompanied the spreading of the Gospel, the *"good news,"* throughout the Gentile world, because it was this joyous melding together in Christ that allowed for *loving one another, as Christ loved us*.

Once the Apostle John had received from the Lord the Book of Revelation, it was further revealed in conjunction with Paul's writings, that those same truths about "two becoming one" became essential for understanding the chronological order of Endtime events. It is unquestioned that the Book of Revelation is completely in sync with what Jesus taught concerning the Endtimes during His ministry, and what Paul had already written about the Endtimes.

During the first number of decades of the New Testament period, through the apostles Paul and John, the Holy Spirit revealed and made more clear than ever the truths in the doctrine of the *Mystery of God*. Today, the *Mystery of God* is **perceived** to be new to those who have not been taught about it in this generation.[137] There have been many great preachers and theologians who have understood the connection between Israel and the Church, and who were not guilty of **Division Theology**. It is interesting that some evangelical theologians have pointed a corrective finger at others who have taught **Replacement Theology** (please see *Appendix C re: Replacement Theology*), and rightly so. **Replacement Theology** is indeed, heretical and offensive to the Lord. Yet at the same time we Bible-believers have done similar harm to the body of Christ by teaching **Division Theology**. Both are grave errors; and they are not merely semantical differences. By the grace of God, this seriously needs to change in the Church worldwide.

We are instructed by the Apostle Paul to understand that it is "high time to wake up out of sleep" with a sense of great urgency in and for these last days.[138] This is not fully possible without an understanding of the *Mystery of God*. We cannot afford to, and we must not, neglect or set that fact aside. Therefore with all of my heart, and by His grace, it is my intent to make the *Mystery of God* clear.

As you sincerely study the *Mystery of God* and it begins to become clearer, you will learn that God has revealed the *Mystery* in great detail for our good and His glory. Remarkably, yet understandably, to most who have their eyes opened for the first time concerning the Mystery, even world events tend to provoke a greater sense of urgency in drawing near to the Lord on a moment-by-moment basis in our daily walk. This is not driven by fear; rather this comes from the same attitude of heart that Jesus had when He faced death on the cross. He looked at what was ahead of Him, that is the horrible suffering of death on the cross, as He was bearing the sins of the world. The writer of Hebrews explains for us that it is our privilege to be "... *looking unto Jesus, the author and finisher of our faith, who for the joy that was set before Him endured the cross* ..." (Hebrews 12:2). What was that joy that was set before Jesus which enabled Him to endure the cross? Have you considered that the joy He longed for was when His Day would come at the *Marriage of the Lamb*?

With this in mind, I want to see with you key reasons each believer and follower of Christ needs to have a thorough understanding of the *Mystery of God*. Concerning this matter, we should be like the "sons of Issachar, who understood the times, and what Israel should do." Understanding the future, or at least that which God wants us to know, is essential for a wise, expectant, watching and prepared believer, who is "*buying the oil*," now, before it is too late.

In a refreshing way, we will see that the entire story of Scripture is about Christ. We will see that the *Mystery of God* is **"A Glorious Revelation,"** precisely because that Mystery is about Him.

Chapter Eleven Notes

[115] Hebrews 10:24-25; Malachi 3:16-18.

[116] Romans 12:4,5; 1 Corinthians 6:16; 10:17; 12:12,13,20; Ephesians 2:16; 4:4; Colossians 3:15.

[117] Romans 9:1-8.

[118] 2 Corinthians 5:8.

[119] *"For he says to Moses, 'I will have mercy on whom I have mercy, and I will have compassion on whom I have compassion.' So then it depends not on human will or exertion, but on God, who has mercy"* (Romans 9:15–16, ESV).

[120] Luke 3:23-38: The genealogy of Christ ("Adam, the son of God; verse 38).

[121] It would be good for all of us to maintain an attitude about covenant *responsibilities* as actually being covenant *privileges* and *opportunities*. Jesus' said that His yoke is easy and His burden is light. Jesus Himself viewed even His covenant responsibility of suffering death on the cross as something that was motivated by the "joy set before Him" (Hebrews 12:1-12).

[122] I have copied only essential parts to avoid irrelevant questions into the idea to which we are looking.

[123] Hebrews 11:10: *"for he waited for the city which has foundations, whose builder and maker is God."*

[124] John 1:1; Isaiah 7:14; Luke 1:30-33, plus too many other reference to list.

[125] John 6:46; 8:42; 13:3; 16:27, 30.

[126] John 3:7.

[127] Zodhiates, S. (2000). "εκκλησια, **ekklēsía**; gen. *ekklēsías*, fem. noun from *ékklētos* (n.f.), called out, which is from *ekkaléō* (n.f.), to call out. It was a common term for a congregation of the *ekklētoí* (n.f.), the called people ...."

[128] Galatians 4:4.

[129] Galatians 6:16.

[130] Hebrews 11:39-40 connects with this truth.

[131] Once, again, I want to emphasize that I am not making any claim that even hints at British Israelitism, or that today's Church is physical Israel, or that the Church is diminished in any way. The opposite is true. I am saying what Paul is saying: *All saints are part of Christ's Body. The Old and New are brought together through the blood of Christ, our Head!*

[132] Zodhiates, S. (2000).

[133] Acts 15:1-31.

[134] Luke 8:10.

[135] It's important to note that the Apostle Paul explained that the Law of Moses was a "schoolmaster" bringing us to Christ. That is, one of the main purposes of the Law was to make sin obvious, and to cause us to realize that ***we cannot keep the Law!*** Our inability to keep it is what drives us to the Savior, because we cannot accomplish keeping the Law. But Jesus kept it and more than that, He fulfilled all of the righteousness of the Law, without sinning. What a Savior, the spotless Lamb of God, who died for sin!

[136] Galatians 3:29.

[137] The more complete answer as to "why" it has ***not*** been taught will be understood more thoroughly as this truth unfolds throughout the remaining chapters.

[138] Romans 13:11-14.

Chapter 12

A GLORIOUS REVELATION

"… God chose to make known how great among the Gentiles are the riches of the glory of this mystery, which is Christ in you, the hope of glory."

Colossians 1:27

Colossians 1:27 is rich in meaning. Ponder the words—*"how great…are the riches of the glory of this mystery, which is Christ in you, the hope of glory."* The primary issue in this verse is not just the **Mystery**. It's not even just about the *riches* of the glory of the *Mystery*. The primary issue in this verse is **"Christ in you."** Christ in you **IS** the riches and the glory! His being in you is your sure hope of glory. Paul is not referring to a hope that is weak and wishful, riddled with doubts. This is a hope that is predetermined in the mind of God by His sovereign will and good pleasure. This is a sure hope, the kind of hope that is an **"anchor,"** as explained by the writer of Hebrews when he wrote:

*"… [we] have fled for refuge to lay hold of the hope set before us. This hope we have as **an anchor of the soul, both sure and steadfast, and which enters the Presence behind the veil**, where the forerunner [Jesus] has entered for us …."*

Hebrews 6:18–20

The *"glory,"* as referred to above, speaks of something far beyond a nice little Bible idea to be read, and then pass on by. This is about God's people obtaining *"glory,"* in, with, and from Christ being in you. That is our living hope of glory. *This glory is rooted in God's* **Glorious Revelation!**

Paul referred to this same *"glory,"* that *hope of glory*, when he wrote:

"For I consider that the sufferings of this present time are not worthy to be compared with the glory which shall be revealed in us."

Romans 8:18

When is this glory going to "be revealed in us?" Five verses later in Romans 8:23, Paul gives us the answer. This glory will be revealed at the moment of the "redemption of our body." Our body will be redeemed at the resurrection of the saints.[139]

It is true that Christ is "in" us, right now; and it is true that we are "in Him." But there is coming a day when our limited comprehension and experience of what that means in its fullness will instantly and radically change when Jesus comes in the rapture. But for now, though He is in us, the fullness of the glory to which Paul refers will not become realized until the redemption of our body, at the resurrection and rapture.[140]

When in conversation with Christians these days, I am often amazed and saddened at the dearth of heartfelt interest demonstrated about this incredibly important issue of *"Christ in you"* and the adjoining issue of *"the hope of glory."* These issues are of great consequence to Christ, as it will be to us if we love Him and His appearing. *"… the riches of the glory of this **mystery**, Christ in you, the hope of glory"* is unpacked and understood in and through the truths of the *Mystery of God*.[141] Among other factors, this *Mystery* is glorious not only because it refers to Christ in us *now*, but it specifically and wonderfully refers to the final completion of His Plan to become one with His Bride at the end of this age. The *Mystery of God* is about His glory. And it is very much about His glory in the Endtimes. It is "the ***revelation*** of Jesus Christ" (the unveiling, the revealing, the disclosure of Jesus Christ). And the **glory** of *"the revelation of Jesus Christ"* is particularly known in the *Marriage of the Lamb*. At the *Marriage of the Lamb*, **His glory will have become our glory!**

Once the judgment and rewarding of the saints are completed, God will once again magnify His Son in the celebration of the perfect wedding: The *Marriage of the Lamb* to His Bride! And as if that weren't glorious enough, that celebration will segue into the next glorious event: The wedding banquet called the "Marriage Supper of the Lamb"! What a time that will be for those who will be there!

At that time, the *Mystery of God*, which **began to be fulfilled** as announced in Revelation 10:7 and then ***initiated*** in Revelation 11:15-18 with the sounding of the "seventh" and last trumpet, will then be ***fulfilled or completed*** at the *Marriage and Supper*.[142] That is not the "end" of the glory; that is the "beginning" of the glory! After that series of events, He—and His Bride with Him—will enter into a new age—the Millennial Kingdom Age—the reign of King Jesus and His Bride on earth!

As we consider the *Marriage of the Lamb* in the context of the *Mystery of God*, some may not have readily seen the link between the two. This is a missing link in most Endtimes studies. It has been missing to our detriment. While the *Mystery of God* had been hidden from before the beginning of the world, God revealed it to the apostles, prophets, and the saints at the beginning of the New Testament age. Since it is now part of the written Scriptures, saints have access to this written revelation, this crucial truth. We should pursue understanding of it wholeheartedly.

A Glorious Revelation

In conjunction with that, I want to draw our attention, once again, to the phrase, *"The revelation of Jesus Christ ...."* The ultimate purpose of the Book of Revelation is to "reveal," to "unveil," to "fully disclose"—*Jesus Christ for Who He is!* Given the fact that Jesus is so great that our limited human faculties cannot altogether comprehend **Who He is** in His fullness, why should it be any surprise that there is much more for us to know about Him, as we continue growing in our relationship with Him? There is an *eternity's-worth* of growth to be gained in the knowledge of **Who He is**, especially once we are face to face!

An astounding and often-overlooked facet of **Who Jesus Christ is** in the Book of Revelation, will be further revealed during His marriage to His Bride. We need to see this from God's perspective. We know that His Bride is His body. Doesn't the "head" and the "body" make up the whole person? When God made Eve, didn't He make her from Adam? God took a rib from Adam and formed Eve. After God did that, didn't He tell us that those two then became *one through marriage?* The fact that Adam and Eve were made to be "one" is the very picture of the Great Mystery the Apostle Paul referred to in Ephesians 5:22-32?[143] Aren't we told repeatedly, that Christ's own Bride, the Church, the "second Eve," is "in Him"? Christ marries His Bride at the *Marriage of the Lamb*, and therefore, does she not become "one" with Him? Is she not already "spiritually and positionally" one in and with Christ in "heavenly places"—during the betrothal period? Isn't that the case, until Christ completes the marriage at the *Marriage of the Lamb*, at which time the two become one in every way God intended? That is, indeed, a major facet of the *Glorious Revelation of Jesus Christ*.

He said that His own, His disciples, were to be "one" with Him, as He was "one" with His Father. Was this not His original and ultimate plan from before the foundation of the world? Why should we be the least bit surprised? The Apostle Paul gives us the following insight into this:

*"Therefore do not be ashamed of **the testimony of our Lord** ... who has saved us and called us with a holy calling ... according to His own purpose and grace which was given to us **in Christ Jesus before time began**, but has now been revealed by the appearing of our Savior Jesus Christ ... who brought life and immortality to light through the gospel ...."*

2 Timothy 1:8–10

And this:

*"Blessed be the God and Father of our Lord Jesus Christ, who has blessed us with every spiritual blessing in the heavenly places in Christ, just as **He chose us in Him before the foundation of the world** ...."*

Ephesians 1:3–4

When I say that the Book of Revelation **IS *"the revelation of Jesus Christ,"*** I am not referring to the title of the Book of Revelation. I am primarily referring to Christ, as and when He is joined with His Bride in marriage: ***That fact will be the revelation of Jesus Christ, for Who He is, like nothing we have ever known in our current lifetime.*** Let's remember the Apostle John's testimony …

> *"Beloved, now we are children of God; and it has not yet been revealed what we shall be, but we know that **when He is revealed, we shall be like Him, for we shall see Him as He is.**"*
>
> 1 John 3:2

While it is true that during this present age the children of God are one with Him now, it must be acknowledged that we are one with Him in our positional relationship with Him. That all changes when the resurrection and rapture take place and we "… see Him as He is."

We want to see this from an additional perspective because it is integral to the *Mystery of God*. The two (that is, the physical children of Abraham who come into relationship with God with the same *Abraham-like* faith, along with born-again Gentiles), become one *"in Christ"* during this life. They will become fully one with Christ, the Bridegroom, in heaven, as His Bride. We are already, in this lifetime, "sitting together in heavenly places,"[144] if we are His by grace through faith. But that is our spiritual condition and position in the here and now. There is coming that day when we will see Him face to face, and we shall "be as He is."

If you are like me, we can easily, unconsciously, slide right past these truths as we read the Bible. We might even inadvertently tend to set aside those places in the Bible where the word *"mystery"* is found, putting them into the *"we can't know or understand it"* category. But concerning this *Mystery* and the glory to be revealed, we are told by the Apostle Paul that the Spirit is the One Who reveals God's future blessing in this Mystery. He wrote:

> *"But we speak the wisdom of God **in a MYSTERY, the hidden wisdom** which God ordained **before the ages for our glory** … But as it is written: 'Eye has not seen, nor ear heard, nor have entered into the heart of man the things which God has prepared for those who love Him"* (emphasis mine).
>
> 1 Corinthians 2:7, 9

Often, when that passage is quoted, the person doing the quoting ends their quoting in the phrase, *"eye has not seen, nor ear heard, nor [has it] entered into the heart of man what God has prepared for those that love Him …."* Perhaps, they stop there because those verses are quoted with the intention of explaining that what God has prepared for the future is so great

A Glorious Revelation

that it simply cannot be expressed, so we are told. There's only one little problem with that idea. The next verse reveals the exact opposite is true. Paul goes on to write:

"… But God has revealed them to us through His Spirit …" (emphasis mine).

Corinthians 2:10

What all has God revealed to us through His Spirit? Has He then revealed everything that can be known? Is that what He is saying? That is not the case. Earlier in verse 9, Paul wrote that those things revealed "to us through the Spirit" were ordained "before the ages *for our glory.*" In this passage, the subject matter is that God is pointing to **our glory**. What glory of ours is Paul referring to? He is revealing the glory that is already "positionally" ours by faith; but he is also pointing to that glory that will be ours throughout eternity with Christ because we are His Bride. While it is true that in the mind of God we are already glorified in Christ[145] as our spiritual position, in our passage in 1 Corinthians 2 God is referring to that glory which **will eventually be revealed** "in us" when we see Jesus, face to face. And that will take place as the *Mystery of God* is being fulfilled. It begins when the last trumpet sounds at the resurrection when our bodies will be changed into new, incorruptible bodies. Is that not at the rapture? Doesn't the rapture happen at the "last trumpet" sounding?[146] Since that is obviously true, then we will literally see Jesus at the last trumpet, precisely when the *Mystery of God* is beginning to be "fulfilled."[147] That is when "our glory" will begin to be known, but it will be this glory which is ours only in and through Christ which will be finally and completely fulfilled in the *Marriage of the Lamb*.

Both Paul and Peter give us additional insights into this important truth, which we should want to understand because of its connection to the Mystery of God. Paul wrote:

*"For I consider that the sufferings of this present time are not worthy to be compared with **the glory which shall be revealed in us**. For the earnest expectation of the creation eagerly **waits for the revealing of the sons of God** … we ourselves groan within ourselves, eagerly waiting for the adoption, **the redemption of our body** [which happens at the sounding of the last trumpet] … we eagerly wait for it with perseverance"* (quoted in part, insertions and emphases mine).

Romans 8:18–19, 23–25

Peter gave testimony: "The elders who are among you I exhort, I who am a fellow elder and a witness of the sufferings of Christ, and also a **partaker of the glory that will be revealed**."[148] Peter speaks of a "glory that **will be revealed** …." So, when will that revealing take place? It will happen at the "revelation of Jesus Christ," when He returns, and we see Him as He is, face to face. It is at that time when His own full glory will be revealed: *"but rejoice to the extent that you partake of Christ's sufferings, that **when His glory is revealed**, you may also be glad with exceeding joy"* (1 Peter 4:13).

The Book of Revelation is all about revealing Him and His glory. Imagine the glory that will be His, when He marries the Bride that He had purchased with such a great price. That scene is foretold with all of its glory:

> *"And I heard, as it were, the voice of a great multitude, as the sound of many waters and as the sound of mighty thunderings, saying, **'Alleluia! For the Lord God Omnipotent reigns! Let us be glad and rejoice and give Him glory, for the Marriage of the Lamb has come, and His wife has made herself ready.'"***
>
> Revelation 19:6–7

Surely, God's people agree that the Book of Revelation is **not** focused on the antichrist, the beast, the false prophet, or anyone else for that matter. It is not focused on the Great Tribulation, although much is revealed about it in the Book of Revelation. Nor is it focused on all of the judgment and wrath that will come upon the earth. That is not to suggest that those things are of no consequence. They surely are of consequence. But all of those things take place because of Who **He** is, and I might add, because of who **we are in Him**. The glory and revelation of Jesus Christ, being revealed in His fullness, as expressed in the context of the end, is the purpose of Revelation. Please don't take me wrongly on this point. The *Marriage of the Lamb* is not the end of all ends, which should be rather obvious. The Marriage will usher in the beginning of a new age in God's dealings with humanity. That next age will be the *One-Thousand-Year Reign of Christ*, as mentioned previously.

It has been rightly said that Revelation is the "sum total" of the rest of the Bible. I agree. If the entire Word of God is a continuous revelation of Jesus Christ, then Revelation rightly sums it all up … it **ties the knot** on the end of the multi-threaded, prophetic cord, namely the revelation and the glorification of Jesus Christ with His Bride/Wife.

In his book, *The Emmaus Code: Finding Jesus In The Old Testament*, David Limbaugh writes:

> "Biblical theologians acknowledge these different types of unity, but apparently no clear consensus has emerged as to what central idea unites the Old and New Testaments. In my view, however, the overarching theme of the Bible is crystal clear: from first to last, it is Jesus Christ."[149]

Arthur Pink, the renowned biblical typologist of the past century, wrote,

"Christ is the key which unlocks the golden doors into the temple of Divine truth. "Search the Scriptures," is His command "for they are they which testify of Me." And again, He declares, "In the volume of the Book it is written of Me." In every section of the written Word, the Personal Word is enshrined—in Genesis as much as in Matthew."[150]

Limbaugh and Pink summarize God's revelation about Jesus Christ, the "first and last" and "Personal Word." Even if it's not so obvious to some who are illegitimate theologians because they are Christ-deniers, Jesus Christ is indeed the overarching theme of the Bible, just as Limbaugh and Pink said. In one sense, this book that you are now reading begins where their thoughts leave off. ***The addendum to their excellent statements is the Mystery of God.***

In order to add the *Mystery of God* to the basic foundation of the fact that *"Christ is the key that unlocks the golden doors into the temple of Divine truth,"* important questions should be answered: In what way does the Bride become one with Jesus Christ in that glorious Marriage of the Lamb? Why is that important? Why does God's Word put Christ's marriage in the context of the Mystery of God in the Endtimes, and then use that marriage as a means of explaining the chronology of the other Endtime events?

I understand that at this juncture some of this may very well be somewhat puzzling to the reader. But I ask you to *"Wait!* As we progress through these prophetic threads, you will eventually see those threads become the completed multi-threaded prophetic cord.

Over time erroneous teachings have smudged the Church's spiritual glasses, making it difficult to see clearly. We need to clean those glasses a bit; otherwise, the *glorious revelation* will not be seen as it should. The reason for the title of this chapter, *A Glorious Revelation*, is to help us do just that—clean those glasses by the washing of the water of the Word!

One of the smudges on our spiritual glasses which has distorted our spiritual eyesight, is *Division Theology* to which I referred earlier. That particular smudge would more correctly be described as a viral disease. It has insidiously taken its toll on the Church over the centuries, beginning not too long after the Apostles had passed off of the Church scene. One only has to research Church history to see this.

We in the New Testament era of God's family, should take note of the fact that what took place in the Old Covenant era of God's family, namely their failure to believe and walk in His covenant, is precisely what we have done. We have been no better stewards of many of the responsibilities God has given New Covenant believers than were the Old Covenant believers. As soon as Moses and Joshua passed off of the scene, Israel began to fail in their mission. In similar form, as soon the apostles passed off of the scene, New Covenant (Testament) believers began to fail. This is one of the primary reasons *Division Theology* took root and began bearing diseased fruit in the Church. The Church began to be "Gentilized," casting aside the "Jewish leadership." That was one of the very things the Apostle Paul warned born-again Gentiles against in Romans 11: "[You Gentiles], *do not boast against the branches* [spiritual Israel]. *But if you do boast, remember that you do not support the root, but the root supports you* ... [You Gentiles], *Do not be haughty, but fear. For if God did not spare the natural branches, He may not spare you either*" (Romans 11:18-21). But who believes that in the Church today?

The idea of *Division Theology* is that Israel and the Church are two different peoples who face somewhat different roles and destinies in the latter days of the Endtimes. I would be the first to agree that ethnic, physical, corporate Israel and the Church are two different peoples. The tragic confusion propagated by many theologians takes place when some of them call **ALL ISRAEL** "enemies of God." It has been that misguided understanding and attitude of heart that has left the door open for the savaging of Jews, costing millions of Jews their lives over the centuries. This can be laid at the feet of those who have made the claims of either Replacement or Division Theology, whether intended or not. Even Evangelicals today are unwittingly participating in this unbiblical *Division Theology*.

Generally and thankfully, the Gentilized, evangelical Church of today is careful not to teach the disastrous *Replacement Theology*. *Replacement Theology* is the belief that the Church, primarily seen today as a Gentilized Church, has replaced Israel as God's chosen people. That is a brief sketch of *Replacement Theology*.

Division Theology on the other hand is deeply rooted among many of the same theologians who repudiate *Replacement Theology*. In all fairness to them, from what I have seen and heard, their position of division is usually not intended as being against Israel in any way. Their lack of understanding of the *Mystery of God* has led them into the error of *Division Theology* as an inadvertent result. Regardless of which of these errors one might fall into, the problem is that both errors have been very damaging to the Church:

> "Another key to properly interpreting prophetic Scriptures is to understand the relationship that exists between God's people Israel and the so-called "Gentile Church." Since they both play major roles in the end-time scenario, if our concept of how they fit together, in the end, is incorrect, our understanding of the end will be incorrect. Many heretical and damaging doctrines have entered the Church by ignoring certain Scriptures on this subject. This has affected not only end-time doctrine but even some aspects of the gospel message itself. For this reason, we need to spend a little time on this vital subject.
>
> "Two common errors that contradict clear statements of Scripture are (1)

A Glorious Revelation

because Israel rejected their Messiah, the "Gentile Church" has taken the place of Israel, and (2) Israel and the Church are two different peoples who face somewhat different destinies and different dealings of God in the end. The first error is known as Replacement Theology, and I have named the second error Division Theology. Both ideas openly contradict New Testament teaching and have given birth to some very unscriptural ideas about the roles of Israel and the Church in the last days."[151]

The Gentilized, westernized Church of today is fully aware and typically agrees, that Romans 11 teaches that born-again Gentiles were and are grafted into the natural olive tree, spiritual Israel. The reader would be well-served to capture the weighty distinctions, which Paul made in Romans 11. Paul's writings about this are admittedly, somewhat complex, which was what Peter indicated in his personal testimony. He wrote, "... *in all his* (Paul's) *epistles, speaking in them of these things, in which are* **some things hard to understand** *which untaught and unstable people twist to their own destruction, as they also do the rest of the Scriptures*" (2 Peter 3:16). Every moment of investment of time and prayer into understanding of what Paul teaches on this matter is worthy, even if complex. Nevertheless, due to this complexity, we seek to make it as simple as possible.

Nothing can be properly understood about the relationship between Israel and the Church in the Endtimes (and for that matter between Jews and Gentiles, in general) if we do not anchor our understanding in the fact that there has always been a remnant among every generation who were and are God's family on the earth. This family eventually became known as the *Israel of God, the Church*. Additionally, I use the term *spiritual Israel*, along with other descriptions, such as *children of Abraham through like-faith*. The men and women of "*faith*" in Hebrews 11-12 include this spiritual remnant of Israel. The very man whom God used to explain the Mystery of God—the Apostle Paul, was part of that remnant.[152]

Paul further testified:

> "... *If anyone else thinks he may have confidence in the flesh, I more so: [because I was] circumcised the eighth day, of the stock of Israel, of the tribe of Benjamin, a Hebrew of the Hebrews; concerning the law, a Pharisee; concerning zeal, persecuting the Church; concerning the righteousness which is in the law, blameless. But what things were gain to me, these I have counted loss for Christ. Yet indeed I also count all things loss for the excellence of the knowledge of Christ Jesus my Lord,* **for whom I have suffered the loss of all things, and count them as rubbish***, that I may gain Christ."*
>
> Philippians 3:4–8

No one made it more clear in the Scriptures than Paul that being a *physical Israelite* was not what made him a part of God's spiritual family. The fact that Paul had become integrated as part of the spiritual remnant of Israel was a testimony verifying his *spiritual relationship with God*, which made him a *"citizen"* of the spiritual *"commonwealth of Israel"* (Ephesians 2:12-22). Does anyone believe that Saul (Paul, after his conversion) had been a part of *spiritual Israel* prior to Jesus encountering him on the road to Damascus? He had been zealously hunting down the Church of God to have them killed or put in prison.[153] His authority came from the same wicked Jewish leaders, who had participated in the crucifixion of Jesus. Saul, quite simply, had not been a part of the spiritual family of God until he met Jesus on the road to Damascus.

Paul's Jewish credentials were of no redeeming value regarding his salvation in Christ. In fact, it was those very credentials which had caused blindness in his prior spiritual life as he went about persecuting Christ's disciples and the other saints in the Churches in the New Testament. We can see that those credentials did what they always do with anyone of any sect, who might trust in them: *They brought about spiritual deadness*. This is why we read that his credentials were considered by him, to be like *"rubbish"* compared to the real prize and joy, which was knowing Christ and being known by Christ. Clearly, before Paul had been born again, he had not been a part of the spiritual remnant from within Israel, as had been the case with the other apostles and disciples. Nor was he a child of Abraham spiritually. He was like all others in Israel, a physical child of Abraham who needed the Savior!

Returning now to the *"natural olive tree,"* we realize that this natural olive tree (the spiritual remnant from within Israel) receives the life-giving sap from the Root, which is Christ![154] But Gentile believers today desperately need to rediscover and understand our grafted-in position and relationship with the pre-existing, natural branches of Christ's tree; they are that remnant of believing Israel. The Root is Christ Himself, and He is the only One from and through whom the life-giving sap flows for both the natural (spiritual) branches of Israel and the grafted-in Gentile branches from the wild olive tree of the Gentile world. The only ones in Israel whom God recognized as His own spiritual family were those who believed on Him. *"... For they are not all Israel who are of Israel, nor are they all children because they are the seed of Abraham ..."* (Romans 9:6–7). That is precisely why John wrote, *"He [Jesus] came unto His own [physical Israel], and His own received Him not. But to as many [from among physical Israel] as received Him to them He gave the power to become the sons of God [spiritual remnant Israel]* (John 1:10). The only children of Abraham who God recognizes as His own regenerated ones, are those who are of the faith of Abraham, that is, spiritual children of Abraham, and not those who are born of the fleshly seed of Abraham.[155]

It is of no little consequence that Paul refers to the *Mystery of God* as he teaches us about these pivotal truths about the "Root," the "natural olive tree branches,"[156] and the "wild olive tree branches." The connection of the *Mystery* in this context is an important part of the threading of this truth throughout the Scriptures, and perfectly parallels Paul's constant declarations about the *two* (Jews and Gentiles) *being made one in Christ*. To the Gentiles Paul wrote:

> *"For I do not desire, brethren, that you should be ignorant of this mystery, lest you should be wise in your own opinion, that blindness in part has happened to Israel until the fullness of the Gentiles has come in."*
>
> Romans 11:25

To be sure, if it were suggested to most evangelical theologians that they have neglected or disregarded Israel, the land of Israel, and the Jews, many would likely recoil at that idea. And I would understand because I would recoil, if someone suggested that I neglected or disregarded the physical children Israel, or that I had neglected concern about the *Land of Israel*. I can assure you that there is no criticism intended in these remarks concerning our brothers and sisters in Christ, who are among those theologians. We are only in pursuit of God's truth in the matter. The truth is that most evangelicals have a certain love for the chosen people of Israel and God's chosen land. That is not the problem. The problem is that, even with the best of intentions, sometimes that love seems to be inadvertently founded in an emotional and intellectual love, more so than sound teaching and belief. This needs a bit of explanation. The balance of the book will clear this up, but it is good to address it to some degree here.

One of the objectives in this chapter is to demonstrate, without condemnation, how Bible-believing Gentiles have been negatively affected by erroneous beliefs about the relationship between Jews and Gentiles, that is, as was taught by the Apostle Paul. To the degree that the Gentilized perspective regarding this relationship has been inaccurate, it is my hope that it has been due to a simple lack of understanding. Paul provides a picture for us of Israel and the Jews as the *"natural olive tree."* If we misunderstand this very important truth, we will have a treacherous blind spot. Our interpretations of God's purposes will be more easily diverted into *Replacement or Division Theology*, both of which are erroneous ideas. *May God remove that blind spot from us, as we turn to Him for understanding about this vital issue!*

Understanding the *Mystery of God* should not be unnecessarily complex. It certainly doesn't have to be. However, the nature of any mystery is that our understanding of it progressively develops. In learning any mystery, we first hear some early details and wonder what it means. Then as we are given more information, we are better able to put the pieces together. Eventually, we begin to gain a picture of what we think it might mean. But at the end of it all, when the mystery is completely disclosed, we confess that only now do we really know what it is about. This *Mystery of God* functions similarly. It is an ah-ha moment; the eyes of our understanding are opened to see! It is a paradigm switch.

So, in the same manner, the threads leading to the understanding of the *Mystery of God* begins in the Garden of Eden with the Seed, and weaves their way down through the Bible and history, being identified in those individuals who believed God's message, in conjunction with the accompanying covenants and promises. It is important for us to see this picture. Some of these important people (who had key roles concerning this multi-threaded cord) are dramatically stated in Hebrews 11, the so-called Hall of Faith. Among other things involved in the Hall of Faith, these Old Testament saints are representative of God's relationship with His Own covenanted people, signified by and within the series of covenants God made with them down through history. These also are to be seen as additional threads in the braided, unbreakable, multi-threaded, prophetic cord of the *Mystery of God*.

When these things have become clearer in our minds and hearts, we will have a greater understanding of the glory that will be ours, in and with Christ, as He gathers His Bride from every part of earth and heaven, just as He has said. Currently, the glory of that moment can be received in the spirit, but in that Day we will have been unfettered from the earthly body, experiencing that glory in a new incorruptible body.[157]

> *"Beloved, do not think it strange concerning the fiery trial which is to try you, as though some strange thing happened to you; but rejoice to the extent that you partake of Christ's sufferings, that **when His glory is revealed, you may also be glad with exceeding joy. If you are reproached for the name of Christ, blessed are you, for the Spirit of glory and of God rests upon you ….**"*
>
> 1 Peter 4:12–14

We will indeed be *"glad with exceeding joy,"* because the *"Spirit of glory,"* which now rests upon us, will reveal the glory that is ours in Christ because He is living *in and through us*. Why? Because, when the *Mystery of God* is finished or completed in that Day, we will have seen Christ face to face, and we will be *"as He is."*[158] What does that look like? We will be **"one with Him,"** as His **"wife."** The Spirit of glory and of God will flow not only in and through Christ but in and through us, His Bride—as one in and with Him. **This IS the Glorious Revelation of Jesus Christ!**

Knowing we have that to look forward to, in **Part III** let's see how and why the **Braided, Multi-Threaded, Unbreakable, Prophetic Cord** illustrates God's astounding Plan in the *Mystery of God* throughout the Bible.

Chapter Twelve Notes

[139] Romans 8:18-25; Philippians 3:20-21; 1 Corinthians 15:51-55; Luke 21:27-28; Ephesians 1:7-14.

[140] *"For in this we groan, earnestly desiring to be clothed with our habitation which is from heaven, if indeed, having been clothed, we shall not be found naked. For we who are in this tent groan, being burdened, not because we want to be unclothed, but further clothed, that mortality may be swallowed up by life. Now He who has prepared us for this very thing is God, who also has given us the Spirit as a guarantee"* (2 Corinthians 5:2–5).

[141] Colossians 1:27.

[142] The fact that the *Mystery of God* is finished and completed at the *Marriage* does not mean that the effects of the *Mystery* will not continue. Of course, it will continue on into the *Millennial Reign of Christ* on earth and into eternity. Nothing in Scripture speaks to the contrary!

[143] Ephesians 5:22-32.

[144] Ephesians 2:6. Also, *"... [God] has blessed us with every spiritual blessing in the **heavenly places in Christ**, ..."* (Ephesians 1:3). The obvious question from that verse is: If those spiritual blessings are ours **"in Christ,"** then where is Christ during this time to which Paul is referring? In Ephesians 2:6, we are told that **Christ is in the "heavenly places."** In that simple fact, we discover why we are presently *"sitting together in heavenly places,"* even though we are alive in this world. This is because we are in Christ, and He is there in heaven, right now. Are we certain of this connection? Yes, indeed! We are certain of this connection, because *"... [God] raised Him from the dead and seated Him at His right hand in the heavenly places ..."* (Ephesians 1:20).

[145] *"Moreover whom He predestined, these He also called; whom He called, these He also justified; and whom He justified, these He also **glorified**"* (Romans 8:30).

[146] 1 Corinthians 15:51-58.

[147] Revelation 10 and 11 (refer specifically to 10:7 and 11:15-18).

[148] 1 Peter 5:1.

[149] Limbaugh, *The Emmaus Code: Finding Jesus in the Old Testament* (Washington, DC: Regnery Publications, 2015), 8-9.

[150] Arthur W. Pink, *Gleanings In Genesis*, (Stilwell, KS, Digireads.com, 2005), pg. 9.

[151] Byers, Marvin, *The Final Victory: The Year 2000?*, 1998, 3rd Edition (Shippensburg, PA, Treasure House)

[152] Romans 11:1-10.

[153] Acts 8:3; 9:1; 22:4-5; 26:9-11; Galatians 1:13, 23; Philippians 3:6; 1 Timothy 1:13.

[154] It is worth noting that some evangelical theologians teach that the "root" of this "natural olive tree" is the "fathers," like Abraham, Isaac, and Jacob. While this might seem plausible to some, we must keep in mind that the fathers don't give life to us, nor do they sustain our spiritual walk, which can only come in, from and through our "Root," and which is none other than Christ Himself! He is the one from and through whom the life-giving sap comes. Figuratively, "life is in the blood." The "blood" of a tree is the "sap." Also, whether we are "natural" branches or "wild branches" grafted in, the whole tree is Christ, as we are "in and of Him," anyhow. The beauty of this tree is the very Tree of Life—Jesus Christ!

[155] It is important at this juncture to state that there are many blessings given to the "physical" Israel, the "physical" children of Abraham, which God has not removed from them. After all, even Jesus was born into this world through them, as Paul wrote, *"... from whom, according to the flesh, Christ came ..."* (Romans 9:5).

[156] Romans 11:24-25: *"For if thou wert cut out of the olive tree which is wild by nature, and wert graffed [grafted] contrary to nature into a good olive tree: how much more shall these, which be the natural branches, be graffed [grafted] into their own olive tree? For I would not, brethren, that ye should be ignorant of **this mystery**, lest ye should be wise in your own conceits; that blindness in part is happened to Israel, until the fullness of the Gentiles be come in."* (Romans 11:24–25, AV, insertions and emphases, mine).

[157] I Corinthians 15:51-58.

[158] 1 John 3:2–3.

PART III

THE BRAIDED, MULTI-THREADED, UNBREAKABLE, PROPHETIC CORD

God's foreknowledge is eternal. Our God is omniscient; that is, He knows all things and has known all things forever. "Known to God from eternity are all His works" (Acts 15:18). In His dealings with humanity through His Word, we can see that God has been in the process of revealing Jesus Christ by many different means, down through history. The revelation of His person in this world is like continuous threads which run from the very Beginning to the very End.

> *"For by Him all things were created that are in heaven and that are on earth, visible and invisible, whether thrones or dominions or principalities or powers. **All things were created through Him and for Him. And He is before all things, and in Him all things consist.**"*
>
> Colossians 1:16–17

Jesus is God[159]—*God doesn't change*[160]—*and Jesus is the same yesterday, today and forever.*[161] In those few statements of Scripture, from one perspective, is the essence of God's revelation of Himself. Consider this profound declaration of Who God says He is:

> *"… For I am God, and there is no other; I am God, and there is none like Me, Declaring the end from the beginning, and from ancient times things that are not yet done, Saying, 'My counsel shall stand And I will do all My pleasure ….'"*
>
> Isaiah 46:9–10

This is one important facet of what our great God and Savior is like! **This** is a snapshot of His sovereign planning! He is the Author and Creator of what we are calling the *Braided, Multi-Threaded, Unbreakable, Prophetic Cord*, which is dynamic throughout the entire Word of God. It cannot be otherwise, because it is about Jesus, and He is seen throughout the Word of God. *He **IS** the Living Word!*

In the simplest of terms, this braided, multi-threaded, unbreakable, prophetic cord graphically assists us in seeing the *Mystery of God* and how God has threaded His purpose for mankind from the beginning to the end.

In **Part III**, we will see that the beginning and the end of the Bible are replete with repetitions, mirroring one another. This speaks to the consistency of God's Word. Because He shows us so many obvious details in the beginning and the end which mirror one another, we should stop and take note. Should we be surprised that God reveals so many details in Genesis, which we then find in Revelation? We can see the thread-by-thread braiding of the Mystery of God in Genesis because Jesus is seen there. That is why I titled Chapter 13, ***In the Beginning Was The Beginning and The End.***

Chapter 13

IN THE BEGINNING WAS THE BEGINNING AND THE END

"In the beginning was the Word, and the Word was with God, and the Word was God. He was in the beginning with God."

John 1:1–2

"I am ... the Beginning and the End," says the Lord, "who is and who was and who is to come, the Almighty ... the First and the Last ...."

Revelation 1:8, 21:6; 22:13

Genesis is a Revelation of Revelation

There is good reason why Genesis should be compared with Revelation, and vice versa: Genesis is a revelation of Revelation in so many ways. By making these comparisons, we will discover additional insights and be better able to understand God's own interpretation of His Word, which is the only interpretation that ultimately matters. To make these comparisons is to simply follow the admonition to compare *"spiritual things with spiritual."*[162]

For instance, in both Genesis and Revelation we find a serpent, the tree of life, an important marriage, and many other comparative details. The mirrored messages between the beginning and the end, are not just found in comparing the beginning of the Old Testament with the end of the New Testament. It is also amazing to see that the same holds true when comparing the beginning of the Old Testament with the ending of the Old Testament, and when comparing the beginning of the New Testament with the ending of the New Testament.

Someone has rightly said that history repeats itself. Expanding on this, it can be said that the nature of individuals, and humanity as a whole, causes the natural flow of human history to repeat itself. Fallen humanity's actions over time are generally predictable. Interestingly, the founding fathers of the United States wrote about this phenomenon. They were excellent students of world history. They used the recorded lessons of history to lay the best foundation for the United States they possibly could. They not only understood secular history, but the influence of the Bible on their considerations, debates, and conclusions reveals the fact that many were informed and passionate students of the Bible. Almost all were readers of the Bible. They could see God's perspective on human history, and they wrote prolifically about it. Most of them believed the Bible, as did the majority of the freedom-hungry colonists. The quotes from America's founders reveal an amazingly balanced view of the nature of humanity and the nature of God, and the blessings and cursings that come from humanity's choices in light of these realities.

Regardless of humanity's actions in the natural flow of human history, history from God's perspective is about Jesus. History and His message are the same at any point. He remains the same at all times. "I am the LORD; I change not" (Malachi 3:6, AMPC). He is the "same yesterday, today, and forever" (Hebrews 13:8). Fallen, sinful human beings, and fallen, sinful civilizations, repeat the same failures. Of this there is no doubt. We would do well to acknowledge that American society is following the same tragic pattern of repeating historical, individual, and societal errors. The same is tragically true about modern Israel.

Since God is the same, and since humanity's nature remains the same, we should not be surprised to see that history and His-Story repeat. Humanity's history repeats its proclivity to run away from God.[163] *His-Story* repeats the fact that God's heart is always about drawing all of humanity to Himself so that none should have to perish.[164]

Pick a book, pick any book anywhere in the Bible. Whether in the beginning, the end, or the middle, or anywhere in between, you will find Christ. He said that He is the One *"who is and who **was**, and who **is to come**."*[165] His proclamation about Himself covers all of eternity—eternity-past, all time from the Creation to the end of time, and on through eternity-future. He calls Himself the *"I AM,"* for good reasons. He appears in the Scriptures one way or another, through prophecy, or by one of His names, or by typology, or by analogy, or when we simply read between the lines in a particular story. In every book of the Bible, He is magnified. With our spiritual eyes wide open, it is easy to see those numerous threads which braid into that multi-threaded, unbreakable, prophetic cord.

Jesus proclaimed that He is *"the Beginning and the End"* in Revelation 1:8. Just as John was about to receive a revelation of the Endtimes events in the Book of Revelation, Jesus wanted John to know the truths found in His names. As we know, Jesus wasn't a person who would waste words. He made it clear that He is [Himself] the End. For this reason, as Revelation 1:1 states, [the Book of] Revelation is a revelation of Jesus Christ. Therefore, it is He who is **the End**. But what some may not notice is that He also emphasized that He is **the**

In the Beginning Was the Beginning and End

Beginning. Notice that Jesus did not say that He is simply *in* the end, or a *part* of the end, or *in* the beginning, or *part* of the beginning.[166] He said that **He IS the Beginning and the End!**

At first glance, the title of this chapter may seem a bit odd: *In the Beginning Was the Beginning and the End.* That is not a typographical error. In the beginning (in Genesis), He Who is the "Beginning and the End" was there—in the Beginning. Of course He was. He "is, and was, and is to come," so how could He not have been there? Or as John put it, "*In the beginning was the Word* [Jesus] *and the Word was with God and the Word was God.*" He was not only "there" in the sense of being present; He is obviously there in the pages and story of the Scriptures. He *is The Story* in Scripture. Since Jesus proclaimed that one of His names is the "*Beginning and the End,*"[167] like all of His other names this name also reveals rich truths about Himself and His desire for humanity, and especially His Bride.

Among others, one of the more noticeable ways you will find the royal cord of Christ throughout Scripture is by His names. There are some 700 names for Jesus in the Bible.[168] God's infinite character requires many names to show Who He is. These names are not mere 'titles'; they are His names, each of which brings Him glory!

Many of those names express His glory, His nature, and His care for us. The reader may be familiar with the Hebrew names of God, which speak to this same point: *El Shaddai (All-sufficient God); Jehovah-Jireh (the Lord will provide); Jehovah-Shalom (The Lord Our Peace),* and many others.

Many of His attributes are found in His names. Jesus said, "*I am the **Way**, the **Truth**, and the **Life** ....*"[169] When He said that He is "*the Way, the Truth, and the Life*" it was more than just an idea. Those are some of His names, and yet, they indeed reveal attributes about *Who He is.*

When Moses was on Mount Sinai, He asked God to show him His glory. God responded with this:

"Then He said, "I will make all My goodness pass before you, and I WILL PROCLAIM THE NAME OF THE LORD before you …" (emphasis mine).

Exodus 33:19

"Now the Lord descended in the cloud and stood with him there, and proclaimed the name of the Lord. And the Lord passed before him and proclaimed, 'The Lord, the Lord God, merciful and gracious, longsuffering, and abounding in goodness and truth, keeping mercy for thousands, forgiving iniquity and transgression and sin, by no means clearing the guilty, visiting the iniquity of the fathers upon the children and the children's children to the third and the fourth generation.'"

Exodus 34:5–7

What a name! He proclaimed, "*The LORD, the LORD God ....*" Those are two of His names, for sure. But He didn't stop there. The attributes of God that follow "*the LORD God*" do not just describe God's nature; they also reveal His name. So, His name is also "*Merciful,*" "*Gracious,*" "*Longsuffering,*" "*Abounding in Goodness and Truth,*" etc.

The Scripture says, "*God is Love.*"[170] Is the word "love" in this verse, only an attribute of God? Love is Who He is, and it is also one of His names, just like "*the **Way**, the **Truth**, and the **Life***" are His names. Through the knowledge of His names, we are able to know and experience the unsearchable riches of Christ in a wonderful and enlightening way!

Are all of the 700 names to which Elmer Towns refers in his book really His names? You might be surprised when you review that list of 700 names. For instance, is the word "*Holy*" one of His names? It is assuredly one of His attributes and speaks to His character, but is it really one of His names? God answers that question very directly.

"*For thus says the High and Lofty One Who inhabits eternity, whose name is Holy ....*"
Isaiah 57:15

Our great God inhabits eternity. I have no doubt that we will experience more and more of His names when we are no longer in these bodies of corruption with our limited mental and spiritual comprehension. In our new bodies, we will have supernatural ability to comprehend Him for we "*shall see Him as He is!*"[171]

In the Beginning Was The Beginning and the End

The first time Jesus spoke in the Book of Revelation, He declared one of His very important names for the Endtimes. "*I am Alpha and Omega, **The Beginning and The End**.*"[172] With emphasis, He said three times in Revelation that He is the *Beginning and The End*, as found in Revelation 1:8; 21:6; and 22:13. But it doesn't stop there. In addition to Jesus saying His name is "*The Beginning and The End*," He compounds the point, when He calls Himself by His name "*Alpha and the Omega*" and then calls Himself by His name "*First and the Last.*" Those names, each mean the same thing. They are simply different ways of saying it, which should grab our attention. He identifies Himself with those names a total of eleven times in six different verses in Revelation.[173]

Anytime in the Bible we see God repeating Himself, we should pay close attention. For example, God says "*He who has an ear to hear, let him hear what the Spirit says.*" In Revelation alone He says that eight times.[174] There are eight similar phrases portraying the same concept in the Gospels.[175] With that much emphasis, it's easy to understand that He greatly desires us to have an *"ear to hear"* His appeals to our hearts. He knows that it is for our good that we hear Him. In other words, we would do well to give close and serious attention to whatever He may be emphasizing!

Why does Jesus repeat such names as *"the Beginning and the End?"* This is not just a random name picked out of eternity by lottery. This name describes Who and what He is. The *"Beginning and the End"* is a Person, the Person of Jesus Christ. From our limited human perspective, we see those words as ideas. From Christ's perspective, He is revealing Himself and His nature through yet another of His names.

In the beginning, He is revealed as the Seed. Therefore the Seed is revealed in the Beginning and the End, since He is the Beginning and the End. Can we not see that there are very good reasons why Jesus can be seen and understood in every book of the Bible: It is all a revelation of Him … from the Beginning to the End!

When our spiritual ears are attuned to hear the Spirit, and our spiritual eyes are enlightened by Him, Jesus' names and person will jump off of the pages of Scripture from Genesis to Revelation, just like it was when Jesus declared to those two disciples on the road to Emmaus that He has been revealed in the writings of *"Moses, the prophets, and **all the Scriptures**."*

So, let's draw the string on this. If the *"Beginning and the End"* is Jesus, and He is the *"same yesterday, today, and forever,"* then shouldn't we be able to understand the **"End"**-times more clearly when we have our eyes opened to see Him in the beginning, the very One Who is the **"Beginning?"** This is why you will notice that I have mentioned the first five words of Revelation 1:1 a number of times in this book. I repeat it because the *"End"*-times is first and foremost about those first five words —"The **revelation** of Jesus Christ …," or Jesus Christ being revealed in the *End*! But do we not know that *"The revelation of Jesus Christ"* could be the title of every book in the Bible? If those who print our Bibles were to include the phrase *"The Revelation of Jesus Christ"* as part of the title of every book in the Bible, it would be wholly appropriate. For instance: If they were to print it like this, *"Genesis, the Revelation of Jesus Christ,"* and *"Exodus, the Revelation of Jesus Christ,"* it would be a correct title. Furthermore, if we were to remove the words "Holy Bible" from our Bible covers and replace those words with *"The Revelation of Jesus Christ,"* it would be wholly appropriate! So when we come to the Book of Revelation, it is about revealing Jesus Christ as the *"End"* which is also *Who He is*!

In my seminars, I often walk through a PowerPoint presentation entitled *"Genesis is a revelation of Revelation."* If Jesus is indeed *The Beginning and The End*, then we will see evidence of that fact in Genesis. That seminar goes into greater detail than the space we will dedicate here.[176] We are able to provide a much broader comparison from Genesis and Revelation. Remember, God gets glory by revealing the end from the very beginning!

Genesis 2:4 through 5:1 contain many details that are also revealed in Revelation. A few comparative details are these:

- First, a new Heaven and a new earth are seen in Genesis 2, as well as in Revelation 21:1-6.

- In Genesis 2:7 man comes forth from the dust of the earth, and the same will happen in the end, at the Resurrection (Compare Daniel 12:2 and Revelation 20:6).

- Also, in Genesis 2:8 God plants a garden. From that garden flows a river of life, and the tree of life is found there (Gen. 2:9-10). Revelation 22:1-2 also reveals a garden with a river of life and a tree of life.

- In Genesis 2:18-25 we find the first marriage between a man and a woman, and in Revelation 19:7, 21:9 and 22:17 we find the last marriage between a Man and a Woman. In I Corinthians 15:45, we are even told that the heavenly Bridegroom of Revelation (who is Christ) is linked as the last Adam (who is Christ), which links Him to the first Adam in Genesis! Please read the following passage carefully. You will see in 1 Corinthians 15:45-52 that the *last* Adam (Christ) is the heavenly Bridegroom, who will marry His bride (the Church, the *last* Eve) at the *Marriage of the Lamb* (Revelation 19; Ephesians 5:32). The last Adam (Christ) is directly linked to the *first* Adam in Genesis, who is the husband of the *first* Eve in the Garden of Eden! We see a picture of Christ in Genesis as the Beginning, and we see Christ in Revelation as the Ending!

- Genesis 3 introduces the Serpent and the Deceiver. God then promises that the "*seed of the woman*" will bruise the head of the serpent. In Revelation 13:14 that same Deceiver is at work, and he "*deceives them that dwell on the earth.*" In Revelation 12:1-11 a woman gives birth to a child (her seed) who crushes the head of the "*old serpent.*"

- In Genesis 3:21 the Lord gave Adam and Eve clothing or a covering. In Revelation 19:8 God gives a covering: "*And to her was granted that she should be arrayed in fine linen, clean and white.*"

In these beginnings and endings, God is providing further insight into His Word, His Plan, and the Person of the Lord Jesus Christ! It has been said; *There's a lot in a name.* Is there any doubt that He is wonderfully glorified by the name, "*The Beginning and the End!*"

Any revelation of Him or His character brings Him glory. In my view one of the most glorious revelations of Christ, especially as it relates to the Bride of Christ's future, is through the revelation of Christ within the truths of the *Mystery of God*. The *Mystery of God* captures many glorious details about God's ultimate purpose for the creation of humanity. But if we look at it from Christ's own perspective, it is not difficult to understand that He is waiting for His *Own Wedding Day*, the *Marriage of the Lamb* to His Bride, and for the *Marriage Supper*. Christ has always had a passionate desire to receive a Bride from among those whom He has created. This is part of His glory! And He is, indeed, going to receive a Bride from among those who are willing to receive Him as their Bridegroom. If we want to get a glimpse of the passion Christ has for His Bride, we need only read the *Song of Solomon*. That story is rich with the love of Christ for us. When a holy and wholesome view is taken of that book, it is breathtaking, to say the least. Oh, how He loves His own! In the *spiritual music* in this song, *The Song of Solomon*, we can see the beautiful picture of the final step or phase to be realized in the *Mystery of God*; that is, the *Marriage of the Lamb* to His bride, the Church, the *last Eve*!

To see this truth in Scripture, and to understand it, let's keep in mind our braided, unbreakable, multi-threaded, prophetic cord introduced in Chapter 5, **WAITING**. The prophetic threads are constantly being braided together to illustrate God's Beginning-to-End Plan, encapsulated in the *Mystery of God*. Some of the unique and astounding details, for understanding the *Mystery of God* at its "Beginning", are what I want to see with you. Are you sure you know what really happened in the Garden of Eden between ***THE SERPENT, THE SEED, AND ADAM AND EVE?***

Chapter Thirteen Notes

[159] Colossians 2:9.
[160] "For I am the LORD, I do not change..." (Malachi 3:6).
[161] Hebrews 13:8.
[162] 1 Corinthians 2:13.
[163] "... light is come into the world, and men loved darkness rather than light, because their deeds were evil ..." (John 3:19).
[164] "... but [He] is longsuffering toward us, not willing that any should perish, but that all should come to repentance (2 Peter 3:9, AV); "For God did not send His Son into the world to condemn the world, but that the world through Him might be saved" (John 3:17).
[165] Revelation 1:4, 8; 4:8.
[166] (Byers, *The Final Victory*, 1998) 62.
[167] Revelation 1:8
[168] Towns, Elmer L., *The Names of Jesus*, (Denver, Colorado, Accent Publications, 1987).
[169] John 14:6.
[170] 1 John 4:8,16.
[171] 1 John 3:2.
[172] Revelation 1:8.

[173] Revelation 1:8,11,17; 2:8; 21:6; 22:13.
[174] Revelation 2:7,11,17, 29; 3:6,13, 22; 13:9.
[175] Matthew 11:15; 13:9, 43; Mark 4:9, 23; 7:16; Luke 8:8; 14:35.
[176] An extensive expansion on this truth is found at http://www.biblestudytools.com/commentaries/revelation/introduction/genesis-and-revelation-as-bookends.html (accessed June 22, 2017). And other details are found in (Byers, *The Final Victory*, 1998).

Chapter 14

THE SERPENT, THE SEED, AND ADAM AND EVE

"And I will put enmity between you and the woman, And between your seed and her Seed; He shall bruise your head, And you shall bruise His heel."

Genesis 3:15

Since the specific Mystery to which we are referring had been hidden *"since the world began"*[177] until Christ and His apostles, we know, therefore, that God did *not* reveal the details of it to Adam and Eve. However, He *did* declare the first prophetic thread to them. It seems clear that they did not understand the fuller implications of the words they heard, as it related to the long-term future of the coming of the Seed, Christ Himself. They did, however, understand all He wanted them to understand in their day: *The knowledge that there was a promised Seed.* From that moment, a four-thousand-year-long process of prophecies began to accumulate, as God was moving the world toward the revelation of His Son, who was destined to come in the *"fullness of time,"* and not a day sooner.

All along the way His Son was gathering His Bride, those who would choose to have a covenantal-love relationship with Him. And all along the way, God carefully braided threads in that very Plan throughout the Old Testament—from Beginning to End. We see this in the ever-increasing threads of prophecy highlighting His coming and His final plan. Again it should be stated that the fuller implication of those threads of prophecy was heard with the ears, but still had been *"sealed"* or *"hidden,"* until it was made known and fulfilled in Christ Himself. Those prophetic threads were braided throughout the entire Old Testament through individuals and events and the covenants, God had made, and then eventually by the covenant God made with Abraham, Isaac, Jacob, and of course the nation of Israel. During the time of those relationships and all of those covenants, there was what can be understood as one overarching covenant: *The Covenant of God's Grace upon humanity.* *"… And let him who thirsts come. Whoever desires, let him take the water of life freely"* (Revelation 22:17). Those who have taken *"the water of life freely"* down through history, have experienced that grace. That is precisely why it was said of Noah that he *"found grace in the eyes of the Lord"* (Genesis 6:8).

There can be no doubt of His grace throughout history. After His resurrection, Jesus appeared to two of His disciples on the road to Emmaus. In His conversation with them, from His own lips He validated those very markers, those prophetic threads, seen as His grace throughout biblical history in the Old Testament, when He said to them:

> *"... foolish men and slow of heart to believe in all that the prophets have spoken ... Then beginning with **Moses and with all the prophets**, He explained to them **the things concerning Himself in all the Scriptures**."*
>
> Luke 24:25–27, NASB95

Let's not skip over that too quickly. That is saying that Jesus revealed to those men those things concerning Himself found in **all the Scriptures from Genesis (Moses' writings) and all the Scriptures (which includes the entirety of the Old Testament)**. Those *"things concerning Himself"* are indisputable threads concerning the *Seed*, which are core prophetic threads, and which had been *"hidden"* and *"secret"* from the *"beginning of the world."* Those were revealed to the *"apostles, prophets, and saints"* in the New Testament in many ways, but especially in the truths concerning the *Mystery of God*. Please understand, while it is true that Christ was known in the Old Testament, it is equally true that He was not yet known in the way that the apostles, and we, know Him.

Concerning those prophetic threads pertaining to the *Seed*, if you wanted to walk back through the Old Testament, book by book, looking for those prophetic threads, how would that be done? Let's illustrate it this way. If a rescue team member, in search of a lost hiker, decides to walk through unknown territory in a forest where there is no trail, one of the most important steps the team members must take is not the footprints of his feet, as important as that is. He must mark his steps on the trail, as he goes along. He might tie a bright marker around trees as he moves along his chosen path. He may not know exactly the steps ahead of him, but he would be able to take that same marked route back to the beginning. Others can find him on that same marked trail. Once the lost hiker is found, the path back is no longer a mystery. If the team member who found the hiker is asked how he found that lost hiker, his answer would be: *Let me show you the way, beginning with the end—starting at the initial marker. There will be markers showing the path, all along the way.* This little analogy is a simplified picture of one of the ways of finding the resolution to the trail to the *Mystery of God*.

Now, we can see in reverse order. Looking backward from the beginning of the New Testament Church, we see Christ's first coming. Then going further back in history, we see the prophets, the calling of the nation of Israel, Jacob (Israel), Isaac, Abraham, and so forth all the way back to Adam and Eve. The markers, that is the threads, on that trail are obvious to us now. Before the Spirit was sent by the Father, and before the revelations of the *Mystery of God* were given through the apostles, all was purposely not obvious. The Old Testament saints and prophets were looking forward to the fulfillment of God's prophesied plan for His own, just as we see in God's commentary about Abraham: *"... for he [Abraham] waited for the city which has foundations, whose builder and maker is God"* (Hebrews 11:10; also, 1 Peter 1:10-12).

This is especially important for our understanding, if we are those to whom the Apostle Paul referred when he pointed to this generation and said, *"on whom the ends of this age will come."*[178] We seriously need to understand how we got here by looking at the markers (threads) left by the Lord throughout the Bible. Didn't Jesus declare on the road to Emmaus that *"all the Scriptures"* were prophetic threads specifically pointing to Himself?

That part which God revealed in the Garden of Eden—that secret, that marriage, and that Seed—were the initial threads to the *Mystery of God* in human history. The full understanding of the *Mystery* would be kept secret until the time of Christ and the Apostles. Then it would ultimately culminate in the full revelation and completion of the *Mystery of God*.

The Little Seed

I want to see with you in more detail the first disclosure of this secret to the world, the part of the Mystery, as it relates to the Seed. Although it was disclosed in the form of a little seed, we have the great advantage of knowing that the seemingly little seed was actually the *ultimate* Seed, Jesus Christ our Lord and Savior.

We can easily agree that a little seed is much more powerful than its superficial size might portray. A seed is power-packed. It contains in itself a specific nature and life—its own DNA, each after its own kind. If a food-seed it produces food. Having been planted in the soil, once it germinates, then like-kind comes forth. The seed will suffer death so that new life can come forth. All of this has been engineered by our Creator-God.

The nature and life of the Seed reveal **Who He, Christ, is**. The Seed also reveals the "first fruits" which is Christ Himself raised from the dead, along with His own fruit which is generated from His seed, planted in believers by the Spirit. Believers are of His own kind, just as Jesus said: *"That which is born of the flesh is flesh, and that which is born of the Spirit is spirit"* (John 3:6).

The Seed in the Garden

When that old serpent Satan tempted Adam and Eve, they yielded and sinned against God. God then pronounced judgment on Satan and on Adam and Eve. What God said and did at that moment was of particular importance because it was a revelation of His way and His heart. On the one hand His justice had to be satisfied; therefore, His pronouncement of judgment. On the other hand it provided the perfect moment to introduce a key marker for His secret, one of those profound, prophetic threads, as Adam, Eve and Satan stood there in the presence of the Creator-God. This was the glorious moment of the introduction of *"the Seed,"* which through mercy provided hope to Adam and Eve in the midst of their sinful shame. The reason this provided them hope, as we will learn more clearly, was because that Seed was the promise of the Redeemer, Christ Himself, the Hope of the world!

Thankfully and simultaneously, the judgment also pronounced doom directly to Satan. During this pronouncement of judgment on Satan, God told him something that was new news to his wicked ears. Satan had already been told that his destruction would come. God had told him so[179] at the point of his rebellion in heaven before he was cast from heaven to the earth. Surely, what Satan did not yet know was by Whom he would be destroyed, and by what means. Satan did not know then, nor has he ever known all things, but was about to find out, namely, his new, bad news!

I love the fact that God pronounced this judgment on Satan to his face, right in front of Adam and Eve. Even though Adam and Eve stood there in shame, they were right there listening in. And they got an ear full!

Let's open our spiritual imagination (part of the following is **speculation**, but it's not hard to see it). We can see Adam and Eve listening to what God said to Satan with their heads bowed in shame. They were likely thinking something along this line: *"We are next! What's He going to say to us?"* One thing was certain, they were feeling completely hopeless in their sinful condition. They faced a very real death, an immediate spiritual death, and an eventual physical death, just as God had promised. Just imagine for a moment their feelings of loss. Previously they had only known the joy of God's presence. Now a whole new feeling. How heavy and hopeless that had to have felt!

During God's pronouncement on Satan, it became clear that Satan's final judgment would not be completed immediately. Since Adam and Eve were going to continue living on earth, they must have realized that their future included the experience of continuing temptations and troubles from the hand of Satan. They had to have felt as though yet another massive emotional and spiritual burden was added to what they already were feeling, and all of it was crushing in on them. Surely each of us can relate due to our own failures, when God opens our eyes to see what He sees. Doubtless they were already feeling like their future would be bleak.

The Serpent, The Seed, and Adam and Eve

After all there was no doubt in their minds that Satan had already won Round One with them. Perhaps, they were thinking: *How can we ever win against Satan, if he is not going to be destroyed now? Why would God allow this wicked serpent to continue at all?*

One thing was certain. They knew the hope for their future would in no way come from within themselves. They had just proven that to be impossible. Their utter failure before God was obvious. So, what was their hope?

Everything was not lost, though Adam and Eve must have felt it had been. What they were about to learn in a new way was that their hope was in God, and in Him alone. And in this case, that hope would come to them contained in the Seed that God was in the process of revealing to them right at that very moment. Satan had received from God *new,* **bad** *news.* Adam and Eve were about to become the recipients of *new* **good** *news.* The Mystery was not yet going to be revealed, but the good news of the Seed was! This was the thread that would stretch throughout human history to the very end: *The Seed, Jesus, and all of the spiritual fruit that would come from that Seed "in like kind," namely, His Bride!*

In this moment of God's pronouncement of judgment on Satan, Adam and Eve had to have been shocked to learn how it was going to happen. That wicked serpent Satan was going to get his head bruised (*"crushed"*).[180] And even more satisfying than the crushing of Satan's head, they suddenly learned that the Crusher would be *a son.* That was amazing news to Adam and Eve—and to Satan! For Adam and Eve, it meant great mercy, great grace, and great hope! What relief they must have felt! But for Satan, who thought he had spoiled God's human creation and Plan, it meant that he would be destroyed through the very *Seed* of the one he had sought to destroy through His tempting lies. Until that very moment, the *Seed* had been a hidden secret. But it was no longer completely locked away, even though the details remained a secret—at least, for the time being!

It's interesting to note that some may have thought that God's announcement about what the Seed would do to Satan, had been directed to Adam and Eve. Not so! It was spoken directly to Satan. But as Adam and Eve stood there listening, it seems doubtless that the revelation of this secret, which they were now hearing from God, would melt and humble their hearts.

> *"So the Lord God said to the serpent: 'Because you have done this, You are cursed more than all cattle, And more than every beast of the field; on your belly you shall go, And you shall eat dust all the days of your life. And I will put enmity between you and the woman, and between your seed and her Seed;* **He shall bruise [crush] your head,** *And you shall bruise [crush] His heel'"* (emphasis mine).
>
> Genesis 3:14–15

Adam and Eve's hearts had to have been melting. They didn't deserve this grace; what God was doing. They certainly didn't earn it. They had been standing there exposed, practically naked, shattered with shame, and feeling hopeless. But God had a perfect plan in place to redeem what had been lost, to rescue them from their souls' enemies: *The flesh, Satan, the world, and this world's system.*

The idea of promising the *Seed* didn't just pop into God's mind on the spur of the moment as a reaction to the terrible situation. It wasn't that God saw the deceitfulness of Satan and the failure of Adam and Eve and then began to wring His holy hands. He didn't say to Himself, *how can this be? I just created this man and woman, and look what they have done! I could never have imagined that it would turn out like this. What shall I do? What shall I do! Hmmm …!* And then, bingo! It finally comes to God's mind what to do. *I know what I'll do*, He says to Himself. *I'll just change what I thought was a perfect plan, and I'll show them what I can do to overcome this shocking dilemma that obviously caught me off guard!*

No! A thousand times, no!

In His perfect timing, God revealed this initial marker, this thread, as part of the unfolding of His foreknown dealings with humanity, and with Satan. God's nature, desire, and will are for every soul to have the freedom to choose to love Him or not to love Him. This was built right into His eternal plan. God had already decided that He would happily allow humanity the responsibility of choice. He did that. And then, they did what they did. He foreknew it all. Therefore, we read:

> *"For God so loved the world that He gave His only begotten Son, that whosoever believes in Him should not perish, but have everlasting life."*
>
> John 3:16

Obviously today's generation looks back, with access to the knowledge and understanding He gives us in the New Testament, and we can see that the promise of the Seed in the Garden of Eden was just the **Beginning** of the revelation of the Mystery of God at that pivotal moment. Didn't John's Gospel begin with these words: *"In the **Beginning** was the **Word** [Jesus Christ]?"* The problem with our understanding of that declaration of John is that we may not have seen the full meaning behind it. From our limited perspective, at first glance, we may not have added the whole counsel of God's Word to it. Jesus Christ is the *"Head;"* and His body is no less part of His person, which should make perfect sense, even though we use a physical analogy to refer to His eternal person. We were in Him *from the very beginning*, which some believers overlook. Our finite perspective can hinder us from seeing this great truth. But God has no such limitation. This is why the Apostle Paul said:

THE SERPENT, THE SEED, AND ADAM AND EVE

> *"Blessed be the God and Father of our Lord Jesus Christ, who has blessed us with every spiritual blessing in the heavenly places in Christ, just as He chose us **in Him** before the foundation of the world ...."*
>
> Ephesians 1:3–4

The concept of being in Him from before the foundation of the world is not a mere spiritualization, nor is it figuratively spoken. It is spoken from God's perspective, which is an eternal perspective. It is more real than our finite flesh has the ability to comprehend to the fullest degree. Thank God, that will change, when *"we see Him as He is!"*[181]

The truth of the *Seed*, the *Word*, in the Garden of Eden is seen as He lives on in unbroken, prophetic threads leading straight through the generations of those who believed God and followed Him by faith, and right on down to the line of Abraham, the friend of God, and His family.

> *"That faith was based on a covenantal thread that began in Eden and knit together the hearts of all true men of faith right up to Abraham's day. They were the men who believed the promise God made to Adam and Eve—that He would send a Redeemer [the Seed] who would die for man's sin"*[182] (bracketed comment, mine).

This blessing continued in a covenantal relationship with Isaac, the son of promise, and then Jacob, whom God changed internally and gave him one of His own names, Israel, and for whom God's chosen nation was named. This *Mystery* proceeds in history through God's chosen people, Israel. The threads continue in the judges, prophets, and kings and people of Israel. And throughout it all, God was gathering a Bride—He continued to braid the multi-threaded prophetic cord.

Then when Jesus, the Seed, the Word, came into the world, He came bringing a New Covenant. Therefore in the Seed was the New Covenant; and in the New Covenant was the Seed! The New Covenant was prophesied by the Prophet Jeremiah:

> *"Behold, the days are coming, says the Lord, when I will make a new covenant with the house of Israel and with the house of Judah ...."*
>
> Jeremiah 31:31

It is in that New Covenant that we can now fully see that God was unveiling His secret, the *Mystery of God*. In that **Seed**, that is, the actual **Person** of the *Mystery*, the ancient, hidden secret is now revealed to the world in the *"fullness of time."*

The events in the Garden of Eden and God's solution to the sin problem relate to the Adamic Covenant through which the early thread of the *Mystery* began to be braided in history.

The Adamic Covenant:
"... God's revelation is progressive. He does not tell us everything at once, but He unfolds His Plan for us over time. Moreover, His successive covenants are not corrective to earlier ones; rather, they explain and add to earlier revelations. For this reason, we assume continuity in God's Plan. Unless we are told otherwise, the stipulations of the earlier covenants are still to be carried out by us."[183]

This remark is nothing new. Christians must be willing to embrace this truth, and continue pursuing the Holy Spirit to open our understanding.

It was the famed preacher, Charles G. Finney, leader of the Second Great Awakening in the United States in the 1800's, who said: *"Christian consistency implies continued investigation and change of views and practice corresponding with increasing knowledge. No Christian, therefore, and no theologian should be afraid to change his views, his language, or his practices in conformity with increasing light ...."*[184] And that same truth was poignantly expressed in the words of Jeremiah, when he prophesied that God's Endtime revelations will be understood at the right time. He wrote explaining that there was coming a time "in the latter days, (when) you will understand perfectly." This clearly indicates that before understanding perfectly, we will understand imperfectly. It is expected, and completely within God's plan in these last days, that more and more understanding is being revealed to His Church! In Daniel 11:32-35, the prophet Daniel was told by the heavenly messenger that in the time of the end there would be those who would have *understanding*. The truth is that today's Church desperately need to be seeking God for greater and greater understanding of the days in which we live.

Come Go With Me

NOTE: I would ask the reader to understand that the following approach to making a point is fictional in form, although there are real quotes and identifiable facts discussed. My goal is to bring emphasis to the truth, and certainly *not to replace* any truth of Scripture. So, I want to take you on a quick fictionalized trip through the Bible!

Imagine that the Lord came to you and said, *"Come go with me. I want to take you on a trip."* Since it is God doing the asking, you decide that it would be a good idea to go. So, you agree. He explains that your trip will be experienced in a completely different dimension. Suddenly you are there. You understand somehow, that on this trip one-thousand years will be as one-day. He feels it is important for you to understand more about this dimension, so He tells you a little bit about it.

He tells you that there is an overlooked biblical concept regularly referred to by the early Church fathers, which affirms that human history on this present earth will cover a six-thousand-year period before the time comes when Christ will set up His Earthly Millennial Kingdom. He asks if you had read the writings of the early Church fathers, who had referred to this seven-thousand-year period as "chiliasm."[185] Without waiting for an answer, He reminds you that He accomplished His creative work in six days, then the seventh is His **day** of **rest**. In other words, He explains that there will be only seven thousand years of human history on this present earth. Peter referred to this. "*But do not overlook this one fact, beloved, that with the Lord one day is as a thousand years, and a thousand years as one day*" (2 Peter 3:8, ESV). The last of the seven sequential one-thousand-year periods will fulfill God's *Millennial* and *Jubilee* rest, as it relates to this present earth.[186]

Then making His point all the more emphatically, He mentions that concerning the matter of how long He will allow mankind the opportunity to believe and trust in Him before He sets up His Earthly Kingdom, one of the early church writers (either Paul's companion named Barnabas, or some say it was Barnabas a Levite) wrote:

> The Sabbath is mentioned at the beginning of the creation [thus]: "And God made in six days the works of His hands, and made an end on the seventh day, and rested on it, and sanctified it." Attend, my children, to the meaning of this expression, "He finished in six days." This implies that the Lord will finish all things in six thousand years, for a day is with Him a thousand years. He, Himself testifies, saying, "Behold, today will be as a thousand years." Therefore, my children, in six days, that is, in six thousand years, all things will be finished. "And He rested on the seventh day." This means: when His Son, coming [again], shall destroy the time of the wicked man, and judge the ungodly, and change the sun, and the moon, and the stars, then shall He truly rest on the seventh day.[187]

He reminds you of when you read about Irenaeus, one of the early Church fathers, who was a student of Polycarp, an earlier Church father. He reminds you of those historical documents from which you had learned that Polycarp was a right-hand man and disciple of the Apostle John. It was Irenaeus who wrote:

> For in as many days as this world was made, in so many thousand years shall it be concluded. For this reason, the Scripture says: "Thus the heaven and the earth were finished, and all their adornment. And God brought to a conclusion upon the sixth day

the works that He had made, and God rested on the seventh day from all His works." This is an account of the things formerly created, as also it is a prophecy of what is to come. For the day of the Lord is as a thousand years, and in six days created things were completed: it is evident, therefore, that they will come to an end at the sixth thousand years.[188]

He tells you that there are other such historical statements, but that those few should be sufficient. When six-thousand-years from the creation of man comes to an end, the Millennial Reign of Christ will begin. And His reign would begin at the *Second Coming of Christ.* He explains further that biblical historians are correct when they agree that the six-thousand-years will come to an end—and much sooner than many have believed.

He continues giving you just a few pointers to help you better understand some things about the trip and finishes His introduction to the time together by telling you this trip is all about the Revelation of Jesus Christ.

Waiting for your question, He pauses. So you ask Him, *"Since it is about the Revelation of Jesus Christ, are you going to show me the Book of Revelation, like you did to the Apostle John?"*

He responds, *"I'm saying that everything you will see on this trip, from the Creation and all the way through the Endtimes, is a revelation of my Son, Jesus Christ. That 'revelation' is not limited to the Book of Revelation. All of this is by promises and covenants and was also shown in types, shadows, and secrets. These things were put into place, one by one all the way down through history, under and through each covenant I made with mankind. They are all connected to one another. The newly added ones did not, and do not, necessarily void the old ones. For instance, do you remember the Word I gave to My faithful servant, Paul: "...the law, which came 430 years afterward, **does not annul a covenant previously ratified by God, so as to make the promise void."**[189] When I make promises or covenants with humanity, those men and women who come under the umbrella, by grace, and through faith, of a given covenant and promise during that period of time—they may not have kept them—but I do. That's Who I Am! I don't allow my faithfulness to fail. What is often overlooked is that each one of those covenants, along with many other details, plays a role in establishing the revelation of My Son to humanity throughout history. So as you will see during our short trip when Jesus is sent to the earth because of Our love for humanity, He fulfills everything necessary in every covenant from the past in order to bring in Our New Covenant. Any part of those previous covenants not needed after the fulfillment of those covenants is set aside. This is not as though they are not true or good; to the contrary, it will be because My Son brings about something better — much better. It is that New Covenant which, obviously came into the world when He came into the world, but that will be both consummated and finished, from the eternal perspective, at the marriage of My Son to His Bride. That marriage is the Marriage of the Lamb! As you will see, the ultimate fulfillment of these things will occur during the days of the sounding of the seventh and last trumpet!"*

THE SERPENT, THE SEED, AND ADAM AND EVE

He also tells you that it is His nature to understand that humanity is frail. Humanity is incapable of keeping covenant completely and perfectly. He had to make mankind with a free will, the ability to choose. He knew they would choose wrongly. Therefore, He knew He would have to swear by Himself that He would keep the covenants that He makes with mankind. Therefore, relationship with Him is a matter of faith, belief, and trust. Those who would choose to believe and trust in Him, He would count as His own special people in His New Covenant.

He says something that grabs your attention, just before the trip begins: *"When Jeremiah, one of My prophets, prophesied that We would make a New Covenant, We foresaw that many Gentiles would fail to understand Our intent. Some of the Gentiles would actually begin to believe and teach that the New Covenant was made with a Gentilized Church, even though this is a direct contradiction to what We said through the prophet. We said that we would make a New Covenant with the house of Israel and Judah. The problem is two-fold: 1) Some in the Church have come to believe that the Gentilized Church replaced Israel as Our chosen people; and 2) some in the Church came to believe that We make a difference between Israel and the Church, because of the covenants made with Abraham and Israel. Those ideas are confusion, and worse. The whole problem with all of that is that the Gentilized Church has now done what the nation of Israel was doing when My Son came to earth for His ministry and sacrifice. Many have turned to men's traditions, rather than Our pure Word. Many have failed to understand our Plan. However, a spiritual remnant, from the beginning with Adam and Eve, has always been in place. When We chose Abraham, Isaac, and Jacob, and then their descendants, there were those among their descendants who did not believe. Those, therefore, were not part of the remnant of believers. But those who believed Me were considered the remnant of the natural olive tree that My servant, Paul, wrote about. And the Gentiles are seen by Us as being grafted into that same tree, whose Root is My Son, the One who gives that tree its life. So, I ask this question: How can the people of Israel, who were chosen to bring My Son into this world, possibly be made jealous by those who don't even understand My Plan? Those whom I chose, that is, those who are of the physical seed of Abraham, will continue to hear a confusing Gentilized gospel message, which completely disregards that which is so obvious—the Mystery of God."*

Then instantly, there you are, high above the earth looking down on events as they begin to unfold in history. You see the first marriage. The two, Adam and Eve, are pronounced by God to be one. At that point, He lets you listen in on the declarations He made to the Serpent and Adam and Eve. The **Seed** is introduced, and He explains that His Son was the *Seed* referred to in the Garden scene. In that Garden was seen a revelation of God's first covenant and the essential relationship between the Seed and the Covenant. And you witness as that Seed continues to be known in the relationships with Abel, and Enoch, Noah, Shem, and eventually, Abraham—the friend of God. Then you see Abraham's son of promise—Isaac, who typified Christ Himself; after all, He says, Jesus was the ultimate *"Son of Promise."* Jacob is seen, who was given one of God's names —Israel. Then comes the nation of Israel to whom was given responsibilities and covenants of promise, along with the privilege of continuing to be the people through whom the very *Seed*, the Christ, would be born into the world.

You can't help yourself; you are overwhelmed with emotions, as you see Joseph and Mary arriving in Bethlehem, seeking a place to sleep. For the first time in your life, you can more fully understand the weight and meaning that the Seed has in Scripture. You remember what the Apostle John wrote concerning every born again child of God: "*… His Seed remains in him* [the believer] *for he is born of God.*"[190] He continues the trek, showing you the lives of the Apostles. He allows you to look over the shoulder of His beloved Apostle Paul, as Paul is given the many details describing the *Mystery of God*. In a flash, you are looking over another shoulder, as you witness the Apostle John being given the Book of Revelation. When He arrives at Revelation 10 and 11, it is as though things went into slow motion, as He highlights the importance of the *Mystery of God*.

Suddenly as you are arriving near the end of your trip, you are awe-struck at what you see: The awe-inspiring, glorious *Marriage of the Lamb*. There you see the throngs, who make up the Bride of Christ. Each one of those who had been gathered from every corner of heaven and earth was there standing in awe of the Bridegroom, the Lamb of God who had been slain before the foundation of the world, and who now will reign, as King of kings and Lord of lords. Suddenly it dawns on you, without Him saying a word, that every member of the Bride of Christ has the Seed in them. Everyone is *"in Christ."* You recall the scene in the Garden, when Eve had been taken from Adam's side, as having been part of Adam. She had became one with Adam in covenantal marriage. You now understand that just as it was with Eve coming from Adam's side, that was a type or a picture of how Jesus got His wife. The heavenly fulfillment of that is now coming into focus. The Lamb's Bride came from His wounded side—through the shedding of His blood. In that very real sense, Christ's Bride was *"in Him."* And Christ—because He is the *Seed*, is in His Bride." They are truly one!

Then after such a humbling and awesome sight, you are directed to look, there! And there He is; the King of kings, and LORD of lords, Jesus Christ, mounted on His white horse along with the host of heaven riding back to the earth to rule and reign for one thousand years in power, majesty, righteousness, justice, purity, and with great glory. Peace is gained and maintained in the earth until Satan is loosed for a short time at the end of that period. Finally, the *Seed of the woman* completely crushes the seed of *the Serpent, Satan*, as He is cast into the Lake of Fire for eternity, along with the antichrist and the false prophet.

The Great White Throne Judgment is suddenly seen with the books opened, and the judgment of the unsaved is meted out, and all are cast into the Lake of Fire, who had chosen to reject Christ and His salvation. A new heaven and a new earth are created. Then, He allows you to get a glimpse of a truly awesome sight. Coming down out of heaven to the new earth as a Bride adorned for her Husband is the New Jerusalem, the City of God.

In a flash, your glorious seven-day—seven-thousand-year trip—is over and what a glorious trip it was! A trip right through the Bible, from beginning to end. He asks, *"What was the one thing you were moved by more than anything else?"* You answer by telling Him that the most profound thing that you came to realize was that it is all about the revelation and glory of Jesus Christ as the Redeemer and Bridegroom of the Bride He gathered throughout history!

As the trip fades away like a dream, you hear Him say those familiar words He spoke several times in the Bible: Jesus *"is My Beloved Son, in Whom I am well-pleased. Hear Him!"*

Who Is The "Seed?"

In the Garden God said, *"He shall crush your head, Satan."* Who then is the "He" who does the crushing? As we have seen, the simple answer is that He, the Seed, is Christ Himself. Of this fact, no Bible-believing pastor, teacher, scholar, professor, or any informed student of the Word of God could disagree. After all, the Apostle Paul referred to the Seed in Galatians, stating that the "*Seed*" is Christ.

> *"Now to Abraham and his Seed were the promises made. He [God] does not say, "And to seeds," as of many, but as of one, "And to your Seed," who is Christ."*
>
> Galatians 3:16

Not only is He the Seed in the Garden, but after a fast-forward from the Garden to Abraham, we learn that the promise was not only made to Eve and Adam, but also to Abraham and his *"son of promise."* We learn from Paul in Galatians that Abraham's ultimate *"Son of Promise"* was not Isaac. Rather in fact, that "son" and that *Seed*, is Jesus.

It cannot go without saying that same *Seed* has been there throughout history. And of course, it can be no other way. The *Seed* is Christ, and Christ was and is the Word, the One who was in the beginning and before the beginning. The *"Seed's"* presence throughout Scripture cannot be dismissed as though He were not there all the way through. Let's put it another way. Any knowledgeable believer would say that once we are born again, from that day forward, we are in Christ for eternity-future. Does that mean that the moment someone has been born again God takes that believer to heaven because they are *"in Him?"* Of course, not. What it means is that our new position spiritually, is *"in Him"* in *"heavenly places"* (Ephesians 1:3, 20; 2:6).

We need a paradigm switch however. What I mean is this. In addition to being *"in Him"* during eternity-future, if we see from God's perspective (which is the ***true reality***), it is equally true that we have been in Christ since before the foundation of the world—as far as God is concerned. Paul made this clear:

*"For whom He **foreknew,** He also **predestined** to be conformed to the image of His Son, that He might be the firstborn among many brethren. Moreover, whom He predestined, these He also called; whom He **called,** these He also justified; and whom He **justified,** these He also **glorified.**"*

Romans 8:29–30

This makes perfect sense in one of the aspects about seeds. We have apples today because of the seeds that came from the first apple trees in God's creation! And through that fact, we finally have the answer to what has been a famous conundrum. How many times have we heard the puzzling question: *Which came first, the chicken or the egg?* The same applies to the question, *which came first, the apple or the seed?* The answer is *Both.* When God made the chicken and the apple, their *seed,* being their *kind,* was already in that which was created by God! Wasn't that true with Adam, too? Weren't Cain and Abel in Adam? For instance, concerning Abraham and Levi, the Book of Hebrews tells us that *"Even Levi, who receives tithes, paid tithes through Abraham, so to speak, for he was still in the loins of his ancestor ..."* (Hebrews 7:9–10).

Since we are *"in Christ"* and Christ is the Seed, we are in and from Him in that sense! This is not just an interesting word picture of Jesus. This is one of God's essential expressions of His Son. He is revealing many things, not the least of which is the consistency of His revelation of who Jesus is throughout history. If Christ is from eternity-past, and He is, then we were *"in Him,"* as far as our sovereign, all-knowing God is concerned. This if nothing else, speaks to His faithfulness, and the *"sure hope"* we have in Him as the writer of Hebrews says.[191]

Additionally this is why it can be said that we are the spiritual children of Abraham. This is because Abraham was of the Seed, Christ. Is there any question as to whether or not the faith that Abraham had was the faith that came from Christ? Christ is the Word of God. *"Faith comes by hearing, and hearing by the Word of God [Christ]."* Was it not Christ Himself whom Abraham met when three men met Abraham on the road at Abraham's tent? It's no wonder that it was prophesied of Abraham that *"in you [Abraham] all of the nations shall be blessed ...."* Of course! This is because Abraham was *"in Him"* before the foundation of the world. An even more amazing truth about Christ and Abraham is this. Christ was of the *Seed* of Abraham, and Abraham was of the *Seed* of Christ. Both are true. The reason this is feasible has little to do with Abraham and much to do with Christ. Jesus said, *"Before Abraham was, I Am ...,"* meaning that Jesus was eternally alive as the ever-present One, the "I Am." He was before Abraham was. To make the full point, it is equally true that Jesus could have also said *Before I came into the world in the likeness of man, Abraham had lived! Concerning being born, according to the physical birth, Abraham preceded me. In that sense, Abraham was physically living in this world before I was.* Can we not see that Jesus Christ is the same *yesterday, today, and forever* The Seed, the very Son of God?

Back to Adam and Eve

Now let's pick back up, where we left off because now we will be able to see things all the more clearly. God had just revealed a secret to Adam and Eve. I say secret because even though they heard the words come from God's own mouth about the promised Seed, they absolutely did not know that God was referring to Christ Himself. This is doubtless one of the things that Jesus was referring to when he said: *"... I will utter things kept secret from the foundation of the world"* (Matthew 13:35). Jesus said that those secrets were among those mysteries he would make known.[192]

Adam and Eve it seems, saw the seed as a *human-only, redeemer-son*. So it seems that they assumed that this seed would be their own birth-son, who was yet to be born. To them, all of this had to have been a mystery, at minimum. This required of them to walk by faith in what God had said, looking forward to the time of that promised seed whenever that seed would come into the world within God's foreknown timing.

Adam and Eve, and all of those in the Old Testament who followed in faith, looked forward by faith to the promised *seed*, the promised son. We, on the other hand, look back at it all, after God had revealed these things in the New Testament. Therefore today's believers can see the first revelation of the promised **Seed**, the promised **Son**. If we have eyes to see and ears to hear, as Jesus said, we can see the conclusion of it all as revealed to us in the New Testament—and that conclusion is found in the truths and events of the Mystery of God.

When Isaiah prophesied, he left no question in the hearts of faithful believers during the Old Testament period that God's Son would be **given** by God, and that He would be **born** into the world. He would be the Deliverer, the Savior. This Prince of Peace would come![193] Even though Isaiah's ability to see was still hazy regarding the Messiah's coming, it was at this time in history that God gave him the privilege of recording those prophetic threads, those secrets. Still we can rest assured that even Isaiah did not fully understand all that had been revealed to him by God, as Peter explained later on.[194] Some may not have considered that the prophets *"searched intently and with the greatest care, trying to find out the time and circumstances"* of the things they themselves, had prophesied. We, on the other hand, have been given these truths in the text of the Scriptures. And Peter tells us that those prophets were not prophesying to serve themselves but to serve those who would be able to understand once Christ came. While we too must search, we have been given so much more than they were given. *"To whom much is given, much is required."*[195] It behooves us to seek His face relentlessly for understanding.

After Adam and Eve had sinned in the Garden of Eden, God's merciful and gracious dealings with them had been demonstrated by the covering He had provided them through the shedding of blood, and in the promise of the seed-son-redeemer. He had bathed them in His love and mercy. It seems Adam and Eve were now ready and willing to walk by faith. Their faith was tested and revealed in the terrible events concerning **Cain and Abel**.

Chapter Fourteen Notes

[177] Matthew 13:35; Romans 16:25–26; 1 Corinthians 2:7; Ephesians 3:1-9.

[178] 1 Corinthians 10:1-11.

[179] See Ezekiel 28, God prophetically uses the "king of Tyre" as His means of addressing Lucifer, a cherub angel, telling him that he is doomed. From this passage, we see that Lucifer knew at least that much about his "end."

[180] (Strong 1995), Strong's Hebrew "#7779 רוּשׁ, שׁוּף [shuwph /shoof/], to bruise, crush ...."

[181] "Beloved, now we are children of God; and it has not yet been revealed what we shall be, but we know that when He is revealed, we shall be like Him, for we shall see Him as He is" (1 John 3:2).

[182] (Byers, *The Mystery*, 2000), 24.

[183] Cited from the online article under Topic Index at *Adamic Covenant*, Ligonier.org/learn/devotionals/ Adamic-covenant/?mobile=off.

[184] https://www.goodreads.com/author/quotes/4645522.Charles_Grandison_Finney.

[185] Tim Warner, *The Time of the End*, (Tim Warner, 2012), 17, 41.

[186] The pattern of sevens in Scripture are pervasive and are addressed later on in Chapter 16.

[187] Roberts, A., Donaldson, J., & Coxe, A. C. (Eds.). (1885). *The Epistle of Barnabas*. In *The Apostolic Fathers with Justin Martyr and Irenaeus* (Vol. 1, p. 146). Buffalo, NY: Christian Literature Company.

[188] Roberts, A., Donaldson, J., & Coxe, A. C. (Eds.), *Irenæus against Heresies* (1885). In *The Apostolic Fathers with Justin Martyr and Irenaeus* (Vol. 1, p. 557). Buffalo, NY: Christian Literature Company.

[189] Galatians 3:17, ESV.

[190] 1 John 3:9.

[191] Hebrews 6:16-20: "For people swear by something greater than themselves, and in all their disputes an oath is final for confirmation. So, when God desired to show more convincingly to the heirs of the promise the unchangeable character of his purpose, he guaranteed it with an oath, so that by two unchangeable things, in which it is impossible for God to lie, we who have fled for refuge might have strong encouragement to hold fast to the hope set before us. **We have this as a sure and steadfast anchor of the soul, a hope that enters into the inner place behind the curtain, where Jesus has gone as a forerunner on our behalf,** having become a high priest forever after the order of Melchizedek."

[192] Jesus said that the secrets he was revealing through His parables were those which were "*given to [My disciples to] know the mysteries of the kingdom of God.*" (contextual bracketed insertion, mine)

[193] Isaiah 9:6-7.

[194] 1 Peter 1:10–12.

[195] "... *everyone to whom much is given, from him much will be required ...*" (Luke 12:48).

Chapter 15

THE PROMISED SEED: CAIN OR ABEL?

"And I will put enmity Between you and the woman, And between your seed and her Seed; He shall bruise your head, And you shall bruise His heel."

Genesis 3:15

"Now Adam knew Eve, his wife, and she conceived and bore Cain, and said, "I have acquired a man from the Lord."

Genesis 4:1

"Then she bore again, this time his brother Abel. Now Abel was a keeper of sheep, but Cain was a tiller of the ground."

Genesis 4:2

What was Eve thinking when she named her first two sons? One thing seems certain. Eve was on a mission. When she named Cain her first son, she believed she had given birth to the coming "Lord;" the one who would crush the Serpent's head. Even though the typical English translation reads as quoted above, Eve's declaration can also be translated from the Hebrew, as saying: "I have acquired (given birth) to a man, **the LORD**." This carries the idea that Eve felt she was giving birth to the promised one himself. I want us to keep that fact in mind, as we walk through this chapter together.

Cain and Abel

Names have meaning. The naming of Adam and Eve's first two sons shows this in a superbly profound way. Can you imagine Eve's thoughts, feelings, and reactions as she went through her first pregnancy? God had said, "... *in pain you shall bring forth children* ....." She must have been petrified when her contractions began. I think it is fair to say that if there ever was a *natural* birth, this was it, in living color and sounds. Yet if there ever was a mother ready and willing to go through suffering to get a child, this mother was that one! She had doubtless been on pins and needles with phenomenal expectations. While she was writhing in pain, surely the promise God had given her about the seed-redeemer had to have given her strength and motivation all the way through the ordeal. You could say that she had a prophetic understanding. But what was her motivation and encouragement to persevere? We can imagine her laying on her back with her fingernails embedded in Adam's arm as she squeezed, allowing him the privilege of feeling just a little bit of her pain. Still we can hear her saying to herself; *I'm ready for the seed, the redeemer-seed, the one who will crush that wicked serpent, Satan, who beguiled me! I am soooooo ... ready!*

Then with pain enveloping Eve's entire being, the moment finally came. A son was born! *"Ahhh! Praise be to God!"* She must have shouted out. It's fascinating and telling that it was Eve, not Adam, who named their son. This is not coincidental. Evidently she and Adam had taken the matter of "her seed" seriously. We can sense her excitement and expectation by understanding the meaning behind the name she chose. The root of the Hebrew word for Cain is "kan" (*qayin*, meaning "spear" or "smith," resembling in sound the root *qanah*, "get," "acquire." The verb form root means *"to acquire"* or *"to create."*[196] To put it in her own words, she said, *"I have acquired a man from the LORD"* (Genesis 4:1). It seems that she had something specific in mind with Cain's name. To her way of thinking, she had **acquired** the promised seed, who would crush the head of that wicked serpent! And further, it seems that she had in mind that Cain might well finish off that serpent with the use of a spear. One thing is absolutely certain. Eve had "acquired" a man from the LORD. And **THAT** was what she had been hoping for.

Time passed. Then bye and bye, Eve became pregnant again. Another son was born into their family—Abel. In the meantime, Cain was the one she perceived to have been the promised seed she had "acquired." According to the name she had given Cain, it is obvious that she was fixated on Cain, as her promised seed, whom she had *"acquired."*

But what does the name Abel mean? His name helps us understand what Adam and Eve were thinking. Abel's name, significantly, means "nothing" or "breath"[197] in the original language. From the perspective of their fixation on Eve's previously *"acquired"* seed, Abel meant *"nothing,"* in a manner of speaking, or in comparison. Doubtless they loved Abel, so that wasn't the issue. It was a practical matter. They wanted to get this business of the crushing of the serpent's head taken care of—as soon as possible.

Sadly for them, the crushing came, but it was not the crushing they had been looking forward to all of those years.

THE PROMISED SEED: CAIN OR ABEL?

Obviously the Bible doesn't tell us in this manner, but our imaginations (and speculations) can just hear Adam and Eve during one of their evening walks together. Speculating what might have happened at that point, Eve might have been heard saying something like this to Adam, "Surely, Cain is old enough now, Adam. Maybe the time has come! I wonder why God hasn't told Cain what he must do? We have told Cain over and again that God promised a seed, the redeemer-seed." Adam might have responded something like this: "Yes, Eve, you are so right. Why does God keep all of this a secret? And by the way, I have been wondering about what God meant when he said to Satan back in the Garden that there would be enmity between Satan's seed and your seed. I wonder who Satan's seed is? Is Satan going to have children too? I hope not; Satan is enough to be concerned about. We don't need any more of his kind around! All of it seems like such a mystery to me."

Then suddenly, their whole world fell apart due to the inconceivable, stunning and tragic news: *Cain had murdered Abel.*

We can hear their heart-cries. *How could that be! The Seed is a redeemer, not a murderer! We thought Cain was the promised seed!* Devastation had come to the home and hearts of Adam and Eve.

In addition to the complete horror of the murder, we have to realize that this first shedding of human blood and physical death on earth was something *new* and *unthinkable* to them. They surely asked themselves, and God, questions expressing perplexity, perhaps even depressing questions. This was a horribly confusing moment; and heart-shattering. This surely left them empty, with their hopes dashed in traumatic fashion. It is not too difficult to imagine that they were tempted to wonder how God could promise the seed who would crush Satan's head, when it was their seed who had just crushed their heads and hearts, instead! Confusion had to be rampant and overwhelming.

Slowly but surely, the identification and understanding of **what was meant by Satan's seed** began to dawn on them. As they recounted those early years with Cain and Abel, they could now look back and see that Cain's choices were not God's ways. Cain's choices were earth-bound, fleshly, selfish, jealous, envious, and hateful. Adam and Eve began to realize how they had allowed themselves to be blinded by their own ideas of the way things should be. Does that sound familiar?

When God allows that which He could prevent, we may find ourselves asking the very questions Adam and Eve must have wondered. Sometimes the deeper meaning of Isaiah's words, sink in on us, causing us to be drawn to God out of sheer necessity, which is not a bad thing: "'… *My thoughts are not your thoughts, nor are your ways My ways,*' says the Lord" (Isaiah 55:8). Isaiah seemed to be filled with such instructions. He also said, "*… some of you want to light your own fires and make your own light. So, go, walk in the light of your fires, and trust your own light to guide you. But this is what you will receive from me: You will lie down in a place of pain*" (Isaiah 50:11, NCV). Is there any doubt that this is the way of the flesh for every one of us? The Apostle Paul responded to this problem, when He said, "*O wretched man that I am! Who will deliver me from this body of death?*" (Romans 7:24).

Abel had been the one who had chosen God's way. It was Abel's offerings God had accepted. We can see God's covering once again, through the shedding of the blood of Abel's animal offerings. This truth was doubtless becoming clearer to Adam and Eve. Cain had demonstrated the seed of Satan's ways. In speaking to the serpent, that is Satan, God told him: "*And I will put enmity between **you** and the woman, And between **your seed** and her Seed; He shall bruise your head, And **you** shall bruise His heel*" (Genesis 3:15). Satan and his seed are seen in Cain. "*There is a way that seems right to a man, but the end of it is the way of death*" (Proverbs 14:12 and 16:25). "*Woe to them! For they have gone in the way of Cain ...*" (Jude 11).

Not only was Cain's offering to God not accepted, but the full proof of Cain's heart-choices was revealed when he killed his brother. Abel may have been named a mere *breath*, or *nothing*, but in his name and his life was a picture of what pleases God. Abel's humility and attitude of heart were revealed. We can see that the attitude of Christ's heart was revealed in him. As we come to the place of **nothing**-ness, having no confidence in our own flesh, we can then please God when His fruit, the fruit of the Holy Spirit—the very life of Christ—flows in and through us. This is where faith is really known—in our heart attitude of our own **nothing**-ness and God's *everything*! The Apostle Paul understood this very well, when he said, "*When I am weak, then I am strong.*"[198] And when He further testified, "*... the life that I now live, I live by faith in the Son of God, who loved me and gave Himself for me.*"[199]

Obviously Abel had made a choice. His choice had required that he lay down his own preferences or wants, counting his own way as *nothing* compared to the will and way of God. He believed and trusted God and His ways, rather than his own—the opposite of the choice of Cain. Paul referred to the principle found in this revelation when he wrote "*... I know that in me (that is, in my flesh) **nothing** good dwells ....*"[200]

When Christ came into the world, there were those within Israel who thought that they were the special ones because they thought they knew who the Seed was. But they didn't. They would have done themselves a favor if they had meditated a bit more on the Seed first mentioned in the Garden of Eden! Had they done so, perhaps they would not have joined hands with the Gentile rulers to "*crucify the Lord of glory.*"[201] Jesus identified those who were envious leaders of Israel with words that also accurately identify Cain:

> "*You are of your father the devil and the desires of your father you want to do. He was a murderer from the beginning* and does not stand in the truth, because there is no truth in him. When he speaks a lie, he speaks from his own resources, for he is a liar ..." (emphasis mine).
>
> John 8:44

The Promised Seed: Cain or Abel?

Clearly Adam and Eve still had a lot to learn; just like the rest of us. At this point, we can see how it would make sense for Adam and Eve to begin to set aside their own speculations and ideas, which had been driving their misguided ambition concerning the promised seed. The walk of faith, which required waiting on God to reveal the Seed whenever He would choose to do so, would be the best and only way to live! That remains the best approach to life, as opposed to our own fleshly approach.

It was Abel who was the righteous one of the two sons. *"By faith Abel offered to God a more excellent sacrifice than Cain, through which he obtained witness that he was righteous, God testifying of his gifts, and through it he being dead still speaks"* (Hebrews 11:4). And what is it that "still speaks" from Abel's life? Abel's blood still speaks. When his blood speaks, it speaks of Christ and not Abel's own righteousness. What a testimony Abel had!

As good as that is, it is Christ's blood that we want to hear from most. *That Seed, which was what spoke to Abel, still speaks to us today.* We are told that Jesus' blood is the *"Mediator of the new covenant, and to the blood of sprinkling that speaks* **better things than that of Abel**" (Hebrews 12:24). Of course it *speaks better things than that of Abel* because only Jesus' blood can redeem Abel, me, you, or anyone else!

Abel's blood cries out from the ground, as it should, telling all of us that no matter the cost, God's way is the right way. But Jesus' blood cries out from the cross telling us that He is the *"Way, the Truth and the Life,"* and that no man can come to the Father except through Him.

God's desire for our lives is the right path, and nothing short of that will work well. If we kick against it, we will be spiritually crushed. Honor Him in it, and we will be blessed, as was Abel. God Himself testified on Abel's behalf. Which would you rather be, Cain or Abel, even though Abel's life had been taken by murder? Truly God's ways and thoughts are not like ours.

Abel was in the line of the *Seed* because the *Seed* was with Him. Abel can be seen as a thread in the prophetic cord, in a manner of speaking.

The Seed: A Hope and a Future

Down through the millennia, women of faith knew about the seed because that message was God's message to the world. Those women prayed to have sons,[202] with the hope that theirs would be the promised seed. Even the wicked ones knew about and had a perverted desire to bear the seed.[203] Satan has always sought to provide his *seed* in place of Christ. The world and history are replete with such examples. But those who are seemingly self-deceived with such grand schemes, are actually deceived by Satan, who does to them what he always does to those who are his own seed: He *"steals, kills and destroys"* them![204]

While godly women knew about the *Seed* and walked by faith in their limited knowledge, God had not yet revealed the broader meaning of the *Seed*! It remained a *"Mystery," "hidden,"* and *"secret,"* waiting for the *"fullness of time."* Other generations would receive additional revelations all of the way to Christ and His apostles. But again, as New Testament believers, we can look back and see clearly what those generations had received without their full understanding.

When Gabriel announced to Mary that she would conceive and Jesus would be born, he also revealed to her that her relative, Elizabeth was pregnant in her old age. (She was pregnant with John the Baptist.) Mary soon took a trip to visit with Zacharias and Elizabeth. Mary was so enthralled that she began to praise and give thanks to God. Those words of praise and thanksgiving were not idle words. She identified the fact that God had honored her with the grace of being the woman who would bear **The Seed**. Not just any seed; but *the* Seed promised in the Garden of Eden. Mary sang and shouted out: *"He has helped His servant Israel, In remembrance of His mercy, As He spoke to our fathers,* **to Abraham and his SEED forever**" (Luke 1:54–55).

Her son was indeed **The Seed**! Every revelation about Him throughout history had become part of the braided, unbreakable, multi-threaded, prophetic cord. This prophetic cord progressed from Adam and Eve, through Abraham and Sarah with the son of promise, and on to Christ in Mary, and as we will see, on to the **Marriage of the Lamb**!

During her moments of praise with Elizabeth, Mary affirmed God's 4,000-year-old promise and its threads which came through Abraham, when she exulted in praise: "to Abraham and his SEED forever." If we put our spiritual glasses on, we will see this clearly. The Seed in Genesis 3:15 was that same Seed referred to by Mary, when she spoke of God's mercy *"from generation to generation."* From the first generation, Adam and Eve, to the last generation, the Redeemer-Seed is the One! This Seed was, indeed, the Seed that would crush the head of the serpent! Paul explains exactly who she referred to:

"Now to Abraham and his Seed were the promises made. He does not say, 'And to seeds, as of many, but as of one, And to your Seed, who is Christ'" (emphasis mine).

Galatians 3:16

Let's confess it. God knows **how and when** to reveal **what** is in His Plan. Again, the complete revelation of the *who, what, how and when* about this *Seed* would not be understood in the Garden of Eden. This is one reason why the apostle Paul wrote about the details of this *Mystery*, again and again:

The Promised Seed: Cain or Abel?

"... by revelation He made known to me the Mystery ... which, when you read, you may understand my knowledge in the Mystery of Christ [**the Seed and the Seed's Bride—Jew and Gentile, believers**] *which in other ages was not made known to the sons of men, as it has now been revealed by the Spirit to His holy apostles and prophets ..."* (emphases and bracketed insertion mine).

Ephesians 3:3–5

The Holy Spirit provided to us the detailed explanation of this *Mystery* primarily through the Apostle Paul. With an understanding of the relationship between the *Seed* and the *Mystery of God*, we can more fully understand the Beginning as well as the Endtimes. To me it is an astounding revelation to realize that as Christ's Bride, we are His seed; that is, He is in us and we are in Him, *as one.*

Having identified *the Seed,* we can begin to see more clearly that Seed, Christ, in relation to the *Mystery of God* throughout the Bible in the next chapter: ***The Mystery of God and The Revelation of Jesus Christ Throughout the Bible!***

Chapter Fifteen Notes

[196] Orr, James, M.A., D.D. General Editor. 1915. "Entry for 'CAIN.'" *International Standard Bible Encyclopedia.*

[197] (Strong 1995) לֶבֶה *[Hebel /**heh·**bel/]* ... Abel = "breath." (also, means "nothing")

[198] 2 Corinthians 12:10.

[199] Galatians 2:20.

[200] Romans 7:18.

[201] 1 Corinthians 2:8.

[202] Of course, they loved their daughters born to them. But there was a special rejoicing in their lives, when males were born, because they knew that the Seed, the Messiah, would come through the seed of the woman.

[203] Babylon was important not only politically but also religiously. Nimrod, who founded Babylon (Gen. 10:8–12), had a wife known as Semiramis who founded the secret religious rites of the Babylonian mysteries, according to accounts outside the Bible. Semiramis had a son with an alleged miraculous conception who was given the name Tammuz and in effect was a false fulfillment of the promise of the seed of the woman given to Eve (Gen. 3:15). Walvoord, John F.; Zuck, Roy B., Dallas Theological Seminary, Bible Knowledge Commentary, 1983.

[204] John 10:10.

Chapter 16

THE MYSTERY OF GOD AND THE REVELATION OF JESUS CHRIST THROUGHOUT THE BIBLE

"And beginning at Moses and all the Prophets, He expounded to them in all the Scriptures the things concerning Himself."

Luke 24:27

"And there are also many other things that Jesus did, which if they were written one by one, I suppose that even the world itself could not contain the books that would be written. Amen."

John 21:25

"Christ is so essential to the Old Testament that one could fill tens of thousands of pages demonstrating it."[205]

From the Seed to the Savior, to the Supper! Those nine words, from one perspective, represent the *braided, multi-threaded, unbreakable, prophetic cord* from Genesis to Revelation. The title of this chapter links the *Mystery of God* and the *Revelation of Jesus Christ* throughout the Bible. This linkage is seen in Jesus Christ, the Seed in the Garden of Eden. It continues from there as the revelation of Jesus Christ to His first coming and as the revelation of Jesus Christ in the Book of Revelation where it is finally seen in the revelation of Jesus Christ in the *Marriage of the Lamb* to His Bride. As I stated earlier, it is both accurate and wonderful to comprehend that the entire Bible can be seen as *"the revelation of Jesus Christ."*

The fabric of the Old Testament is woven in the prophetic threads of the promised Christ. If there are nearly four hundred direct prophecies of Christ in the Old Testament, then there are, additionally, thousands of details within those four hundred. We see Him in stories, illustrations, and word-pictures, applicable to Him without distorting or disturbing the intended meaning. Again David Limbaugh says it well, "Christ is so essential to the Old Testament that one could fill tens of thousands of pages demonstrating it."

A myriad of beautiful threads are woven into both the Old and New Testaments testifying of Jesus. These make the fabric of Scripture come alive through many profound patterns,[206] each of which speaks of Christ. His tapestry is woven. On the one side of the tapestry are indistinguishable patches of threads, as we tend to see them, until He opens our eyes and we see the other side of things. When by His grace, we are privileged to have Him move us into His viewpoint, we see beautiful patterns of a glorious, vibrant, brilliant Plan. He is pictured in patterns; all of which serve to reveal Christ. A complete study of these is outside of the scope of this book, the following provide a few snippets of broader insights:

- The *Seven Days of Creation, including God's Sabbath Day of Rest* are a pattern.
- The *Seven Men of Faith* in Genesis are a pattern.
- The *Seven Primary Parts of the Tabernacle and Temple* are a pattern.
- The *Seven Feasts of the Lord* are a pattern.
- The *Seven Millennia*: That period, during which God is dealing with humanity. Six days of "work" (six-thousand-years), and then, the seventh day (one-thousand-year) "rest," called the Millennial Kingdom, which are another amazing pattern.

A Thread Is Worth More Than A Thousand Words

Rightly, we say that *a picture is worth a thousand words*. But in this book we will adapt that saying: **A thread is worth more than a thousand words.**

In the *Introduction* and in *the Panoramic View of the Bible* in The Scofield® Study Bible, Rev. C. I. Scofield and his Consulting Editors included notes which provide a scholarly perspective on the whole of the Bible.[207] They express much of what this chapter is about.

"The greater covenants of God ... and their relation to each other and Christ [are] made clear."

"The Dispensations are distinguished, exhibiting the majestic, progressive order of the divine dealings of God with humanity, "the increasing purpose" which runs through and links together the ages, from the beginning of the life of man to the end in eternity ...."

"... no particular portion of Scripture is to be intelligently comprehended apart from some conception of its place in the whole [Bible]. For the Bible story and message is like a picture wrought out in mosaics: each book, chapter, verse, and even word forms a necessary part and has its own appointed place. It is, therefore, indispensable to any interesting and fruitful study of the Bible that a general knowledge of it be gained."

"... The Bible forms one continuous story—the story of humanity in relation to God ..."

"... The Bible is a progressive unfolding of truth. Nothing is told all at once, and once for all."

"From beginning to end the Bible has one great theme—the person and work of the Christ."

Like the commentaries of so many other writers, what these men wrote refers to some of the basic truths found in the *Mystery of God*, even though they did not identify it as such. To see this more clearly, let's make one paraphrased sentence of their thoughts:

"The greater **covenants** of God, ***and their relation to each other and to Christ***, provide us with the "majestic, ***progressive order of the divine dealings of God with humanity***, demonstrating the ***increasing purpose running through and linking together the ages*** as a story and message, ***like a picture*** wrought out in mosaics, in which **the Bible forms one continuous story.**" And I would add: ***ALL of which pertains to the Mystery of God!***

That "one continuous story" is the story of the revelation of Jesus Christ, and that story is revealed in and through the *Mystery of God*, as concealed in the Old Testament, revealed in the New Testament and fulfilled in *the End*.

We saw previously that in Genesis, beginning with that single thread of the Seed, speaking of Christ Himself, God reveals a seed. A picture could be worth billions of words, but this little thread, this little seed, *the actual Prophetic Cord* Himself, is worth an infinity of words which only eternity can contain!

Let's follow the reasoning here. Christ is seen throughout the entire Bible from the very beginning. We were *"chosen in Him before the foundation of the world."*[208] We were in His heart, mind and plan before the foundation of the world. Is it not obvious? He foreknew each and every one who would become His very Bride. *Christ's Bride has been in the center of Christ's heart from before the foundation of the world!*

With that basic thought in mind, consider the fact that the revelation of Jesus Christ is seen in every book of the Bible. Recently, a friend sent me a copy of Kevin J. Conner's book: *Interpreting The Symbols and Types*. There have been many authors who have provided us with listings of how Christ is seen in each book of the Bible. Among others, Conner's book is certainly on target in that genre. Utilizing Conner's graphic provides an excellent picture of Christ throughout the Old Testament, which in turn reveals the prophetic cord of the *Mystery of God*. Providing the entire graphic at this point in the book is unnecessary. So I will only include Genesis and Exodus here, and provide the balance of the details in Appendix B for your reference. Here is the sampling, assisting us to understand the evidential point.

CHRIST THE MYSTERY IN THE OLD TESTAMENT

THE BOOK	OLD TESTAMENT Chapters	NEW TESTAMENT Chapters
CHRIST Revealed In GENESIS		
The Creator	Genesis 1, 2	Colossians 1:16
The Beginning	Genesis 1, 2	Revelation 1:8
The Seed of the Woman	Genesis 3:15	Matthew 1:23
The Ark of Salvation	Genesis 6:18; 7:23	Luke 2:30
Isaac, Only Begotten Son	Genesis 22:1-19	John 3:16
Joseph, the Beloved Son	Genesis 37:4	Matthew 3:17

CHRIST Revealed In EXODUS		
The Deliverer	Exodus 6:1-8	Acts 5:31
The Mediator	Exodus 32:30-35; 33:12-14	Hebrews 8:6
The Lawgiver	Exodus 20:1-12	Hebrews 8:10
The High Priest	Exodus 28,29	Hebrews 2:17
Passover Lamb	Exodus 12	1 Corinthians 5:7
Tabernacle of God with Man	Exodus 40:34,35	John 1:14

The initial listing, above, carries forward throughout every book in the Old (and New) Testament, revealing Christ in every book of the Bible.[209]

THE MYSTERY OF GOD AND THE REVELATION OF JESUS CHRIST THROUGHOUT THE BIBLE

So here are some questions and answers that should help us understand more clearly what is being said by all of this. Why does Christ reveal Himself this way, book by book? To whom is He revealing Himself and for what reasons? One of the most salient answers to those questions is this: *Throughout the Bible, Christ can be seen as being in the process of calling to and for Himself a special people, His Bride. His revelation of Himself—book by book, covenant by covenant, type by type, and by illustrations provided through certain events, especially in the beautiful picture of marriage—is a statement of His love for and pursuit of His Bride.* How beautiful it is to see Christ's heart and Word in this light.

My personal testimony is that since these truths began to impact my heart and mind, I have found greater grace in daily living and walking in the Spirit. The kind of knowledge and understanding that God offers us always brings grace with it. But God warns, "*My people are destroyed because of lack of knowledge.*"[210] (Couldn't the antithesis of that verse read something like this: "*My people will not be destroyed, if they receive God's intended knowledge?*"

God's written Word is not about what we think He means by what He is saying! God's knowledge is **what He says in His Word, which can only be known by confirmation in His Word, demonstrating what He means by what He says elsewhere in Scripture. And all of this is taught and revealed to us by His Spirit, our Teacher.** This kind of knowledge has life, and only by the Spirit! Yes, I understand that He has given us a mind to think with. God's objective is different than ours. His objective is that we will receive from the mind of the Spirit that which He means in His Word. We cannot merely receive His truth in the "mind," expecting that to be the conclusion of the matter. God's Spirit first communicates with our spirit *and* soul (including the mind and heart together) to meet His objective. It should be obvious that we must learn to keep our conclusions firmly rooted in God's Word. For example, concerning the *Mystery of God*, walk through the following steps of thought to see how God's Word reveals truth while keeping in mind that this is not intended to be an exhaustive test of the matter:

- Why did the Apostle Paul emphasize that *the* **Mystery** [about which this book is written] was hidden and kept secret, since before the foundation of the world?
- Why did Jesus indicate that *the revelation of Himself and His Kingdom* was among the **mysteries** and that these things had been kept **hidden** and **secret** from the foundation of the world in Matthew 13:10, 11, 34 and 35?
- Why did the Apostle Paul belabor with emphasis in Ephesians 5:25-32 that the marriage of Christ and His Church is the **Great Mystery, the Mega-Mystery**?
- What connection does that **Great Mystery** have to the Endtimes?
- Why did Paul and John refer to that same **Mystery** nearly 20 times, identifying it by ten different factors with some 35 distinctive details contained in 13 different chapters in 7 books of the New Testament?

- Why did the Apostle John write about this *Mystery* in Revelation 10:7? In the context of Revelation chapters 10 and 11, he deals with the finale, the finish, the completion, the fulfillment of the prophecies concerning the resurrection, judgment, and rewards of the saints.
- Furthermore, in the context of the seventh and last trumpet in those same chapters (Revelation 10 and 11), John specifically reveals the chronological sequence of those prophesied events.
- Additionally, because the message given to John in Revelation chapters 4-13 is repeated by John in Revelation chapters 14-19, the *Marriage of the Lamb* is also directly linked to the *Mystery* (this marriage and this mystery links with *Christ and His Bride, the Church*, in Ephesians 5:22-32).

From one perspective, the heart of this book can be found in those statements and questions, and the answers to them. Furthermore the answers enable us to understand more clearly the Endtimes. The braided, prophetic cord will bring us to our desired goal in the end. Every thread of the way, we will continually see Christ, as He ceaselessly gathers His Bride.

Imagine with me a trip, as we travel into the Endtime events within the Book of Revelation. There we find the sounding of the seventh and last trumpet, the resurrection, rapture, judgment, rewards, the *Marriage of the Lamb*—and all of this, as the fulfillment of the *Mystery of God*. That fulfillment happens to be *The (further) Revelation of Jesus Christ*. The book of Revelation is so named for a very good reason: *It is the ultimate revelation, the unveiling of Jesus Christ, for all to see. In this revelation, we see Him in great glory at the Marriage of the Lamb!*

Starting from the point of that fulfillment, I want us to travel back through the Bible, all the way to Genesis. As we travel back through biblical history, we acknowledge that because we are New Testament believers, therefore the secret-ness, hidden-ness, and the mysterious-ness of the *Mystery of God* has already been removed—because it has been revealed already. God's title or description of the *Mystery of God*, remains the same until He has completely fulfilled this *Mega-Mystery* at the *Marriage of the Lamb*. In this sense, New Testament saints enjoy a privilege, opportunity, and responsibility, but with no disadvantage to the Old Testament saints. From the Endtimes perspective, as we travel back in time through the Old Testament, we will find that the hints, the markers, the threads, which God had put there, begin to jump off of the pages at us. (One needs only refer to the Conner graph above, to track the obvious presence of Christ from the end of the Old Testament back to the beginning of the Old Testament.

However when we join Adam and Eve in the Garden of Eden, and we then turn around to look forward in time (with all of that yet-to-be-revealed biblical knowledge being hidden from the Old Testament saints' understanding), that secret-ness and mysterious-ness surrounding the

Mystery of God naturally required faith to follow God's way, going forward. Every one of God's people in the Old Testament, from Adam and Eve forward, were confronted with the necessity to walk with God by faith in the face of what we now know have been God's secrets and mysteries during those times. The Old Testament prophets searched diligently to understand but their understanding was limited by God Himself. His revelation of Himself to them and their reception and trust in Him were matters of grace, just as it is today.

It was not that God was playing games with the saints in the Old Testament. Far from it. Their inability to see was only because in His Plan the *fullness of time* had not yet come for certain things to be revealed. He was carrying out His Plan, which did not include the need for them to know more than He had revealed to them at that particular time. Each prophetic thread was braided into humanity's time line as God determined would be necessary. Each additional thread was braided into the prophetic cord for His glory—for their good, and our good too.[211] Their privilege, opportunity, and responsibility was to walk with Him by faith in what He had revealed up to that point and to walk by faith concerning that which He chose not to reveal. To this day, nothing has changed in that regard. There is much yet to be understood in the prophetic near-term future and longer-term. We too, must look ahead, walking by faith!

For instance, it is true that the promise made to Abraham about *the whole earth being blessed through him* was given in Genesis. The question that would remain until the New Testament period was this: *How would God fulfill that promise to Abraham? What would that look like? If Abraham's family was, by God's sovereign purpose and will, the chosen family, then how would God bring the Gentiles into that family and into that nation?* These questions, I believe, are much more important than many in the Church today notice. We should notice.

Before the creation of the world, God had already established His Plan. That plan from its initiation into human history was initially revealed to them, and us, as the **Seed**—who is of course, the promised Redeemer, God's Son, the Word, the Christ! Why then, was the fullness of the central theme of His Plan to be kept hidden and secret as a *Mystery?*

This *Mystery* is a fundamental and pervasive biblical truth from beginning to end. God switched on His floodlight and gave us the New Testament, so that we are able to see what had been previously hidden.

- *Since* we now know that the truths about the *Mystery* were planted in prophecy throughout the Old Testament, and;
- *Since* the *Mystery* reveals that the Gentiles who receive Christ as Savior, are grafted into His family, and;
- *Since Jews and Gentiles* are one-together-in-and-with-Christ, and;
- *Since* the **Marriage of the Lamb** (Christ) with His Bride takes place at the end of the age, and;

- **Since** we know that this **Great Mystery,**[212] which Paul referred to, specifically refers to the Marriage of the Lamb found in Revelation 19:7-8;
- **Therefore,** we are able to see that Christ, **the Seed**, is the very essence and strength of the *Mystery* cord from the Beginning to the End.

In the end, as that multi-threaded prophetic cord reaches its fulfillment and the *Mystery of God* becomes finished, we can know that He is seen in and through that *Mystery* from Genesis to Revelation. He said that He is *The Beginning and the End*. He meant precisely what He said!

God reveals Christ in various ways within the Old Testament. In the New Testament, He was definitely revealed in a human body, which had been foretold in the Old.[213] All of the *Mystery* details, bullet-pointed above, are seen in the analogies of the *"waiting"* and the *"braiding"* of threads-into-a-cord, as referred to in Chapter 5, **WAITING**. Even though the things directly pertaining to the *Mystery* were secret and hidden for God's sovereign purposes, God planted indisputable shadows, types, illustrations, and analogies from the beginning of the Old Testament and all of its revealed covenants, all of the way to the very end of it. This is why Jesus could tell those two disciples on the road to Emmaus after His resurrection, that He is seen in all of the Scriptures.

INDISPUTABLE

If we understand that all things were created through Him and for Him, we will realize the utter preeminence of Christ in all things. This is indisputable, and must be brought to the forefront of our hearts with the most thorough humility.

"For by Him all things were created that are in heaven and that are on earth, visible and invisible, whether thrones or dominions or principalities or powers. All things were created through Him and for Him. And He is before all things, and in Him all things consist. And He is the head of the body, the Church, who is the beginning, the firstborn from the dead, that in all things He may have the preeminence."

Colossians 1:16–18

Those three verses are consequential, when it comes to understanding just how pervasive the truths of the *Mystery of God* are throughout the entire Bible. The Apostle Paul highlights many vital things in this passage:

- All things…in heaven and earth;
- All things…visible and invisible;

- All things…whether thrones or dominions or principalities or powers;
- All things…were created through Him and for Him;
- All things…Christ is before all things;
- All things…in Him, all things consist.

Paul continues without skipping a beat, saying *"And He (Christ) is the head of the body, the Church."* When we take into consideration that the Church is the Body and Bride of Christ, it is simple to see that the Apostle Paul was not just throwing words out to take up space. Paul is saying by multiple proofs throughout his writings, that Christ's bride has been in Him since before the foundation of the world, as far as God is concerned. God has the majority vote on this matter!

From beginning to end Jesus Christ rightly has and will have preeminence in all things, including the **Marriage of the Lamb** to which Paul refers to in Ephesians 5:22-32. Let's keep in mind that the subject matter of this chapter is *The Mystery of God: The Revelation of Jesus Christ Throughout the Bible*. What I am saying is that any time we see Jesus revealed in the Bible, it should be taken into account that His Bride, in His heart, is part of Him. Some might feel this is a bit of an overreach, a bit of a stretch. First, I am not saying that the word bride itself is to be found at every instance where Christ is seen in the Bible. I am saying however, that His bride has been chosen *"in Him before the foundation of the world."* That cannot be denied, nor should it be neglected.

One way of looking at it is to once again see Christ as the *Seed*. Let's remember that a seed contains the DNA for everything that comes forth from that seed. Whenever we read that we are in Him, we can see ourselves in the context of His eternal DNA,[214] His spiritual DNA, in a manner of speaking. We are in Him, and we are one with Him, as He is one with the Father.[215] We have **exactly** the life of Christ within us! He is our life, and we are hidden with Christ in God!

> *"For you died, and your life is hidden with Christ in God. When Christ who is our life appears, then you also will appear with Him in glory."*
>
> Colossians 3:3-4

The principal idea intended, from the above statements, is this: *Because Jesus Christ is obviously, intrinsically, and pervasively seen in the entire Bible, from beginning to end, it is equally true that the Mystery of God is seen throughout!*

Throughout the Old Testament, God was laying the groundwork in every symbol, shadow, type, illustration, covenant, and promise for the eventual and complete revelation of who Jesus Christ is. I am **not** referring to the revelation of Jesus when He came as a man only. That revelation was only part of the unveiling of Jesus. Until Jesus' first coming, the clearest and most profound understanding of it all was contained, hidden in the *Mystery*, much like the life that is hidden in a seed. That revelation was purposefully, but only partially, fulfilled in His first coming but will be further fulfilled in the Endtimes; for when we see Him face to face, we will see the fullest **"*revelation of Jesus Christ.*"** John said, "*... but we know that, when he shall appear, we shall be like him; for we shall see him as he is.*"[216] Certainly so! We shall be like Him because His Bride will finally be one with Him in the fullest sense of His Plan at the *Marriage of the Lamb*. This is not some mystical idea conjured up in Scripture. This revelation of Jesus Christ is exactly that glory, which is and will be known in us when He returns.

Another indisputable example: When referring to the ***shadows*** found in the *Old Testament* (Covenant) and the transition to the prophesied ***substance*** of the *New Testament* (Covenant), the Apostle Paul explained to the Church at Colosse:

> "[Christ] *wiped out the handwriting of requirements* (Old Covenant related) *that was against us, which was contrary to us. And He has taken it out of the way, having nailed it to the cross. So let no one judge you in food or drink, or regarding a festival or a new moon or sabbaths, which are a* **shadow** *of things to come, but* **the substance is of Christ** [revealed in the New Covenant]" (emphases, mine).
>
> Colossians 2:14,16–17

It should not be overlooked that from the beginning of humanity "*God, who* **at various times and in various ways spoke in time past** *to the fathers by the prophets, has* **in these last days spoken to us by His Son** *...*" (Hebrews 1:1–2). God was **definitely speaking** back in the Old Testament, but "*in these last days,*" in the New Testament, He has spoken "*to us by His Son ....*" As the Father said on the mountain of transfiguration, we are to "*Hear Him!*" (Matthew 17:5).

Throughout biblical history, God consistently spoke to us through types, covenants, promises, illustrations, and examples concerning the overarching prophecy of the *Mystery of God*. Let's remember that the fulfillment of the Mystery of God was declared beforehand by God to the prophets. "*... the Mystery of God will begin to be completed,* **as He declared to His servants the prophets.**" Christ, His Bride, and the *Mystery of God* are melded together in the Old Testament, and not just in the New Testament. That statement might raise questions for some. But Jesus, Paul, and John had no difficulty with it. The Old Covenant was filled with *"shadows"* of *"things to come,"* but the *"substance"* was and is always found in Christ. "*For by Him, all things were created that are in heaven and that are on earth, visible and invisible, whether thrones or dominions or principalities or powers. All things were created through Him and for Him. And He is before all things, and in Him, all things consist*" (*Colossians 1:16–17*). I think we can agree those verses cover it all!

THE MYSTERY OF GOD AND THE REVELATION OF JESUS CHRIST THROUGHOUT THE BIBLE

Previously I referred to the meeting between Jesus and two of His disciples on the road to Emmaus on the very day of His resurrection. One of the telling parts of that story was when …

*"… He said to them, 'O foolish ones, and slow of heart to believe in **all that the prophets have spoken!** Ought not the Christ to have suffered these things and to enter into His glory?' And beginning at Moses (Genesis) and all the Prophets, **He expounded to them in all the Scriptures** the things concerning Himself"* (emphasis and parenthetical insertion mine).

Luke 24:25-27

Jesus said that He *"EXPOUNDED TO THEM IN ALL THE SCRIPTURES."* And what was it that he expounded to them? He expounded *"the things **concerning Himself.**"* Yes, "all the Scriptures … concerning Himself." This cannot be repeated too strongly. Once we understand what Jesus was saying, awe should rise in our hearts and praise should flow out!

If I were texting on my smartphone, instead of typing on my computer, the capitalized, emboldened words, above, would be considered **SHOUTING**, as far as the rules of texting etiquette are concerned. The writing of this book is obviously not in the form of texting, but I admit that I am still SHOUTING. These are glorious truths, worth shouting about.

Much of what we accomplish with social communication is quite useful. Thankfully, it's not completely a generational thing. I understand that SHOUTING may not conform to good book writing etiquette. If you are under forty years of age, my comment about SHOUTING may be one of the more fun side notes in this book. If you are among those who simply do not text, because it is just one more new-fangled and unnecessary facet of technology, I can appreciate that you may find this whole paragraph to be a complete waste of space. I can't help but ask: When was the last time you and I stepped up and texted our grandchildren? I'm **SMILING**—and yes, I'm **SHOUTING** about **SMILING**, too!

What is definitely not a waste is the fact that Jesus *"expounded to them in **all the Scriptures**"* about Himself. Is He, or is He not, revealed in *"all the Scriptures?"*

The only reason we may not have seen it this way before is likely because we have failed to see it through the lens of the *Mystery of God*. In His wisdom, God foretold and **connected** this truth throughout the Bible for His own glory. I say for His own glory because God is glorified when He foretells and then fulfills what He foretold.[217]

Like Monday morning quarterbacking, we can now look back over our shoulder through the historical record in the Bible. We are privileged to see many things in the Old Testament that even the prophets did ***not fully understand***[218] even though they were the ones who were used by God to give us these prophecies in the first place. As New Covenant believers, we have many advantages in our walk with God, like the joy of unfettered understanding of the hundreds of prophecies fulfilled in Jesus Himself, in His first coming; and the fulfillment of some of the prophecies in our current times, such as when Israel became a nation again. When Jesus spoke of the *"mysteries of the kingdom"* in Matthew,[219] we see Him connecting Himself directly to those very mysteries. Those mysteries are dominated by one great mystery, the *Mystery of God*[220] since that *Mystery* is called the *Great Mystery*, or the *Mega-Mystery*.

As the doors of the New Testament swung open, the time had come to declare and explain *the Mystery*, so that they, and we, would understand it, and be guided in the light of it. Such guidance was much needed because the *Mystery of God* answered many of the then-present complications in the historical relationship between Jews and Gentiles. Now that the two were brought together as one in Christ, those practical complications had to have practical solutions for daily interaction and understanding. God did not leave them or us to chance. Nevertheless, as important as it was to know how to function together back then, and even though the *Mystery* gave guidance and answers to many complications at that time, we must not lose sight of the crowning fulfillment of the *Mystery*, which was and is yet to be completely fulfilled.

Just because the Holy Spirit **revealed** the *Mystery* to the Apostle Paul, this did not mean that the *Mystery* had been, therefore, instantly and completely ***fulfilled*** or ***finished***. By knowing the purpose of and then the beginning and completion of the *Mystery of God*, we will be able to more clearly understand the *"times and seasons"* of the rapture and Christ's second coming, along with other principal events of the Endtimes. *The Revelation of Jesus Christ Throughout the Bible*, as seen in this chapter, is intended for us to see Christ and His Bride in a new light. This enlightened view of Him comes through that braided, multi-threaded, unbreakable, prophetic cord, the *Mystery of God*.

Let's allow the Word of God to further unveil the *Mystery of God* to us, as we peer deeper into the amazing and humbling relationship between **The Lamb and His Bride**.

Chapter Sixteen Notes

[205] Limbaugh, The Emmaus Code: Finding Jesus in the Old Testament, (Limbaugh 2015), 6.

[206] Byers, Marvin, *Six Days and A Day*, (Shippensburg, PA., Treasure House, 1995), 240.

[207] The Scofield® Reference Bible, Copyright 1909, 1917, copyright renewed, 1937, 1945 by Oxford University Press, Inc., p. iii-vi.

[208] Ephesians 1:4.

[209] See Appendix B for the remainder of this graphic illustration, Leviticus through Malachi. Additionally, I encourage the reader to purchase a copy of the book, *Interpreting the Symbols and Types*, by Kevin Conner. http://citychristianpublishing.com/collections/all-resources/products/interpreting-the-symbols -and-types; or call 1-800-777-6057. Please note that the title for this graphic (*Christ the Mystery in the Old Testament*) is mine, and not that of Kevin Conner or City Christian Publishing.

[210] Hosea 4:6; Ephesians 4:29-30.

[211] Hebrews 11:39-40; 2 Peter 3.

[212] Ephesians 5:32.

[213] For example, Psalm 40:6-8; referred to in Hebrews 10:5-7; and Isaiah 9:6-7.

[214] A few examples of "in Him": Ephesians 1:4,7,10,11,13. There are many more throughout Paul's letters, and in Jesus' prayer in John 17.

[215] John 17:20-23.

[216] 1 John 3:2.

[217] Isaiah 42:8–9.

[218] 1 Peter 1:12.

[219] Matthew 13:10.

[220] Revelation 10:7; Ephesians 5:32.

PART IV

THE LAMB AND HIS BRIDE

Jesus is going to get married. His wedding is called *The Marriage of the Lamb*. "*And I heard, as it were, the voice of a great multitude, as the sound of many waters and as the sound of mighty thunderings, saying, "Alleluia! For the Lord God Omnipotent reigns! Let us be glad and rejoice and give Him glory, for the Marriage of the Lamb has come, and His wife has made herself ready*" (Revelation 19:6–7).

Perhaps unintentionally, concerning His wedding, we disregard Jesus' already demonstrated passion for His bride on the cross! In fact, wouldn't you agree that the very words *"Jesus' feelings"* are not words that come out of our mouths often, if ever? It's not that Jesus is *thin-skinned* (in today's vernacular). The Spirit of Christ can be grieved; do we not know this? (See Ephesians 4:30). Imagine Jesus, our Bridegroom, sitting down with us to discuss the *Marriage of the Lamb,* and we sit there distracted, disinterested, and therefore, disrespectful and rude. Do we not know that the angels and others in heaven, who are before the throne of God right now, are excitedly awaiting the *Marriage of the Lamb*. In Revelation 19, as we see His *Marriage* being announced prophetically, all of heaven breaks out in loud shouts, singing, and praise. Why? Because they know just how much this means to Him, and for us.

Maybe we don't express our disregard with our mouths, but if we never teach, preach or talk about His upcoming *Marriage*, how can we sincerely claim that we care about what He cares about? Does the Church seem to care today? When was the last time you heard teaching or a sermon strictly about the *Marriage of the Lamb?*

I am making much about this because of how much Jesus cares about His own wedding. He has been in preparation for it for a long time humanly speaking, and for eternity in His heart and mind! Didn't He say to His disciples just before the cross, "*I go to prepare a place for you?*" (John 14:2). Doesn't the Book of Hebrews tell us that both Old and New Testament saints "*look for a city, whose builder and maker is God?*" (Hebrews 11:10). Isn't that city ultimately called the "*New Jerusalem?*" (Hebrews 12:22). Isn't the "*New Jerusalem*" also called the "*Lamb's wife?*" (Revelation 21:9-22:5). Yes, yes, yes, and yes!

So who is this Bride, this Wife of Christ? In Part IV, I seek to answer that question and others, such as *Does God have two wives: Both Israel and the Church?* And I provide further insight into the chronology of Revelation, especially the timing of the rapture of the saints. We will expand our understanding of the relationship of the *Mystery of God* to the *Marriage of the Lamb*.

If you fail to understand the relationship of the *Mystery* to the *Marriage*, along with the timing of the *Marriage of the Lamb*, you cannot understand the Book of Revelation! The lack of understanding about these things is key reason Christians read Revelation, and then give up trying to understand it. But I want to encourage you: Don't give up! You are about to learn a truth that will greatly encourage you. I want to see with you another way in which Jesus the Bridegroom sees His bride: **THE LAST EVE and THE GREAT MYSTERY.**

Chapter 17

THE LAST EVE AND THE GREAT MYSTERY

"And so it is written, 'The first man Adam became a living being.' The last Adam [Jesus] became a life-giving spirit."

1 Corinthians 15:45

"... Adam ... is a type of Him [Jesus] who was to come ...."

Romans 5:14

The First Adam and the Last Adam

There is a **first Adam**, and there is a **last Adam**.[221] "The first man Adam became a living being." "The last Adam became a life-giving spirit" (1 Corinthians 15:45). "... Adam ... is a type of Him [Jesus] who was to come ..." (Romans 5:14). When the Apostle Paul wrote about this, he knew full well the amazing truths he was revealing. He plainly indicated that this is a "type," a "picture." One of the amazing things to me, is not only that the first Adam is a "type" of the last Adam, Christ; rather, by simple deduction, we know that the **first Eve** is a "type" of the **last Eve**. We've all read of the **first Eve** in the Garden of Eden, but have we ever noticed that the **"last Eve,"** the Church, who is betrothed as the very bride of Christ, will be seen in a "Garden" setting, when God makes a "new heaven and a new earth?"

NOTE: From Revelation 21:9 - 22:5, the entire passage is in the context of the Bride/Wife of Christ.

> *"'Come, I will show you the bride, the Lamb's wife.' And he ... showed me the great city, the holy Jerusalem, descending out of heaven from God, having the glory of God ... And he showed me a pure river of water of life, clear as crystal, proceeding from the throne of God and of the Lamb. In the middle of its street, and on either side of the river, was the **tree of life**, which bore twelve fruits, each tree yielding its fruit every month. The leaves of the tree were for the healing of the nations."*
>
> Revelation 21:9–11; 22:1-2

Sound familiar? It should. The Garden of Eden where the first Adam and the first Eve resided is a picture, a type, of where the last Adam and the last Eve will reside.

The connections between the first Eve and the last Eve are further revealed in this statement by the Apostle Paul when he wrote to the church at Corinth:

> *"For I am jealous for you with godly jealousy. For I have **betrothed you to one husband** that I may **present you as a chaste virgin to Christ**. But I fear, lest somehow, **as the serpent deceived Eve** by his craftiness, so **your minds may be corrupted** from the simplicity that is in Christ."*
>
> 2 Corinthians 11:2–3

Whose minds might be corrupted? The Eve, the last Eve, who is called the Church of Jesus Christ, His bride.

To affirm this truth, consider the relationships between these two pairs of two and their two separate marriages. While there are many parallels, I want to see with you only one for now, which is at the heart of the issue.

Eve was deceived by Satan when she chose to eat of the forbidden fruit of the tree of the knowledge of good and evil.

> *"And **Adam was not deceived**, but the woman being deceived, fell into transgression."*
>
> 1 Timothy 2:14

Not only was Adam *"not deceived,"* he made a conscious decision to identify with his wife Eve in her condition. The issue is not that Adam was better than Eve since she was deceived and he was not! The opposite would be truer. The fact that he consciously and willfully chose to disobey God is obviously worse. The Scripture does not say that *by one **woman** sin entered into the world*. It says that sin entered the world by one **man's** sin. What then is the message God has given us here? Adam and Eve both sinned against God.

Perhaps, you have heard the joke some men tell. It goes something like this: *Well, if Eve—the woman—hadn't failed, we wouldn't be in this mess.* Of course, women have their response ready to defend themselves from such things. They say: *If Adam—the head of the home—had fulfilled his responsibility given to Him by God, Eve would have been protected from the serpent's temptation, and she wouldn't have been deceived in the first place.* If Adam was not deceived—and *he wasn't*, then why didn't he help Eve avoid being deceived? While we guys might joke, saying that Eve was responsible for the problems, the fact that Adam was responsible before God as the "head" of his wife is obviously not a joking matter! Eve transgressed, **having been deceived**. About that there is no question. Adam transgressed, but he did so, not having been deceived. He did what he did, knowingly. *"... through one man [Adam] sin entered the world, and death through sin ..."* (Romans 5:12).

But then there's the rest of the story: *"... **Adam ... is a type of Him** [Jesus] **who was to come** ..."* (Romans 5:14). What does God mean when He says that Adam is a *type* of Jesus? They are similar in type, and that similarity is indispensable for the message God is giving us; keeping in mind that there are differences also, as is usually true with types.

In Romans 5:15–17 we read more about this *type*. I would encourage taking the time to understand this classic statement by the Apostle Paul. It is somewhat complicated so let's not fly through it. Let's read with meditative intentionality, and we will get through it just fine. To assist, I have inserted bracketed wording for easier understanding.

"But the free gift [of eternal life, which came through the "last Adam, Jesus Christ"] ***is not like the offense*** [the sin of the "first man Adam"]. *For if by the one man's offense* [Adam's offense] *many died, much **more the grace of God and the gift by the grace** abounded to many* [which came through] **the one Man, Jesus Christ. And the gift** [which came through the last Adam, Jesus Christ] **is not like that which came through the one who sinned** [the first man Adam]. *For the judgment which came from one offense* [of the first Adam] *resulted in condemnation,* **but the free gift which came from** [the last Adam, Jesus, who became sin for us, due to the] **many offenses** [of every human who ever lived; His having paid for those offenses of sin] **resulted in justification. For if by the one man's offense** [the first Adam's offense] **death reigned through the one** [the first Adam], **much more those who receive abundance of grace and of the gift of righteousness will reign in life through the One, Jesus Christ** [the last Adam]."

What we are seeing in these verses is this. Even though it is clearly stated that the *"first man Adam"* was a type of the *"last Adam"* (Christ), the use of a type of comparison is an acknowledgment of the fact that the comparison is intended to go only so far in explaining the comparisons between Christ and Adam. But that which is given to us as a type is precisely where we find an astounding picture of what Jesus has done for His Bride.

What did Jesus do that made Him to be the last Adam? After all, Jesus never sinned or trespassed like the first Adam did. Obviously the entire Bible makes it clear that Jesus did not sin. Hebrews 4:15: Jesus *"was in all points tempted as we are, **yet without sin** ...."* What then is so important about this type?

After we look at the similarities of the type, things are seen to be extremely different in the comparison, which again is the point Paul makes. The picture of what happened with Jesus, as He took upon Himself the sins of humanity, is so horrible and so radical that only God could possibly explain it. I want to see with you that what Jesus did in identifying with His Bride made His personal circumstance far worse than that of the first Adam.

Rather than leaving Eve alone in her fallen condition, Adam joined her where she was. Some have condemned Adam for his foolish and weak choice. They say he succumbed to Eve's choice. Might I say that it depends on what God is saying about it all. Perhaps there is a much deeper truth and message here than we may have thought.

First of all, Adam's sin cannot be condoned. Nevertheless from a different perspective, Adam's choice was far from being foolish and weak. In one sense, it was one of the greatest demonstrations of love that any husband could have for a wife. He literally laid down his life for her! He knew what he was doing.

What was he doing? Imagine this picture. Eve is deceived by Satan, and she eats of the fruit. Adam's mouth drops open in horror, because he knows that she will die. After all God had made that clear from the beginning. What, then, was Adam to do? In one sense, it's quite simple. He could have said to himself, *Adam, don't eat! You will sin, and you'll die too.* But what does he do instead? I can see him staring at Eve, as she turns to him and offers him the fruit from which she had already eaten. And rather than him looking at the fruit, he keeps his eyes locked onto her eyes. His eyes are eyes of love, compassion, care, concern, and a desire for togetherness, oneness. I'm imagining, speculating that he never once looked at that fruit as he reached out to take it. In his heart was both a deep, painful sorrow, along with the joy of his desire for being one with her. This is a type, though not an exact picture of what Jesus did for His Bride, the Church. I think it is as close as can possibly be pictured from the human perspective, yet with an eternally important difference.

Jesus Christ, our Savior, *the last Adam,* did something even more drastic than *the first Adam* in order to identify with His Bride; and He did so unselfishly for her benefit! Here's what that looks like. We know that Jesus loves humanity and that His love has been active since before the creation and continues to be active in all of his dealings with humanity. Jesus proved His love, God's love, by His ultimate, personal sacrifice. The Bible shows us that His personal sacrifice is pictured in the Garden, when God replaced Adam and Eve's fig leaf clothing with the skin of an animal. The picture of Christ's sacrifice is seen in the sacrifice of that animal; its blood being shed to make their ***covering*** possible. That picture, that type, that shadow, could *"never take away sin,"* just as the blood of bulls and goats under the law of Moses could not. All of these things were necessary shadows.

"And every priest stands ministering daily and offering repeatedly the same sacrifices, **which can never take away sins.** *But this Man* [Jesus, the last Adam], *after He had* **offered one sacrifice** [of His own body] *for sins forever, sat down at the right hand of God, from that time waiting till His enemies are made His footstool"* (insertion and emphasis).

Hebrews 10:11–13

The Last Adam is the Last Lamb

It is not difficult to see that the **last *Adam, Christ,*** can be pictured as the ***"last Lamb;"*** after all, Christ is the *"Lamb of God who takes away the sins of the world."* And, after all, His marriage is called the *Marriage of the **LAMB***. The last-Lamb-sacrifice was foreshadowed in the nation of Israel's story. The lamb had to be sacrificially offered—their blood being shed—year after year. *"But in those sacrifices, there is a reminder of sins every year. For it is not possible that the blood of bulls and goats could take away sins"* (Hebrews 10:3–4). Those sacrifices were a type, a shadow of better things to come, as the writer of Hebrews makes plain.²²² The animal sacrifices could never take away sin. Only Jesus' sacrifice could do that! He is not only the *Lamb;* He is the *Last Lamb,* the only Lamb acceptable to **take away** sins!

How Did Jesus Accomplish Taking Away Sin?

How did Jesus accomplish taking away sin? Before Jesus came into the world, God required sacrifices with the shedding of blood in order to cover man's sin. This has always been God's way, from the Garden of Eve to the cross of Christ. Animal sacrifices had no redeeming power in and of themselves. They were a shadow of the real thing, a type of what was already accomplished in God's mind and heart before the foundation of the world. This is why we are told that Jesus was *"… the Lamb slain from the foundation of the world"* (Revelation 13:8).

Imagine this picture before the world began. There was God the Father, God the Son and God the Holy Spirit sitting in the throne announcing that is it time to "create" the heavens, the earth, and Adam, and then Eve from Adam. The plan was set. It had always been set. Once He had finished creating man, God's brilliant light from eternity-past was, as always, shining on Jesus, the *"Lamb slain from the foundation of the world."* Because the Light was on that Lamb, a shadow was cast into the Garden of Eden, in a manner of speaking. That shadow took the form of the sacrifice of an animal, when the animal's blood was shed for Adam and Eve's sin, as acknowledged by the covering God made for them from that animal.

Eventually that same shadow and type would be revealed in greater detail in the form of the sacrificial system, which God would eventually command Israel to follow.

This specific shadow, along with every other shadow or type given to us in the Bible, was just that—only a shadow or type. They were important messages from the heart of a loving God. Those shadows offered a revelation of Christ Himself specifically designed for that particular moment in time. While it is true that God's light was shining, it is equally true that, for the most part, Old Testament saints were still seeing shadows cast by His eternal Light. But let's not take away too much from the beauty and value of those shadows, because shadows guarantee that light is shining, and that the light has encountered something of substance, which is the reason why the shadow is seen. The shadow is a forecast of the substance. In this case, it is easy to realize that the "substance" is Christ and the light is that of the Father.

Once Jesus came into the world, He, being the "Light of the World," overwhelmed the shadows! The real "SUBSTANCE," the very "LIGHT" of God Himself, the Lamb slain, had come. In Him, there is no shadow or variableness. *"Every good gift and every perfect gift is from above and comes down **from the Father of lights, with whom there is no variation or shadow of turning"*** (James 1:17). Jesus is *"the Light of the world"* (John 8:12).

What did the world see when the Lamb, the Light, came? He was, is, and forever will be, the most beautiful, invariable Light! No matter how you look at Jesus, there is no shadow cast in, around, by or through Him! *"… there is no variation or shadow."* When Jesus moved, only light was seen. Isn't this also why Revelation 22:5 foretells us, concerning our eternity with Him, *"There shall be no night there: They need no lamp nor light of the sun, for the Lord God gives them light …"* (Revelation 22:5).

He came into this world and *"He … put away sin by the sacrifice of Himself"* (Hebrews 9:26). *"… John saw Jesus coming toward him, and said, "Behold! The Lamb of God who takes away the sin of the world!"* (John 1:29)

The above Scripture verses about Jesus' sacrifice tell us what happened, but only a partial picture of how He took away sin. The question remains in need of a more complete answer for us to learn how He accomplished taking away our sin.

When Israel's priest laid his hands on the scape goat, it symbolized the sins being transferred on to that animal. The goat was then sent outside of the camp of Israel. This action was symbolic. It was a type, a picture, a shadow of Jesus' crucifixion outside the gate. (Refer to Hebrews 13:11-13.)

In explaining how Jesus took away sin, there is a particular verse which explains it very graphically. I will confess that while I am able to read the words of this verse, the actual depth of the richness and meaning of these words are far too deep for me. But let's attempt to understand it as well as possible.

*"For He [God] made **Him** [Jesus] **who knew no sin to BE sin for us,** that we might become the righteousness of God in Him"* (emphases mine).

2 Corinthians 5:21

May I ask that you re-read that verse because in the truth of that verse is found the secret of how Jesus was able to accomplish taking away the sin of all people of all time. Also found in that verse is a great truth about the *Last Adam* and His Bride.

Unlike the first Adam, Jesus clearly did not join his Bride by sinning[223] because Jesus *"knew no sin!"* Unlike the first Adam, however, Jesus **did more** than merely identify with His Bride. Rather as I stated earlier, Christ's circumstance was much worse than Adam's circumstance. God's justice, judgment, and wrath against all sin required the only sacrifice sufficient to satisfy God for all of humanity's sin. That was Jesus' own sacrifice of His own body, shedding His own blood, on the cross. The only way to define and see the full picture of that justice, judgment, and wrath is in Jesus' offering of Himself as the satisfactory sacrifice.

*"Therefore, when He came into the world, He said: 'Sacrifice and offering You did not desire, But **a body** You have prepared for Me.'"*

Hebrews 10:5

*"... [Jesus] **bore our sins in His own body** on the tree ...."*

1 Peter 2:24

What was completely and eternally impossible by any other means, that is, to satisfy God's wrath against sin and to reconcile humanity to God, was completely and eternally accomplished by means of Jesus going beyond the inadequate shadows and types seen under the Old Covenants. Unlike the first Adam, we see the fullest degree of Jesus' sacrifice: *"For He [God] made **Him** [Jesus] who knew no sin to BE sin ...."*

When we unpack that verse, we see the incredibly beautiful, yet indescribably horrific, thing Jesus suffered. He didn't just die for our sin. He actually **BECAME SIN!** It was God Himself who *"made Him to BE sin."* That is *how* Jesus accomplished what He did on behalf of the last Eve, His Church, His Bride!

"... He humbled Himself and became obedient to the point of death, even the death of the cross. Therefore, God also has highly exalted Him and given Him the name which is above every name ...."

Philippians 2:8–9

THE INCREDIBLE KEY

In order to satisfy God for the payment for our sin, our Lord Jesus Christ had to experience becoming sin itself! He was seen as sin itself in God's eyes, and so much so that God turned His back on His own Son! As a result, the Son cried out on the cross, *"My God, my God! Why have You forsaken Me?"* (Mark 15:34) It had to be so. Otherwise you and I would have zero hope of coming near to God. It was specifically because the wrath of God's judgment was poured out onto Jesus on the cross that God's judgment is no longer against the one who believes and receives Him as their Savior, because of what He did and Who He is. This is why John 3:36 reads, *"Whoever believes in the Son has eternal life, but whoever rejects the Son will not see life, for God's wrath remains on him."* (John 3:36, NIV84).

God was indeed satisfied with Jesus becoming sin, paying the price for our sin, and thereby, reconciling the world to God through the offering of His body and the shedding of His own blood! Oh, what a Savior! How *"unsearchable are the judgments and His ways past finding out,"*[224] and how rich are the *"good and perfect gifts"* Christ's Bride has received, through her Bridegroom, Jesus Christ, the Lamb slain before the foundation of the world?[225]

Move over first Adam! The *Last Adam* has arrived! Praise God! *"And so it is written, "The first man Adam became a living being. The last Adam became a life-giving spirit"* (1 Corinthians 15:45). The life He, the last Adam, gives is like none other—it is eternal life. But it came at a great price. This is precisely why the Scripture says that **His bride is His purchased possession.**

Eve ate of the forbidden fruit first, having been deceived. Adam could have said no. But at that moment, those two who had been "one" since they were created, became distinctly, spiritually, separated. When Eve initially ate of the fruit, she had transgressed, but at that moment Adam had not. He was then faced with a decision. What was he going to do! The choice he made brought the two of them together again; but they were now together in their fallen, sinful condition. Even though the separation from each other ended, their separation from God began. Therein is the problem. The solution was planned before the foundation of the world. The last Adam (Christ) was called upon by God to save the last Eve (Christ's bride).

Our last Adam, the Church's Bridegroom, truly is the Savior of His Bride which is the Church, just as Paul stated. In admonishing Christian husbands to love their wives, Paul records the Holy Spirit's glorious picture of all of this in Ephesians 5. That message, that vital message, includes the commonly applied admonition to Christian husbands and wives, to love and respect one another. But that passage is first and foremost about Christ's marriage to His Bride, the Church. What does Paul say?

"Husbands, love your wives, **as Christ loved the Church and gave himself up for her…** *This is a GREAT MYSTERY, but I speak concerning Christ and the Church."*

Ephesians 5:32

The Great Mystery and the Last Eve

We have seen that the last Adam is Christ Himself, and therefore, we are able to see Christ's bride as the last Eve.[226] We, this *last Eve*, had sinned. We were in need of a Savior. In keeping with this picture or type, we have seen that the Church's Bridegroom has more than *identified* with His Bride; He *became sin* on her behalf to redeem her!

How interesting and important it is that Paul writes about the *Mystery* in the same context as the *"first man, Adam"* and the *"last Adam."* Only six verses later, in that same discussion of the last Adam, Paul continues the discussion, directly and contextually linking it to the *Mystery*. And it is this Mystery which is specifically linked to the *last trumpet* and the *resurrection*. Paul makes sure that we get the point, by making that linkage in 1 Corinthians 15:45-52.[227] The *Mystery* in 1 Corinthians is the same mystery as the *Great Mystery* to which Paul referred in Ephesians.

"Behold, I show you a Mystery. We shall not all sleep (die), but we shall all be changed … at the last trumpet … [which is when] *the dead will be raised …."*

1 Corinthians 15:51-52

And then, this in Ephesians 5:

"… the two shall become one flesh. This is a Great Mystery, but I speak concerning Christ and the Church." (emphasis mine).

Ephesians 5:25-27, 31–32

How do we know that this first Adam, last Adam, the *Mystery*, the last trumpet, and resurrection are the same subject matter as that of Ephesians 5, where He talks about the marriage of Christ to His Bride, the Church? There are three connecting reasons, at minimum, which should not be overlooked in understanding this truth: 1) the subject of the *Mystery* is exactly and contextually, found in both places (the Bible interprets the Bible); 2) the *Marriage of the Lamb* is the Marriage of the last Adam and the Church, His Bride, who is the last Eve. It is introduced in both places in context; and 3) In Revelation 10 and 11, in the context of the trumpet, we find the same things; that is, the *Mystery*, the last trumpet, and the resurrection. As we have seen, these factors have inseparable direct links to numerous other factors concerning the *Mystery*, all of which are braided together as a multi-threaded, unbreakable, prophetic cord.

Often today's pastors teach and preach with the goal of making the Bible applicable to daily living. The Bible says "such and such," and this can be applied like "such and such." It is as though the practical application of God's Word as affecting "our behavior" is the goal of preaching. The pendulum of applicational Bible teaching has swung so far to the extreme of practicality that we are guilty of failing to see the Word of God from the perspective of God's supreme and primary purposes in those same Bible passages. There is no better example of this than the "husbands and wives" discussion in Ephesians 5:22-32. It is indeed practical for us to teach truths from that passage as it relates to the relationship between Christian husbands and wives. But, we are told in no uncertain terms that the ***supreme and primary*** purposes for this passage is about the ***great, "mega" Mystery, concerning Christ and the Church*** [His Bride]. It's about the relationship and the preparation of the Bride of Christ for the Marriage of the Lamb! Yet, too often, this is not even mentioned. We are practical, which is good. But, there's an old saying, which goes like this: *Good, better, best; never let it rest, until the good is better, and the better is best! In this scenario, Christ is best!*

Without His heart's passion and eternal perspective, our practical teaching can be like feeding the flock processed fast foods. This can result in draining the spiritual nutrition out of the food the sheep are being fed. Application is good and necessary as pastors attempt to get their message across for daily living. But if the sheep are not fed the ***spiritual meat***, which includes the sure and confirmed Word of Prophecy, then the sheep will attempt to look good, but they will not understand the ***spiritual meat***. God's Holy Spirit can take out our heart of stone, replace it with a heart of flesh, and write His laws on our heart. This would allow Christ's life to be what is seen in and through our lives, as lived out from the heart and not from rules, or applications of those rules by human determination and mandate. The Holy Spirit can and does use His Endtime prophetic Word to empower us so that we will not "cast off restraint." The lack of teaching and preaching in most churches today, especially as it relates to the "*sure, confirmed word of prophecy,*" stands as an indictment and reason as to why the Church is spiritually failing without even knowing why we are failing.

It is a bit disheartening when pastors and teachers make every effort to make the Bible practical and applicable to our daily lives, without feeding their flock God's ever-present spiritual value and meaning in this eternally important passage. Again it must be said that practical application of the Word of God is so pervasive today that is as though the earthly practicalities of God's Word are the end of all ends.

Similar to the American diet of nutritionally-drained food, Christians, in general, are crying out for healthy Biblical food. In many cases, they don't know what they need, because those responsible for feeding them fail to put the quality of food needed on the menu.[228] They may not even know they are malnourished. "*Where there is no prophetic vision* [understanding] *the people cast off restraint …*" (Proverbs 29:18, ESV). "*My people are destroyed for lack of knowledge*" (Hosea 4:6).

In our all too often it's-about-me Church, we would do well to give our glorious Bridegroom the attention He deserves, rather than grasping for center stage. It's about our Bridegroom, Christ Himself, and His Bride, is it not? The English Standard Version translation says it well: "***This mystery is profound,*** *and I am saying that* ***it refers to Christ and the Church***" (Ephesians 5:32, ESV).

Have we become so set on the issue of the self-improvement gospel, which is at best the milk of the Word, that our teaching can too often leave out the glory of Christ—*the meat of the Word?* If we fail in the *meat of the Word*, we make what we are teaching mundane, earthy and anything but eternal. We are living for eternity. Is there ever a time when sound teaching becomes unsound teaching because we leave out the part that is closest to the heart of God? We must concern ourselves with the warning the Apostle Paul gave: "*… for the time will come when they will not endure sound teaching ….*" Some might suggest that we can become so heavenly-minded that we are of no earthly-good. That too is true. But as I saw it first in myself, and now see it as being far too pervasive in the Church, we have already become so earthly-minded that we are in danger of becoming of too little heavenly-good. Yes, God's Word provides the most practical instruction for this life. And yes, we must learn how He wants us to live in this life. We must have practical instructions of course! But what was Jesus' commanded privilege and gracious offer: "*Seek first the kingdom of God, and all of these things will be added to you*" (Matthew 6:33). Perhaps the Church has swung too far one way, and we must come back to God's complete Word. "*All Scripture is given by inspiration of God, and is profitable for doctrine, for reproof, for correction, for instruction in righteousness, that the man of God may be complete, thoroughly equipped for every good work*" (2 Timothy 3:16–17).

Which brings us back to this: It's truly an amazing insight to see the references to the Mystery as being inseparable; pertaining to the same truths: *1 Corinthians 15:51-52, Revelation 10, 11 and 19, and Ephesians 5:25-32*, along with *1 Thessalonians 4:13-18*. They refer to a set of events, all of which are connected to the *Marriage of the Lamb*. When was the last time you heard someone address the *"Mystery of God,"* as it relates to the Endtimes scenario, especially with a direct connection to the *Marriage of the Lamb*? (The reader will notice that I repeat that question throughout this book. Rather than it being a point of repetition turned to ad nauseam, I appeal to allow that question to impact us in a positive way.)

When the Endtimes is taught, it's as though the word mystery is not in the text at all, or if it is acknowledged as existent, it is not explained. With the inclusion of the truths of the *Mystery of God*, it is impossible to disconnect all of those unbreakable details. **IF** these comparisons, correlations, and connections in 1 Corinthians 15, Thessalonians 4, Revelation 10, 11, 19 and 22, and Ephesians 5 are not collectively the correct way to interpret, then under what circumstance could we ever confidently interpret any comparative passages? How can we possibly come to a sure conclusion about anything in the Bible? How much evidence is enough to find a conclusion on anything? And isn't the process of comparing *"spiritual things with spiritual"*[229] eternally better than the results derived from our limited human speculation, opinion and conjecture? Our own private, human interpretation is precisely what Peter warns us against, while the Bible is replete with instructions to compare passages in order to come to God's intended interpretation.

For example, follow the questions below to determine in your own mind whether or not this list of questions is a legitimate means of comparison. I would encourage a review of the context of each of the verses listed below to gain the broadest and clearest understanding.

- Is Christ identified as the *last Adam* in 1 Corinthians 15:45? **Yes.**
- Since Christ is the last Adam, and since Christ is the Bridegroom at the *Marriage of the Lamb*, does the last Adam then, have a Bride? **Yes.**
- Does Ephesians 5:22-32 specifically and primarily refer to the marriage relationship between Christ and His Bride, the Church? **Yes.**
- Does Paul call Christ's marriage the *Great Mystery* (the *Mega-Mystery* in the original Greek) in Ephesians 5:32? **Yes.**
- In Revelation 19:6-9, does the marriage between Christ and His Bride occur **after** Revelation chapters 10 and 11, where we find the resurrection, the judgment of the saints and the rewarding of the saints, which is **after** the sounding of the seventh and last trumpet found in the Book of Revelation and the entire Bible? **Yes.**
- Does 1 Thessalonians 4:13-18 connect the resurrection with the trumpet? **Yes.**
- And does the resurrection, the judgment of the saints and the rewarding of the saints occur in the context of the *Mystery* in Revelation 10 and 11? **Yes.** Aren't Revelation chapters 10 and 11 specifically within the context of the sounding of the seventh (last) trumpet? **Yes.**
- Doesn't 1 Corinthians 15:51-57 refer to the time of the resurrection of believers? **Yes.** Then doesn't that same context of the resurrection also include the context of the *"last trumpet"* and the *"Mystery."* Doesn't that fact bear sufficient weight to interpret that passage as being the same events referred to in Revelation 10 and 11, where those same three items (the Mystery, last trumpet, and resurrection of the saints) are seen? **Yes, and Yes.**
- Shouldn't the fact that the two passages (1 Corinthians 15:51-57 and Revelation 10 and 11) are the **only** places in the entire Bible that include those three specific details in the context of the Endtimes convince us that these are the same events? **Yes.**

By following that simple series of questions and answers, it seems to me that unless we are blinded by preconceived notions, the obvious conclusion is this: *Christ, the Last Adam, will be married to His Bride, the Church, after the seventh (last) trumpet, the resurrection, the judgment and rewarding of the saints.* The sequential details (resurrection, judgment, rewards) are each directly linked to the Mystery and Marriage spoken of by the Apostle Paul in 1 Corinthians 15 and Ephesians 5, in conjunction with the Apostle John in Revelation 10, 11 and 19.

The previous paragraphs are an important example of interpretation of the Endtimes events.

The Scriptures are replete with pictures, types, and shadows showing truths, which further verify that we are talking about the same subject matter. Notice the parallels between the first Adam and his Eve, and Christ and His own "Eve"—His Bride, the general assembly, the Church.

Let's review the following picture, which is limited to the comparisons between the first Adam (and Eve) and the last Adam, Christ (and His Eve, the Bride), even though there are many other comparisons that could be made in the same manner:

1) *Genesis 3 and 1 Timothy 2:13-14; Luke 4:1-13; Hebrews 4:15*
   a. The *first Eve* was deceived by the Serpent, Satan, but the *first Adam* was not.
   b. We were deceived by Satan, but *Christ, the Last Adam*, was not.
2) *Genesis 3 and 1 Timothy 2:13-14; Matthew 26:50-54*
   a. The *first Adam* could have chosen to *not* eat of the fruit. This would have left the *first Eve* alone in death while Adam lived on.
   b. *Christ, the Last Adam*, could have chosen to *not* take upon Himself our sin. This would have left us alone in death while Christ lived on.
3) *Genesis 3:12; 2 Corinthians 5:21*
   a. Instead the *first Adam* chose to identify with His wife, the *first Eve*, by eating of the fruit she had eaten. In those moments before he ate, he hadn't yet transgressed as Eve had. He chose to identify with her.
   b. Instead *Christ, the Last Adam*, chose to identify with us by taking our sins upon Himself, when He had never sinned. *"But God demonstrates His own love toward us, in that while we were still sinners, Christ died for us"* (Romans 5:8). The picture becomes crystal clear when we realize that Jesus **didn't merely identify** with His Bride. He so completely identified with her that He actually **became sin** for the sake of His bride; yet without sinning. *"For we do not have a High Priest who cannot sympathize with our weaknesses but was in all points tempted as we are, yet without sin"* (Hebrews 4:15).
4) *Genesis 3; Colossians 1:15-18; Ephesians 5:30-32*
   a. The *first Adam* existed before the *first Eve*, and the *first Eve's* life came from the *first Adam*.
   b. The *Last Adam*, Christ, existed before His Bride (the *last Eve*); and His Bride's life comes from Him, the *Last Adam*.

The Incredible Key

The Last Eve, the bride of Christ, is obviously essential to the *Mystery* and *Marriage*, as I have shown here and throughout. If a Christian does not learn to understand the prophetic Endtimes through the spiritual glasses of the *Mystery* and *Marriage*, he or she will be incapable of clearly seeing the Endtimes. Christ wants His bride to see, and He wants her to be looking for His appearing with a passion. It is His desire for us to see *things to come*. As Jesus was preparing His disciples for His death, resurrection, and ascension back to His Father in Heaven, He emphasized His desire and plan for His disciples to know truth, including *things to come*. He said, *"However, when He, the Spirit of truth, has come, He will guide you into all truth; for He will not speak on His own authority, but whatever He hears He will speak; and He will tell you things to come"* (John 16:13). The relationship between the *Last Adam* and the *last Eve* is not only one which begins when a person is born again; it is an Endtimes relationship, completed at the *Marriage of the Lamb*! The *Last Eve*, the *Mystery*, and the *Marriage* are inseparably intertwined in the *"braided, multi-threaded, unbreakable, prophetic cord!"* As we will see in the last chapter in this book, Jesus, the Lamb of God, will *"tie the knot"* in that prophetic cord at His own wedding: *The Marriage of the Lamb!*

From eternity-past to Genesis through Revelation, we can see God's plans moving toward the event of the *Marriage of the Lamb*. When it comes to the greatest wedding of all weddings, can you think of a better wedding planner than God the Father? *After all, once Christ's wedding has taken place, there will never be another marriage!* His wedding will be the last! In Genesis, God showed us the first marriage, when He made the first Adam and Eve to become one. Then as planned, He has shown us the last marriage, the *Marriage of the Lamb and His bride*; that is, the marriage of the *last Adam and the last Eve*! Is it any wonder that one of Jesus' names is *"Alpha and Omega, the Beginning and the End, the First and the Last?* His marriage to His bride has been planned *from before the world began by* **The Perfect Wedding Planner and His Plan.**

Chapter Seventeen Notes

[221] 1 Corinthians 15:45-49.

[222] Hebrews 10:1-18

[223] *"But the gift is not like the trespass. For if the many died by the trespass of the one man, how much more did God's grace and the gift that came by the grace of the one man, Jesus Christ, overflow to the many! Again, the gift of God is not like the result of the one man's sin: The judgment followed one sin and brought condemnation, but the gift followed many trespasses and brought justification. For if, by the trespass of the one man, death reigned through that one man, how much more will those who receive God's abundant provision of grace and of the gift of righteousness reign in life through the one man, Jesus Christ."* (Romans 5:15–17, NIV84).

[224] Romans 11:33.

[225] James 1:17.

[226] I wish to be clear that the Bible does not use the phrase "last Eve." I have chosen to insert it to emphasize a particular truth because it perfectly parallels what God makes clear about our relationship as Christ's Bride to our Bridegroom, Christ, our "last Adam."

[227] Most of us have understood 1 Corinthians 15:51-56 as being a favorite portion of Scripture telling us about the last trumpet, the resurrection and the conquering of "death." But we do not often take into consideration the greater context. In this case, the context includes the "first man, Adam" and the "last Adam." This is important because it brings into the picture the connection of not only the two Adams, but the two Eves. That fact therefore, brings the Bride of Christ (the Last Eve) and the Marriage of the Lamb into the context. The Marriage of the Lamb is inextricably part of the Mystery of God.

[228] Hebrews 5:12–14; 1 Corinthians 3:1–4.

[229] *"These things we also speak, not in words which man's wisdom teaches but which the Holy Spirit teaches, comparing spiritual things with spiritual.* (1 Corinthians 2:13).

Chapter 18

THE PERFECT WEDDING PLANNER AND HIS PLAN

Christ's Wedding Plan Seen in the Garden

"Therefore, a man shall ... be joined to his wife, and THEY SHALL BECOME ONE flesh."

Genesis 2:24

-Christ's Wedding Plan Seen in the Great Mystery

"... For no one ever hated his own flesh, but nourishes and cherishes it, just as the Lord does the Church. For we are members of His body, of His flesh and of His bones. 'For this reason a man shall leave his father and mother and be joined to his wife, and the two shall become one flesh.' This is a GREAT MYSTERY, BUT I SPEAK CONCERNING CHRIST AND THE CHURCH ..." (emphasis mine).

Ephesians 5:29-32

Christ's Wedding Plan Seen in the Marriage of the Lamb

*"Let us be glad and rejoice and give Him glory, for **the Marriage of the Lamb has come, and His wife has made herself ready** ... Blessed are those who are called to the Marriage Supper of the Lamb!"* (emphases mine).

Revelation 19:7–9

The Incredible Key

We have just finished reviewing the most familiar passage of Scripture we hear in our churches regarding the relationship between a husband and wife, which is found in Ephesians 5:22-33. Ironically, as was pointed out, the human marital relationship is not Paul's primary focus and meaning in this pivotal passage. He simply uses the marriage relationship of a husband and wife as the appropriate (God-designed) analogy to help us understand key elements of the marriage relationship between Christ and His Bride, the Church. He gives us a glimpse of the preparations God desires for His bride in advance of the *Marriage of the Lamb*, as seen in Revelation 19.

The insights about Christ's relationship with His Bride found in Ephesians 5:22-32 are profound for the believer, if we see them through the eyes of a bride focused on the Bridegroom. We will see His **Salvation** of His Bride; His **Sanctification** of His Bride, and finally, the **Supper** after His **marriage** to His Bride, whom He calls His body. (The Bridegroom fulfills His betrothed Bride becoming "one with Him".)

1. *Salvation*: "... He is the **Savior** of the body..." (5:23); "... Christ also loved the Church and gave Himself for her ..." (5:25);
2. *Sanctification and cleansing*: "... that He might **sanctify and cleanse her** with the washing of water by the word ..." (5:26);
3. *Supper at the Marriage of the Lamb*: "... that He might **present her to Himself** a glorious Church (Bride), not having spot or wrinkle or any such thing, but that she should be holy and without blemish" (5:27).

But it gets even more intriguing than that. Describing the relationship between Christ and His Bride, He says something that is often completely overlooked or under-emphasized, but which we continuously emphasize in this book. Paul ties Christ and His Bride to a vitally important truth found in just two words. Those two words have deep significance, not only in our present relationship with Christ, our Bridegroom, but for the wedding celebration at the *Marriage of the Lamb*! He describes the marriage of Christ to His Church as the **Great Mystery**. Let's carefully read this significant passage, noting the highlighted text.

> "*Wives, **submit** to your own husbands, **as to the Lord**. For the husband is head of the wife, as also **Christ is head of the Church** [His Bride]; and **He is the Savior of the body** [which, is His Church, His Bride]. Therefore, just as the **Church is subject to Christ**, so let the wives be to their own husbands in everything. Husbands, love your wives, just as **Christ also loved the Church and gave Himself for her, that He might sanctify and cleanse her with the washing of water by the word, that He might present her to Himself a glorious** [Bride] **Church, not having spot or wrinkle or any such thing,*

*but that she should be holy and without blemish. So husbands ought to love their own wives as their own bodies; he who loves his wife loves himself. For no one ever hated his own flesh, but **nourishes and cherishes it, just as the Lord does the Church** [His bride]. **For we are members of His body, of His flesh and of His bones.** For this reason a man shall leave his father and mother and be joined to his wife, and the two shall become one flesh. **This is a GREAT MYSTERY, but I speak concerning Christ and the Church**"* (emphases and parenthetical insertions mine).

Ephesians 5:22–33

The English Standard translation reads like this: "*This **mystery** is profound, and I am saying that **it refers to Christ and the Church***" (Ephesians 5:32, ESV).

I want to see with you more about those two key words. They carry tremendous significance in this passage which is why I capitalized and emboldened them to read as **GREAT MYSTERY**. The Apostle Paul had just said that he was speaking about the marriage of "Christ and the Church," and he called this marriage the **Great Mystery**! The three key elements of this are simple and profound:

1) Human marriage illustrates the marriage relationship between Christ and His Church, His Bride;
2) The two, Christ and His Bride, will become one;[230] and
3) This relationship, including the event of the *Marriage of the Lamb*, represent the ultimate goal and conclusion of the **Great Mystery**!

The marriage of Christ and His Church has been the *Perfect Wedding Plan* made by the *Perfect Wedding Planner*, "*since before the foundation of the world*," that is, from all eternity. "*Known to God from eternity are all His works*" (Acts 15:18).

His marriage plan for Christ and His Bride was before He made Adam and Eve. As we may recall, from the very moment God took a rib from Adam and made Adam's helpmate, Eve, God has been continuously giving us messages in His Word about marriage. But not just any **marriage.** He has been giving us His message about **His Son's Marriage, the Marriage of the Lamb.** It is that same continuous messaging in the Old Testament Scriptures. It has been given to us in the form of types or shadows of better things to come. It is described as a natural (or earthly) event until the heavenly event is fulfilled among the Endtime events of the *Mystery of God* at the *Marriage of the Lamb*. After the Mystery of God is completed or fulfilled, then there will be no other marriage.

It helps to understand God's order of things. In the same context of the "first man Adam, and the last Adam," we are told something very interesting. "*But it is not the spiritual that is first but the natural, and then the spiritual. The first man was from the earth, a man of dust; the second man is from heaven*" (1 Corinthians 15:46–47, ESV). The natural, earthly marriage came first and then will come the spiritual marriage. Why? All of this is done to foretell, to prophecy, the *Perfect Wedding Planner's* prophesied desire and goal: The marriage of His Son!

In both the earthly marriage and the heavenly marriage, the two become one. God's numbers matter. When God says *two become one*, take it to the bank; two does become one! That is the way it is in God's created order. He has always used the natural marriage as a picture of His Plan for His Son and Bride.

Those kinds of pictures are all throughout Scripture. For instance, Noah was saved in the flood, but he wasn't the only one saved. Noah's family was spared. In very practical terms, it wouldn't have made sense to have flooded the earth to rid it of its wickedness, if God had saved only one man, Noah, and not saved his family as well. The only exception to that would have been if God were to start from scratch. But that could suggest that God had made a mistake in creating Adam and Eve in the first place. That idea is out of the question. God doesn't make mistakes. He foreknew that Adam and Eve would sin and that problem was included in His redemption plan. He knew that humanity would become continually wicked and that He would have to destroy humanity—except for Noah and his family. God knew that He had to allow humanity the free will to do what they would choose; otherwise, they could not choose to love (or not love) Him. He knew what all of this would require. Christ knew full well that He Himself would provide redemption through the shedding of His own blood for their sin. No surprises there!

Let's remember the *Perfect Wedding **Plan*** has a *Perfect Wedding **Planner.*** I repeat, "*Known to God from eternity are all His works*" (Acts 15:18). Even in the Garden of Eden, as stated earlier, God had a wedding plan that was just beginning to unfold. And Adam and Eve (and most importantly, the Seed, which is Christ) were central to His *Wedding Plan*. There was no way that God was going to allow His Plan to fail because He is by nature the Sovereign-Savior of the body: "*For the husband is head of the wife, as also Christ is head of the Church; and He is the Savior of the body*" (Ephesians 5:23). From the very beginning, marriage was central to God's sovereign plan for the future of his dealings with humanity. And He is jealous about the future of His Son's marriage.

No Marriage In Heaven? It Makes Sense

In Matthew 22:23-33, Jesus was encountered by the Sadducees, a sect of the Jews. These attempted to challenge and trip him up with a question. The Sadducees didn't believe in a resurrection, but that didn't stop them from asking Jesus a question about the state of marriage after the resurrection. They gave Jesus a hypothetical story. Jesus' answers stopped their mouths, but also astonished the crowds who were listening in.

> *"The same day the Sadducees, who say there is no resurrection, came to Him and asked Him, saying: "Teacher, Moses said that if a man dies, having no children, his brother shall marry his wife and raise up offspring for his brother. Now there were with us seven brothers. The first died after he had married, and having no offspring, left his wife to his brother. Likewise the second also, and the third, even to the seventh. Last of all the woman died also. Therefore, in the resurrection, whose wife of the seven will she be? For they all had her."*
>
> Matthew 22:23–28

Those so-called spiritual leaders thought they had given Jesus a real stumper-question, except for a couple of little complications that Jesus pointed out to them:

1) He explained that **there will, in fact, be a resurrection.** Remember, the Sadducees didn't believe in the resurrection;
2) Secondly, He explained to them that *there will be* **NO** *marriage in heaven!*

Here are His words, which blew their minds!

> *"Jesus answered and said to them, 'You are mistaken, not knowing the Scriptures nor the power of God.* ***For in the resurrection they neither marry nor are given in marriage,*** *but are like angels of God in heaven. But concerning the resurrection of the dead, have you not read what was spoken to you by God, saying, 'I am the God of Abraham, the God of Isaac, and the God of Jacob'? God is not the God of the dead, but of the living.' And when the multitudes heard this, they were astonished at His teaching."*
>
> Matthew 22:29–33

I had mentioned that God is jealous about the future of marriage, both in this world but especially in eternity. God, the *Perfect Wedding Planner*, has been perfectly planning the marriage of His Son to His Bride since before the world began. After He created humanity, the *Perfect Wedding Planner* initiated the process of two things:

1) Getting the redemption story to every living soul after the creation. He did so by every possible illustration, types, example, picture, all of which, in one form or another, are connected to the future marriage of Christ to His Bride; and

2) He began gathering that Bride during each covenantal age from Adam and Eve and on through to the end. The ones He has been gathering as His own are those who believed and trusted Him by grace through faith. Each was connected to God by covenant. Individually and collectively, He has brought them and us into the New Covenant, the new marriage covenant, in which *"He will be our God, and we shall be His people,"* as one, just as Jesus, the prophets, Paul, and the entirety of the Word of God proclaim.

All of this had been the *Mystery of God*, yet to be fulfilled. But things changed, beginning with Christ's first coming, death, and resurrection. It was a New Covenant. That *Mystery* has now been revealed and is waiting to be completed at the end of the age at the *Marriage of the Lamb*.

Why will there be no new human marriages or marriage relationships in eternity? *The ONLY MARRIAGE that will be known or needed in eternity will be the Marriage of the Lamb.* Who will He be married to? His Bride. One thing is certain. Those who did not believe and have faith in Him during this life will not be part of His Bride in the next. Woe to them!

Our focus and our eternal satisfaction will be with our husband, **the** *Husband,* **the** *Lamb of God*. When we are finally with Him, face to face, we will be completely consumed, yielded, and submissive in our relationship with Him. It's pretty obvious in Scripture where our attention will be—on Him and His glory! So much so that He says He will give to us His glory because we are one with Him; His Body, His Bride! Even more amazing to me is that it seems that His attention will be on us.

Some have suggested that the *Marriage of the Lamb* to His Bride is symbolism. The suggestion is that the Marriage of Christ to His Bride won't be a real marriage. How thoughtless and insensitive some can be! How earthly and carnal we tend to be! Are we so bound to this life that we do not understand what reality is, and what the real marriage will be? When Jesus met the Samaritan *Woman at the Well*, engaging her in a simple but profound conversation, one of the most important things He said to her was the explanation of what true reality is.

"The woman said to Him, "Sir, I perceive that You are a prophet. Our fathers worshiped on this mountain, and you Jews say that in Jerusalem is the place where one ought to worship." Jesus said to her, "Woman, believe Me, the hour is coming when you will neither on this mountain, nor in Jerusalem, worship the Father. You worship what you do not know; we know what we worship, for salvation is of the Jews. ***But the hour is coming, and now is, when the true worshipers will worship the Father in spirit and truth; for the Father is seeking such to worship Him. God is Spirit, and those who worship Him must worship in spirit and truth."***

John 4:19–24

So the question is about true reality. Jesus was emphatic. God's reality is Spirit! Whatever else that entails, there is one thing certain. God's personal reality is the supreme reality. Whatever the reality of the *Marriage of the Lamb* will be, that will be *the real reality*. In Paul's instructions to the Church in Colosse, he addressed where our reality is to be. It's not that we don't live in a very real world. Of course we do. However, was Jesus' body after the resurrection like our current bodies? No! It was a "resurrected body", which cannot be affected by death. It's no wonder when he entered the room where the disciples had huddled after the cross, He didn't need to open the door. He simply appeared without regard to the walls or doors! He was on earth, but things had changed. First, when He came for ministry, He came in the natural body; but after the resurrection, He came in the spiritual body, which was unhindered by natural, earthly matter, and in fact, overwhelmed it, since He was in an eternal body!

Our heart's affection currently, however, is privileged to be on another Person and another Place!

"... you have been raised with Christ, set your hearts on things above, where Christ is seated at the right hand of God. Set your minds on things above, not on earthly things. For you died, and your life is now hidden with Christ in God. When Christ, who is your life, appears, then you also will appear with him in glory."

Colossians 3:1–4, NIV84

And what a day that will be! When Jesus came to this earth, He came giving life, abundant life, real life, eternal life. This is because He was a "life-giving Spirit," just as 1 Corinthians 15:45 says.

Throughout eternity, as it is throughout the pages of the Bible, God is consistent with His emphasis on His Wedding Plan for His Son. Using Noah, once again, for an example, we can see the obvious continuation of His Plan in God's covenant with Noah. Most of us realize that the story of Noah is a "choke-point" in history, due to God choosing to spare one family. These are the only people who survived the whole-earth flood. If God had not chosen to spare this one family, humanity would have ended. That part of the story is pretty well understood and acknowledged for what it is. However, there is more to the story than the physical eye sees. The fact that he spared Noah—***and His wife, and his three sons and their wives***—shows the obvious sparing of the *physical line of the physical seed of humanity*. God's mercy shown to Noah, his wife, his sons and their wives was essential when viewed through the paradigm of God's eternal Plan. The physical seed and the spiritual Seed are inseparably ensconced in the story of Noah! Some might feel that this is a bit of a stretch. But to them, I pose this question. Obviously how could Noah's sons have had children without wives? First, and most importantly:

*"Noah found grace in the eyes of the Lord." Then, we read, "Then God spoke to **Noah and his sons** with him, saying: "And as for Me, behold, I establish My covenant with you and with your descendants after you …."*

Genesis 9:8–9

And this is why Peter wrote, numbering the souls who went into and came out of the ark to repopulate the earth:

"… the Divine longsuffering waited in the days of Noah, while the ark was being prepared, in which a few, that is, eight souls, were saved through water."

1 Peter 3:20

We know God's will was the spread of the message of His covenant throughout the earth because it was through Shem, Ham, and Japheth, the three sons of Noah and their wives, that the world was divided and repopulated.[231]

Furthermore the story of Abraham's marriage to Sarah, along with the promised son, illustrates this truth. Isaac and Jacob and their marriages, also speak about Christ and His marriage to His Bride. Isaac was the *"son of promise,"* but that was physical, it was in the natural. On the spiritual side of the equation, Jesus Christ Himself was and is the *"Son of Promise,"* just as the Apostle Paul explained in detail in the Book of Galatians.

Also the beautiful story of Isaac and Rebekah and how they became husband and wife, shouts with illustrative beauty concerning the marriage of Christ and His Bride. There are also Jacob and Rachel; Joseph and Asenath; Moses and Zipporah; the High Priest and the bride; Salmon and Rahab; and Ruth and Boaz. The Song of Solomon beautifully portrays Christ's relationship and marriage to His Bride. And on and on it goes!

One more example: The betrothal between Jehovah and Israel! Why did God call Israel His wife?[232] How does that fit into all of this? After all, does the Scripture somehow teach that God the Father has a wife and simultaneously Christ has a wife? How could that be? The question deserves to be answered. It's a good question, not a foolish one, which is asked by many Christians when they learn that Jehovah had a bride and then we see that Jesus has a bride. The idea of God and Christ having separate wives is weird, mind-boggling and wrong thinking. It is an important issue, which must be resolved. We will get some answers to that dilemma in Chapter 20, **ONLY ONE BRIDEGROOM AND ONLY ONE BRIDE.**

Rest assured of this: *In all of these illustrations of marriages, God was certainly working in the day-to-day lives of all of them, like He is with us. Remember that these are shadows and types. Those references and stories are part of the Perfect Wedding Planner's eternal plan to bring about the Perfect Wedding of His Son to His Bride!*

We will begin to find answers to the amazing truths found in the betrothal of Jehovah and Israel as we read about the **BETROTHAL**.

Chapter Eighteen Notes

[230] Please note that we are already "one in Christ," positionally and spiritually. But just as "death" has been conquered already by Christ's resurrection, and yet, in the future the "last enemy to be destroyed will be death"; so it is in this passage regarding the "two becoming one" in and with Christ. We are His Bride, now and we will become His Wife in the future, when the marriage is completed! (See Revelation 19:7 and 21:9, plus context)

[231] A thorough review of this is outside the scope of this book. But the reader is encouraged to study the migration of Noah's sons' families, beginning in Genesis 9.

[232] Jeremiah 3:14.

Chapter 19

BETROTHAL

*"Now in the sixth month the angel Gabriel was sent by God to a city of Galilee named Nazareth, to a virgin **betrothed** to a man whose name was Joseph, of the house of David. The virgin's name was Mary."*

Luke 1:26–27

What is *betrothal*? Is it *marriage*? Is it *engagement* such as we have today? I want to see with you what betrothal is in the Bible. But first, let's repeat our question from the previous chapter once again. Do God the Father and Christ, each, have a bride or wife? We will answer this question in this chapter and the next. We will see how this fits into the matter of the Endtimes. This is actually a very important issue. One of the solutions to the confusion in the Church about the Endtimes is found in answering this and other related questions. I believe that one of the reasons for the spread of *Division Theology* is rooted in the mistaken idea that the betrothal of Jehovah and Israel has nothing to do with the betrothal of Christ and the Church.

After all, the Bible shows us that Israel was God's betrothed wife. *"For **your Maker is your husband** The Lord of hosts is His name …"* (Isaiah 54:5). *"Return, O backsliding children," says the Lord; '**for I am married to you** …'"* (Jeremiah 3:14). *"'And it shall be, in that day,' Says the Lord, 'That you will call Me '**My Husband**' And no longer call Me 'My Master,'"* (Hosea 2:16).

The Bible states that Christ has a bride, His *betrothed* wife. For many this can be confusing, even disconcerting. It is that confusion which can lead to ideas that often skew the understanding of God's design of things. For instance, if God the Father and Jesus, God the Son, *each* has a wife, does the Holy Spirit also have a wife? If not, why not? If each One has a wife, what does that do to our understanding of the unity of the trinity, the Godhead? Before you flip to the next chapter, seeking to avoid a spiritual headache, please read on. These truths are the aspirin required to get rid of this nagging headache in the Church.

THE INCREDIBLE KEY

The eternally important truths about the bride/wife is often misunderstood. One of the reasons for this misunderstanding is because the truths concerning the *Wife of Jehovah* and the *Bride of Christ* is rarely dealt with in the context of Endtime prophecy study, except to indicate that the bride will marry the Lamb of God. But we must come to understand that our relationship to Christ as His bride, and His relationship to us as our Bridegroom, is at the heart of God's plan for His Son since before the world began. And furthermore, once humanity had been created, God didn't skip over the entire Old Testament to finally reach His goal of gathering a bride for His Son. He began executing the plan of gathering His Son's bride from day one in the Garden of Eden, as we will see.

Consider the ***beginning*** and the ***end*** of God's dealings with humanity. At the very beginning of Genesis when God created Adam, He made Eve from Adam, and at that moment, God Himself introduced marriage. In marriage Adam and Eve became one. This is how it worked: He *created* one—Adam. Then God *created* one, Eve, from that one, Adam. Then He made the two to be one, that is, the two became one in the marital relationship. *From one, God made two; and from the two, God made one.* That was at the beginning of the Old Testament.

Then look at the very end of the Old Testament; what do we see? In Malachi 2, in the Old Testament, as if Christ is appealing to His people about His heart toward His own bride, we hear Him saying through Malachi:

> *"'... Because the Lord has been witness Between you and the wife of your youth, with whom you have dealt treacherously, Yet she is your companion And your **wife by covenant**. But did He not make them one, Having a remnant of the Spirit? And why one? He seeks godly offspring. Therefore take heed to your spirit, and let none deal treacherously with the wife of his youth. **For the Lord God of Israel says That He hates divorce**, for it covers one's garment with violence,' Says the Lord of hosts. 'Therefore, take heed to your spirit, that you do not deal treacherously.'"*
>
> Malachi 2:14–16

What an impassioned plea, by God Himself! That plea is about His passion for continuing what He started in the Garden of Eden with Adam and Eve: *Marriage.* In this marriage He is seeking *"godly offspring."* In order to be what is needed in that relationship, it required that we take *"heed to your spirit,"* specifically because **He made them to be one.** This is none other than the heart of Christ showing up in the beginning and end of the Old Testament with the same message: *I am gathering a bride for Myself for eternity.*

His marriage plan was in Genesis, and then Malachi, the last book of the Old Testament, and throughout the interim books. Then the Holy Spirit turns right around, in the continuation of Scripture in the New Testament, and reveals the first miracle Jesus performed, which was at the Wedding in Cana at the beginning of His ministry. Is it any wonder then, that in the end of the Bible, in Revelation, He concludes with the ultimate wedding: *Christ's own wedding—the Marriage of the Lamb?* In Revelation 20, an angel shows John the very *"Wife"* of Christ coming down out of heaven, as a Bride adorned for her husband.

Are these seemingly little coincidences actually little coincidences? Once we understand the heart of Christ and the price He paid to purchase a bride with His own blood, these cannot be seen as coincidences at all. This matter of the bride of Christ was His Grand Plan for this world—it is, in fact, the **Great Mystery** of Ephesians 5:25-32!

Jehovah's Wife

When we look into the Old Testament, we see that the Scripture refers to Israel as God's **wife**. Was God already married to Israel, or was something else going on there? I repeat. *Does God the Father and Christ, each have a wife?* While this question may not be raised as the everyday, ordinary Bible study question, it is very important to you as a believer. Let's be careful to not yield to the tendency to push away from the intensity of so-called deep truths. Such truths are often "priority-truths" in God's heart and plan. And this particular one is definitely a profound priority-truth.

Figuratively speaking, there is a field of spiritual diamonds to be found in the truths pertaining to Christ's marriage to His bride. The Lord wants us to find those diamonds, those deeper truths! Let's do some digging together. He has promised that His Spirit will help us.

Betrothal or Engagement?

In our culture, we tend to have what's called an engagement period before the marriage. In our western culture, our engagement arrangement has a lot of flexibility, a lot of wiggle room. An engagement is a relationship that announces to others that we *might* marry—or, we *might not* marry. A couple can become engaged one day and decide to call it off for any reason whatsoever, the next day, the next month, or next year. No problem.

But that was not the case among the Israelites, and it's still not the case today in Jewish orthodoxy.

The Incredible Key

> *"Until the time of the actual marriage, the bride–to–be remained in her own family. It was not permissible to betroth her to any other man except by action amounting to divorce, and any violation of the rights established by the betrothal was as serious as if the two persons had been ceremonially married."*
>
> Deut. 22:23, 24[233]

As is recorded in the Gospels, Joseph and Mary were betrothed. *"Now the birth of Jesus Christ was as follows: After His mother **Mary was betrothed to Joseph, before they came together,** she was found with child of the Holy Spirit"* (Matthew 1:18).

Let's not misunderstand this. Mary was indeed Joseph's betrothed bride. Legally, they were bound together, preserved to be husband and wife. The only events that could legally break the betrothal were divorce due to fornication with another person before the marriage; or death. That is why Joseph reacted the way he did when he discovered that Mary was already pregnant before the end of the betrothal period. He was in the state of shock and considered divorcing her, even though they had never come together, physically, nor had the marriage process been completed and consummated. Notice in the following verse that Joseph, before they were permitted to live together (because they were still in the betrothal period), was said to be Mary's "husband." ***"And her husband Joseph,*** *being a just man and unwilling to put her to shame,* ***resolved to divorce her quietly"*** (Matthew 1:19, ESV). What? How could he divorce someone to whom he had not yet taken to his own home in the marriage relationship? This can be a bit confusing to the western mind, but this was not in the western mind when it took place. This was about the soon-to-be birth of the Son of God, the Lamb of God, who would not only take away the sins of the world but who would, Himself, *marry* His own Bride in the future! This is an important story for understanding the whole scenario of the bride of Christ, who is currently Christ's *betrothed wife*. It is not a misstatement or mistake when we read the following words concerning the *Marriage of the Lamb* in Revelation 19:7. As the wedding ceremony is being announced, **but BEFORE the wedding**, we read that the **BRIDE** of Christ is called His **WIFE**, who has made herself ready for the wedding to begin. *"… Let us be glad and rejoice and give Him glory, for the marriage of the Lamb has come, and* ***His WIFE has made herself ready"*** (Revelation 19:7, emphasis, mine). That description is perfectly correct. The *bride* of Christ is the *wife* of Christ! This is precisely because His bride was already **betrothed** to Him as His purchased possession.

A betrothal is **not an engagement**, as we use that term today. Betrothal is part of an actual marriage covenant—a binding marriage relationship, though not yet completed.[234] The moment a betrothal was covenanted, the couple were bound together, religiously, as a very **real** husband and wife in marriage, even though there would be a process to go through, including legally registering the covenant before they would or could live together.

Once the purchase price had been paid to the father of the bride (a sobering and essential act), there still remained the betrothal period to process through. According to the Jewish Encyclopedia, the betrothal period was twelve months, unless the bride was a widow, or the groom was a widower. In the case of the widower the betrothal period was to be three months. The betrothal period was designed to allow the committed couple to put their lives into good order prior to cohabitation, while fully committed covenantally and legally. Pitts Evans, author of *The Wife of God*, and a prolific student of the subject of the *Bride of Christ* quotes Ronald L. Eisenberg's remarks in *The JPS Guide to Jewish Traditions*:

> In Israel's early history, espousal [betrothal] was far more binding than engagement is for us. To be espoused [betrothed] meant that the couple was legally set apart and committed to each other, but they had not yet been intimate. Most people would have treated them as if they were already married [living together in marriage]. There were formal writings detailing the espousal, drawn up by the religious authorities and kept on file. This sacred relationship could only be dissolved by divorce or the death of one of the parties.[235]

Among the things that were put in order was the preparation of a place to live together which was often a room in the home of groom's father. Cohabitation was not allowed until preparations were completed.

Another key preparation was that this betrothal period would provide sufficient time for the family and community to be assured that the bride was not pregnant. Virginity was of great concern to all involved. Betrothal meant that they were lawfully bound in marriage all the way through until the time came for cohabitation. However if it became known that either the groom or the Bride was guilty of fornication, the non-guilty party could divorce because of the evidence.

While this may be foreign and a bit confusing to a non-Jewish mind today, it was not the least bit confusing to Joseph and Mary. They knew full well what they were doing, and were committed to each other in marriage betrothal. This was the standard and accepted practice. So for Joseph to still take Mary to be his wife, especially after he learned that she was pregnant, was a life altering matter, to say the least. He knew that she was not pregnant by him. In that time in history, this complication held the potential of great shame, severe punishment, or even death.

Both Joseph and Mary were in an extremely difficult situation, both spiritually and culturally. Rather than a wonderful marriage, there could have been a very bad ending to their story. After all, as we saw already, Mary was with child (pregnant) before they were free to cohabitate. Joseph had not yet taken Mary to his home to live together. Their betrothal period had not been completed. As further proof that betrothal was as we have described it, the Scriptures tell us that Joseph is called a *"just man."* But why was he called a just man? He was a good and just man because he didn't want to put Mary to open shame, publicly. He determined within himself to divorce her but not put her to public shame. Given all of the facts as Joseph understood them, his approach was that of a good, kind and thoughtful man.

The truth is that it would take a miracle for Joseph to complete the marriage. And that is exactly what happened. That miracle came in the form of an angel sent from God, appearing in a dream to Joseph, to convince him, and to keep him from divorcing Mary. Yes, I said, *divorce*, legally and religiously, before God and everyone else, because that is exactly what would have happened. God in His sovereign and gracious plan needed to make it clear to Joseph that even though Mary was pregnant, she had nevertheless remained holy and pure. The Child in her womb was conceived by the Holy Spirit, and that Child would be the promised Messiah, the Savior. Only then by God's grace, did Joseph take her as his wife in cohabitation (though not in physical relationship until after Jesus was born),[236] just as the angel of the Lord had commanded him in his dream. He finalized the marriage by taking her to himself in his home. *"When Joseph woke from sleep, he did as the angel of the Lord commanded him:* **he took his wife,** *but knew her not until she had given birth to a son. And he called his name Jesus"* (Matthew 1:24–25, ESV).

That process is how a legitimate betrothal works. In this case Joseph decided to follow what God had shown him in his dream; he was to marry Mary.

Having said all of that about Joseph and Mary, I want to see with you how the story of the betrothal of Joseph and Mary can help us with a previous question. Do God and Christ each have a wife? The short answer is no. From the Garden of Eden through to the actual *Marriage of the Lamb*, God (Christ) has always and only had **one "betrothed wife."**

All of the people of biblical faith, beginning with Adam, Eve, and including Abel, Enoch, Noah, Abraham, Isaac and Jacob, the tribes of Israel, David, and the others who believed by grace through faith, along with the New Testament assembly of believers, are together, as one—*spiritual Israel, the Israel of God, the Church, the betrothed bride/wife of Christ.*

In his great teaching concerning Israel and the Church the Apostle Paul made a definite distinction between his *"countrymen according to the flesh"* [that is, natural Israel] and those who were the spiritual children of Israel. Paul said: *"… **they are not all Israel who are of Israel, nor are they all children because they are the seed of Abraham;** But "In Isaac, your seed shall be called." That is, **those who are the children of the flesh, these are not the children of God; but the children of the promise are counted as the seed**"* (Romans 9:6–8, emphasis mine).

The same principle was referred to when Jesus spoke His message to the Church in Smyrna in Revelation 2:9: *"I know the blasphemy of **those who say they are Jews and are not, but are a synagogue of Satan**"* (Revelation 2:9). Someone being born a Jew did not satisfy *the*

BETROTHAL

Jew of Jews, Jesus Himself! He showed us that those who were not *believing Jews* were of the synagogue of Satan.

Furthermore, when Jesus was talking to the unregenerate Pharisees who were part of the so-called spiritual leaders of Israel, they claimed that they were children of Abraham, and therefore, they had a relationship with God. But Jesus responded with strong words. Here's how the story goes.

> *"They answered and said to Him, "Abraham is our father." Jesus said to them, "If you were Abraham's children, you would do the works of Abraham … You are of your father the devil, and the desires of your father you want to do …."*
>
> John 8:39, 44

Wow! Can it be any clearer or stronger! There were those in Israel that believed God, and there were those in Israel who did not; even though they both carried the name of Israel. This troubling fact is also true in the Church today. There are those in our churches who believe God today, and there are those who do not, even though all of them may claim the name of Christ, and lay claim to being part of the Church, and refer to themselves as Christian! In God's wheat field there have always been wheat and tares growing together, awaiting the great harvest at the end of the age as we find stated in Matthew 13:24-30. Only the true wheat will be harvested into God's barn! The tares will be burned! Thus the saying, *Turn, or burn!*

Which ones are those throughout history who make up His Betrothed Bride? Friend, let there be no mistake. God is the same yesterday, today and forever. He does not change. He has shown us over and again in His Word what His Plan has always been. *He has been gathering for Himself a Bride all along. That gathering is His betrothed wife.*

What we have seen in these references is that God's betrothed wife, Israel, was only one of many expressions of the same truth. God's types and examples on earth are representative of the heavenly realities. Earthly realm; earthly marriage. Heavenly realm; heavenly marriage!

From before the foundation of the world, **God had only one Bride in mind: The Bride of Christ**. Though she is betrothed to Him and has not yet been gathered to His Home ("I go to prepare a place for you."), she will transition from being a betrothed bride to being one with Christ at the *Marriage of the Lamb* as His *wife*. It needs to be understood that the bride, being the Church as a body, is not primarily addressed to us as individuals only. The Church though a *"many-membered body"* is still *"one body."*[237] She, the Church, is the collection of the many members of that body. We should not view the Bride of Christ through the eyes of ourselves as individuals only; rather as Jesus views her: His Church, a many-membered body. In that sense, it is not an individually, personal marriage to Christ; rather the gathering of all of the *called-out ones* into *one body, the Bride*.

At the *Marriage of the Lamb*, He will have gathered His Bride to Himself by means of the rapture. *"Then they will see the Son of Man coming in the clouds with great power and glory. And then He will send His angels, and **gather together His elect from the four winds, from the farthest part of earth to the farthest part of heaven**"* (Mark 13:26–27). All saints on earth and all saints in heaven will be gathered to Him in the rapture, and ultimately transition to the *Marriage of the Lamb*. Those who are gathered are both Old and New Testament saints.

From that point forward, His Bride will be completely one *in* Christ and one *with* Christ. This is the point at which it is critical to understand the fact that the *Marriage of the Lamb* is inseparable from the *Mystery of God* —the *Great Mystery*—found in Revelation 10:7 and in Ephesians 5:32; and many other references. One would do well to read and re-read those important passages, in context, to become completely familiar with them.

Relationship By Covenant

What about covenant relationship? Do the biblical covenants pertain to marriage covenants? Pitts Evans speaks to this point.

"In the Old Testament, the Lord often speaks of His marriage covenant promises to Israel. Many of the Biblical authors refer to the relationship between God and Israel in terminology that is normally reserved for marriage. Under the inspiration of the Holy Spirit, they used this language, even though they may not have fully understood that the Old Covenant was always intended to be a Marriage Covenant ...."[238]

He continues:

"In Exodus, the Lord initiated a covenant with the nation of Israel through Moses at Mount Sinai. Many rabbis have taught that this was actually a marriage covenant between the Lord and Israel. A well-known Messianic Jewish writer from the last century said, "Moses brought forth the people out of the camp to meet with God; while Jehovah, as the bridegroom, meets His Church at Sinai. The modern Jewish scholar Ronald L. Eisenberg said, "For the Rabbis, marriage symbolized other perfect relationships, such as those between God and Israel." Rabbinic sages have long understood that the Old Covenant is not a Jewish law book; it is a Marriage Covenant."[239]

Betrothal

Each time God initiated each of His several covenants with His people throughout history, He revealed more and more of His heart, purpose, and plan for those who were spiritually His own by covenant. How many times have we said to ourselves that we are so amazed and humbled due to the fact that God showed us such great mercy by drawing us to Himself for salvation? That is how it was for Old Testament saints when they would discuss the covenants God had made with them. With them there was and is a constant blessing of grace and truth: *"The secret of the Lord is with those who fear Him, And He will show them His covenant"* (Psalm 25:14).

There is a richer and more powerful correlated truth. That truth is found in another verse which was spoken prophetically: *"I, the Lord, have called you in righteousness; I will take hold of your hand. I will keep you and will* **make YOU to be a COVENANT** *for the people and a light for the Gentiles"* (Isaiah 42:6 NIV). Who is *"the Lord"* talking to in that passage? Whoever that person is, God says that He will make that person to be a *"Covenant!"* In this passage, God, the Father, is recording His promise to His Son, Jesus, prophetically.

So when we are told in Psalm 25:14 that God will show the *"secret"* of the *"covenant"* to those who fear Him, He is saying something quite mysterious by calling it a *"secret."* The ultimate meaning of that mysterious promise is that the One who **IS** the **COVENANT** will be made known to those who fear (reverentially love) Him by grace through faith. Those who fear Him with reverential love are being described in marriage covenant terms; His bride! The Person, the Covenant Himself, will be made known to them; that is Jesus will be made known to them. This very fact that Christ Himself is The Covenant is intrinsic, a direct and essential connection, to the Great Mystery. Let's remember that the terms New Testament and New Covenant are the same. And the prophecy concerning God making a New Covenant is where we first learn this promise: I will be their God, and they shall be My people, as seen in Jeremiah 31:33. This is the same New Covenant seen as having been completely fulfilled in Revelation 21:3. This is every bit directly related to the *Mystery of God* and the *Marriage of the Lamb!*

Every one of the covenants was a message, type, picture, sign, or love-letter from His heart, telling humanity through many different means that God was gathering a people for His own possession. He was collecting a body, a household, a family, a nation, a temple, a kingdom, a Church, and a Bride. He was saying, *"Come to Me, all you who labor and are heavy laden, and I will give you rest. Take My yoke upon you and learn from Me, for I am gentle and lowly in heart, and you will find rest for your souls. For My yoke is easy and My burden is light"* (Matthew 11:28–30). How gentle, loving and thoughtful He is with His bride.

Some believe that the bride of Christ is exclusively the New Testament assembly of believers; and that the assembly, the Church, is *only made up of New Testament Christians.* Some even believe that the Jews who become born again today, and who want to please God have to become part of a Gentilized Church to get it right, not that they would overtly or even intentionally call it the Gentilized Church! I want to be clear that I am not putting Gentile believers down or attempting to separate them from those who are children of Abraham. Far from that, I am seeking to explain that the Gentilized Church has by default erred from biblical teaching regarding the way Christ looks at His body, though perhaps not intentionally.

God's plan concerning Christ's marriage, always included every soul who received Him by grace alone through faith alone (in Christ, as He was being revealed through covenants, in types and shadows, etc.), no matter which covenant they lived under from Genesis through Revelation. The blood of Jesus applies retroactively, after His cross and resurrection. Or, have we as pastors, teachers, seminarians, and theologians, just been preaching, teaching and writing these things? Those who were His own under the previous covenants were accounted to Him as His bride-in-*waiting*—**betrothed**! The blood of Jesus Christ that redeems New Testament believers is the same and only blood that redeems Old Testament believers. Without the shedding of Jesus' blood, there is not now, nor was there ever any redemption! All believers, Old and New Testament, are part of what the Apostle Paul called the *Mystery*. Tragically the *Mystery of God* has been missing in so many pulpits, books, Bible colleges, and seminaries throughout the world. The *Mystery is The Key* that God has given to us which was long ago revealed to the *"apostles and saints,"* and about which we need a revival in this area of doctrine to understand how *The Incredible Key* unlocks these truths.

One of the clearest descriptions of the ultimate results of the fulfillment of the *Mystery of God*, the Great Mystery, is the *"holy city, New Jerusalem"* in Revelation 21 and 22:1-14. Keep in mind that one of the fundamental tenets of the *Mystery of God* is the fact that believing Jews and Gentiles became *"one in Christ," "one new man," "one body,"* one Bride. Don't forget that all [believing Jews and believing Gentiles] are included in *the commonwealth* [citizenship] *of Israel*, through His death, burial, and resurrection (Ephesians 2:12-13).

Believing Gentiles became part of the household of God, the family of God, citizens of the commonwealth of spiritual Israel. Those who were born into physical Israel who do not come to know God spiritually, but who are simply Israelites in the flesh, **were not counted** and **are not counted** among the *Israel of God*. Without redemption through the blood of Christ, those who are not part of the *Israel of God* will end in hell like any other soul who rejects the Savior.

When we read the following biblical description, we can see that the bride or wife of Christ is that same spiritual Israel, His Church, which is unequivocally described over and again in these phrases and others. *"But you have come to* **Mount Zion** *... the* **city of the living God** *... the* **heavenly Jerusalem** *... the* **assembly of the firstborn who are enrolled in heaven** *... the spirits of the righteous made perfect ..."* (Hebrews 12:22–24, ESV). Who are those people? Who is *"Mount Zion?"* Who and what is the *"city of the living God?"* Who is the *"heavenly Jerusalem?"* Who is the *"assembly of the firstborn who are enrolled in heaven?"* Who are the *"spirits of the righteous made perfect?"* These are Old and New Testament saints, as defined in Hebrews 11 and 12, from the Garden to the rapture of His Bride! Who can deny this, and why would they deny this?

Is there any doubt that the Church is the spiritual bride of Christ? The Bible is clear, and there is no doubt! Is there any doubt that the Gentiles were grafted into and became part of the spiritual *Israel of God?* The Bible is clear and there is no doubt! As we have made abundantly clear, the Apostle Paul stated over and again that the Gentiles who become born again are grafted into the olive tree of spiritual Israel, and that whole tree (the original olive tree and those grafted in) are described as both spiritual Israel and the body of Christ. Furthermore, and very importantly, these details are intrinsic to the *Mystery*.[240]

It simply must be repeated:

> *"Therefore remember that at* **one time you Gentiles in the flesh,**—*remember that* **you were at that time** *separated from Christ,* **alienated from the commonwealth of Israel and strangers to the covenants of promise, having no hope and without God in the world. But now in Christ Jesus you who once were far off have been brought near by the blood of Christ."*
>
> Ephesians 2:11–13, ESV

It cannot be made more clear, nor should it have to be!

We find insight into the truths listed in Hebrews 12:22–24 and Ephesians 2:11–13 in the Book of Revelation. We see there the holy city, the New Jerusalem, coming down out of heaven as Christ's Wife, a bride adorned for her Husband. Let's keep in mind that before the New Jerusalem comes down out of heaven in Revelation 21 the following events and details will have already taken place:

- The resurrection, rapture, judgment and rewarding of the saints, the Marriage and the Supper of the Lamb and the Millennial Reign of Christ on earth.
- Satan, the antichrist, and the false prophet will have already been thrown into the lake of fire for eternity.
- Every soul whose name was not written in the Lamb's Book of Life will have already been cast into the lake of fire.
- God will have already caused the current heaven and earth to have passed away, and He will have created a new heaven and a new earth.

After all of that, this is what we see next in Revelation 21:

> *"I saw a new heaven and a new earth, for the first heaven and the first earth had passed away ... Then I, John,* **saw the holy city, New Jerusalem,** *coming down out of heaven from God,* **prepared as a bride adorned for her Husband.** *And I heard a loud voice from heaven saying, 'Behold, the tabernacle of God is with men, and He will dwell with them, and they shall be His people. God Himself will be with them and be their God.' ... Then one of the seven angels...came to me and talked to me, saying, 'Come,* **I will show you the bride, the Lamb's wife.'** *... she (Christ's bride; Christ's wife) had a great and high wall with twelve gates, and twelve angels at the gates, and* **names written on them, which are the names of the twelve tribes of the children of Israel** *... Now the wall of the city had* **twelve foundations, and on them were the names of the twelve apostles of the Lamb ...."**

I want to emphasize a few key factors in those verses.

First, this New Jerusalem is prepared as a *"BRIDE adorned for her HUSBAND."*

Second, the angel tells John, **"Come, I will show you the BRIDE, the LAMB'S WIFE ...."**

Third, notice the fact that the "names of the **TWELVE TRIBES OF THE CHILDREN OF ISRAEL**" are on the gates of this image of the **"WIFE"** of Christ.

Fourth, we can see on the **"twelve foundations** [of Christ's **"WIFE"**] are *names of the* **TWELVE APOSTLES OF THE LAMB ...."**

It is an amazing truth that each and every one of those twelve tribes of Israel and each and every one of those twelve apostles were Israelites, both physically and spiritually, all of which are part of the *spiritual remnant.* Those twelve tribes aren't there because of the idea that they were a part of physical Israel; rather they are there because they are part of the spiritual remnant from within physical Israel; they were part of the spiritual "olive tree," which Paul referred to in Romans 11.

No one can make the claim that a person, any person, whether in the Old Testament or the New Testament, has ever become part of God's spiritual family because they are physically born into a specific physical family or nation. Neither a citizen of historical Israel or today's Israel, nor a member of a Church (any Church), nor one who is a member of a specific denomination, and for that matter, any other religion, cult or otherwise, can claim that they are a child of God *due to their physical connection or their particular religious affiliation.* God's children are **only** those *purchased by the* blood of Christ. *"That which is born of the flesh is flesh; and that which is born of the Spirit is spirit,"* just as Jesus said.[241]

It's important to restate that God's covenant with the physical or natural children of Abraham guaranteed certain promised benefits and blessings. Therefore this holds true to this day, not because of their faithfulness to Him, but because of His faithfulness to His own promise; and therefore they benefit from His faithfulness. But that pertains to earthly blessings in the earthly, natural realm. Those earthly blessings were intended to lead them to Christ. Even the Law of Moses was given as a "tutor" to bring them and us to Christ. *"Therefore the law was our tutor to bring us to Christ, that we might be justified by faith"* (Galatians 3:24). To be sure, those physical and earthly blessings which were given to the physical children of Abraham **did not, do not, and cannot save any one— not one soul!** The truth is that the greatest blessing the physical children of Abraham received from God was the privilege of His promise that **the Seed**, their Messiah, would be brought into the world through that physical line of Abraham, that is *"according to the flesh."*[242]

Just as it is with them, isn't it also true that God is faithful in His covenant with those who are His own, and not we who are faithful to Him in His covenant? No one in the New Covenant is registered in heaven as a child of God because that person has been faithful. First of all, let's confess that none of us is always faithful and without fault. Rather it is because of grace alone, through faith alone, in Christ alone, by which we are born again and made to be part of His family. It is not through our own faithfulness! Any faithfulness we demonstrate in our lives is ultimately, nothing more and nothing less than a result of our willingness to allow His faithfulness, by the Spirit, to be lived through us.

In order to rightly connect these vital truths, it is important to understand that something very special takes place when a Gentile is born again. That born again Gentile becomes a **spiritual citizen of spiritual Israel, the Israel of God.** Too often there is a ho-hum attitude among many Christians regarding this glorious fact. Without a spirit of condemnation but rather with a spirit of concern, can we see that such a ho-hum attitude would grieve the heart of Christ? When our ill-informed attitude and words demonstrate an indifference about that which Christ did for us, we are, at minimum, unwittingly confessing a great lack of understanding of the very heart of Christ for His Bride, His Church.

Paul brought eternal weight to bear on this point when he wrote:

*"Therefore remember that **YOU**, [who were] **ONCE GENTILES** in the flesh ... were without Christ, being aliens from the commonwealth of Israel and strangers from the covenants of promise, having no hope and without God in the world. **BUT NOW in Christ Jesus** you who once were far off have been brought near by the blood of Christ."*

Ephesians 2:11–13

> *"Now, therefore, you are **NO LONGER STRANGERS AND FOREIGNERS, BUT FELLOW CITIZENS WITH THE SAINTS AND MEMBERS OF THE HOUSEHOLD OF GOD**, having been built on the foundation of the apostles and prophets, Jesus Christ Himself being the chief cornerstone, in whom the whole building, being fitted together, **grows into a holy temple in the Lord, in whom you also are being built together** for a dwelling place of God in the Spirit"* (emphasis mine).
>
> Ephesians 2:19–22

If we look through spiritual eyes, we will see Christ's heart in those verses. His desire is focused on His Bride, spiritually. Again the *natural* (earthly marriage) speaks of or typifies, the *spiritual* (heavenly marriage). This is why our citizenship is already in heaven. *"For our **citizenship is in heaven**, from which we also eagerly wait for the Savior, the Lord Jesus Christ ..."* (Philippians 3:20). The **betrothal** is already in progress, typified on earth, but spiritually situated with Him *"in heavenly places,"* as Paul explained. *"... even when we were dead in trespasses,* [He] *made us alive together with Christ ... and made us sit together in the heavenly places in Christ Jesus"* (Ephesians 2:5–6).

Now let's turn our attention back to the earlier question: *Do the Father and Jesus each have a wife?*

In referencing the final scenes of the entire Bible, a so-called Gentilized Church is nowhere to be found. The Church is there in Revelation, but a Gentilized Church is not. Gentiles are grafted into the Church, which is the body of Christ, which is His Bride, which is the spiritual *commonwealth of Israel*, the *Israel of God*. It is for a good reason that the so-called Gentilized Church is not seen.

This does not mean that the Church should not be called the Church. Far from it. The word "Church," in the New Testament Greek, means "called-out ones," or "called-out assembly" (called-out by God to Himself). The called-out ones are easy to find, from cover to cover in the entire Bible. They are easily found in the Garden of Eden; it's quite simple because they were the only ones whom God could call out. And He did call them out! He did so, covenantally, in the promise of the *Seed*. God always had believing individuals, a believing remnant, i.e., Abel, Enoch, Noah, Abraham, etc., who made up His household, His spiritual family!

Like He did with Noah at a pivotal time in human history, God ramped up things with Abraham, as is witnessed in the promises He made to Abraham, even though His covenant with Abraham didn't leave the saints of earlier times behind. Not at all! His covenant with Abraham was an awesome addition of promises, threads, to that *braided, multi-threaded, unbreakable, prophetic cord*. God continued covenantally calling out those who would receive Him, all the way down through the historical record to the covenantal nation of Israel. Those from within the nation of Israel who believed the message of God's grace through faith[243] became His spiritual children. To that point, the Apostle Paul leaves no ambiguity.

> *"... For they are not all Israel, who are of Israel, nor are they all children because they are the seed of Abraham; But "In Isaac your seed shall be called." That is, those who are the children of the flesh, these are not the children of God; but the children of the promise are counted as the seed."*
>
> Romans 9:6–8

Christ's future sacrifice would become the price paid for the children of Israel's redemption, though that redemption had been typified through the shedding of blood sacrifices from the very beginning. They would be His purchased possession, and evidence of His continuous threads in the cord.

Furthermore the Gentiles who believed (during the Old Testament) and chose to become citizens of Israel, and who also chose to believe in the God of Abraham, Isaac, and Jacob, were added—grafted in—to those who were already part of the spiritual remnant of Israel. They became part of those who were already called-out ones, *children of promise destined for the land of promise.* The Apostle Paul said in Romans 11 that Gentiles were wild olive branches. God being the master husbandman, personally grafted the believing Gentiles into the natural olive tree, which is the tree of Christ Himself. With that perspective, it is easy to see that all of them are *"in Christ;"* therefore, the entire Tree is Christ. The Gentiles were spiritually assimilated into one household, one body, one temple, one family, one commonwealth, one Church, His Bride.

The Answer to Our Question

The answer to our question is that *there has only always been one wife—one wife, only.* And that wife is made up of only those who choose to trust in Him. All of these were and are betrothed to Him. There is a reason why we see the Promised *Seed* in the Garden of Eden. Beginning at the beginning and throughout, we see the Seed typified in the marriages of the *called-out ones*—Adam and Eve, Isaac and Rebekah, Boaz and Ruth, and the others. Their *natural relationship* typified their *spiritual-faith-relationship.* Again I say, these were and are *betrothed* to Him. We see the *Seed* in the lives of Abraham and Sarah. And their son, Isaac the son of promise, typified Christ the Son of Promise! These were *betrothed* to Him. We see the *Seed* in the life of Jacob, whose name was changed by God to "Israel." Jacob was betrothed to Him. We see the *Seed* in the *called-out ones*, the people of Israel, as they drank of the spiritual drink and were led by the "Rock"[244] out of Egypt to the Promised Land. That Drink and that Rock was Christ. These were *betrothed* to Him. We see the *Seed* in the lives of God's prophets, who were, indeed, *called-out ones*. They were *betrothed* to Him. We see the *Seed* in the lives of each of those *called-out ones* listed in Hebrews 11 in the "Hall of Faith." These were *betrothed* to Him. *"These (the saints listed in 11:1-38) were all commended for their faith, yet none of them received what had been promised. God had planned* [the wedding plan of two becoming one in and with Christ] *something better for us so that **only TOGETHER with us would they be made perfect*** [complete] ...." Keep in mind that the Book of Hebrews was initially written with **Hebrew Christians** in mind, but not exclusively.

Once all of the *covenants (plural)* of promise[245] of the Old Testament had been established, then in the fullness of time Jesus brought in the New Covenant (Testament). Under the New Covenant, the *called-out ones*, the Church, were shown by the Apostle Paul to be the *commonwealth of Israel, the Israel of God*. Those who are the *commonwealth of Israel* (both Jews and Gentiles) were *betrothed* to Him, just as the Apostle Paul made clear when he linked it all together in Ephesians:

> "...*that at that time you* [Gentiles] *were without Christ, being aliens from the **commonwealth of Israel** and strangers from the **covenants** of promise, **having no hope and without God in the world**. But now in Christ Jesus you who once were far off have been brought near by the blood of Christ."*
>
> Ephesians 2:12–13

In that declaration, Paul was explaining how Gentiles became one in and with those who were already part of the spiritual commonwealth of Israel: "*... to create in Himself one new man from the two, thus making peace, and that He might reconcile them both to God in one body through the cross ...*" (Ephesians 2:15–16). And who does Paul tell us this one new man from the two is? "*...[that] you may understand my knowledge in the **mystery of Christ** ... that the **Gentiles should be FELLOW HEIRS, of the SAME BODY**, and partakers of His promise in Christ through the gospel*" (Ephesians 3:6). So what is that *same body* that Paul was referring to? That body is the Body of Christ, the Church, and Paul names her as the *commonwealth of Israel*; and in Galatians 6:16, Paul calls this same people, the *Israel of God*.

> "*For we* [Jews and Gentiles, the whole commonwealth of Israel] *are members of His body, of His flesh and His bones. "For this reason a man shall leave his father and mother and be joined to his wife, and the two shall become one flesh." **This is a Great Mystery, but I speak concerning Christ and the Church.**"*
>
> Ephesians 5:30–32

The entire spiritual *"commonwealth of Israel,"*[246] which is the *"olive tree,"*[247] "the *"one new man from the two,"* "the entire *"building,"*[248] the *"temple,"*[249] "*in whom you also are being* **built together for a dwelling place of God in the Spirit.**"[250] These are in fact **the Church.** There is only one corporate dwelling place of God in the Spirit in the New Covenant; and that is, *The Church, the Bride of Christ, the New Jerusalem!*

So, do God the Father and Jesus, each, have a wife?

No!

God is One, and that One has one bride, one wife, only! He is not a bigamist!

We will see in the next chapter that there has always been **Only One Bridegroom and Only One Bride.**

Chapter Nineteen Notes

[233] *"If a young woman who is a virgin is betrothed to a husband, and a man finds her in the city and lies with her, then you shall bring them both out to the gate of that city, and you shall stone them to death with stones, the young woman because she did not cry out in the city, and the man because he humbled his neighbor's wife; so you shall put away the evil from among you."* (Deuteronomy 22:23–24, NKJV).

[234] *The unedited full-text of the 1906 Jewish Encyclopedia*, http://jewishencyclopedia.com/articles/3229-betrothal.

[235] Evans, H. Pitts. *The Wife of God: Fresh Revelation on the Bride of Christ* (Kindle Locations 454-455). Xulon Press. Kindle Edition. Quoting Ronald L. Eisenberg, The JPS Guide to Jewish Traditions (Philadelphia: The Jewish Publication Society, 2004).

[236] Matthew 1:24-25.

[237] 1 Corinthians 12:12-20.

[238] (Evans 2016) (Kindle Locations 318-323).

[239] (Evans 2016) (Kindle Locations 343-350).

[240] Romans 9 and 11 (for complete context).

[241] John 3:6.

[242] Romans 9:3–5.

[243] *"And the Scripture, foreseeing that God would justify the Gentiles by faith, preached the gospel to Abraham ..."* (Galatians 3:8–9).

[244] 1 Corinthians 10:1-4.

[245] Ephesians 2:12–13.

[246] Ephesians 2:15-16.

[247] Romans 11.

[248] Ephesians 2:21.

[249] Ephesians 2:21.

[250] Ephesians 2:22.

Chapter 20

ONLY ONE BRIDEGROOM AND ONLY ONE BRIDE

Jesus said, "For this reason a man shall leave his father and mother and be joined to his wife, and the two shall become one flesh …."

Matthew 19:5

"Hear, O Israel: The Lord our God, the Lord is one! You shall love the Lord your God with all your heart, with all your soul, and with all your strength."

Deuteronomy 6:4–5

"For we are members of His body, of His flesh and of His bones ... one flesh. This mystery is profound [great], and I am saying that it refers to Christ and the Church."

Ephesians 5:31–32, ESV

"Let us be glad and rejoice and give Him glory, for the Marriage of the Lamb has come, and His wife has made herself ready."

Revelation 19:7

There is nothing quite like a wedding ceremony! It is initially, the most important event in the lives of a bridegroom and bride. Preparations, though exciting, are so tedious that few couples avoid exhaustion. When the moment finally arrives, the anticipation gives way to emotions never to be forgotten. Once the wedding march begins and the bride is walking down the aisle, exhilaration fills the room, and everyone present feels the joy of the moment, many with tears. The bridegrooms' countenance is filled with joy, a sense of awe and expectation as he watches her approaching. The bride's joy is running over!

The current generation's wedding ceremonies exploit the moment to the fullest. The preparations are phenomenal, including scheduling the Church sanctuary, the minister, and wedding planner, buying the dress and tuxedo, the cake, the decorations, selecting the bride's maids, the groomsmen, the ushers, the ring bearer, the flower girl, the honeymoon trip plan, and arrangements of VIP's schedules. Then let's not forget that we not only have photographers to capture it all, but we add videographers into the mix. On top of that, social media gets its fair share of the moment, as the newlyweds often post their entire wedding online for the whole world to see. Any and everything that can be done to capture the moment is planned. And why not? A marriage should be a treasured experience in every couple's life. Typically for the couple, things feel somewhat surreal as the entire event progresses. The vows, the rings, and the minister's pronouncement of man and wife are things which become more meaningful after the event is over. The experience of married life takes on more reality; certainly more than those few moments of the wedding ceremony and vows can explain.

Marriage was designed by God! So from the Christian perspective, there is much to learn about the wedding and marriage in Scripture. The Jewish marriage process was different in several ways during the time of Christ's first coming than that which we experience today. As we just learned, one of the major differences is that of the betrothal of the bridegroom and bride, which many have mistaken to be the same as an engagement. While there are some similarities, as we now know, the betrothal was very different in substantial ways. It was a period during which the couple was as good as married, because they were legally and religiously registered as such. During the betrothal period, each partner would be vetted, to determine whether each was faithful and pure, and that they were keeping themselves for their marriage. Plus it was during that period that the bridegroom would prepare a place for the couple to live. Typically that place was an addition built onto the bridegroom's father's house; sometimes merely a room in the house.

Another interesting difference is that it was in fact, the bridegroom who was the one who would walk to his bride. The bride would most often remain at her parents' home with her maidens, and the bridegroom would walk from his home with his friends to the bride's home. One of the friends of the bridegroom would run ahead of the bridegroom preparing the way. This friend would announce the coming of the bridegroom, alerting the bride and her maidens that the bridegroom was coming.[251] Once the bridegroom arrived at the bride's home, he would then receive her, and finally take her to his home, as the final joyful step in the process, leading to cohabitation.

The intent in highlighting this betrothal period is not to suggest that we should change our western tradition of the bride walking down the aisle. Rather, it is to point out that this scenario has a connection to the Endtimes and the *Marriage of the Lamb*. When we read Ephesians 5:22-32 about that *Great Mystery, the Mega-Mystery,* we learn that the entire Bible, beginning in Genesis, is leading up to Christ's *Marriage* before He sets up His Kingdom on earth. When Christ's betrothal period is completed, it will have been taking place during the period from the Creation in Genesis down through history and up to and including those key Endtime events, beginning with the sounding of the *"trumpet"* in Revelation 11:15-18.

We want to see that the *Marriage of the Lamb* was first and foremost designed with our Bridegroom, Christ, as the center of attention. This should be very easy to understand since it is His glory that we, as His Bride, will be experiencing. Our glory in that moment will be derived from His glory. Our glory obviously does not originate with us. Let's remember that Christ's marriage is not called the Marriage of the Lamb AND *the bride!* It's simply called the *Marriage of the Lamb.* "The bride" is not used in the name of the marriage, because all eyes and all hearts will be on the Bridegroom!

All Eyes Will Be On The Bridegroom!

Christ's own wedding day is coming! Do we believe for a moment that Christ is sitting in heaven without a thought about His coming marriage? God has always foreknown His sovereign plan, including the *Marriage of the Lamb.* "*Known to God from eternity are all His works*" (Acts 15:18). Christ's death and resurrection was predetermined in God's purpose and foreknowledge. "*Him* (Jesus), *being delivered **by the determined purpose and foreknowledge of God**, you have taken by lawless hands, have crucified, and put to death …*" (Acts 2:23). It is irrefutable that from before the foundation of the world, Jesus Christ, the Creator of all things, purposefully determined and foreknew the way things would work in this life and in eternity. No believer would dispute that.

He is the One who created the institution of marriage with Adam and Eve. In that marriage, as it is with so many events in Genesis, it is intended by God that we see Christ. As we will see throughout this book, God has structured the Word of God so that we are able to learn about the *end* by learning about the *beginning*. The key is found in Who Jesus says He is. In Revelation Jesus says that He is the *"Beginning and the End."*[252] As we saw in Chapter 13, **In the Beginning Was the Beginning and the End**, this descriptive name of Christ is deeper than some may have realized.

So significant is the event of Christ's marriage that God uses it in the Book of Revelation to identify what the timing and order of events will be throughout the entire book. Once we are able to identify the chronology in Revelation of the resurrection, rapture, judgment of saints, rewarding of the saints and the *Marriage of the Lamb*, it is then that the outline of Revelation clears up, and the confusion referred to earlier fades away.

His wedding will be a monumental time for Christ, and yes of course, for His Bride. During all of human history, since the creation of Adam and Eve, Christ has been looking forward to His own marriage. We *say* that we are made in His image. Didn't He *create marriage* as a part of this image? We anticipate our own wedding. And whatever else that may mean, it should seem fairly obvious that Christ has every reason, and has earned every right to enjoy great anticipation. The simplest proof of that anticipation is when we look in on that very moment in Revelation 19, where we witness the Marriage ceremony as it is time for it to begin. We are privileged to read for ourselves how all heaven breaks out singing a Hallelujah Chorus, in honor of Jesus the Lamb of God—giving Him glory!

*"And I heard, as it were, the voice of a great multitude, as the sound of many waters and as the sound of mighty thunderings, saying, 'Alleluia! For the Lord God Omnipotent reigns! Let us be glad and rejoice and give Him glory, **for the Marriage of the Lamb has come, and His wife has made herself ready.**'"*

Revelation 19:6–7

In the very beginning of the Bible after creating Adam, God declared that it was not good for him to be alone. Some may not have noticed that after each day of creation, God finished His work by saying, *"… it was good."*[253] He finished it all by saying that it was *"very good."* Then we see that God said something was *"not good"* for the first time, when he saw Adam alone, without a soulmate, and He said, *"It is **not good** that man should be alone"* (Genesis 2:18). Was the *"not good"* because God was surprised by the look on Adam's downcast face, and therefore, He figured He had better do something about that? So God got busy, and made Eve? Did God make a mistake that He needed to correct? Of course not!

Think about this from Christ's viewpoint for a moment. Christ is the Creator. Before the world began, He had Eve in mind when He created Adam, just as He Himself had His own Bride in mind from before the world began. It was not good for Adam to be alone, just as Christ chose within Himself to love His own Bride, and to not be alone. Simply put, His wedding plan was being initiated.

Christ created Adam's Bride, Eve. At that moment, He sovereignly declared the *"**two shall be one**"* (in marriage).[254] In God's math, *one became two, then two became one!* From that day forward, Christ has been declaring that same truth to the world through a myriad of messages. But have we considered that His messages have been declaring who He is and what His Plan is, and that He has been and continues in the process of gathering a Bride for Himself?

He has been gathering a Bride all the way from the beginning of the Beginning and will continue to do so until the end of the Endtimes. He has been doing this from the creation and marriage of Adam and Eve, to the example of the believing remnant from within Israel being the betrothed wife of Christ, to the first sign and miracle Christ gave us during His ministry (the wedding in Cana), and on to the culmination of the *Mystery of God*[255] at the *Marriage of the Lamb* to His Bride, His own gathered assembly, which is called the Church. And yet, according to His consistent nature, His Bride will receive glory in, through, and with Him. *"For I consider that the sufferings of this present time are not worthy to be compared with **the glory which shall be revealed in us**. For the earnest expectation of the creation eagerly waits for the revealing of the sons of God"* (Romans 8:18-19). Any glory received by anyone in His presence at His coming, will only be as a result of the Holy Spirit having flowed in and through yielded lives. When His Big-Day comes, all eyes will be on Him. He is the one to whom all glory began and belongs.

An Unintended Consequence

Just a bit earlier, we reviewed the fact that Israel was referred to as Jehovah's wife. Furthermore, we mentioned the fact that there are those who teach that not only was she God the Father's Bride and wife, but in addition, Jesus also has a different Bride and future wife who is the Church. There are various theological opinions about this idea. But such teaching creates unintended consequences, because this has direct implications for the Endtimes.

I do not believe that those who teach that *God has two wives*, intend to demean the God they love. But the two wives idea is nevertheless, dangerous and erroneous, regardless of good intentions. This idea has many complications which deserve responses. To assist in resolving this troubling concept, it seems useful to state the obvious on several related points:

1) Jesus Christ is God. No true believer would disagree with that.
2) God is One God. Our One God eternally exists in three Persons: Father, Son and Holy Spirit. No true believer would disagree with that.
3) God hates divorce. No true believer would disagree with that.
4) God's law regarding kings in ancient Israel disallowed them from having multiple wives. (Deuteronomy 17:17) No true believer would disagree with that.

In those fundamental biblical facts are fairly straightforward answers to the doctrinal dilemma of whether or not God has two wives. But let's verify this.

The notion that God the Father and Jesus each has a wife is tragic. God has always and only had one wife. She was and is a betrothed wife. This wife is a spiritual wife. She was not and is not a physical wife, as we humans think of these things. God does not have, and never has had, two wives. When Jesus marries His Bride, it will not be his second marriage. Putting it another way, God the Father didn't have one wife, and then Jesus will marry yet another wife in the future. That is not only absurd; it is near to blasphemous.

Theologians who say that God the Father had a wife named Israel, and Jesus has another wife, the Church, are complicating God's declarations about Himself. One key reason for such a confusing teaching in the Church is primarily because of the catastrophic impact of a lack of teaching and understanding of the *Mystery of God*.

The Apostle Paul was specifically called to preach the Gospel and to preach with great emphasis on the *Mystery*. Many who are in leadership in the Body of Christ today, rarely if ever, teach anything about this *Mystery*. That is truly strange when that lack is compared to the backdrop of the Apostle Paul's calling and passion for teaching and preaching the *Mystery*. Tragically, many have been and will be adrift on the sea of speculation and confusion concerning the issue of the *Marriage of the Lamb* and the Bride of Christ without the inclusion of these and other insights and understanding of the *Mystery of God* throughout the Bible.

Without examining the Bride of Christ in the Old Testament, it would be difficult to gain clarity about the *Mystery* and *Marriage*. I want to see with you that the Church of Jesus Christ needs a paradigm shift because there is *Only One Bridegroom and Only One Bride*. We desperately need to remove ourselves from Division Theology and move into Theology of the Lamb of God. The next chapter will help us to make that move as we learn about **Old Testament Saints and the Bride of Christ**.

Chapter Twenty Notes

[251] In one sense, it seems that this was pictured in the role that John the Baptist filled, when he fulfilled Isaiah's prophecy: *"Prepare the way of the Lord …."*

[252] Jesus calls Himself the Alpha and Omega, the Beginning and the End, or the First and the Last a total of 11 times in Revelation. He is emphasizing "Who" He is. He is the "Beginning and the End."

[253] Genesis 1:4, 10, 12, 18, 21, 25.

[254] Genesis 2:24.

[255] Ephesians 5:32 (the **Great Mystery**); Revelation 10:7 (the **Mystery of God**); Revelation 19:6-9. The inseparability of these sections of Scripture is explained more fully throughout this book.

Chapter 21

OLD TESTAMENT SAINTS AND THE BRIDE OF CHRIST

Where Do Old Testament Saints Fit Into God's Wedding Plans?

For the sake of discussion, a better question than "*Where Do Old Testament Saints Fit Into God's Wedding Plans*, would be: "*Before the cross of Christ, where did Gentiles fit into God's Wedding Plans?*

To help us with those questions, let's look to one of the great theologians of years gone by. Due to some of the older British English wording in the following quote, I have taken the liberty to offer [bracketed] explanation where necessary to assist in providing clearer understanding of the use of old English terminology used by Charles Haddon Spurgeon,[256] when he wrote the following:[257]

Only One Covenant of Grace

"Difference of dispensation [different periods of God's dealings with His own in this world] does not involve a difference of Covenant, and it is according to the Covenant of Grace that all spiritual blessings are bestowed. So far as dispensations reach they indicate degrees of knowledge, degrees of privilege, and variety in the ordinances of worship. The unity of the faith is not affected by these [dispensations], as we are taught in the eleventh chapter of the Epistle to the Hebrews. The faithful of every age concur in looking for one city, and that city is identically the same with the New Jerusalem described in the Apocalypse [Book of Revelation] as "a Bride adorned for her husband ....

> The testimony to the Bride [of Christ] is not peculiar [restricted] to the New Testament. Her praise and her destiny were sung [believed] by those who went before [in the Old Testament].
>
> 'And I say unto you, that many shall come from the east and west, and shall sit down with Abraham and Isaac and Jacob in the Kingdom of Heaven ....' Those blessed patriarchs are undoubtedly heirs of the promises. Christ has acknowledged them. You need not ask whether they shall sit down with you [which is what is implied within the teaching of some in dispensationalism], but your inquiry may well be [should be] whether you shall sit down with them [the Old Testament saints] in the kingdom of heaven."

Spurgeon taught that the Old Testament saints and the New Testament saints are one in the *unity of the faith*; and that both were, and are, "*looking for one city ... the New Jerusalem ... as a Bride adorned for her husband ....*" The late Charles Haddon Spurgeon was a renowned theologian who is broadly praised among most Evangelicals for his deep and clear-headed understanding of Scripture. Those quotes are good examples of why he is still so respected after his decease one-hundred-and-twenty years ago.

To amplify Spurgeon's point, let's visit Hebrews 11:39-40 once again: "*These (Old Testament saints in 11:1-38) were all commended for their faith, yet none of them received what had been promised. God had planned something better for us so that only* **together with us would they be made perfect (complete)** *....*" Therefore, in being "*made complete*," both Jew and Gentile are made to be one new man in Christ, both Old and New Testament saints! Both Old and New Testament saints were and are in God's foreknown will together! Both are part of His "*... general Assembly and Church of the firstborn who are registered in heaven ...*" (Hebrews 12:23) and both are represented in the gates and foundations of the New Jerusalem—Christ's Wife since all believers are part of spiritual Israel in Christ (Revelation 19).

Division Theology inherently hinders a clear understanding of the true relationship in which the Old and New Testament saints come together as one in Christ. Previously in this book, I mentioned the misguided concept of *Division Theology*. The use of the word "*division*" in this case, does not mean division in the sense of a conflict among believers. This phrase, *Division Theology*, refers to making a division or distinction between Old Testament saints and New Testament saints as far as the overarching Covenant of Grace is concerned, and as far as its relationship to the doctrine of the Bride of Christ is concerned.

By the term Covenant of Grace, I am saying that salvation has only always been by God's grace, expressed in each and every covenant God made with His own people throughout history from the Garden to the End. This Covenant of Grace is an overarching covenant of promises, which includes all covenants and promises beginning with the Garden of Eden.

This overarching covenant progresses into the New Covenant in Christ, and the New Covenant will come into its completed fullness when Christ delivers the Kingdom to God the Father at the end of the age.

> *"... Christ the firstfruits, afterward those who are Christ's at His coming. Then comes the end, when He delivers the kingdom to God the Father, when He puts an end to all rule and all authority and power."*
>
> 1 Corinthians 15:23–24

> *"Now I saw a new heaven and a new earth, for the first heaven and the first earth had passed away. Also, there was no more sea. Then I, John, saw the holy city,* **New Jerusalem***, coming down out of heaven from God,* **prepared as a bride adorned for her husband***. And I heard a loud voice from heaven saying,* <u>**'Behold, the tabernacle of God is with men, and He will dwell with them, and they shall be His people. God Himself will be with them and be their God.**</u> *And God will wipe away every tear from their eyes; there shall be no more death, nor sorrow, nor crying. There shall be no more pain, for the former things have passed away.' Then He who sat on the throne said, 'Behold, I make all things new.' And He said to me, 'Write, for these words are true and faithful.'"*
>
> Revelation 21:1–5

This is the very same New Covenant that Jeremiah prophesied would come:

> *"Behold, the days are coming, says the Lord, when I will make a* **new covenant** *with the house of Israel and with the house of Judah—not according to the covenant that I made with their fathers in the day that I took them by the hand to lead them out of the land of Egypt ... this is the covenant that I will make with the house of Israel after those days, says the Lord:* **I will put My law in their minds, and write it on their hearts; and I will be their God, and they shall be My people.***"*
>
> Jeremiah 31:31-33

"... He [Jesus] is the Mediator of the **new covenant** ..." (Hebrews 9:15). The New Covenant expresses the pure grace of God for both Old and New Testament saints because He is the Mediator of this covenant. Jeremiah prophesied that God would make a New Covenant with the house of Israel and the house of Judah. And who are these that are called Israel and Judah? Are they not the Israel of God?[258] Those are the Old and New Testament saints who are referred to as being brought into completion together in Hebrews 11:39, 40. Are these not the same ones who are referred to as the New Jerusalem;

that New Jerusalem whose gates are named for the tribes of Israel, and whose foundations bear the names of the Apostles?[259]

We should be humble as Christians in this age. Instead of claiming that the saints of the New Testament are completely separate from the Old Testament saints, we would do well to listen carefully to the continuation of the previously quoted admonition from Charles Haddon Spurgeon.

> "And I say unto you, that many shall come from the east and west, and shall sit down with Abraham and Isaac and Jacob in the Kingdom of Heaven ….." Those blessed patriarchs are undoubtedly heirs of the promises. Christ has acknowledged them. You need not ask whether they shall sit down with you [**which is what is implied within the teaching of dispensationalism**], but your inquiry may well be [should be] whether you shall sit down with them [**the Old Testament saints**] in the kingdom of heaven." (**Inserted clarifications are mine.**)

The only way anyone ever has come, or ever will come, into relationship with God is through the redemptive sufficiency of the blood of Jesus Christ. That sufficiency has been revealed from covenant to covenant.

Threads, Threads, and More Threads

Think about it. The threads braided into our prophetic cord continue. Before God made His covenant with him, Noah already had the specific knowledge of prior covenants and promises which God had given, especially His promise to Adam and Eve concerning the Seed, Christ Himself. God's Word was not some foreign thing to Noah at the time at which God made His covenant with him. According to the biblical record, Adam lived to be 930 years old. Adam was alive when Methuselah was born in 622 (622 years after Adam was created), so Adam lived another 308 years after Methuselah was born. Many do not consider that Adam and Eve's message of their personal relationship with God in the Garden was fresh in the minds and hearts of those who were living then. These families were not strangers on the earth. Methuselah was 369 years old when Noah was born. Methuselah was, in today's terms, just beyond qualifying to be a young *Millennial* adult of sorts, because he lived to the ripe old age of 969 years. Methuselah was the son of the man who walked with God in such a way that God just decided to take him to be with Him. That was Enoch.

The stories of Adam and Eve, Enoch, Methuselah, and others were still fresh in Noah's mind and heart, when Methuselah died the same year as the Flood. God's covenant promises remained fresh with Noah. So what we are saying here is that Noah's knowledge of the covenantal promises of God was fundamental to his life and family. The promises were handed down to Noah through the righteous line of saints, God's spiritual family.

Being born into this world does not qualify as being a spiritual child of God. This is why the *Fatherhood of God* is a false idea. God is the Creator of all, but not the spiritual Father of all. Jesus made that very clear when He declared that the spiritual hypocrites among the Jewish leaders, had a father, but that father was none other than the Devil.

"You are of your father the devil, and your will is to do your father's desires. He was a murderer from the beginning, and does not stand in the truth, because there is no truth in him ...."

John 8:44, ESV

God doesn't change. He didn't just show up one day, and out of the blue, introduce Himself to Noah, and then tell Noah—"Hey, I want you to build a boat!" God's relationship with Noah was long-standing; not only with Noah, but with his family line. The spiritual heritage continued in Noah's sons. Many are not even aware that it was through Noah's son, Shem, by whom Abraham was instructed in the things of God. Noah was still alive when Abraham came to live with Shem to learn the ways of the Lord. And Abraham was nearly sixty years old when Noah died.[260] The direct and personal relationship between those who followed the God of Adam and Eve, Abel, Enoch, Methuselah, Noah, and Abraham was directly handed down from the very Beginning in the form of the covenants and promises made to each and every one along the way.

The Old Testament saints looked by faith, toward Christ and His sacrifice and blood, and we as New Testament saints, look back by faith to Christ and His sacrifice and blood. Both are redeemed by the same blood. Both are anchored in the same hope. Both are in the family of God. Both are in His Beloved Bride! The two have truly become one new man in Christ. Again, this is intrinsic to the *Mystery of God*.

The understanding of the Covenant of Grace should naturally be more fully understood during this present era of the New Covenant than they could have during the Old Testament.[261] This is because Christ and the Holy Spirit have now come and they have opened our understanding more so than in the time of the Old Testament. The inclusion of **all** saints of **all** history into one body is precisely why Hebrews 11 discusses the well-known Hall of Faith. Those were *"looking for a city, whose builder and maker is God ...."* Old Testament saints were looking for that city and saw it by faith. New Testament believers have been privileged to know more fully what that city is, the New Jerusalem. But still, neither we nor they have yet to see that city. We have all come to that city by faith. Both the Old and the New Testament believers were and are looking for that *"city."* The day will come, after the Millennial Reign of Christ on earth, when we will do more than look for that city. Both Old and New Testament saints are shown to be that city and it is that city which is represented as His Wife coming down out of heaven.[262] Both Paul and John tell us that this is the same city for which they longed, and for which we all long; and which is specifically referred to as the *New Jerusalem, the Bride, the Wife.*

To suggest that the Old Testament saints are not a part of Christ's Bride is an affront, even if unintentional, to the heart and plan of God. Those who suggest otherwise should ask themselves, *Why does Romans 11 teach us that the Gentiles are grafted into spiritual Israel?* There is no clearer portion of Scripture about the status of Gentiles who are born again; they are grafted into spiritual commonwealth of Israel.[263] And who were those who would have been part of the commonwealth of Israel prior to Christ's coming? The spiritual commonwealth of Israel didn't just pop up on the radar out of nowhere. That commonwealth, that people was and is the accumulation of all covenants and saints down through the ages, beginning at the Beginning. The answer is found, in part, when the Apostle Paul tells us in Romans 9:1-9 that *"… they are not all Israel, who are of Israel; nor are they all [spiritual] children because they are the [physical] seed of Abraham ….."* What does that mean? Addressing this issue, once again, Paul is referring to *two different Israels* and *two different children*. Was he confused? The Apostle Paul was not a man in whom you might find confusion. Besides the Holy Spirit, through Paul, meant exactly what He said. In Romans 9 Paul identifies two separate Israels! Both have a special place in the heart and plans of God. Those two can be identified as Physical Israel and Spiritual Israel.

1. *Physical Israel*
    a. Isaac, the son of promise, came through Abraham's physical lineage, as Paul wrote in Romans 9:6–8 (NIV84), *"It is not as though God's word had failed. For not all who are descended from Israel are Israel. Nor because they are his descendants are they all Abraham's children. On the contrary, "It is through Isaac that your offspring will be reckoned." In other words, it is not the natural children who are innately God's children, but it is the children of the promise who are regarded as Abraham's offspring."* We see in this passage that Israel came from the line of Isaac, the son of promise. We also see a clear distinction made between physical Israel and spiritual Israel.
    b. But that distinction does not negate nor disregard, the fact that God made certain promises to Abraham and his promised physical seed, Isaac. Jesus, the Seed promised in the Garden of Eden, came through that physical seed. Those who by grace and through faith received God's covenantal message were counted into the lineage of the spiritual line. The *Seed* of Eden, Christ Himself, is seen

in these men and women of faith in each and every one of the old covenants, as mentioned in Galatians and Hebrews.

c. It was the same physical people about whom the Apostle Paul wrote explaining God's call on them and His work through them. These people were Paul's kinsmen according to the flesh, as he said, "*... my countrymen **according to the flesh**, who are Israelites, to whom pertain the adoption, the glory, the covenants, the giving of the law, the service of God, and the promises; of whom are the fathers and from whom, **according to the flesh**, Christ came ...*" (Romans 9:3–5). In other words, it was this physical people to whom Paul was kin, and to which those things pertained. This included the physical birth of Christ, His physical lineage. We could picture those "*countrymen according to the flesh,*" Paul's kin, as a special group of physicians. These physicians have been licensed and authorized (by covenant) to carry in their physician's bag a very special medicine that will heal anyone who chooses to take it. The physicians carry the medicine, but not all of them believe in the medicine. Then picture that the whole group of physicians contract a deadly sickness. Some take the medicine, as prescribed by the Inventor; but many do not. Paul's fellow physical-countrymen were given the medicine. Some took it; some did not. Those who did were considered by God as the spiritual children in the spiritual line of the Promised Son; Jesus! The same applies today.

d. To this day, there are certain promises made to Abraham's physical children which are still active, but which pertain to this earth, this world, and this life. Those things have always been theirs by covenant. But they are not spiritual children of Abraham because of those natural covenantal promises. They were a chosen people for God's purposes, and to whom He made covenantal promises. Therefore, if these physical descendants of Abraham fail to turn to God through Christ, they will end up in hell, like anyone else. This reminds us of those who grow up in Church and who feel they are okay because they are from the *right family* or the *right Church*. That's not the way it works with the Promised Son and those who are His. God has no grandchildren.

2. **Spiritually Born Israel**

a. Again, quoting Paul: "For not all who are descended from [physical] *Israel are* [spiritual] *Israel. Nor because they are his* [physical] *descendants are they all Abraham's* [spiritual] *children."* This begs the question about what Paul meant when he said that "not **ALL** are ...." There is an old saying that goes like this: *All means all, that's all all means.* That's true. The **"NOT ALL"** means that some are not included in the *all* of Abraham's spiritual children.

b. This is profoundly important. New Testament saints are called children of Abraham in the faith. *"Therefore know that only those who are of faith are sons of Abraham"* (Galatians 3:7). This is true, if we are born again, whether we are Jew or Gentile; we are spiritual sons of the faith of Abraham.
c. Furthermore Paul tells us that the spiritual Israel (Abraham's children in faith) pertains to prophecy, and to the Gospel to the Jews and the Gentiles, and to the *Mystery of God*:
   i. The very next verse reads: *"And the Scripture, **foreseeing** [prophesying] that **God would justify the Gentiles by faith, preached the gospel** [the Gospel of Christ] **to Abraham beforehand saying, 'In you all the nations shall be blessed.'** So then those who are of faith are blessed with believing Abraham"* (Galatians 3:8–9). When Paul referred to *"all the nations"* being blessed with believing Abraham, the *"all the nations"* to which he referred, were the Gentiles. The *Mystery of God* involves the *"two being made one."* That was specifically declared by the Apostle Paul.
   ii. That's interesting, is it not? Paul tells us that the Scriptures *"preached the Gospel to Abraham."* Is that right? Did Abraham hear the Gospel? Yes, he did! It was that very Gospel which Paul tells us about. This should not be difficult to grasp. There are many examples of Christ being present with the Old Testament saints. For instance, didn't Christ Himself join with the children of Israel as they traveled in the wilderness? *"… all ate the same spiritual food, and all drank the same spiritual drink. For they drank of that **spiritual Rock** that followed them, and **that Rock was Christ**. But with most of them God was not well pleased, for their bodies were scattered in the wilderness"* (1 Corinthians 10:3–5).
   So we see that the Gospel of Christ involved the inclusion of the Gentiles. What did that Gospel say to Abraham? ***"In you all the nations shall be blessed ….."*** Abraham's Gospel came in the form that included the Gentiles in the Good News. This was reflective of Abraham's spiritual relationship with God. He was justified by faith. *"For what does the Scripture say? "Abraham believed God, and it was accounted to him for righteousness"* (Romans 4:3).
   iii. "In you **ALL THE NATIONS** shall be blessed." The ALL was the inclusion of the Gentile nations, who through that promise were included in the Good News of the Gospel. The tearing down of the *"middle wall of separation"* between the children of Abraham and the Gentiles was being prophesied in those words spoken by God to Abraham. God was telling Abraham and the world that Christ's sacrifice was His Plan of mercy for bringing the Gentiles into the *"family;"* grafting them into the *"olive tree!"*

iv. Paul also tells us that this *Gospel that was preached to Abraham* is directly connected to the *Mystery*: "... *by revelation He made known to me* **the Mystery** ... *which in other ages was not made known to the sons of men, as it has now been revealed by the Spirit to His holy apostles and prophets:* **that the Gentiles should be fellow heirs** [fellow heirs with spiritual Israel, spiritual children of Abraham], *of the same body* [the body of Christ, the Church, His Bride], **and partakers of His promise in Christ through the gospel** [the Gospel to Abraham] ..." (Ephesians 3:3–6). Once again, Paul clearly linked all of this to both (Jew and Gentile, and Old and New Testament saints) being *"made complete together,"* as also seen in Hebrews 11:39-40.

The New Jerusalem and the Old Testament Saints

All of this helps us understand why the New Jerusalem, which Revelation tells us is Christ's Wife, has the names of the *"twelve tribes of the children of Israel"* on the gates and the names of the *"twelve apostles"* on the twelve foundations of that *"city, whose builder and maker is God!"* All saints, Old and New Testament, are part of His Bride, His Wife! All saints, Old and New Testament, are part of God's olive tree, spiritual Israel (Romans 11), the *Israel of God* (Galatians 6:16)! All saints, Old and New Testament, have come to God through and in the Covenant of Grace! All saints, Old and New Testament, are redeemed by the same blood of the same Lamb of God![264]

The Old Testament saints, in their day, could not yet receive the promise, according to Hebrews 11:39-40. Something was missing. It wasn't that they were not children of God by grace alone through faith alone. They were indeed, children of God. However, the truth in that statement, *by grace alone through faith alone*, could not be fully activated until Christ had actually shed His blood. The blood was then, applied to both the Old Testament saints and to the New Testament believers, both Jews and Gentiles, all saints of which were made to be one in Christ. That is such a beautiful part of the *Mystery of God*.

Still let's not misunderstand. Even with the application of the blood of Jesus to Old and New Testament saints, the ultimate completion or fulfillment, of that *Mystery* has not yet taken place. It was the shedding of His blood, His redemptive work, that provided our position in Him and His promises, His New Covenant. But the ultimate finale doesn't happen until the completion of the final part of the Mystery at the *Marriage of the Lamb*.

Before we delve further into Hebrews 11:39-40, the graphic, which we had originally seen in the Introduction, provides a snapshot of the *Mystery of God* throughout biblical history and on through the Endtimes. Now, with the background of the truths we have been seeing, let's pause and consider this graphic.

The Mystery of God

From the Garden of Eden
To the Marriage of the Lamb

From Genesis to Jesus' First Coming	From Jesus' First Coming to Last Trumpet	From Last Trumpet to the Marriage of the Lamb
The Mystery of God <u>CONCEALED</u> *in the Old Testament*	**The Mystery of God <u>REVEALED</u>** *in the New Testament*	**The Mystery of God <u>FULFILLED</u>** *in the END*
Romans 16:25-27 1 Corinthians 2:6-8 Ephesians 3:3-5 Ephesians 3:8-12 Colossians 1:24-29	Romans 9-11 Romans 16:25-27 1 Corinthians 2:6-8 1 Corinthians 15:42-58 Ephesians 1:1-22 Ephesians 2:11-3:12 Ephesians 6:14-20 Colossians 1:24-29 Colossians 2:1-2 Colossians 4:2-4 1 Timothy 3:16 Revelation 10-11	1 Corinthians 15:42-58 Ephesians 5:22-33 Revelation 10-11 Revelation 19:6-9 Revelation 21:2-3, 9-10

OLD TESTAMENT SAINTS AND THE BRIDE OF CHRIST

This graphic expresses the *Mystery of God* over the span of human history. The *Mystery* was **Concealed,** then **Revealed,** and will be finally **Fulfilled** at the *Marriage of the Lamb*.

It would be nearly impossible for the reader to have missed the fact that I repeatedly point to Hebrews 11:39-40 as being a profound revelation and explanation of God's eternal plan, even if it comes to us in such succinct terms. I ask the reader to not become weary with these short verses, but rather to revel in their truths. It starts out with the Old Testament saints as listed in Hebrews 11:1-38. Then both Old and New Testament saints are connected as those who receive the promise together.

> "And all these [Old Testament saints],[265] *having obtained a good testimony through faith, did not receive the promise, God having provided something better for us, that they* [the Old Testament saints] *should not be made perfect* [that is, "made complete"] *apart from us* [the New Testament saints (Jews and Gentiles)]."
>
> Hebrews 11:39–40

In other words, now that Jesus has come and broken down the middle wall of separation through His cross, Old and New Testament saints are completed as one in Christ to receive the promise. **BOTH and ALL** are part of His *one body*, His *one family*, His *one temple*, His *one people and nation*, His *one new man*, His *one general Assembly and Church of the first-born*,[266] His *one Bride and Wife*! This was always God's Wedding Plan for His Son!

That Wedding Plan **will in the end be finished.** That plan was, and is, that He would gather a Bride throughout all of human history, all the way up to the time at which Christ gathers or assembles the saints to Himself at the Rapture. It is upon Christ's return in the Rapture that the ultimate fulfillment of the promise to Abraham will begin to come to full completion.

> "*Then they will see the Son of Man* **coming in the clouds** *with great power and glory. And then He will send His angels, and* **gather together** *His elect from the four winds,* **from the farthest part of earth to the farthest part of heaven** [all saints, Old and New Testament saints]."
>
> Mark 13:26–27[267]

It is incredibly important to note that Abraham was a "friend" of God. Still, God has only always known the physical descendants of Abraham as just that—the physical descendants of Abraham. They were granted many blessings or cursings due to the covenant God made with Abraham, Isaac and Jacob (Israel). The physical lineage of Abraham includes Isaac, Jacob (Israel) and all of the nation and lineage of Israel throughout history, down to this very day and on to the end of these last days.

Separately God even made promises to Ishmael. To emphasize the distinctions between the "physical" compared to the "spiritual", one need only look at the promises God made to Hagar and Ishmael, Abraham's oldest son, birthed by Hagar the concubine, as opposed to Sarah, Abraham's wife.

"And as for Ishmael, I have heard you. Behold, I have blessed him, and will make him fruitful, and will multiply him exceedingly. He shall beget twelve princes, and I will make him a great nation. But My covenant I will establish with Isaac, whom Sarah shall bear to you at this set time next year. Then He finished talking with him, and God went up from Abraham."

Genesis 17:20–22

But like any and every unregenerate soul in the physical line of Abraham through Isaac, the same applies to those who are unregenerate souls in the physical line of Abraham through Ishmael. Blessed they were and are, in this world, during their lifetime on this earth, to be in the physical line of Abraham. But the truest, spiritual and eternal blessing comes only upon those who are the children with the faith of Abraham, whether they are through Isaac or Ishmael, or whether they are Jews or Gentiles.

The assimilation of the majority of the *northern tribes of Israel* among the nations of the world makes it impossible to discern who those tribes are in today's global population. The *southern tribes of Judah*, along with the mixture of some of all of the other tribes of the northern kingdom of Israel, seem to be those who make up the people who now have repopulated the land of Israel. The "chosen [physical] people" will **NOT** "inherit the land [of Israel]" or anything else in God's eternal kingdom, unless they have received God's gift of eternal life through Jesus Christ.

Just because they have the physical DNA connection back to Abraham, that physical fact does not have and never has had any eternal merit regarding salvation. Otherwise Christ's death on the cross would have been unnecessary. But that doesn't remove God's heart-of-love for them. He chose them for His purposes, and His eye is still on them because He is faithful! But the promises in God's covenants that have a lasting and eternal value are for His *spiritual children*, whether they be Jew or Gentile! It has always been that way.

Abram the Gentile: The First Hebrew

From time to time, I ask folks, *Who was the first Hebrew?* Some know the answer: Abram. Then I ask, *If Abram was the first Hebrew, then what was Abram before he was a Hebrew?* Typically eyes glaze over a bit.

Abram and Sarai were Gentiles, who then became the *first Hebrews*. The word *Hebrew* means *"to cross over"* (or, *"one from beyond"*[268] the river). God called them to leave Ur of the Chaldees and to travel to the promised land. Abram was seventy-five years old, when they traveled to *cross over* the Jordan River. He would now be known as one of God's own spiritual children (along with those others listed before him in Hebrews 11 in the Hall of Faith).

When Abram was ninety-nine years old, God met with Abram again. The covenant God made with Abram was the point at which God changed Abram's name ("exalted father")[269] to Abraham ("father of a multitude").[270] This was in specific relationship to the covenantal relationship God made with him. The name change had great meaning, but what really mattered was that God had made a change inside of Abraham in his soul and spirit, thereby changing *who he was!* As part of God's family, he was in the same spiritual line as Adam and Eve, Abel, Enoch, Noah, etc., and every believer who has ever entered into the family of God! In Abraham and the others, the braiding of the multi-threaded, unbreakable, prophetic cord was being revealed continuously down through history.

Righteousness was imputed to Abraham by and through faith, not by some innate greatness of Abraham that God happened to like about him. *"For we say that faith was counted to Abraham for righteousness"* (Romans 4:9). *"But the words "it was counted to him" were not written for his sake alone, but for ours also. It will be counted to us who believe in him who raised from the dead Jesus our Lord, who was delivered up for our trespasses and raised for our justification"* (Romans 4:23–25, ESV). In that sense, nothing has changed. It was counted to Abraham by faith, and it is counted to us by faith.

The **physical** descendants of Abraham received promises for this life on earth. But the **spiritual** children of Abraham are those who are known by God as His own, spiritually, no matter who they are, where they are from, or their ethnicity, or color of their skin, whether they are from physical Israel and are physical Jews, or they are physical Gentiles; but to the *"Jew first, and also for the Gentiles"* (Romans 1:16). No matter who they formerly had been, they are now children of God by grace alone through faith alone in Christ alone.[271]

It is difficult for some to reconcile the fact that we as New Testament Christians *could not have received the "promise"* in Christ without the Old Testament saints being included. By not reconciling these two, we foolishly and grievously limit God's Word. If we see from God's perspective, which is a perspective not tethered to time, and if we understand that Jesus' blood is applied to their sin, just like it is applied to the sin of New Testament believers, then we will be able to see this clearly.

Whether we had been among those Old Testament saints, who looked forward by faith to Jesus, the promised Seed, as did Adam and Eve, or whether we are looking back by faith, as New Testament saints do now, it is clear that we all must believe God with the same faith as Abraham had! **When** we look is not the operative issue. **Who** we are looking to is the great issue! God doesn't have our problem of being a finite creature with limited knowledge and insight. He lives in and *"inhabits eternity."*[272] This is why God can say that Jesus was *slain before the foundation of the world*. The shedding of Christ's blood on the cross was effective from the very beginning from God's eternal perspective! For us, His bodily sacrifice was an event in history, at which time Jesus who was God incarnate, died on the cross when He was 33 ½ years old in the context of time and history. What is *eternally correct* in God's mind (that Christ was slain before the foundation of the world) is not contradictory to what is *historically correct* in our minds! They are the same event. The Old Testament saints were redeemed by that same blood and sacrifice of Christ, as are we. There is no other way to be redeemed!

For as long as I can remember, Bible believing Churches have correctly said that those who were believers, prior to Christ shedding His blood on the cross, were redeemed by grace through faith, just as we who came after the cross have been and are being redeemed by grace through faith. But this is where some of our brothers' and sisters' trains go off the tracks. Some say that those who were in God's family before the cross are not part of Christ's Bride. Strange! Unbiblical! Can we not see this for what it is?

Those unbroken threads which began in the Garden when God shed the blood of an animal to clothe Adam and Eve, the first in the long line of believers throughout history, to demonstrate His purpose and plan. They were shadows, types, of Him who was to come.[273]

When He did come, the shadows went away! *"Every good gift and every perfect gift [including Jesus, John 3:16] is from above and comes down from the Father of lights, with whom there is* **no variation or shadow** *of turning"* (James 1:17). He covenanted from the beginning concerning the *Seed*. To facilitate God's continuing message to be made known going forward, not only did the *Seed* continue, but God also provided revelatory covenants, events, and individuals, from the Garden of Eden and throughout history. All of those were God's threads in the braided cord to reveal the promised One. These were references to the *Mystery of God*, which to them (though prophesied by and through them) were concealed, hidden, and secret in the Old Testament. Once the promised One, Christ, came, He brought with Him the New Covenant. In fact as we learned earlier, He is Himself **the Covenant**!

The many covenants God made with men down through history, all of which are threads in the prophetic cord, can be described in principle by what the Apostle Paul wrote:

"For I am not ashamed of the gospel of Christ, for it is the power of God to salvation for everyone who believes, for the Jew first and also for the Greek (Gentile). For in it **the righteousness of God is revealed from <u>faith to faith</u>;** *as it is written, 'The just shall live by faith.'"*

Romans 1:16–17

This has never changed. We see this truth in the ark of safety with Noah; the obedient offering of Isaac by Abraham, and the graphic substitutionary animal caught in the thicket; through the sacrificial system God gave to Israel, and many, many other thread-pictures—from *"faith to faith,"* from *covenant to covenant* (Galatians 3:15-18), and from *"glory to glory."*[274] The righteousness of God was revealed in the Garden of Eden which was received by Adam and Eve by faith. *The righteousness of God was and is revealed from faith to faith to all of those who hear His voice, trusting in Him; thus becoming part of the braided, multi-threaded, unbreakable, prophetic cord, and ultimately going from glory to glory, until His glorious Day!*

But it was the humble and meek Lamb of God, Jesus, who became the only acceptable sacrifice, who could and did completely fulfill God's requirement for redemption. By laying down His own life, shedding His own blood, He redeemed and is now redeeming, every believer from creation through to the end. His redemption plan remained the same since before the foundation of the world. Jesus was, and always has been, the Lamb slain before the foundation of the world, as Revelation 13:8 reveals.[275] The blood of bulls, lambs, goats, etc., never did and never could be sufficient for the salvation of even one soul.[276] Those things were true, but only in that they were shadows, types, and analogies of the true redemptive work of Christ!

Without going into an even broader discussion about what Jesus did to apply His redemptive work to the Old Testament saints,[277] I think we can all agree that Jesus' blood is sufficient for and is applied to every soul who was, is and ever will be saved, whether they lived before Christ's redemptive work on the cross and His resurrection, or whether they lived afterward. This is one of the great truths showing how, in the fullness of time, God reached back into time and applied His redemptive work of Christ to all. Only God has the sovereign authority, power and right to accomplish that. He is not bound by time. He created time. He inhabits eternity.[278] This was His *Mystery*-Plan all along.

What I am saying is that even though we have taught that Christ's redemptive work is the only way any person can ever be saved, whether it is applied before or after the cross, it remains a tragic and harmful fact that sometimes Bible teachers treat the Old and New Testament believers differently. This is especially true when it comes to redemption's effect regarding the relationship between the Israel and Gentiles, and how they both fit as the Bride into the *Marriage of the Lamb*.

What we see in reading the Scriptures through the lens of the *Mystery of God*, is that there was not, and there is not, any difference between the Old Testament believers and New Testament believers, except when they lived, as it related to the timing of Jesus' death, burial, and resurrection. Some theologians may question this, but they have doubtless ***not*** taken into consideration the *Mystery of God*. The failure to consider the Mystery in this context leaves our understanding of the Plan of God languishing.

The Incredible Key

Words Matter

Words matter! If there are any words that the father of lies, Satan, strives to keep the Church confused about, the words in the following discussion are always one of the prime targets in the crosshairs of his weaponry!

Semantics is all about determining the meaning of words, sentences, phrases, ideas, and so on. Semantics play a role in the Church's confusion about what the relationship between Israel and the Church is supposed to be. Each believer should take personal responsibility for examining the Scriptures, *"showing yourself approved"* in **God's eyes.** (2 Timothy 2:15) Preconceived notions of men, rather than God's perspective about the Church and Israel, have given the "spirit of error"[279] a foothold in this eternally important issue. When our eyes are opened to see the truths in these words, things can begin to clear up.

Many have come to believe that the Church, the so-called Gentile Church, has no spiritual connection with the physical people of Israel (whether in the Land of Israel or elsewhere); today called Jews. They will agree that we are to pray for the peace of Jerusalem. They will agree that the Church should seek to win Jews to Jesus so that they can become part of the Church. This is where it can get confusing. From what I can tell, rarely is there a malicious intent of any kind, when we say that we should love Israel, and the people of Israel, because they are God's chosen people. And we want them to become part of the Church by receiving their Messiah. The truth is that we want them to be born again, no differently than when Jesus wanted Nicodemus to be born again!

Christ's eternally important objective in coming into this world in the fullness of time (when His Plan determined He was to come) was to break down that *"… middle wall of separation, having abolished in His flesh the enmity … **so as to create in Himself one new man from the two, thus making peace, and that He might reconcile them both to God in one body through the cross, thereby putting to death the enmity**"* (Ephesians 2:14–16). Then as *one new man from the two,* that *one new man,* which is Christ's Bride, in the fullness of time becomes one in marriage with Christ at the *Marriage of the Lamb.*

So then where did the modern Church come up with the idea that God makes a distinction between the faith of the Old Testament saints and the faith of the New Testament saints? This so-called distinction is nothing more and nothing less than the result of the ignorance of, or the disregard of, *The Key;* the *Mystery of God.*

Spurgeon points to the Plymouth Brethren of his own day as a leader in the misguided doctrine on this point.[280] In fact, the article quoted at the beginning of this chapter is a rebuttal to the Plymouth Brethren's divisive doctrine. For our purposes, I refer to John Darby and Cyris (C. I.) Scofield. Darby, who was from Europe, impacted Scofield, who was from the United States. This is the same Scofield who developed the popular *Scofield Reference Bible.*[281] Scofield's set of study notes ensconced in his reference Bible became popularized in the United States, when it was first published in 1909. That reference Bible affected a substantial change in biblical understanding, especially the study of the Endtimes, in America and eventually, around the entire English-speaking, western world. Though not single-handedly, his notes have left evangelical Christianity wrapped up in many speculations and opinions, which cannot be substantiated in the Scripture. Even without verifiable substantiation through the means of multiple, Scriptural evidences, these opinions have prevailed as a prominent eschatological system.

However, I am happy to report that there is an awakening beginning to take root. Many are beginning to realize that the Church is not going to be kept from coming Endtime trials, troubles and tribulation. The truth is that God will use the time of tribulation to gain a harvest of souls at the very end. Persecution of the Church has always ultimately led toward the spread of the Gospel. In this case, we will see an outpouring of His Spirit and God will be glorified in and through His people, especially under the coming tribulation.

How Did We Get To This Place

One of the great complications derived from the Gentilization of the Church is that the Church, to some degree, has morphed and disconnected itself from the truths about the *natural olive tree, spiritual Israel*. Some may be quick to push back on that idea because today's evangelical Church cares very deeply about physical Israel, the people, and the land. Of course, we do. God has instructed us to care and to pray for the peace of Jerusalem. But what I am referring to is that we have lost the critical key to our connection with Israel. That lost key is described in many of Paul's writings, but especially in Romans 11. The Church's typical view about the subjects of *physical Israel* and *spiritual Israel* make it seem as though there has been a role reversal in the minds of Gentile believers. We have come to see the Church through eyes of Gentile-believers, rather than through eyes of believers who are from among the physical people of Israel, who like so many before them, became part of God's spiritual Israel also. The apostles and early disciples, all of which were Jews, were perfect examples of spiritual Israel. Were they Israelites in the flesh? Yes! Did they become spiritual Israelites? Yes! The early Church was a Jewish-led Church. There was a remnant back then and there always has been and will be, a remnant of Jewish believers. We seem to have lost the connection the way that Paul so clearly laid it out.

The apostle makes it abundantly clear that saved Gentiles are grafted into spiritual Israel, and not the reverse! It is not the born again Jews who are grafted into the wild olive tree of the Gentiles. The true olive tree (spiritual Israel) is a tree of life, whereas the wild olive tree (Gentiles) is a tree of death. The only spiritual life that a Gentile can ever have is the life that comes from the *"Root."* Jesus is that Root, and it is only in Him that a Gentile *"branch,"* grafted into the spiritual "olive tree" of "spiritual Israel," can have "life"! That life does not come from the nation of Israel in the physical sense; rather, it comes from the "life-giving sap" of Jesus Christ, the Root of the tree of spiritual Israel, the very family of God! (Please refer to Roman 11 for textual details.)

The Bride of Christ and Old Testament Saints

The betrothed Bride of Christ is identified as the eventual New Jerusalem in Revelation 21:9 –22:5; and she is also seen at that point, as His *wife*. Let's once again recall that in that passage is highlighted the fact that the twelve gates have the names of the twelve tribes of Israel, and the twelve foundations have the names of the twelve Apostles. These two groups of twelves, at minimum, are key designated descriptives of the spiritual structure of the New Jerusalem. They are essentials of the same city in Revelation 21-22. This terminology fits precisely within all of the Apostle Paul's writings regarding the *Mystery of God* and the *Marriage of the Lamb*.

It should be noted that those twenty-four *"names,"* relating to the 12 gates and the 12 foundations, obviously do not encompass every facet of the New Jerusalem. So let's ask a question to help discover a better understanding: *Beyond the 12 gates and the 12 foundations, who are those who make up the remainder of the New Jerusalem? Are they New Testament saints, or Old Testament saints, or both?*

Consider the following passage; it answers the question above. Paul wrote to the believers who **had previously been Gentiles** in Ephesus, explaining that when they had been unsaved Gentiles in the flesh, they were without God, but now had become fellow citizens in the spiritual commonwealth of Israel, and therefore had become members of the household of God, and part of the whole building of God, and were growing into a holy temple, and were being built together for a dwelling place of God in the Spirit. Carefully consider Paul's words!

> *"Therefore remember that you, once Gentiles in the flesh … that at that time you were without Christ, being aliens from the commonwealth of Israel and strangers from the covenants of promise, having no hope and without God in the world. But now in Christ Jesus, you who once were far off have been brought near by the blood of Christ …. **Now, therefore, you are no longer strangers and foreigners, but fellow citizens with the saints and members of the household of God, having been built on the foundation of the apostles and prophets, Jesus Christ Himself being the chief cornerstone, in whom the whole building, being fitted together, grows into a holy temple in the Lord, in whom you also are being built together for a dwelling place of God in the Spirit."***
>
> Ephesians 2:11-13, 19–22

I have to pause here to encourage the reader not to allow yourself to skip and skim through the following vital Scripture passages. Taking the time to read these few passages carefully is very important. Otherwise, we fail to understand *the city, the whole building,* that God is putting together. (I have emboldened key phrases for special attention.)

*"Then one of the seven angels who had the seven bowls filled with the seven last plagues came to me and talked with me, saying, 'Come, I will show you the bride, the Lamb's wife.' And he carried me away in the Spirit to a great and high mountain, and **showed me the great city, the holy Jerusalem,** descending out of heaven from God, having the glory of God. Her light was like a most precious stone, like a jasper stone, clear as crystal. Also **she had a great and high wall with twelve gates, and twelve angels at the gates, and names written on them, which are the names of the twelve tribes of the children of Israel:** three gates on the east, three gates on the north, three gates on the south, and three gates on the west. Now **the wall of the city had twelve foundations, and on them were the names of the twelve apostles of the Lamb.** And he who talked with me had a gold reed to **measure the city, its gates, and its wall.** The city is laid out as a square; its length is as great as its breadth. And he measured the city with the reed: twelve thousand furlongs. Its length, breadth, and height are equal. Then he measured its wall: one hundred and forty-four cubits, according to the measure of a man, that is, of an angel. **The construction** of its wall was of jasper; and the city was pure gold, like clear glass. The **foundations** of the wall of the city were adorned with all kinds of precious stones: the first foundation was jasper, the second sapphire, the third chalcedony, the fourth emerald, the fifth sardonyx, the sixth sardius, the seventh chrysolite, the eighth beryl, the ninth topaz, the tenth chrysoprase, the eleventh jacinth, and the twelfth amethyst. The twelve gates were twelve pearls: each individual gate was of one pearl. And the street of the city was pure gold, like transparent glass. But I saw no temple in it, for **the Lord God Almighty and the Lamb are its temple.** The city had no need of the sun or the moon to shine in it, for the glory of God illuminated it. **The Lamb is its light."***

Revelation 21:9–23

Notice that Revelation 21:1–3 is the passage which introduces what we just read above:

*"Now I saw a new heaven and a new earth, for the first heaven and the first earth had passed away. Also, there was no more sea. Then I, John, saw **the holy city, New Jerusalem,** coming down out of heaven from God, **prepared as a bride adorned for her husband.** And I heard a loud voice from heaven saying, 'Behold, the tabernacle of God is with men, and He will dwell with them, and they shall be His people. God Himself will be with them and be their God ...."*

For many students of the Word, some of these details sound very familiar, because they tie into other threads in the prophetic cord.

*"I will establish my covenant between me and thee ... **to be a God unto thee, and to thy seed after thee** ..."*

Genesis 17:7 KJV

*"And in thy seed shall **all the nations of the earth** be blessed ...."*

Genesis 22:18 KJV

*"Therefore it is of faith, that it might be by grace; to **the end the promise might be sure to all the seed**; not to that only which is of the law, but to that also which is of the faith of Abraham; who is the father of us all ...."*

Romans 4:16 KJV

What are the basics of what we are seeing in those passages?[282] What is he referring to when he says that the *"tabernacle of God is with men?"* This is about the housing or the *"dwelling place"* in the New Covenant. God dwelling in and with His own. This covenanted relationship, among other things, is a marriage covenant. He explains by saying, **"He will dwell with them, and they shall be His people. God Himself will be with them and be their God ...."** That is what all saints of all time, Old and New Testament, are looking for and waiting for! That New Covenant is already in place in our spiritual position in Christ. The Holy Spirit was sent to **live within us**. He now dwells in and with us, and we are already His people! But the ultimate fulfillment of that is yet to come!

These very words repeated in Hebrews 8:7-13 were prophesied by Jeremiah in very specific terms:

*"Behold, the days are coming, says the Lord, when **I will make a New Covenant with the house of Israel and with the house of Judah**—not according to the covenant that I made with their fathers ... But this is the covenant that I will make with the house of Israel after those days, says the Lord: **I will put My law in their minds, and write it on their hearts; and I will be their God, and they shall be My people.** No more shall every man teach his neighbor, and every man his brother, saying, 'Know the Lord,' for they all shall know Me, from the least of them to the greatest of them,' says the Lord. For I will forgive their iniquity, and their sin I will remember no more."*

Jeremiah 31:31–34

Where else do we read about the New Covenant? "... *For **you are the temple of the living God. As God has said: "I will dwell in them and walk among them. I will be their God, and they shall be My people**"* (2 Corinthians 6:16).

Do we not even notice that this New Covenant promise is completely wrapped in marital relationship terminology? Note the verse that led up to the passage above: "

*Do not be **unequally yoked** together with unbelievers. For what **fellowship** has righteousness with lawlessness? And what **communion** has light with darkness? And what **accord** has Christ with Belial? Or **what part has a believer with an unbeliever?** And what **agreement has the temple of God with idols?** For you are the temple of the living God. As God has said: "I will dwell in them And walk among them. I will be their God, And they shall be My people."*

2 Corinthians 6:14–16

When Paul wrote those words, "... what agreement has the temple of God with idols," he was telling Christ's Bride, the Church, the same warning message of the prophets, who chastised Israel. "*My people ask counsel from their wooden idols, And their staff informs them. For the spirit of harlotry has caused them to stray, And they have played the harlot against their God*" (Hosea 4:12).

In Paul's first letter to the Corinthian Church, he had instructed them about immoral relationships. He warned them sternly, telling them the impact on their betrothed relationship with Christ. "*Do you not know that your bodies are members of Christ? Shall I then take the members of Christ and make them members of a harlot? Certainly not! Or do you not know that he who is joined to a harlot is one body with her? For "the two," He says, "shall become one flesh." But he who is joined to the Lord is one spirit with Him*" (1 Corinthians 6:15–17).

Paul's admonitions in both of his letters to the Corinthians, were stated in unequivocal terms, and they specifically pertained to the marital relationship, between Christ and His Church.

The subtitle of this section of this chapter is **The Bride of Christ and Old Testament Saints**. Perhaps there are those who can find a way to dismantle the Bride of Christ through Division Theology, by removing the Old Testament saints from the Bride, but in the process it would seem that they will have to do violence to the heart of Christ to do so. The price he paid to purchase every Old Testament soul and every New Testament soul are demeaned by such pseudo-theology. We should join with the Apostle Paul who reveled in the sum of all believers, all of whom are woven into that *braided, multi-threaded, unbreakable, prophetic cord* of believers. Paul could hardly contain himself, expressing his joy in the riches of this truth, as he concluded his teaching about the born again Gentiles being grafted in among the natural branches of the olive tree of spiritual Israel:

The Incredible Key

> *"Oh, the depth of the riches both of the wisdom and knowledge of God! How unsearchable are His judgments and His ways past finding out! For who has known the mind of the Lord? Or who has become His counselor? Or who has first given to Him And it shall be repaid to him?* **For of Him and through Him and to Him are all things**, *to whom be glory forever. Amen."*
>
> Romans 11:33–36

Among the ***"all things,"*** *to which Paul refers are both Old and New Testament saints, and the Jews and the Gentiles— the very Israel of God!*

And I couldn't agree more!

Both and all are found to have become one in the Apostle Paul's writings over and over again, which this book seeks to demonstrate in detail. The fact that those two are seen as key parts of the New Jerusalem should cause us to stop and ask *why*! For one thing, the two are one. That is, the fact that the twelve tribes and the twelve apostles are seen together as integral parts of the New Jerusalem, pictures for us the spiritual makeup of Christ's Bride. For the student of the Word, who loves to go deeper into the truths of Scripture, I would like to drop a hint in the form of a question. *Who are the "twenty-four (24) elders" referred to twelve times in the Book of Revelation?* The answer is found in the twelve foundations and twelve gates of the New Jerusalem. Typically, evangelical theologians say that the twenty-four elders represent the "Church". I would agree—100%—that they are representative and they themselves are "members" of the Church, the Body of Christ. (See Revelation 4:4 and all references in Revelation to these twenty-four elders, comparing them with Revelation 19-21.)

Let's keep in mind that we are discussing **Old Testament Saints and the Bride of Christ**. This is completely consistent with God's promise to Abraham. This is completely consistent with the **Great Mystery** (Ephesians 5:22-33). It is completely consistent with the **Mystery of God** (Revelation 10:7). This is completely consistent with the Apostle Paul's profound graphic picture of the olive tree. It's not about Israel, the nation! It's not about Gentiles! What it is all really about is Christ Himself, and because we are in Him it applies to those before and after the cross, the cross where the wall of separation was destroyed.

> *"Where is boasting then? It is excluded ... Therefore we conclude that a man is justified by faith apart from the deeds of the law. Or is He the God of the Jews only? Is He not also the God of the Gentiles? Yes, of the Gentiles also,* **since there is one God who will justify the circumcised by faith and the uncircumcised through faith**.*"*
>
> Romans 3:27–30[283]

There it is! There is one God and this one God justifies both the circumcised (Jews) by faith and the uncircumcised (Gentiles) through faith! Why do we then divide them through *Division Theology*?

This is precisely why we see that spiritual Israel (Jews and Gentiles made to be one in Christ) are called the Church, and called His Bride. We are *one* positionally in Christ. His Bride will become completely and fully *one* with Christ at the *Marriage of the Lamb!* His promises concerning His overall called-out assembly of believers, both Old and New Testament believers—His Bride—will be completely fulfilled at that time. In each of the above passages, Revelation, Ephesians, and Romans, we can see and sense the heart of Christ, preparing in anticipation of His future —His marriage to His Bride.

The Bride IN Christ

When we become justified by faith, whether we are of the *circumcised* or the *uncircumcised*, we transition from being **outside** of Christ into **"being in Him."**

> *"For he is not a Jew who is one outwardly, nor is circumcision that which is outward in the flesh; but he is a Jew who is one inwardly; and circumcision is that of the heart, in the Spirit, not in the letter [the law]; whose praise is not from men but from God."*
>
> Romans 2:28–29

Because we are in Him, we are His Body.[284] Christ is Head and we are His Body. This is a great truth and one that brings peace and joy to our hearts, as we understand it's richness. The New Testament reveals this truth in no uncertain terms.

- "... To the saints ... and faithful **in Christ Jesus** ..." (Ephesians 1:1);
- "... blessed us ... in the heavenly places **in Christ** ..." (Ephesians 1:3);
- "... He chose us **in Him** before the foundation of the world ..." (Ephesians 1:4);
- "... He made us accepted **in the Beloved**" (Ephesians 1:6);
- "**In Him** we have redemption through His blood ..." (Ephesians 1:7);
- "... gather together in one all things **in Christ**, both which are in heaven and which are on earth—**in Him**" (Ephesians 1:10);
- "**In Him** also we have obtained an inheritance ..." (Ephesians 1:11);
- "... sit together in the heavenly places **in Christ Jesus** ..." (Ephesians 2:6);
- "... all the saints **in Christ** ..." (Philippians 1:1);
- "Greet every saint **in Christ Jesus**" (Philippians 4:21);
- "... saints and faithful brethren **in Christ** ..." (Colossians 1:2);
- "... that we may present every man perfect **in Christ Jesus**" (Colossians 1:28);
- "... the dead **in Christ** will rise first" (1 Thessalonians 4:16);
- "... every good thing which is in you **in Christ Jesus**" (Philemon 6).

Those *in Christ* statements allow us to see all the more clearly the impact of the New Covenant. These demonstrate God's *Marriage* promise: **"I will dwell IN THEM and walk among them. I will be their God, and they shall be My people ...."** This promise was prophesied by Jeremiah. But the completion of this promise could not be understood or seen clearly until Christ had paid the price to purchase His Bride. Until then, it had been *hidden* and *secret* until the *fullness of time*, when the *Mystery of God* was to be made known in Christ. Once He had paid the price, then Hebrews 11:39-40 reveals the bringing together of Old and New into one new man, in Christ!

> *"These were all commended for their faith, yet none of them received what had been promised. God had planned something better for us so that only together with us would they be made perfect."*
> Hebrews 11:39–40, NIV84

As I have mentioned, the Old and New Testament saints are seen in Hebrews 11:39-40 being made *complete* or *perfect* together in Christ. Most of us can relate to how we are made complete in Christ through salvation. But what about the Old Testament saints, about whom it is said that they are among those who are made *perfect* or *complete* concerning the promises? Do we see this verified anywhere else in Scripture in very clear terms so there is no guess work or speculation? It just so happens, to no surprise, God has faithfully provided that for us to see in very specific terms.[285] In describing the privileges and blessings of those who are part of His assembly of believers from all of history, Hebrews speaks to this matter of those Old Testament saints being *made perfect* (made complete). Please remember that we had just been told in 11:39-40 that both Old and New Testament saints were made perfect/complete together. Then we continue to read in Hebrews 12:22-24:[286]

> *"But you have come to Mount Zion and to the city of the living God, the heavenly Jerusalem, and to myriads of angels,* **to the general Assembly and Church of the first-born who are enrolled in heaven, and to God, the Judge of all, and to the spirits of righteous men made perfect,** *and to Jesus, the mediator of a new covenant, and to the sprinkled blood, which speaks better than the blood of Abel."*

Did you catch that? We are part of the general assembly! We are part of the *"Church of the first-born who are enrolled in Heaven!* So then, who are these who are the **New Jerusalem?** Among other descriptive terms used in that passage, we and they are **"the spirits of righteous men made perfect,"** Old and New Testament saints together!

He has let us know the place He is preparing for His Bride! What is that place? That place is the New Jerusalem. That city is what Jesus is preparing; and in it are seen those names of the twelves tribes of Israel and the names of the twelve Apostles to which we have referred several times. We will see all the more clearly, that it was for all of us—Old and New Testament saints, to whom Jesus said, *"I Go to Prepare a Place for You."*

Chapter Twenty-One Notes

[256] Charles Haddon Spurgeon. The renowned Bible author, theologian, teacher, preacher and pastor of Metropolitan Tabernacle in London for 38 years, who died in 1892.

[257] From Sword and Trowel, March, 1867, pbministries.org/Theology/Spurgeon/spurgeon01_02.htm. *"Old Testament Saints: Members of the Church"*. (This article is attributed to Charles Haddon Spurgeon, as editor of the magazine.)

[258] Galatians 6:16.

[259] Revelation 21 and 22:1-5 (see "twelve gates" and "twelve foundations").

[260] Johnson, Dr. Ken, ed. 2008. *The Book of Jasher*. CreateSpace Independent Publishing Platform. I encourage all to read the *Ancient Book of Jasher*. I am **not referring** to either of the two well-publicized, completely debunked, fraudulent books also called the *Book of Jasher*. Though Jasher is not part of the Bible, it is referred to in a positive light, by name, in the Bible (Joshua 10:12-14; 2 Samuel 1:17-18, for example). According to Dr. Johnson, this *Book of Jasher* is an "extremely accurate history book, highly recommended by Scripture itself." This book possibly contains scribal errors or idiomatic statements or embellishments. In my eyes, this does not negate this book as an important historical asset. After all, this scroll may well be over 3,500 years old, and there is no claim by anyone that it is part of Scripture, though referred to, by name. As an historical asset, the reader can decide its personal value. Josephus, the renowned historian who lived in Jerusalem when Jesus was there said: *"…by this book [Jasher] are to be understood certain records kept in some safe place on purpose, giving an account of what happened among the Hebrews from year to year, and called Jasher or the upright, on account of the fidelity of the annals."* (Please refer to **www.biblefacts.org** for obtaining a copy.)

[261] Romans 16:25-27; 1 Corinthians 2:6-8; Ephesians 3:1-12; 3:1-9; Colossians 1:24-29.

[262] Revelation 21. I realize that some readers may be unfamiliar with the ending chapters of the Book of Revelation. Be encouraged to read and re-read them, asking God to give you greater understanding of the truths pertaining to the New Jerusalem, some of which are outside of the scope of this book. One suggestion is to not let yourself get caught up into all of the descriptive imagery. Just take it in and learn over time with greater and greater understanding.

[263] It should be noted that those who are natural "children of Abraham" were "broken off" of the "natural olive tree," as stated by the Apostle Paul in Romans 11. So it is clear that those who are physical "children of Abraham" were not "children of God," until they were born again, and then they were grafted back into the olive tree to join with the others.

[264] For further study about the New Jerusalem, especially as it relates to these 12 names of Israel's children and the 12 names of Christ's apostles, I would simply encourage the reader to review each occasion in the Book of Revelation in which the 24 elders are referred, and realize that these 12 and 12 represent the 24 elders. For some, this should clear up a great deal of confusion about those 24 elders. (See Revelation 4:4,10; 5:8,14; 11:16; 19:4) A good question to ask about the 24 elders is this: Can you think of any other total of 24 elders in the entire Bible who would explain who they are? It's something to consider!

265 If someone believes that Hebrews 11:33-38 includes New Testament saints, I would not argue the point. Either way, both Old and New Testament saints, as one new man, are in view in verses 39-40, and the point remains the same. Both Old and New Testament saints are included "together" in the "promises."

266 Hebrews 12:22-24.

267 I am aware that some teach that the Old Testament saints will not be resurrected until the end of the Great Tribulation; and I agree, but not for the same reasons. Some who teach this, generally teach that the New Testament Church will be "raptured" at the beginning of a seven-year Tribulation. But because they also teach that the Old Testament saints **are not part of "called out assembly" of believers (the Church or the Bride of Christ)**, their eschatology doesn't allow for those Old Testament saints to be raptured until the end of the Great Tribulation. But since the Scriptures tell us that the "saints and prophets" of God, both Old and New Testament, will be resurrected, judged and rewarded at the end of the Great Tribulation (see Revelation 10:7 and 11:15-18, all within the context of the 7th and last trumpet in Revelation and the Bible), then there is no need to relegate Old Testament saints to a different resurrection in the Endtime plan of God.

268 (Strong 1995) **5680** יִבְרִע [*'Ibriy /ib•ree/*] "one from beyond."

269 Ibid, **87** סרבא [*'Abram /ab•rawm/*] Abram = "exalted father."

270 Ibid, **85** סהרבא [*'Abraham /ab•raw•hawm/*] Abraham = "father of a multitude" or "chief of multitude."

271 See Romans 11. Also, see Ephesians 2:12-3:12, where the Apostle Paul makes it unequivocally clear that those Gentiles who had now come to be part of God's family, are now made to be citizens of the commonwealth of Israel. That "commonwealth" is the "spiritual Israel" about which I have written here. Gentiles of all ages, who became part of the family of God, became—and still do become— part of the spiritual commonwealth of Israel.

272 Isaiah 57:15.

273 Colossians 2:15; Hebrews 8:5; Hebrews 10:1.

274 2 Corinthians 3:17-18.

275 "… the Lamb slain from the foundation of the world." (Revelation 13:8).

276 "For it is not possible that the blood of bulls and goats could take away sins." (Hebrews 10:4)

277 Some disagreement exists about the meaning of Psalm 68:18 and Ephesians 4:7ff: "Therefore He says: 'When He ascended on high, He led captivity captive…' (Now this, 'He ascended'—what does it mean but that He also first descended into the lower parts of earth? He who descended is also the One who ascended far above all the heavens, that He might fill all things.)" (Ephesians 4:8–10) It is suggested that those who had been "in the place of the dead" from the previous ages, Jesus took with Him to heaven after His resurrection, when He was taken up. This would mean that the Old Testament saints were "in waiting." But now that Christ has risen from the dead, Paul taught, "to be absent from the body is to be present with the Lord."

278 "For thus says **the High and Lofty One Who inhabits eternity,** whose name is Holy: "I dwell in the high and holy place, with him who has a contrite and humble spirit, to revive the spirit of the humble, and to revive the heart of the contrite ones." (Isaiah 57:15)

279 1 John 4:6.

280 (Spurgeon 7).

281 (Scofield 1909, 1917, copyright renewed, 1937, 1945).

282 A full exposition of these passages is not possible, here, but I will highlight several items.

283 Also, see: Romans 9:22-29.

284 Ephesians 1:22-23.

285 More is said about this in the following chapter, *I Go to Prepare a Place for You.*

286 NASB95 version.

Chapter 22

I GO TO PREPARE A PLACE FOR YOU

"Let not your heart be troubled; believe in God, believe also in Me. "In My Father's house are many dwelling places; if it were not so, I would have told you; for I go to prepare a place for you. "And if I go and prepare a place for you, I will come again, and receive you to Myself; that where I am, there you may be also."

John 14:1–3, NASB95

Many important shadows,[287] types, analogies, and prophecies of the Old Testament began to be understood during the beginning of the New Testament era, as a direct result of the revelation and understanding of the Mystery of God. Notice what the Apostle Paul wrote: "*Now to Him who is able to establish you according to my gospel and the preaching of Jesus Christ*, **according to the revelation of the mystery kept secret since the world began but now made manifest, and by the prophetic Scriptures** *made known to all nations, according to the commandment of the everlasting God, for obedience to the faith …*" (Romans 16:25–26). Do we even slow down long enough to seriously meditate on the apostle's profound statement? Without understanding the *Mystery of God*, some of the most fundamental truths we need in our spiritual arsenal for spiritual warfare in these latter days are not completely accessible, leaving us vulnerable to *"deceiving spirits"*[288] and *"doctrines of men."*[289] That is how important this truth is, not only for understanding the Endtimes but for understanding God's will and plan throughout the ages, just as the Apostle Paul explained.

Those shadows, types, and analogies, prophesied in the Old Testament began at the very beginning in Genesis. Let's take another look at Adam and Eve to see another facet of this diamond called the *Marriage of the Lamb* to His bride. We will see how Paul links these truths together.

The natural man, the *"first Adam"* is a type of the spiritual man, the *"last Adam,"* who is Christ Himself.[290] "*The first man Adam became a living being. The last Adam [Christ] became a life-giving spirit*" (1 Corinthians 15:45). And the *first Eve* is analogous of the spiritual *last Eve*, Christ's Bride.[291] No one can legitimately deny that believers are in Christ. As we have seen, the Apostle Paul repeatedly emphasized this. Believers are "*created in Christ Jesus.*"[292] As such, Christ's Bride is taken out of His side, in a manner of speaking, and we are created in, from and through Christ. Let's see if this idea holds true! Where did the first Eve, the Eve in the Garden of Eden, come from? God brought her forth from within Adam, from his side. God took a rib from within Adam and **created** Eve. That is not just a sweet little idea from the creation story or a cute little graphic snapshot. It is a remarkable reference to where Christ's Bride comes from, and **how she is created**.

When we read about the *Marriage of the Lamb* in Revelation 19, it is easy to see what I believe to be Christ's greatest anticipated joy. That joy will soon be witnessed by the fanfare surrounding the awesome events taking place in God's presence at the *Marriage*. We are specifically told in Hebrews 12:1-2 that we are to set our heart on "*Jesus, the author and finisher of our faith, who for the joy that was set before Him endured the cross, despising the shame, and has sat down at the right hand of the throne of God*" (Hebrews 12:1–2).

In the middle of His sufferings—the torture of body, soul, and spirit; enduring the cross; despising the shame—Jesus was full of the *joy* that was set before Him. What was this joy that was set before Him? Some say that the *joy* was the fact that He would soon leave this life and suffering, and finally be with His Father again in Heaven. It is true that He would soon be with His Father, and there had to be great joy in that. But Jesus' personal joy, the joy He had anticipated since before the world began is found in the fulfillment of the *Mystery of God*, when He marries His Bride! When it comes to the idea that God is love, nothing expresses it more in our human terms, than that of a wedding and a marriage. When that happens in the *Marriage of the Lamb*, His New Covenant will have become as much alive, fulfilling, and relevant as it ever will be. It is at that time that the Lord will begin to fulfill His New Covenant's promises (in the most real terms) made to the Old Covenant saints and the New Covenant saints: *I will be their God, and they will be My people.*

The *Marriage of the Lamb* can be seen as the crowning event in the prophesied fulfillment of the *Mystery of God*. It is the moment of Jesus' personal joy! We are privileged to read some of the sights and sounds of that joy as that fulfillment is seen taking place in Heaven:

> "And I heard, as it were, the voice of a great multitude, as the sound of many waters and as the sound of mighty thunderings, saying, "Alleluia! For the Lord God Omnipotent reigns! Let us be glad and rejoice and give Him glory, for the Marriage of the Lamb has come, and His wife has made herself ready."
>
> Revelation 19:6–7

This scene in Heaven is the beginning of a wedding celebration to which none other will ever compare! And rightly so! It's the beginning of the celebration of the wedding of the Lamb of God to His Bride, His saints. Shouldn't our own joy and anticipation, as individual believers, be gained by a heartfelt commitment and attachment to that same marriage, if we are part of His Bride?

Surely we all realize that once a wedding has been set, the Bridegroom does not want his Bride to be unnecessarily distracted by things not related to their future; and the same holds true vice versa. Rest assured that our Bridegroom, Christ, is not, and will not be, distracted from His Bride and His marriage. On the other hand, as we are anticipating the coming of our Bridegroom, we should be avoiding the distractions of the world, the flesh, and the devil—by and through the power of the Holy Spirit. Is there any doubt, based on the myriad of biblical references, that Jesus holds a special place in His heart and in His Kingdom for overcomers, and rewards them accordingly (Revelation 2 -3)?

Are We Living Like Jesus Is Preparing A Place For Us?

Jesus' heart is full of love for His Bride. Consider His attitude about His Plan for the future with His Bride. As He was preparing His disciples for His death, we can hear the joy in His voice as He told them that even though He was going away, they should not let their hearts be troubled.

> *"In My Father's house are many dwelling places; if it were not so, I would have told you; for I go to prepare a place for you; And if I go and prepare a place for you, I will come again, and receive you to Myself; that where I am, there you may be also."*
>
> John 14:2–3, NASB95

The love He is expressing in those promises is much deeper than is sometimes suggested. Christ was not down in the dumps as He spoke to His disciples about dying and returning to His Father. He was certainly sober, but He was not without love, hope, faith, and joy! In fact, what is seen in His statements in John 14-17 have to do with a truth which had not yet been fully revealed to them at that point. That truth had to do with the New Jerusalem; that is, the broader understanding of the Bride and Wife of Christ. Some might wonder where that is found in the text. To answer that question, I want us to ask this: What was *Jesus referring to* when He talked about there being many "dwelling places," and preparing "a place for you;" and "receiving you to Myself;" and "where I am, you may be also?"

The Incredible Key

There is only one place He was talking about. It is ultimately not Heaven, in the general sense. Rather, Jesus was referring specifically and prophetically to preparing the New Jerusalem. You will recall that we had previously reviewed the description of the New Jerusalem in Revelation 21. In John 14, Jesus was expressing to the disciples His joy and anticipation of preparing that great city, the New Jerusalem!

Some have said that He was trying to comfort His disciples. That is no doubt true. However, while He was comforting them about the importance of Him going away, He was simultaneously expressing His personal joy about that future moment in which He will experience the *Marriage of the Lamb* to His Bride. Hebrews 11 and 13 expand on what Jesus was referring to:

> *"By faith Abraham obeyed when he was called to go out to the place which he would receive as an inheritance ... for he waited* **for the city which has foundations, whose builder and maker is God"**
>
> Hebrews 11:8,10

Also this: *"But you have come to Mount Zion and to city of the living God, the heavenly Jerusalem ...."* (Hebrews 12:22). Then we see precisely what this city is! *"Then I, John, saw the holy city, New Jerusalem, coming down out of heaven from God, prepared as* **a Bride adorned for her husband"** (Revelation 21:2). *"Then one of the seven angels ... came to me and talked with me, saying, 'Come, I* **will show you the Bride, the Lamb's wife.'** *And he carried me away in the Spirit to a great and high mountain, and* **showed me the great city, the holy Jerusalem, descending out of heaven from God,** *having the glory of God. Her light was like a most precious stone, like a jasper stone, clear as crystal"* (Revelation 21:2, 9–11).

Yes, this is what Jesus had in mind when He was telling His disciples to *"Let not your hearts be troubled..."* in John 14. Jesus' heart was **not troubled**! Jesus' heart was full of joy and anticipation as He ministered to them. We are not talking about Jesus being *giddy*, as though what He was facing concerning His sufferings was a light matter. Far from that, He was looking forward to the glory that awaited Him, as we read two chapters later in John 17, where His prayer leaves no doubt about His anticipated glory and joy. Not only was He to be glorified by and through the Holy Spirit,[293] who would soon indwell His disciples and fill them, but Jesus goes on to pray to His Father.

> *"And the glory which You gave Me I have given them, that they may be one just as We are one: I in them, and You in Me; that they may be made perfect in one, and that the world may know that You have sent Me, and have loved them as You have loved Me."*
>
> John 17:22–23

I Go To Prepare A Place For You

In John 14, Jesus promised the disciples that He was going away to prepare a place for them (and us). John 14-17 are during the same event covering four chapters. These chapters were clearly special to Him. Many vital prophecies were being fulfilled, and His redemptive sacrifice was knocking at the door of His time. His prayer in John 17 was therefore an extremely intimate and powerful time with His Father (and with them) just before His crucifixion. Not only was Jesus aware that His death on the cross was immediate, all that accompanied His death was in the forefront of His mind. Yet John 14-17 are full of expressions of His joy and His glory. Have we considered what caused Jesus to be so full of joy at that moment?

There were at least three major things on Jesus' heart as expressed in these four chapters. His care for them as He prepared them for His death, resurrection and departure; His joy of returning to His Father and to His own glory; and His anticipation and joy as He was looking forward to the Marriage of the Lamb. It is the Marriage I want to highlight here.

In Jesus' prayer, He mentioned two key things which specifically speak to the Marriage. In John 17:17 Jesus asks His Father to "sanctify them" by the truth, that is, by the Word:

*"Sanctify them by Your truth. Your word is truth. As You sent Me into the world, I also have sent them into the world. And **for their sakes I sanctify Myself, that they also may be sanctified by the truth.**"*

John 17:17–19

This is specifically what Jesus does for His Bride, as the Apostle Paul explains in Ephesians 5:25-26. "Husbands, love your wives, just as Christ also loved the church and gave Himself for her, that He might **sanctify and cleanse her with the washing of water by the word** ...." (see also Hebrews 9-10). Regarding the "anticipation and joy" Jesus experienced concerning His disciples in John 14-17, He mentions "joy" seven times. Why all of the expressions of joy? From this moment forward, all the way through to and including His death, joy became one of the ruling and motivating factors of His determined spirit, empowered by the Holy Spirit (See Isaiah 50:7 where Jesus is prophesied as having His face set like a flint—sharp and honed for precision of direction—toward His cross.) Yes it is true that Jesus suffered. But through it all, even during His suffering as He hung on the cross, He was looking forward with joy to the future with His Bride and His Father. Hebrews 12:2 portrays in exquisite terms:

*"... Jesus, the author and finisher of our faith, who **for the JOY that was set before Him** endured the cross, despising the shame, and has sat down at the right hand of the throne of God."*

Hebrews 12:2

THE INCREDIBLE KEY

This joy specifically pertains to His coming Marriage to those very disciples whom He was comforting, and all who will be part of His Bride!

In John 14-17, Jesus expressed the joy that was in His heart. Where did that kind of joy come from, especially in the face of the coming suffering in a matter of hours? Hebrews 1:9 quotes the prophetic passage from Psalm 45:7, which gives us an insight into His deep well of joy. "You (Jesus) have loved righteousness and hated wickedness; therefore God, your **God, has anointed you with the <u>oil of gladness</u>** beyond your companions." (Hebrews 1:9, ESV) Furthermore this joy is rooted in His love, both for His Father and for His Bride, the saints. Let's read His words:

*"As the Father loved Me, I also have loved you; abide in My love. If you keep My commandments, you will abide in My love, just as I have kept My Father's commandments and abide in His love. These things I have spoken to you, that **My joy may remain in you, and that your joy may be full.**"*

John 15:9–11

Among other things that Christ is preparing for His Bride, He is preparing a city!

*"… God is not ashamed to be called their God, for He has **PREPARED** a city for them."*

Hebrews 11:16[294]

"For here we have no continuing city, but we seek the one to come."

Hebrews 13:14

In this context, I want to revisit the discussions in Chapters 19-21. This key issue is about whether or not God the Father and Christ each have a wife. In Revelation 21, we saw that the New Jerusalem, the great city, comes down out of heaven. There she is called the Bride and Wife of Christ. The description of the New Jerusalem gives us credible and sufficient evidence that the Godhead, through Christ, has only ever had, and will only ever have, one Bride, one Wife. She is revealed in types, shadows, and analogies in the Old Testament. We see her in Eve.

From the Creation to the END we have seen that the Bible reveals only two families. The Bible reveals God's spiritual family. It also reveals the natural human family, composed of those who lived in this world, but who would not turn to God, who are without excuse[295] in light of all that God has done to draw all to Himself.

"… if I am lifted up from the earth [crucified on the cross], I will draw all peoples to Myself."

John 12:32

God has gifted each of us with free will. While it is true that He draws each person to Himself, it is equally true that He does not force us beyond our will to make us choose to love Him, as though we were robots. He wants us to freely choose to love Him, and to freely become part of His spiritual family by faith. Without choosing to become part of His spiritual family we will remain a part of the created human family, but we will not be part of His spiritual family, those who are born(again) into His spiritual family.

Beginning with Adam and Eve, there have always been two lines, from the point at which Adam and Eve sinned. On an imaginary sheet of paper draw two separate timelines, running parallel, one above the other. The lower timeline represents where everyone begins in our drawing.

The upper timeline represents those who had previously been on the lower timeline, but who have become part of God's eternal family by faith trusting in Him. You could say the lower timeline represents those who choose not to believe God and therefore, remain on the lower timeline. Whereas, the upper timeline represents those who choose to believe God, and therefore, become part of God's spiritual family, moving them to the upper timeline. On the upper line are the names of every soul who has become part of God's family by faith, from Adam through to the last soul who becomes part of God's family. This would include Adam and Eve, Abel, Enoch, Noah, Seth, Abraham and so on, and along with them, all of the other names written in the Lamb's Book of Life.[296]

God's created human family are those who chose to remain on the lower timeline, such as Cain (Adam and Eve's eldest son), Nimrod, and all those who would not trust God down through the ages. These are those whose names will not be found in the Lamb's Book of Life at the Great White Throne Judgment,[297] and who will end up in *"the lake of fire."* Each person on that lower line is one of those about whom it is said that "the wrath of God abides on him." (John 3:36).

These two timelines are perfectly synchronized with each other throughout history. They both begin at the Garden of Eden and they both continue to the end.

Friend, which line are you on? There is an eternity. Life is short! If your name is not on the upper timeline, hopefully you want to be there!

I trust that our two-timeline picture is clear because all of this brings to the forefront that important question about who the Bride of Christ is.

As time moves along down through history on our two timelines, we come to the point at which we learn that God says that He is the "husband" of His people, Israel. But who is this ISRAEL? Was He a Husband to those who were a part of physical Israel, yet who had remained on the lower timeline because they were unbelievers? Or was He referring to being a Husband to those on the upper timeline—spiritual Israel, those who were believers who had moved to the upper timeline? Again, the Apostle Paul gives us the answer, when he states the same truth in this passage: "But it is not that the word of God has taken no effect. For they are not all Israel who are of Israel ..." (Romans 9:6). The reader should note that, ultimately, spiritual Israel includes all saints, Old Testament and New Testament. It is so helpful to understand that one of Christ's names is, in fact, Israel.[298]

The upper timeline is "... *the Israel of God* [**spiritual Israel**]"(Galatians 6:16). Keeping in mind that **spiritual Israel** is all believers, Old and New Testament believers; including all of those who were before Abraham because all prior covenants were brought into that covenant. Therefore, we rightly remember that when Jesus went to *"prepare a place,"* it was a place with twelve (12) gates with the names of the twelves tribes of Israel (the upper timeline) and twelve (12) foundations with the names of the twelve apostles (the upper timeline). This prepared place is called the New Jerusalem, the Bride, the future Wife of Christ. Those who will be going to that prepared place will be people who are preparing in their hearts and lives, looking for His appearing. And all of these are on the upper timeline.

Are you waiting, watching, looking for His appearing? **THE BRIDEGROOM IS COMING**!

Chapter Twenty-Two Notes

[287] "... a shadow of things to come, but the substance is of Christ." (Colossians 2:17) This specific verse refers to the shadows pertaining to the "law." But, the "substance is of Christ." And, it is the "substance" of Christ about which we are focused in this book, and especially concerning the truth of the Mystery and the Marriage.

[288] 1 Timothy 4:1.

[289] Colossians 2:22.

[290] Zodhiates, S. (2000). "... Adam ... is a type of Him who was to come (Christ)." Romans 5:14. The word, "type" is the Greek term "tupos." *The Complete Word Study Dictionary: New Testament* states the meaning of this word like this: "Figuratively of a person as bearing the form and figure of another, as having a certain resemblance in relations and circumstances."

[291] Ephesians 2:9-10.

[292] This is something we enlarged upon in Chapter 17, *The Last Eve* and *The Great Mystery*.

[293] John 16:14.

[294] In Revelation 3:12, we are told by Christ that those who are overcomers will experience having the name of that city, New Jerusalem, written on them. This is a special honor! He makes that "city," and them, important by that declaration. Furthermore, He calls that city the "holy city, New Jerusalem, coming down from God out of heaven." To be a part of that city will be a glorious moment.(Revelation 21).

[295] Romans 1:20.

[296] Revelation 13:7 and Revelation 21:27.

[297] Revelation 20:12.

[298] A broad study of the fact that one of Jesus' names is "Israel" is not within the scope of this book. But this is a very important truth, and I want to address it. If the reader will take the time to read Isaiah 49:1-8, Hosea 11:1, and Matthew 2:15, you will be able to conclude only one thing; and that is that the Scriptures specifically refer to one of Jesus' names as Israel. It's not a play on words in the Scripture. One of Jesus' names is, in fact, Israel. That fact helps us understand that all believers are part of spiritual Israel, because all saints are in Christ, who is Himself, Israel.

PART V

THE BRIDEGROOM IS COMING

Jesus told us that we are to "eagerly wait" for His appearing, and those who are doing so will be taken with Him at His return. *"... To those who eagerly wait for Him He will appear a second time ..."* (Hebrews 9:28; 1 Corinthians 1:7; Titus 2:13). This begs the question: *Are you eagerly waiting for His appearing?* That is not a *ho-hum, mundane* question to be answered merely intellectually. This is a matter of the heart. Should we allow ourselves to believe that we are actually **"looking"** for His appearing, if we are not experiencing a growing intimacy with Christ; as well as experiencing a growing love for our brothers and sisters in our daily interactions.

When God's people are discouraged, frustrated and giving up on understanding the Endtimes, we should recognize this as a short step to giving up on looking for His appearing. This is how the slippery slope toward becoming a scoffer operates. *"... knowing this first: that scoffers will come in the last days, walking according to their own lusts, and saying, "Where is the promise of His coming? For since the fathers fell asleep, all things continue as they were from the beginning of creation"* (2 Peter 3:3–4; Jude 17-19).

The next chapter is such a wonderful truth: **We Can Know the Times and Seasons of His Coming.** It is a spiritual Vitamin B shot for discouraged believers. If we can know the approximate time of Christ's coming—not the *day or hour*, but the **times and seasons** of His coming, our faith will be excited and increased by having such knowledge. To live in the foggy, smoggy cloud of ambiguity, which God has not intended, is more than dismal. It is potentially spiritually debilitating. Knowledge—truth-knowledge made alive by the Spirit—brings grace! We need grace concerning the Endtimes. As we eagerly await His appearing at the last trumpet sound, we have much to look forward to. Think about it. We have His Word in our hands and hearts. We have His Spirit within us to *teach us all things and to show us things to come.* We have the promise of the resurrection. We look forward to rewards, at which time we should hope to hear from Him these words: *"Well done, good and faithful servant"* (Matthew 25).

Finally, after all of that, imagine being ushered into the wedding, the *Marriage of the Lamb and the Marriage Supper.* It is at that moment that the Lamb of God, Jesus our Lord, our Bridegroom, will **TIE THE KNOT!** Throughout this book, I have referred to the *Braided, Multi-threaded, Unbreakable, Prophetic Cord.* Metaphorically speaking, this is that cord in which He "ties the knot" in marriage with His bride at the glorious *Marriage of the Lamb.* We should ask ourselves the question, *Are we really, honestly, getting ready for our Bridegroom?* As that "Day is approaching", it is encouraging to know and have confidence that **We Can Know the Times and Seasons of His Coming.**

Chapter 23

WE CAN KNOW
The Times and Seasons of His Coming

*"But of that **day and hour** no one knows, not even the angels in heaven, nor the Son, but only the Father. Take heed, watch and pray; for you do not know when the time is."*

Mark 13:32–33

*"He said to them, "It is not for you to know **times or seasons** that the Father has fixed by his own authority. But you will receive power when the Holy Spirit has come upon you, and you will be my witnesses in Jerusalem and in all Judea and Samaria, and to the end of the earth."*

Acts 1:7–8 ESV

*"But concerning **the times and the seasons,** brethren, you have no need that I should write to you. For you yourselves know perfectly …."*

1 Thessalonians 5:1–2

Jesus said that *"no man knows the hour nor the day"* of His coming. Of course, that is true! Our Father does not seem to have said anything in His Word that would give us reason to believe that he ever made a decision to make the *hour or day* of His coming known. It remains just as He said. No exceptions!

But what about the "times and seasons" of Christ's coming? There is a distinct and important difference between hour and day, and times and seasons. God's Word is precise; we can rely on that. When the Holy Spirit brings further explanation or revelation to a previously introduced concept in Scripture thereby creating a different perspective, we must be able to support that revelation by additional Scriptural evidence. Such is the case regarding *"times and seasons"* of Christ's coming.

In this chapter, we learn that our Heavenly Father did *not* choose to initially provide the apostles with an understanding of the *"times and seasons"* of Christ's coming. However, by the time the Apostle Paul wrote his first letter to the church at Thessalonica, our Heavenly Father had made the *"times and seasons"* known. This was some time prior to approximately A.D. 54.

There is a tendency for each of us to make the mistake of simply believing and repeating what we have been taught as though it were truth; when, in fact, there could be more to the picture. We must have open eyes and ears to the Holy Spirit, our Teacher. If a clarification is required, He will ALWAYS confirm that change or clarification in and through the Word of God; and not by our own speculations.

This was just such the case when Jesus was asked, "… Lord, will You at this time restore the kingdom to Israel?" And He said to them, 'It is not for you to know times or seasons **which the Father has put in His own authority**'" (Acts 1:6–7). The question and Jesus' answer were specifically in reference to the Endtimes. Here, Jesus told the disciples that it was **"not for you to know** *the times or seasons ….*"

It is true that it seems that you and I are **NOT** going to know the **hour or the day** of His coming. Many assume that the **hour or the day** is the same biblical idea as the ***times and seasons***. However, each and every word of and from God matters. "*… It is written, 'Man shall not live by bread alone, but by* <u>every word</u> *of God'"* (Luke 4:4);[299] that is, the "whole counsel of God."[300]

When Jesus said that the **hour and day** of His coming *"the Father has put in His own authority,"* Jesus also said the same was true regarding the ***times and seasons***. "And He said to them, *"It is not for you to know* **times or seasons which the Father has put in His own authority**" (Acts 1:7). So, is that all that the Bible has to say about whether or not we can know the times and seasons?

I want to draw our attention to the phrase, *"… which the Father has put in His own authority."* In that declaration, there is something very big that he ***did not*** say. He did not say that His Father would not ever reveal the *times and seasons*. After all, this was in the *Father's authority* to do with it whatever He decided, if or when He would so choose—to reveal it or not to reveal it, which was part of what Jesus was saying!

What if the Father wanted the disciples, and you and me, to eventually know the ***times and seasons of Christ's coming, but NOT the hour or day of His coming?*** (What difference would it make, anyhow?) An obligatory, yet rhetorical, question to ask and answer is this: *Did the Father have that prerogative?* Of course He did. What if He decided that after Jesus ascended back to sit at the right hand of the Father on His throne, there would come a time when the Father would choose to reveal further understanding about the ***times and seasons?*** *Would the Father have the authority to do so?* The same Father who had the authority ***not to let us know*** the times and seasons during one point in time is the same Father who has the same authority ***to let us know*** the times and seasons at another point in time, for reasons He would eventually make clear. If that is true, and we will see that it is, wouldn't you want to know the

We Can Know the Times and the Seasons of His coming

times and seasons of Jesus' coming? I do. Let's be clear. I am not setting a date, nor will I be setting a date of His return. A date is not necessary.

According to some, Jesus is coming "soon", and there are many signs that tell us His coming is "soon." I believe this is true. According to others, they are looking for Jesus' return, believing that there are no other signs, which have to be fulfilled, or that would hinder His coming. We are also told by the same teachers that we cannot understand nor do we need to understand what the *time and seasons* are before the rapture.

But, then, we read this, which flies in the face of clear statements made by the Apostle Paul. He makes it clear that the Holy Spirit has brought about a change in our understanding regarding "things to come". Here, Paul tells us that "concerning the times and seasons", we can, and therefore, should know "perfectly" not only the times and seasons, but the "day of the Lord".

> *"But concerning **the times and the seasons**, brethren, you have no need that I should write to you. For you yourselves know perfectly that the day of the Lord so comes as a thief in the night. For **when they say: "Peace and safety!" then sudden destruction comes upon them, as labor pains upon a pregnant woman. And they shall not escape.** **But you, brethren, are not in darkness, so that this Day should overtake you as a thief.** You are all sons of light and sons of the day. We are not of the night nor of darkness. Therefore let us not sleep, as others do, but let us watch and be sober."*
>
> 1 Thessalonians 5:1–6

I want to see with you two concepts found in those few verses, which are sometimes taught in the Church, but which are more often than not, taught incorrectly. We will want to clear up the confusion, because of their importance in Endtimes study.

1) We have been told that we cannot know the times and seasons of Christ's return, but here Paul makes it unequivocally clear that we can *"know perfectly"* these things; and

2) We have been told that Jesus will come like a thief in the night for us. Yet, Jesus **WILL NOT** come as a thief in the night for those of us who are His and who are looking for His appearing.

First, concerning the *times and seasons*, believers are specifically instructed to keep *watching*. Watching for what? We are not told to get up each morning, open the drapes, look into the sky (hoping that there are clouds so that Jesus can come in the clouds), and then to check it off of the list for the day because we have looked for His coming. I have no doubt that there are many sincere believers who say that Jesus could come at any moment, even this very moment. Concerning this, is it possible that we all have things to learn? We have nothing to fear about examining what we believe, holding our beliefs up to the light of the Word to make sure we are not missing something in our understanding!

Here in 1 Thessalonians 5, Paul is instructing the Church to *watch* for Christ's coming. He tells the Church to watch by identifying and understanding the *times and seasons*. After that instruction, Paul then followed up with a few very specific things that we should be looking for. In a moment, I want to see those things with you, and to provide commentary based on these verses, and other key Bible passages dealing with the identified details.

Because this is, indeed, a pivotal passage concerning the *times and seasons* of Christ's coming, I can't emphasize enough to you just how important this section is in any pursuit of a greater understanding of the Endtimes. He wants us to know and understand the Endtimes! Did God only leave us with some *generalized* idea that we are to watch *generally*, and to wait *generally* for His *general* return, while He gives us no idea, generally or otherwise, of when that might be? I think not. More importantly, His Word declares that He did not leave us adrift on a sea called the Endtimes.

Let's remember that there were many who had, or were given, understanding of the times and seasons of Jesus' first coming into the world. The priest, Zacharias, and Elizabeth, his wife (parents of John the Baptist); Joseph and Mary; the shepherds; Simeon; and Anna, and the wise men, all had understanding about His coming. These are the only ones we are told about in Scripture. These seem to have been blessed with understanding, to one degree or another. It is not difficult to see that they had a spirit much like *"the sons of Issachar who had understanding of the times ..."* (1 Chronicles 12:32). And that is the same spirit we are offered to enable us to understand the prophetic Word in our day. It has been offered to us to know the times and seasons of His coming. Also, keep in mind, that it was the religious, especially the religious leaders, who failed to receive the King of kings, Jesus, when He came into the world. It was they who crucified the Lord of glory. I think it is fair to say that His Body, His Church is going to face the same type of death to self, whether in physical death or internal decision making as to whether or not we will deny our Lord, during the soon-coming days of trauma.

There are theologians who make an emphatic claim that Christ's coming has always been imminent—that He could come at any moment. That would mean that for the past 2,000 years Jesus could have come at any moment without the necessity of any further fulfillment of prophecy. Many, if not most, if not all, of those same theologians, tell us that in order for Jesus to return in the rapture, *"Israel had to regain her land and the Jews had to return to their promised land—the Land of Israel! How can we possibly be expected to accept such an irreconcilable contradiction?* It is absolutely true that Israel had to become a nation again before Christ would

We Can Know the *Times* and the *Seasons* of His coming

come in the rapture. To that, we agree. But if that is true about physical Israel's nationhood, and it is, then in order for that to be true, Jesus could not have come prior to 1948. In other words, Jesus' coming could not have been at any moment before Israel was birthed as a nation in modern times! To suggest otherwise, would be an erroneous attempt to fit a square peg into a round hole.

Do these theologians even hear what they are saying? No matter how some attempt to explain this serious contradiction, it remains a misleading and confusing contradiction. It's the kind of thing that confuses the sheep, the Church.

Furthermore, the Apostle Paul tells us,

*"Now, brethren, concerning the coming of our Lord Jesus Christ and **our gathering together to Him** … Let no one deceive you by any means; for **that Day will not come** unless the falling away comes first, and the man of sin is revealed, the son of perdition, who opposes and exalts himself above all that is called God or that is worshiped, so that he sits as God in the temple of God, showing himself that he is God."*

2 Thessalonians 2:1-4

We are plainly told that *the Day of **our gathering to Him*** will not come unless the man of sin is first revealed. Here, again, those who teach that we cannot know the *times and seasons*, also teach that this man of sin is the antichrist. If that is the case, and I would not argue against it, we can know that before Jesus comes to gather[301] His saints, the antichrist will first come onto the world scene. If Israel had to have gained their land again before Jesus would come, and if the antichrist has to come onto the world scene before Jesus would come, then how can it be that *no other signs need to be fulfilled before Jesus comes again?* Yet pretribulation-rapture theologians claim that Jesus could come at any moment? This is another confusing and unnecessary contradiction.

God is not the author of such confusion or contradiction. If we do not engage in speculation and opinion, and if we, in reliance on God's mercy and guidance of the Holy Spirit, rightly divide the Word, examining and comparing Scripture with Scripture, we learn that His Word is not one bit contradictory, nor does God intend it to be confusing for us. The problem has been, and remains, that we (I emphasize we, me included) are so prone to add our two cents worth, muddying the water of the Word, at times! But God through Paul did not have that problem, as we will see.

The Apostle Paul examined these Endtime events, again, as he wrote to the Thessalonians, addressing details that should not be overlooked. Paul didn't go into extended detail; he didn't need to. He provided vital keys, or biblical handles, for our study and understanding, proving that we should know the times and seasons of Christ's coming. We are not to speculate here.

We are to trace Paul's thoughts back into the Scriptures and allow God's Word to interpret itself. He basically said to us through his letter to the Thessalonian Church, the following, which is my paraphrase: *"I have no need to review with you the 'times and seasons' again in any great detail, because of what I have already taught you. But I do want to point out a few important things concerning what I have taught you already.*

Then we can see that Paul continues, explaining like this:

1. *You know that when Christ comes, He will come as a thief. But He will only come like a thief upon those who are in darkness. But as I have told you before, this darkness does not refer to you. You are not in darkness; you are children of light.*
2. Paul goes on: *In this letter that I am writing to you in Thessalonica, I use the word "you." When I use the word "you," I am specifically referring to you in Thessalonica, and the Church as a whole, and all of those saints who will read this letter, which I have intended for circulation throughout the Churches.*[302] *But pay close attention, my dear children. In this same letter, when I use the word "they," I am specifically referring to those who are in darkness. You know the difference because you are children of light.*
3. *So now that you know who the* **"you"** *are that I refer to, I want to explain who* **"they"** *are. "They" are those who, "When they say 'Peace and safety (security),' sudden destruction will come upon them, as labor pains upon a pregnant woman. They shall not escape."*
4. *Let's look into specific "hints," which describe who "they" are. I have trained you to find God's own explanation of these detail by means of a thorough examination of the whole counsel of God, the Scriptures.*
5. *So, my question is this: Where else in the Scriptures does God tell us about these who are called "they?" These are the ones who say "Peace and safety," which is then followed by "sudden destruction." Such destruction will be like the "labor pains of a pregnant woman" from which "they will not escape."*

So Paul says that the times and seasons of the Endtimes will include **"labor pains like those of a pregnant woman"** for someone; and that someone is "they." Let's not speculate. We must find in Scripture someone about whom it is said that they will suffer the "labor pains" in the Endtimes. The Old Testament prophets tell us that *Israel* will experience travail like a woman with child in the last days (Jer. 30:6-7; Mic. 4:9-10).[303] Jeremiah confirms that this will be the same *"great tribulation"* that Jesus and Daniel mention. Jeremiah writes:

> *"Ask ye now, and see whether a man doth travail with child? ... Alas! For **that day is great, so that none is like it**: it is even the time of **Jacob's trouble**; but he shall be saved out of it."*
>
> Jeremiah 30:6-7

We Can Know the *Times* and the *Seasons* of His coming

Jesus and Daniel refer to this worst time of trouble in history. By definition, there can only be one "worst time." Jesus calls it a time of "great tribulation" (the greatest trouble in history). As Jeremiah does here, Daniel also assures us that Israel will be saved out of it (Dan. 12:1). Paul is revealing, in 1 Thessalonians 5, the sudden and tremendous tribulation that will come on Israel at a time when they are saying "Peace and safety" which are the very bywords of the nation today! Note also that Paul gives this declaration in the context of his explanation of the end and the Rapture (1 Thess. 4:15-5:3).

Furthermore, I would add that the Apostle Paul referred to that same time period when he said that *"all Israel shall be saved."*[304] He explained that he was referring to that remaining remnant that would come out of that *"sudden destruction,"* which Jesus called the Great Tribulation or which Jeremiah called the *"time of Jacob's trouble."*

Jesus told us to *watch*. Paul tells us to watch. We are told that He will come for those who *"love His appearing."* Surely, this is one of the reasons you are considering the truths of the Scriptures in this book. Very likely, your heart is curious, or even hungry, to know better the Lord, and to better understand the Endtimes. As for me, when my eyes were opened by a clearer understanding of the Endtimes, I sincerely wanted to know as much as He would show me. I asked the Lord to open my eyes more and more.

Is that your heart? Are you hungry to come nearer to Him? Perhaps, you are one, who is willing to review biblical truths that you may not have been familiar with before. Or, perhaps, you might be described as one who is careful to *"search the Scriptures to find out if these things are so,"* as were those in Berea.[305] That's basically where I was when I was first introduced to some of the key details that I have written in this book; those have impacted my life and my walk, in Christ, in the most profound ways. One thing had been certain. I had not been, nor am I now, one who would easily change my beliefs. I needed to see the proof. What's wrong with that? We should see the Scriptural proof, when it comes to such important things, which affect our daily lives, now, and in eternity.

We know that God and His Word have no contradictions. This does not mean that everything is always easy for us to understand. Even when they are complex, complexity should not be equated with contradiction. Even the Apostle Peter confessed that there were things that the Apostle Paul wrote in his letters to the Churches that were, in fact, *"hard to understand."*[306] When it comes to knowing about the Endtimes, we are faced with many difficult and complex things. For some of these things, this difficulty is because *it is not yet God's timing for us to understand them*. God reveals things *in the fullness of time*. He reveals His truths at the best time; *His time*, which is always for His glory.

God is sovereign and in control of time and eternity, and always works things *"for the good of those who love Him, and who are the called according to His purpose ..."* (Romans 8:28). I want to be very clear: I am not saying that God will give us "new Scriptures" for these Endtimes. That is certainly not the case, nor would I ever affirm anyone who would teach such a thing. All I am saying is that we should pray what the Apostle Paul prayed for the Ephesians.

> *"That the God of our Lord Jesus Christ, the Father of glory, may give to you the spirit of wisdom and revelation in the knowledge of Him, the eyes of your understanding being enlightened ...."*
>
> Ephesians 1:17–18

That is what we need!

As God rolled out each of the covenants, He was revealing things not known before. The good news is that God and His Word do not contradict in any of it. We can rest assured that if God has chosen to reveal something that had not been previously understood, then that change will be true and trustworthy. Just such a change took place regarding the Father's desire for us to know the **times and seasons**, while there remains *no such change* regarding the **hour and day**.

For thirty years, I had *dogmatically* believed one way, but *I had been wrong*. I can openly say, now, that I am so very glad He gave me mercy and grace to be willing to reconsider my previous understanding. I became willing to search the Scriptures to see *if those things were so*. This matter of the **times and seasons** is just one of many great examples.

On the one hand, Jesus plainly stated that the knowledge of the **times and seasons** of His return was in the **authority of the Father**. Later on, the Apostle Paul, inspired by the Holy Spirit, when addressing the *times and seasons*, wrote that things had changed. Nothing had changed concerning the matter of whether or not the Church could know the hour or day of Christ's coming. Paul wrote in his letter to the Thessalonian Church that the *times and seasons* could be known. Not only could they be known, but he also declared that the believers in Thessalonica knew *perfectly* the times and seasons of Christ's coming. Did Paul contradict Jesus? Absolutely not, as we will see. At the time when Jesus was about to leave and return to heaven, He told His disciples that they could not (at that moment) know the times and seasons of His coming.

What the Apostle Paul wrote was completely enclosed in his discussion in 1 Thessalonians. The context is clear. 1 Thessalonians 4:13-18, and continuing into chapter 5, Paul is writing about the last trumpet of God, the resurrection, and when He gathers His own in the rapture of the saints.

In 1 Thessalonians 4:13-18, he explains those details, then he continues in 1 Thessalonians 5:1 (please keep in mind that the chapter break between the end of chapter 4 of 1 Thessalonians and the beginning of chapter 5 is man-made). The text of Scripture simply continues:

We Can Know the Times and the Seasons of His coming

*"But concerning **the times and the seasons**, brethren, you have no need that I should write to you. **For you, yourselves know perfectly that the day of the Lord so comes as a thief in the night.** For when they say 'Peace and safety!' then sudden destruction comes upon them, as labor pains upon a pregnant woman. And they shall not escape. But you, brethren, are not in darkness, so that this Day should overtake you as a thief. You are all sons of light and sons of the day. We are not of the night nor of darkness."*

1 Thessalonians 5:1–5

Let's make a simple list of what we know to be the clear facts found in those few verses:
1. Paul is writing *"concerning the **times and seasons**;"*
2. He declares that those believers knew *"perfectly"* about *"the day of the Lord,"* and that the day of the Lord" comes as a *"thief in the night;"*
3. He uses two different pronouns to make a distinction between two groups of people: *"you"* and *"they."* This distinction could not be more clear;
4. He states that a group, which he identifies as *"they"* will be saying *"Peace and safety!"*
5. And while *"they"* are saying *"'Peace and safety!', sudden destruction comes upon them, like labor pains upon a pregnant woman;"*
6. The ones that are saying *"Peace and safety!"* *"**THEY**"* will *"not escape."*
7. This part is pivotal, as Paul writes: **"But YOU, brethren, are not in darkness so that this Day should overtake you as a thief."**

Amazingly, many in today's Church still teach that Jesus will come for them like a thief in the night. If that is true, then the Word of God is totally contradictory. The only problem with that idea is that it is ***impossible*** for His Word to have a contradiction. The Holy Spirit sees to it that God's Word ***never contradicts***. Not only is there no contradiction here, but there is also, instead, a revelation we need to grasp.

The fact is that Jesus coming as *a thief in the night* is for those who are in darkness. Concerning those who are God's own, the apostle, as we just read, plainly stated that **"You are all sons of light and sons of the day. We are not of the night nor of darkness ...."** That is why that **"Day will not overtake you as a thief."**

Think about it! Many in the Church have been teaching the opposite, despite what the Scripture plainly states. First, Paul writes that the Thessalonian Church knew perfectly about these things. He also taught that concerning the times and seasons, there was **"no need"** for Paul to write to them about that. Why? Because he had already taught them, and that they had already learned about the ***times and seasons*** of His coming.

Jesus said to His disciples that the times and seasons of His return was a subject that the Father had put into His own authority. So, why did the Apostle Paul seemingly say the exact opposite? And on top of that, what difference could it possibly make in our personal lives, right here, and right now?

Some have believed that because of what Jesus had previously said, the door, therefore, was shut on the Father ever revealing the *times and seasons*. Jesus was asked,

> "… 'Lord, will You at this time restore the kingdom to Israel?' And He said to them, **'It is not for you to know times or seasons** which <u>the Father</u> has put in His own authority.'"
>
> Acts 1:6–7

That is where this discussion usually ends. That is *not all* that Jesus said. Notice carefully: "**But** *you shall receive power when the Holy Spirit has come upon you …*" (Acts 1:8). That emboldened word, "**but**" is a conjunction, and the weight it bears in this declaration by Jesus is great. We can read it this way: "*But concerning the times and seasons, once you receive power when the Holy Spirit comes upon you as witnesses unto me…; it will be the Father Who will have the authority* [to reveal what He chooses to reveal]."

Some might ask, *On what basis, or what authority are you interpreting this passage this way?* Think about it, and let's compare Scripture with Scripture. Something has to reconcile Jesus' declaration and that of Paul's declaration, both of which addressed the *times and seasons* of His coming. There are *not* two different *times and seasons* in Scripture concerning His return. Something happened between the time Jesus spoke to His disciples and when Paul made his written declaration that the Church knew *perfectly* the *times and seasons*. What happened?

Very simply: *The Holy Spirit* happened! Luke gives us the insight into this exact moment when Jesus was talking with His disciples, just before He returned to His Father in Heaven, and shortly before the Day of Pentecost when the Holy Spirit was poured out upon them. "*Behold, I send the* <u>**Promise of My Father**</u> *upon you; but tarry in the city of Jerusalem until you are endued with power from on high*" (Luke 24:49). This is the same event to which Luke, who also wrote the Book of Acts, gives the "key" additional insights: "*And being assembled together with them, He* [Jesus] *commanded them not to depart from Jerusalem, but to wait for the* <u>**Promise of the Father,**</u> "*which,*" *He said,* "*you have* [already] *heard from Me*" (Acts 1:4). Did you catch that? When was it that Jesus had told about the Holy Spirit coming as the Promise of the Father? We remember that He told them this in John 14.

So the question is this: *What is the* "**Promise of the Father?**" As stated, the "*… Promise of the Father*" is the Holy Spirit. That "*Promise*" is a Person. Jesus tells His disciples that the Holy Spirit, when He comes, will provide them with many things. What Jesus was telling them was not news to them, when He told them to "*… wait for the Promise of the Father, which you have heard from Me ….*"

We Can Know the Times and the Seasons of His coming

You will recall the scene in the Gospel of John 14, where Jesus, knowing that He was about to be betrayed and crucified, began to tell them that his death and resurrection was going to happen. Because of that fact, He also began to offer them comfort, encouragement, and instruction.

> "Let not your heart be troubled; you believe in God, believe also in Me ... I will not leave you orphans; I will come to you ... A little while longer and the world will see Me no more, but you will see Me. These things I have spoken to you while being present with you. But the Helper, **the Holy Spirit, whom the Father will send** [the Promise of the Father] in My name, He will teach you all things, and bring to your remembrance all things that I said to you."
>
> John 14:1, 18-19, 25-26

At this juncture, Jesus begins to explain the meaning of the *"Promise of the Father,"* the Holy Spirit, and His purpose in their lives and for the Church, as a whole. Who is it that will be sending the Holy Spirit? Jesus said, "... the Father will send [the Holy Spirit] in My name ...."

There were to be many blessings and benefits, many reasons, for the Holy Spirit to come and live in His disciples and to do so with power as Jesus announced. But a key blessing was that when He, the Holy Spirit, did come, He would *"bring to your remembrance all things that I said to you."* In John chapters 14 through 16, He continues teaching them about many things. Then He returns to the matter of the Holy Spirit and says:

> "But when the Helper [the Holy Spirit] comes, whom I shall send to you **from the Father**, the Spirit of truth who proceeds **from the Father**, He will testify of Me."
>
> John 15:26

And then the clincher:

> "Nevertheless I tell you the truth. It is to your advantage that I go away; for if I do not go away, the Helper will not come to you; but if I depart, I will send Him to you. However, when He, the Spirit of truth, has come, **He will guide you into all truth;** for **He will not speak on His own authority**, but whatever He hears He will speak; and **He will tell you THINGS TO COME."**
>
> John 16:7 and 13

This was the *"Promise of the Father"* that was to come upon them, and who did, in fact, come upon them. Once the Holy Spirit had come upon them, then at that time the Holy Spirit began to show the disciples **"things to come."** Among the *things* to come that the Holy Spirit eventually revealed to them was the *"times and seasons"* of Christ's coming. This is why the Apostle Paul could teach the Church *"perfectly"* concerning the **times and seasons.** Nothing else can or should explain why the *times and seasons* were made known to the Church. Only the Holy Spirit, as a gift from the Father, had been given the authority to transition the Church from **not knowing** to **knowing** the *"times and seasons"* of His coming, as Paul revealed to us in 1 Thessalonians 5:1. We do not find anywhere that the Holy Spirit revealed the hour or day of Christ's coming; only that we should know the *"times and seasons* of His coming!

Our Heavenly Father has not been trying to keep this truth from us; the opposite is true. Didn't Jesus scold the religious leaders of Israel, when He said that they *did not know the day of their visitation?* (Jesus was referring to the fact that He was right in front of them, and that His coming was their day of visitation.) Didn't Hosea the prophet prophesy about the people of God, saying:

"My people are destroyed for lack of knowledge."

Hosea 4:6

Let's repeat this verse, because it is so important:

"Where there is no prophetic vision [understanding], *the people cast off restraint."*

Proverbs 29:18

Let's understand that we not only **CAN know the times and seasons,** but it is also *critical* we know. As Zephaniah, the prophet said about the Endtimes in which we live:

"Seek the Lord, all you meek of the earth, Who have upheld His justice. Seek righteousness, seek humility. ***It may be that you will be hidden In the day of the Lord's anger."***

Zephaniah 2:3

I am not at all pursuing to know the *"hour or the day"* of Christ's coming. I am pursuing Him and His Word for understanding *"perfectly"* the *"times and seasons,"* so that He might find me all the more useful in helping others during these days of growing stress and trouble on the earth, during the coming trauma before our Lord returns. This is precisely why the writer of Hebrews admonished us:

"And let us consider how to stir up one another to love and good works, not neglecting to meet together, as is the habit of some, but encouraging one another, and all the more as you see the Day [of His appearing] *drawing near."*

Hebrews 10:24–25, ESV

We Can Know the Times and the Seasons of His coming

Seeing the "Day drawing near" is **not** referring to seeing and knowing the *"day and hour"* of His coming. The writer of Hebrews is plainly indicating that we will see that day at a distance, or while it is still some distance in time, which would naturally be referring to *times and seasons*, rather than a precise *day and hour*. It is the times and seasons that He is saying that we are to *"SEE."* And on top of that, we are to *"all the more"* encourage one another as we are seeing that Day approaching. We have the right and responsibility to see that Day approaching. **God wants us to foresee that Day through the lens of the times and seasons, which He has revealed already. Let's "eagerly wait" and "watch" together for His appearing! Let's wake up Church, and spend more time together encouraging one another while we wait and watch!**

Is it in your heart to know the times and seasons of His coming? Friend, we must spend time with Him, to know Him and His prophetic Word. He reveals His covenant to *those* who fear (reverentially love) Him! Do we love Him? Are we really looking for Him, and for that Day of His coming as it is drawing near? If we choose to "eat" the prophetic Word, we will experience what the Apostle John experienced when he ate the little book in Revelation 10. His truth will go into your mouth sweet as honey, but it will become bitter in your spiritual stomach. To know, believe, and live in the truth will be a great honor and privilege; but it will require of you to yield your own will to His will. I believe that this is a lopsided exchange; His truth and His will is best for us anyhow! Nevertheless, that choice when seen through the eyes of Christ will carry the same attitude as that of Christ as He faced His own death. Before He died on the cross, He died to His own will, which is why He could lay down His life for others. Jesus prayed: *"Father ... not My will, but Your will be done."* This attitude of heart and action of yielding of our own will allows our lives to be changed through His Spirit, as we hope in His coming. *"And everyone who has this hope in Him purifies himself, just as He is pure"* (1 John 3:3). Remember, *if we have a true prophetic understanding, we will live restrained lives by the power of the Holy Spirit.* (Proverbs 29:18). These things show us the heart of a Bride for her Bridegroom. The humility, love, commitment, devotion, yieldedness, and the pursuit of Him and His truth are the fruit of the Holy Spirit flowing in power, authority and usefulness in and through such a Bride!

Friend, are you one who wants to be part of the Bride of Christ? Are you one who wants to be there when **The Bridegroom Ties the Knot** at the *Marriage of the Lamb?*

Chapter Twenty-Three Notes

[299] Deuteronomy 8:3; Matthew 4:4; Luke 4:4.

[300] Acts 20:27.

[301] Matthew 24:30-31. In this very context of the "gathering" of Christ's elect, He is seen coming in the "clouds"; and there is the sound of the great trumpet; and the elect are gathered from all of the corners of heaven and the earth. This is the moment of the gathering of the saints at the rapture. Some teach that either this is the second coming, or that Matthew is written to Jews, and not to Gentiles, or both. Whatever else it is teaching, this gathering is the rapture. Also, see: Mark 13:24-27; Luke 21:25-28. In this last reference in Luke, as if to leave no question about what Jesus is referring to, He says that when you see these things coming to pass, "*look up and lift up your heads, because your* **redemption** *draws near.*" What is this redemption? Paul says in Romans 8:23 that this redemption is the resurrection and changing of our body, which he further explains in 1 Corinthians 15:51-58.

[302] The Apostle Peter wrote concerning the Apostle Paul's letters, such as this letter to the Church in Thessalonica: "*… our beloved brother Paul, according to the wisdom given to him, has written to you,* **as also in all his epistles,** *speaking in them of these things …*" (2 Peter 3:14–16) That same chapter, in 2 Peter 3, refers to matters of the Endtimes, which we will not be able to expand on.

[303] Note the context of Micah 4:9-13. This is not referring to the historical Babylonian captivity, because that captivity did not involve all nations being gathered against Israel nor did it involve the victory that Israel obtains over her enemies here. This captivity has to be related to the Babylon of the end found in Revelation 17-18.

[304] Romans 11:26.

[305] Acts 17:10-15.

[306] 2 Peter 3:16.

Chapter 24

THE BRIDEGROOM TIES THE KNOT!

"Let us be glad and rejoice and give Him glory, for the Marriage of the Lamb has come, and His wife has made herself ready."

Revelation 19:7

What has Jesus been doing, since the day He ascended back to heaven to His Father? He has been busy, *waiting*. **Waiting** as was defined in Chapter 5 of this book. The *waiting* that Jesus is currently doing doesn't mean that He is sitting on His heavenly throne doing nothing: *He has been busy preparing a place for His bride.* He has been overseeing the braiding of the *Multi-Threaded, Unbreakable, Prophetic Cord.*

When the time is right, and it won't be long, the very last days will play out in accordance with God's "sure" prophetic Word.[307] After having prepared a place for His bride, Jesus is going to return in the rapture when the last trumpet sounds. The saints will then experience the last prophesied events, as we edge toward the glorious *Marriage of the Lamb*. We will first proceed to the Judgment Seat of Christ, and then the rewarding (or lack thereof). When those necessary events come to an end, Jesus, the Lamb of God, is going to **Tie the Knot**. This will be that moment in which He brings to a prophetic fulfillment the braiding of that beautiful, *multi-threaded, unbreakable, prophetic cord*, which began with the first thread in the Garden of Eden! Jesus has been "waiting" for this glorious day, which has been planned since before the world began. Can it be denied that this will be a glorious day for Jesus? Didn't He create the world and everything in it? And didn't He give to humanity the free will to choose to love Him, or not? For those who have chosen to turn to Him, to trust in Him, to love Him—as part of the bride, they will enter the glory of the *Marriage of the Lamb*. All of Scripture points to that day of Jesus' glory! At that day, the *Mystery of God* will have been completely fulfilled, finished,[308] just "as was spoken by the prophets!" Revelation 10:7 reads:

The Incredible Key

"... in the days of the trumpet call to be sounded by the seventh angel, the mystery of God would be fulfilled [finished, completed], just as he announced to his servants the prophets."

NOTE: I encourage the reader to not skip past the essential Chapter Notes at the end of this chapter, but rather, to take the time to carefully read each of them (footnotes 309 and 310). They provide vital insights into Revelation 10:7; 1 Corinthians 15:51-56; and John 19:30.[309]

We are told in Revelation 10:7 that the *Mystery of God* will be fulfilled or *"finished,"* during the time period, or "days", of the sounding of the seventh, that is, the last trumpet. Is it a mere coincidence that the word *"finished"* has a kinship to Jesus' statement on the cross at the moment of His death? On the cross, Jesus cried out saying, **"It is finished."** Many things were "finished" on the cross. But there is one thing we want to emphasize : On the cross, *Jesus the Bridegroom of heaven paid the price required* to purchase His Bride. (John 19:30).[310] He will celebrate the **eternal result** of the purchase price He paid for His bride at the *Marriage* and *Marriage Supper of the Lamb*.

The Lamb deserves to marry the bride for whom He paid in full! At the moment in which the *Mystery of God* is finished, the perfect will of the Father regarding this marriage will have been *"finished, fulfilled, completed"* by Jesus Christ, the Bridegroom. The clearest evidence of that complete fulfillment will be this: Immediately after the *Marriage of the Lamb and the Marriage Supper*, Jesus will enter into His *Kingdom-on-Earth* mode. He will demonstrate that the complete fulfillment of the *Mystery of God* has been accomplished, completed, and finished. As the **"Lamb of God,"** He mounted the cross, offering Himself as the eternal sacrifice for sin, declaring *"It is finished."* At the conclusion of the **Marriage of the Lamb**, that glorious Lamb will proclaim *"It is finished"*—the *Mystery of God* at that moment will have been finished! Although He had mounted the cross of Calvary as the **Lamb**, after the Marriage and Marriage Supper, He will mount His white horse as the **"Lion of the tribe of Judah"** and as **"King of kings, and LORD of lords."** At that time, He and His Bride, the hosts heaven, will leave the celebrations of heaven to go to the earth to make war with the dragon (Satan), the Beast Antichrist, the False Prophet, and the doomed souls who have rejected Him!

"They will make war with the Lamb, and the Lamb will overcome them, for He is Lord of lords and King of kings; and those who are with Him are called, chosen, and faithful"
                                                                                    Revelation 17:14

Then He will lead His Wife in the Millennial Reign of One Thousand Years, His Kingdom on Earth! The true Lion King will take over the earth, and rule with a rod of iron!

Friend, there is soon coming a day, in the fullness of time, when Jesus will have finished gathering His Bride. That gathering is in process all the way up to the last second prior to the sounding of the last trumpet at the resurrection and rapture.[311] Simultaneous to the last trumpet sounding, the Bible says that at that very moment *"delay will be no longer."*[312] Jesus will have **waited**, braiding thread by thread, as long as possible[313] for *"whosoever will come."* Come and *"drink of the Water of Life freely,"*[314] while there is time.

In *"a moment, in the twinkling of an eye"*[315] that important series of prophesied events will have been initiated—the resurrection, rapture, judgment and rewarding of the saints and the prophets. *Too late* will be the mantra at that point, much like when the door to Noah's ark was closed by God Himself.

It is a travesty that most Christians I speak with have little to no idea about the relationship of the *Mystery of God* and *the Marriage of the Lamb*, or how, when and why it will all take place. Most I speak with are aware of the list of the primary events involved Endtimes, but they are not the least bit aware of their connection to or the understanding of the *Mystery of God* itself, or for that matter, the relationship of these things to their own Christian life and the future. Tragically, for many, there is little to no real *hungry-hearted* love of His appearing, and the joys that are to follow for those who do love His appearing. The Church, generally speaking, seems to be distracted by day to day life, and worldly concerns. *"Then the Lord said … when the Son of Man comes will He really find faith on the earth?"* (Luke 18:8) It's as though this world has already captured the affection of many believers. The Apostle Paul gives us a strong warning and challenge concerning the very time in which we now live:

"… Knowing the time, that now it is high time to awake out of sleep; for now our salvation is nearer than when we first believed. The night is far spent, the day is at hand. Therefore let us cast off the works of darkness, and let us put on the armor of light. Let us walk properly, as in the day, not in revelry and drunkenness, not in lewdness and lust, not in strife and envy. But put on the Lord Jesus Christ, and make no provision for the flesh, to fulfill its lusts."

Romans 13:11–14

What will it be like when He appears? We are warned against sleeping and slumbering. (Matthew 25:5) Is it any wonder that in Revelation 3, we see Jesus standing at the door, knocking, wanting to come in to be with us, now, in this life? And do we not understand what He meant when He said, *"I am a jealous God?"*[316] Christ is the ultimate Love and Lover! Do we not know what He meant when He said through the Apostle John:

"Do not love the world or the things in the world. If anyone loves the world, the love of the

Father is not in him. For all that is in the world—the lust of the flesh, the lust of the eyes, and the pride of life—is not of the Father but is of the world. And the world is passing away, and the lust of it; but he who does the will of God abides forever."

1 John 2:15–17

Are We Really, Honestly Getting Ready?

Dear Friend, the Spirit of God will enable and empower any believer who has a hungry heart and who wants to to know Jesus intimately. Hungry-hearted believers are those who desire to draw nearer to Him in love, learning to yield to His Spirit on a moment by moment basis, day by day, until we see Him face to face. If they get knocked down, they get up.

"Some of the wise will stumble, so that they may be refined, purified and made spotless until the time of the end …."

Daniel 11:35, NIV84

Even though you or I may not have come into perfect rest, our hearts can be fixed on yielding to the Holy Spirit, as a way of life. Years ago I heard it said, *The Holy Spirit is a total Gentleman! He doesn't force Himself on anyone.* Why should He? He respects our God-given will to choose! But of course, with choosing comes the consequences of those choices. Each of us has experienced that in our lives. Besides, we would be complete fools not to want to know and love Him more and more intimately. He is worthy! But let's remember that in order to truly see with spiritual eyes, we need to recall what Jesus said:

"For where your treasure is, there your heart will be also. The lamp of the body is the eye. If therefore your eye is good, your whole body will be full of light. But if your eye is bad, your whole body will be full of darkness. If therefore the light that is in you is darkness, how great is that darkness! No one can serve two masters; for either he will hate the one and love the other, or else he will be loyal to the one and despise the other …."

Matthew 6:21–24

Didn't Jesus also say,

*"Blessed are the **<u>pure in heart</u>**, For they shall <u>see God</u>."*

Matthew 5:8

If the following Bible quotes and remarks are anything, they are an expression of the love of and from the Bridegroom, the Lord Jesus Christ, toward us. He is reaching out to you and me, yearning for us to draw near to Him, because if we do so, He has promised to draw near to us. He has been standing at our heart's door knocking. He loves us, and wants to *"come in, and dine"* with us in deep, rich, loving fellowship.[317] He also wants His Bride to be clean and pure, and wholeheartedly faithful toward Him. While there are time and breath in our bodies:

> *"… let us lay aside every weight, and the sin which so easily ensnares us, and let us run with endurance the race that is set before us, looking unto Jesus, the author and finisher of our faith, who for the joy that was set before Him endured the cross, despising the shame, and has sat down at the right hand of the throne of God."*
>
> Hebrews 12:1–2

Is that what you want? Are you really hungry for intimacy with Him? If you wonder what that really means, don't be discouraged. He will make Himself known to you, as you draw closer and closer to Him. And in so doing, we can "understand the times" we live in; prophetic understanding will be opened to us. We need God's mercies, because we need God's prophetic Word opened. We need our understanding "enlightened." Daniel the Prophet prayed for God's mercies concerning Israel. In God's mercy, He allowed Daniel to have understanding of the times. The Church's current condition is similar to that of Israel in Daniel's day. We are in spiritual demise. We need to "understand the times" we live in. Israel is becoming more isolated by almost all of the nations of the world. The enemies of the Church are the enemies of the land of Israel. They want to wipe Israel[318] and the Church off of the map.[319] The Bible tells us that when the land of Israel is surrounded by armies, while they are crying *"peace and safety, then, sudden destruction"* will come upon them. When you look at the way things are going in this world, it is easy to believe that this, in the most practical of terms, will happen soon? When it does, the *"time of Jacob's trouble,"* the Great Tribulation, will begin, and the desolation will be like no other time in human history.

This **will happen**! Our Lord, the Bridegroom, will allow this time of trouble in the world to accomplish two things: the purification of His Bride in preparation for His coming and the salvation of all of Israel; that is, those who survive the trauma that will come upon them during the *"time of Jacob's trouble."* He loves us enough to allow us to go through the *cleansing process*[320] before He comes to take His Bride to the *Marriage*.[321] Some suggest that the Church will not have to go through the Tribulation, because we will not have to go through the "wrath". But let's take another look at what is stated about the time of the Great Tribulation as found in Daniel. What we will see is that it is precisely the process of going through time of trouble that will cause us to be "refined, purified and spotless" until the very end!

"Some of the wise will stumble, so that they may be refined, purified and made spotless until the time of the end ...."

Daniel 11:35, NIV84

This is precisely the process Christ's Bride will have to go through in preparation for the Wedding, if she is to come into His presence "spotless"! Where do we find that truth?

*"... Christ also loved the church and gave Himself for her, that He might sanctify and cleanse her with the washing of water by the word, **that He might present her to Himself a glorious church, <u>not having spot</u> or wrinkle or any such thing, but that she <u>should be holy and without blemish</u>.**"*

Ephesians 5:25–27

What is the practical takeaway from this book? We must wake up to the reality that on the other side of the *Marriage of the Lamb* is the *Millennial Reign of Christ*, that 1,000-year-period on this very earth. We will not be raptured in order to just *"be with the Lord"* in heaven.

Again, I emphasize, that the capacity and role in which we will be allowed to serve the mighty Jesus in His 1,000-year Kingdom will be dependent on how we lived for and loved Him, now! Do you love Him, now? Do you prioritize Him, now? Have you chosen to turn your heart away from the *love of the world, and the things in the world, the lust of the flesh, the lust of the eyes, and the pride of life* and to replace that love with your love for Him by the work of the Spirit in your life?[322] Are you walking in the Spirit, now? Are you allowing the Holy Spirit to live the life of Jesus in and through you, now? Those are the things that will show up on the other side. It will not be all fun and games for those who deny Him in this life! There will be deep regrets, sorrow, and tears for those who refuse to put Him first, now. Some mistakenly believe that once we are "raptured out," everything and everyone will be on equal ground and all will be bliss. Not so! How insensitive to Him could we be to think like that, after the price He paid to redeem us, and after the Father sent the Holy Spirit to empower us to become "overcomers" in this life?

None of us lives this life without regrets. We have all failed, to one degree or another. I have, but that is not where I want to end my life; and I am quite certain that you don't want to end your life in that condition, either. We have the privilege of learning to ask Him for the grace to run after Him wholeheartedly—moment by moment. Surely, that is what you want?

Do you remember that little chorus among the children's songs? *I have decided to follow*

Jesus. No turning back, no turning back. We could add an addendum to that little chorus, which says, *I have decided to follow from where I am to where He wants me. I have decided to follow Jesus in and through the power of the Spirit. No turning back, no turning back.* That is where we are privileged to be in order to become "overcomers." Becoming an "overcomer" is completely impossible without the power and fruit of the Spirit flowing in and through our lives.

One thing is certain. We need only look at ourselves, and the rest of the Church, to know that we as His Church lack the power of God. We are, as a Church, as His Bride, in a condition, which is untenable and undesirable. He gives us warning of our condition.

> *"…These things says the Amen, the Faithful and True Witness, the Beginning of the creation of God: 'I know your works, that you are neither cold nor hot. I could wish you were cold or hot. So then, because you are lukewarm, and neither cold nor hot, I will vomit you out of My mouth. Because you say, 'I am rich, have become wealthy, and have need of nothing'—and do not know that you are wretched, miserable, poor, blind, and naked—I counsel you to buy from Me gold refined in the fire, that you may be rich; and white garments, that you may be clothed, that the shame of your nakedness may not be revealed; and anoint your eyes with eye salve, that you may see. As many as I love, I rebuke and chasten. Therefore, be zealous and repent. Behold, I stand at the door and knock. If anyone hears My voice and opens the door, I will come in to him and dine with him, and he with Me. To him who overcomes I will grant to sit with Me on My throne, as I also overcame and sat down with My Father on His throne. He who has an ear, let him hear what the Spirit says to the Churches.'"*
>
> Revelation 3:14–22

As the "Revelation of Jesus Christ" comes to a close, we read the passion in Jesus' heart for us:

> *"**I, Jesus**, have sent My angel to testify to you these things **in the Churches**. I am the Root and the Offspring of David, the Bright and Morning Star." And **the Spirit and the bride say, 'Come!'** And **let him who hears say, 'Come!'** And **let him who thirsts come. Whoever desires, let him take the water of life freely** … He who testifies to these things says, 'Surely I am coming quickly.' Amen. Even so, come, Lord Jesus!"*
>
> Revelation 22:16–17, 20-21

Are you hearing His call to "Come" to Him? Are we willing to allow Him to *"sanctify and cleanse us by the washing of the water of the Word,"* so we can be ready for Him; so that He can present us to Himself as a virtuous bride having been *"refined, purified and made spotless"* by the power of the blood, Word and Spirit? We now have, in hand and heart, *The Key That Unlocks the Book of Revelation and the Endtimes*. And we have learned together how and why the *Mystery of God* is the Key to unlocking our own ending before time runs out!

Let's humble ourselves before Him, choosing to allow the Holy Spirit to live the life of Christ in and through us by the power of His Spirit! By choosing to allow this work of the Word and Spirit in our daily walk, we will bless and please our Bridegroom, Jesus, the Lamb of God.

"You shall love the Lord your God with all your heart, with all your soul, and with all your mind."

Matthew 22:37

"He must increase, but I must decrease."

John 3:30

All glory to our great God and Savior, Jesus Christ—our glorious Bridegroom!

Chapter Twenty-Four Notes

[307] 2 Peter 1:19.
[308] Revelation 10:7; Revelation 11:15-18; Revelation 19:1-10.
[309] The Greek "proleptic aorist" grammatical structure makes it clear that the *Mystery of God* will be fulfilled during the "days" of the seventh trumpet. During those same "days" more fulfillment-events will also occur, namely, the resurrection, rapture, judgment, rewards, and the Marriage of the Lamb!
[310] Zodhiates, S. (2000). "Although *teléō* and *teleióō* have much the same meaning: "to carry through, complete, reach the end." Yet, at times in the Greek language, there is a difference between the two. *Teléō* signifies the reaching of an end or goal meaning to finish or accomplish a task, to terminate a course ..." "*Teleióō,* however, speaks of the **continued realization of a purpose throughout the performance of a task**. The former word has in view the point of termination. The latter word has in view the entire process."

In John 19:30 at His death on the cross, Jesus cried out, *"It is FINISHED."* The Greek word Jesus used for the word "finished" is *"tetelestai,"* (which is rooted in the word *"teléō"*). In Revelation 10:7, where the angel said to John that *"the Mystery of God will be finished,"* the word *"teleióō"* is used, which is also related to the word *"Teléō."*

This is precisely what we see happening concerning the *Mystery of God*. We are told in Revelation 10:7 that as the seventh trumpet begins to sound the Mystery of God will be FINISHED (fulfilled, completed). And, this *beginning* of the conclusion is **not the final conclusion of the Mystery of God.** Naturally then, other events included in the *Mystery of God* must follow, until the ***final conclusion*** is reached. Therefore, it is no surprise when we immediately see those expected and continuing events occurring after the sounding of the seventh trumpet. These continuing events are all in the context of that last trumpet in Revelation 11:15-18. (Review Revelation 10 and 11 to see that they are both in the same context of the seventh and last trumpet.) The continuing events are in the correct order; they are chronologically where they should be. In Revelation 11:15-18 *the seventh (last) trumpet sounds*; then we see the *resurrection, the judgment of the saints and prophets*; and *the rewarding of the saints and prophets*. Of course! These are the precise events which the whole of Scripture point to, in the very order in which we should be seeing them; and they are all now being brought to the conclusion. Interestingly, and profoundly, the ultimate conclusion will be at the *Marriage of the Lamb!*

[311] Matthew 23:31; Mark 13:27; Ephesians 1:7-10; Colossians 1:20; 1 Corinthians 15:51-58; 1 Thessalonians 4:13-17; 2 Thessalonians 2:1; Revelation 10:7; Revelation 11:15-18, etc.

[312] Revelation 10:6 The word "delay" is the same word as the word "time" in the Greek. The context determines the meaning. I agree with many excellent scholars that this context lends toward the application of the word "delay," rather than the word "time." It cannot mean that *time will be no longer*, because the Millennial Reign of 1,000 years of time follow this "delay", which obviously means that time continues.

[313] 2 Peter 3:9.

[314] John 4:14; Revelation 22:17.

[315] 1 Corinthians 15:51-52.

[316] Exodus 20:5; 34:14; Deuteronomy 4:24; 5:9; 6:15; Joshua 24:19; Nahum 1:2; James 4:5

[317] Revelation 3:20.

[318] Psalm 83: "They have said, 'Come, and let us cut them off from being a nation, That the name of Israel may be remembered no more'" (Psalm 83:4).

[319] Revelation 13:7.

[320] Ephesians 5:26-27: "that He might sanctify and cleanse her with the washing of water by the word, that He might present her to Himself a glorious Church, not having spot or wrinkle or any such thing, but that she should be holy and without blemish."

Deuteronomy 8:2–5, ESV: "And you shall remember the whole way that the LORD your God has led you these forty years in the wilderness, that he might humble you, testing you to know what was in your heart, whether you would keep his commandments or not. And he humbled you and let you hunger and fed you with manna, which you did not know, nor did your fathers know, that he might make you know that man does not live by bread alone, but man lives by every word that comes from the mouth of the LORD. Your clothing did not wear out on you and your foot did not swell these forty years. Know then in your heart that, as a man disciplines his son, the LORD your God disciplines you."

[321] "All these are the beginning of sorrows. Then they will deliver you up to tribulation and kill you, and you will be hated by all nations for My name's sake. And then many will be offended, will betray one another, and will hate one another. Then many false prophets will rise up and

deceive many. And because lawlessness will abound, the love of many will grow cold. But he who endures to the end shall be saved." (Matthew 24:8–13).

[322] 1 John 2:16.

SIGNIFICANT CLOSING THOUGHTS TO MY READERS

The antichrist will be revealed (2 Thessalonians 2) **before** the rapture. The problem for many Christians is that they are expecting the antichrist to come onto the world stage **after** the rapture. They have believed that they will have been raptured already before the antichrist shows up— so tragically, they have the feeling of "no worries!"

Are you expecting Christ to come before the Tribulation begins? What do you think will happen if you are expecting to be taken out of this world in the rapture before the Tribulation begins, but instead the antichrist shows up first? Have you ever considered the fact that you will not believe it is the antichrist, even if it is? How could you understand what is happening, if your Endtime theology says that the antichrist will not come until after the rapture? This person, whom you are believing cannot be the antichrist, would have to be another leader other than the antichrist, right? That misidentification is precisely what many "believers" are going to face soon, very soon. As a result, some who claim to know Christ will even take the mark of the beast because of their lack of understanding.

This very scenario is one of the reasons there will be a great falling away from within Christianity. Jesus said, *"You will be betrayed even by parents and brothers, relatives and friends; and they will put some of you to death. And you will be hated by all for My name's sake."* (Luke 21:16–17) Most western Christians feel that the kind of persecution Jesus referred to simply does not and cannot apply to them, because—as they would see it—they will not be around to go through it. They will have already been raptured. Yet, our eastern brothers and sisters are already suffering precisely what Jesus prophesied. Soon we will face harsh realities, which do not fit into the current popularized Endtime teaching. Over the next few years, many who call themselves Christians will deny Him to save their own necks.

Believers must realize that Satan's strategy is deception. Jesus forewarned this "rapture"-generation of that very deception (Luke 21:8). For Christians, and the whole world, the only hope of not being deceived is to have a "love of the truth." Having a love of the truth allows the Holy Spirit to prevent deception by the antichrist (2 Thessalonians 2:10). This love of the truth is really a love for Him who is The Truth.

The Church needs a paradigm switch, a clearer understanding of the Endtimes, without which many are going to fall into the trap of believing the popularized way, only to experience something traumatically different. This traumatic difference will spiritually debilitate many. Because of this situation, the Holy Spirit alone will be able to "open the eyes of our understanding"! One of the more important reasons for this book is to offer a clearer understanding of the Endtimes. *"Without a prophetic understanding* (revelation) *the people will live unrestrained."* (Proverbs 29:18)

The closer we get to Christ's return and the rapture, the clearer our understanding can be. We are told that we can *"see the day approaching"* (Hebrews 10:25); and we are told that we can *"know the times and seasons"* of His coming (1 Thessalonians 5). Therefore, we *can* and *should* have knowledge of the *times and seasons*, and not be blinded by our preconceived notions, which are not based on Scripture.

The *Mystery of God* is intended to be the key to understanding the Endtimes for hungry-hearted Christians. Jesus warned that these days would be like the days of Noah. *"For as in the days before the flood, they were eating and drinking, marrying and giving in marriage, until the day that Noah entered the ark, and did not know until the flood came and took them all away, so also will the coming of the Son of Man be"* (Matthew 24:38-39). I believe this refers to many ordinary things will continue all the way up to the very end, even in the middle of chaos about many things. This is a precise picture of deception. The Apostle Paul challenges the *rapture generation* to consider what happened to Israel in the wilderness. Most of Israel *"did not enter into the land (rest)."* Paul warns, *"Now these things happened to them as an example, but they were written down for our instruction, on whom the end of the ages has come."* (1 Corinthians 10:11, ESV)

These are sobering times for the whole world, but especially for Christians who happen to be biblically uninformed. We see the prophesied events of the Endtimes unfolding right before our eyes. The truths in this book can open our eyes; they certainly have opened mine. I am not saying that it is **the** answer to all things. I am saying that we desperately need to understand the *Mystery of God*, not only as it relates to the Endtimes, but as it answers many perplexing questions in Scripture, which only the truths of the *Mystery* can explain. Such questions as: *Why does God picture Himself as a "Husband" to His people? What is the difference between Israel and the Church? Why does the Book of Revelation contain a chronological repetition of forty-two (42) astoundingly similar elements? Does the fact that those elements are repeated help explain the correct outline of the Book of Revelation; and what difference does that make to how we live our lives? Where is the "last trumpet" in the Bible and is that the same last trumpet that Paul referred to in 1 Corinthians 15:51-52? Why are Replacement Theology and Division Theology erroneous and how does the Mystery of God explain those erroneous ideas? How does the Mystery of God explain the two (Jews and Gentiles) becoming one in Christ?* These and many other questions are answered by understanding the truths of the Mystery of God.

The greatest truth in this book is not the *Mystery of God*, per se, even though the *Mystery* is **the Key That Unlocks the Book of Revelation and the Endtimes**. The greatest truth in this book is not about the *Mystery of God*, rather it is about the *God of the Mystery!* Our great God is carrying out His plan for the revelation of the Mystery of God from beginning to end. This *Mystery* was planned before the beginning of the world. He planned for it to unfold throughout history. The *Mystery* was <u>**concealed**</u> by God in the Old Testament (though nestled within every book of the Old Testament), only to be <u>**revealed**</u> in the New Testament. And it will begin to be <u>**fulfilled**</u> during the days of the sounding of the last trumpet. At that very moment, a series of events will begin to occur as initial events in the **_final fulfillment_** of the *Mystery*; those events are the resurrection, the rapture, the judgment and rewarding of the saints and prophets. Yet, the ultimate and crowning event in which the *Mystery* is completely fulfilled is the *Marriage of the Lamb* to His Bride.

Without understanding the *Mystery of God*, we will fail to understand many facets of God's plan for humanity during history and during eternity. And without understanding the *Mystery of God*, it is **_impossible_** to understand the Book of Revelation and the Endtimes. On a very personal level, without understanding the *Mystery of God*, we will lack a critical advantage for growing in spiritual intimacy with the Lover of our souls, the Lamb of God, the Bridegroom of Heaven, who has gone to prepare a place for us.

I encourage the reader to pour over Appendix A (which begins on page 379), and to do so in conjunction with the graphic which demonstrates the linkage and interconnection between all of the Bible verse references to the *Mystery* (page 140). If you really want to understand why the *Mystery of God* determines when and where the rapture is shown to take place in the Book of Revelation, then review in detail the graphic outline and the textual outline of the Book of Revelation. Those outlines can be reviewed on pages 73-75.

May God grant you His mercies as you seek to grow in the grace and knowledge of our Savior and Lord; and may you also receive mercy for "understanding the times" as you humble yourself, submit yourself, and yield to the work of the Spirit of Christ as He prepares to present you to Himself at the *Marriage of the Lamb*! *Christ...loved the church and gave Himself for her, that He might sanctify and cleanse her with the washing of water by the word, that He might present her to Himself a glorious church, not having spot or wrinkle or any such thing, but that she should be holy and without blemish.*

> "*For we are members of His body, of His flesh and of His bones. ... and the two shall become one flesh.* **This is a great** [Greek: "great" is "mega"] **mystery, but I speak concerning Christ and the church.**"
>
> Ephesians 5:25–27,30-32

"The testimony of Jesus is the Spirit of Prophecy."
"Without a prophetic vision (revelation),
the people cast off restraint."

"And everyone who has this hope in Him purifies himself,
just as He is pure."

And the Spirit and the bride say, *"Come!"* And let him who hears say, *"Come!"* And let him who thirsts **come**. Whoever desires, let him take the water of life freely ...
He who testifies to these things says,
"Surely I am coming quickly."
Amen. Even so, come, Lord Jesus!

WORKS CITED

Billheimer, Paul E. 1975. *Destined for the Throne.* 1996. Edited by Edwin Messerschmidt. Bloomington, MN: Bethany House Publishers.

Byers, Marvin. 1995. *Six Days and a Day.* Shippensburg, PA: Treasure House.

—. 1998. *The Final Victory: The Year 2000?* Third. Shippensburg, PA: Treasure House.

—. 2000. *The Mystery: A Lost Key.* Miami, FL.

Conner, Kevin J. 1992. *Interpreting the Symbols and Types.* Portland Oregon: City Christian Publishing. Accessed October 7, 2016. www.citychristianpublishing.com.

Evans, H. Pitts. 2016. T*he Wife of God: Fresh Revelation on the Bride of Christ.* Xulon Press, April 19.

—. n.d. *How Do I Search for Diamonds?* The Arkansas Department of Parks and Tourism. Accessed October 15, 2016. http://www.craterofdiamondsstatepark.com/digging-for-diamonds/how-do-i-search-for.aspx.

Ice, Dr. Thomas. 2013. *The Last Trumpet.* July 29. Accessed October 2016. www.bibleprophecyblog.com.

James Orr, M.A., D.D. General Editor. 1915. Entry for 'CAIN" in *International Standard Bible Encyclopedia.* 1915. Edited by James Orr. 5 vols. The Howard-Severance Company.

Johnson, Dr. Ken, ed. 2008. *The Book of Jasher.* CreateSpace Independent Publishing Platform.

Limbaugh, David. 2015. *The Emmaus Code: Finding Jesus in the Old Testament.* Washington, DC: Regnery Publications.

Pink, Arthur W. 2005. *Gleanings in Genesis.* Stilwell, KS: Digireads.com.

Roberts, A., Donaldson, J., & Coxe, A. C. (Eds.). 1885. *The Epistle of Barnabas.* Buffalo, NY: Christian Literature Company.

Scofield, C. I. 1909, 1917, copyright renewed, 1937, 1945. *The Scofield Reference Bible.* Oxford University Press, Inc.

Spurgeon, Charles Haddon. 7. pbministries.org/Theology/Spurgeon/spurgeon01_02.htm. Accessed October 2016.

Strong, J. 1995. *Enhanced Strong's Lexicon.* Woodside Bible Fellowship.

Swanson, J. 1997. Dictionary of Biblical Languages with Semantic Domains: Hebrew (Old Testament). Oak Harbor, WA: Logos Research Systems, Inc.

1995 electronic ed. of the 1769 edition of the 1611 Authorized Version. The Holy Bible: King James Version. Bellingham, WA: Logos Research Systems, Inc.

Vine, W. E. & Bruce, F. F. 1981. *Vine's Expository dictionary of Old and New Testament Words.* Old Tappan, NJ: Revell.

Warner, Tim. 2012. *The Time of the End.* CreateSpace Independent Publishing Platform.

Writing Tutorial Services, Indiana University, Bloomington, IN. n.d. Using Outlines. Accessed October 2016. http://wts.indiana.edu/pamphlets/outlines.shtml.

Zodhiates, S. 2000. *The Complete Word Study Dictionary: New Testament* (electronic ed.). Chattanooga, TN: AMG Publishers.

APPENDIX A - MYSTERY DETAILS 1-12

"MYSTERY OF GOD"

	Context	Text Verse(s)	Text
	\multicolumn{3}{c}{The Mystery Was Hidden In God From The Beginning}	
1	Romans 16:25-27	Romans 16:25	"… the Mystery kept secret since the world began …"
2	1 Corinthians 2:6-8	1 Corinthians 2:7	"… Mystery, the hidden wisdom which God ordained before the ages …"
3	Ephesians 3:1-12	Ephesians 3:5	"… the mystery … in other ages not made known …"
4	Ephesians 3:1-9	Ephesians 3:9	"… the mystery, from the beginning of the ages has been hidden in God …"
5	Colossians 1:24-29	Colossians 1:26	"… the mystery which has been hidden from ages and from generations …"
	\multicolumn{3}{c}{It is The Mystery of God and of Christ}	
6	Colossians 1:24-29, 2:1-2	Colossians 2:2	"… the knowledge of the mystery of God, both of the Father and of Christ, … in whom are hidden all the treasures of wisdom and knowledge."
7	Colossians 4:2-4	Colossians 4:3	"… that God would open to us a door for the word, to speak the mystery of Christ …"
8	Ephesians 3:1-12	Ephesians 3:4	"… when you read, you may understand my knowledge in the mystery of Christ …"
	\multicolumn{3}{c}{We Are Called To Be Ministers of This Mystery}	
9	Ephesians 3:1-12	Ephesians 3:4-7	"… the Mystery of Christ … now revealed … that the Gentiles should be … partakers of the promise … of which I became a minister …"
10	Ephesians 6:14-20	Ephesians 6:19	"… praying always … for me … that I may open my mouth boldly to make known (minister) the mystery …"
11	1 Corinthians 2:6-8	1 Corinthians 2:7	"… we speak (minister) the wisdom of God in a mystery, the hidden wisdom …"
12	Colossians 4:2-4	Colossians 4:3	"… for us … to speak (minister) the mystery of Christ …"

APPENDIX A - MYSTERY DETAILS 13-25

"MYSTERY OF GOD"

The Mystery Has Been Revealed to the Saints, Apostles, and Prophets

13	Ephesians 1:3-14	"… *having made known (revealed) to us the mystery of His will* …"
14	Ephesians 3:1-12	"… *the fullness of time He might gather together in one all things in Christ* …"
15	Colossians 1:24-29	"… *by revelation He made known (revealed) to me the mystery … as it has been revealed by the Spirit to His holy apostles and prophets* …"
16	Colossians 4:2-4	"… *the mystery which … now has been revealed to His saints* …"
		"… *the revelation of the mystery … now made manifest (revealed)* …"

The Mystery Is Related to Preaching to the Gentiles

17	Ephesians 3:3-12	"… *the mystery … that the Gentiles … should be partakers of the promise in Christ … of which I became a minister (to the Gentiles) … that I should preach among the Gentiles* …"
18	1 Timothy 3:16	"… *great is the mystery of godliness: God was … preached among the Gentiles* …"
19	Colossians 1:24-29	"… *the mystery which … now has been revealed to His saints* …"

The Mystery Is Related to Spiritual "Riches" Among the Gentiles

20	Colossians 1:24-29	"… *the riches of the glory of this mystery among the Gentiles* …"
21	Ephesians 3:1-12	"… *the mystery of Christ … that the Gentiles … should be fellow heirs* …"
22	Ephesians 1:1-22	"… *having made known to us the mystery of His will … that the God of our Lord Jesus Christ the Father of glory may give to you (Gentiles) … the riches of the glory of His inheritance* …"

It Is The Mystery of the Gospel, the Mystery of our Faith

23	Ephesians 6:14-20	"… *that I may open my mouth boldly to make known the mystery of Christ* …"
24	1 Timothy 3:1-12	"… *holding the mystery of the faith with a pure conscience.*
25	Galatians 3:6-9	[Galatians 3:8 specifically links the faith with the gospel.] *"And the Scripture foreseeing that God would justify the Gentiles by faith, preached the gospel* …"

APPENDIX A - MYSTERY DETAILS 26-31

"MYSTERY OF GOD"

			It Is A Mystery For Which Paul Was In Prison
26	Eph. 1:22-23, 2:11-22, 5:5; 1 Tim. 3:25; Rom. 9 & 11; Rev. 19 & 21; I Cor. 15:24	Colossians 4:2-3	"… meanwhile praying also for us, that God would open to us a door for the word to speak the mystery of Christ, for which I am also in **chains** …"
27		Ephesians 3:1-12	"For this reason I, Paul, the **prisoner** of Christ Jesus for you Gentiles … how that by revelation He made known to me the mystery …"
28		Ephesians 6:14-20	"… that I may open my mouth boldly to make known the mystery … for which I am and ambassador in **chains** …"
			This Mystery Reveals Israel and the Gentiles Become One in Christ
29		Romans 11:13, 17, 25-26	"For I speak to you Gentiles … you, being a wild olive tree, **were grafted in among them** (the natural branches—the spiritual remnant of Israel), and with them (you Gentiles) **became a partaker of the root and fatness of the olive tree**, **For I do not desire**, (Gentiles) **brethren … that you should be ignorant of this MYSTERY** … that blindness in part has happened to Israel until the fullness of the Gentiles has come in …" (A remnant of believers, that is, "spiritual Israel," from among "physical Israel," is ever-present. Romans 11:1-5).
30		Ephesians 2:11-22	Romans 11 (above vitally links with the following in Ephesians 2:11-22. "… at that time you (Gentiles) **were separate from Christ**, excluded from citizenship in Israel and foreigners to the **covenants of the promise**, **without hope and without God in the world**. But now in Christ Jesus you (Gentiles) who were once far away have been brought near through the blood of Christ. For He Himself is our peace, who has **made the two one His purpose was to create in Himself one new man out of the two** (Jew and Gentile), thus making peace, and in this one body to reconcile both of them to God through the cross … Consequently, you (Gentiles) **are no longer foreigners and aliens**, **but fellow citizens with God's people and members of God's household**, built on the foundation of the apostles and prophets, with Christ Jesus Himself as the chief cornerstone. In Him the whole building is joined together and raised to become a holy temple in the Lord. And (Gentiles) **in Him** you too are being built together to become a dwelling place in which God lives by His Spirit."
31		**THE MYSTERY OF GOD: JEWS AND GENTILES** Made To Be One IN Christ and WITH Christ	"THE TWO ARE: **One Body, One People, One Holy Temple, One New Man, One Church, One Bridegroom, and One Bride, One Kingdom**

APPENDIX A - MYSTERY DETAILS 32-35

"MYSTERY OF GOD"

The Mystery is Fulfilled at the Last Trumpet, the Resurrection, the Judgment and Rewarding of the Saints, and in the Marriage of the Lamb

#	Reference	Text
32	I Corinthians 15:42-57	I Cor. 15:51-52 — "Behold I tell you a *mystery* ... we shall all be changed ... at the last trumpet ... sound, and the dead will be raised (resurrection) ..."
33	Revelation 10 and 11	Revelation 10:7 and 11:15-18 — "Then the seventh angel sounded (his trumpet, then the elders) *worshiped God, saying, "The kingdoms of this world have become the kingdoms of our Lord and of His Christ, and He shall reign forever and ever! (Now has come for) the time of the dead (resurrection) that they should be judged, and that You should reward Your servants the prophets and the saints ..."*
34	Ephesians 5:22-33	Ephesians 5:29-32 — THESE VERSES LINK THE MYSTERY TO THE MARRIAGE OF THE LAMB: "... the two shall become one flesh. This is a great mystery (*marriage*), but I speak concerning Christ and the church (the Marriage of the Lamb)."
35	Revelation 19:6-9 and 21:1-3, 9-10	Revelation 19:7 — "Let us be glad and rejoice and give Him the glory, for the *marriage of the lamb has come, and His wife has made herself ready.*"

APPENDIX B

CHRIST THE MYSTERY IN THE OLD TESTAMENT

THE BOOK	OLD TESTAMENT Chapters	NEW TESTAMENT Chapters
CHRIST Revealed in LEVITICUS		
Sacrifice and Oblation	Leviticus 1-7	Hebrews 10:12
Holy High Priest	Leviticus 8, 9, 10	Hebrews 7:26
The Atonement	Leviticus 16	Hebrews 9:14
Way of Approach to God	Leviticus 16	Hebrews 7:25
CHRIST Revealed in NUMBERS		
The Tabernacle	Numbers 3,4,9	John 1:14 (Greek: Dwelt)
Sanctuary in the Wilderness	Numbers 3, 4, 7	John 1:14; Ezekiel 11:16
The Nazarite	Numbers 6	Hebrews 7:26
The Serpent of Brass	Numbers 21:8, 9	John 3:14
The Smitten Rock	Numbers 20:8-13	1 Corinthians 10:4
The Star out of Jacob	Numbers 24:17	Matthew 2:2
CHRIST Revealed in DEUTERONOMY		
The True Prophet	Deuteronomy 18:15-19	Acts 3:22
The Rock	Deuteronomy 32:4,18,31	1 Corinthians 10:4

Christ in the Old Testament Continued

THE BOOK	OLD TESTAMENT Chapters	NEW TESTAMENT Chapters
CHRIST Revealed in JOSHUA		
Joshua (Jehoshua)	Joshua 1-24	Hebrews 4:8
Captain of our Salvation	Joshua 5:13-15	Matthew 1:21-23
The Man with the Sword	Joshua 5:13-15	Ephesians 6:12-18
Inheritance Giver	Joshua 13-19	Hebrews 4; Ephesians 1:3, 14
CHRIST Revealed in JUDGES		
Judge/Deliverer/Savior	Judges 2:13-23	Matthew 1:21-23
Anointed by Spirit of Lord	Judges 13	John 1:41-42
CHRIST Revealed in RUTH		
The Mighty Man	Ruth 2:1	Luke 1:49
Lord of the Harvest	Ruth 2:14-17	Luke 10:1-2
Kinsman Redeemer	Ruth 4:1-12	Revelation 5:9-10
CHRIST Revealed in 1 SAMUEL		
Anointed Prophet/Priest/King/Intercessor	1 Samuel 16:1,13	Luke 1:31-35; Matthew 27:37
CHRIST Revealed in 2 SAMUEL		
Son of David	2 Samuel 7	Matthew 1:1

Christ in the Old Testament Continued

THE BOOK	OLD TESTAMENT Chapters	NEW TESTAMENT Chapters
CHRIST Revealed in 1 KINGS		
King of Peace and Glory	1 Kings 1, 2, 3, 4	Matthew 1:1
The Wisdom of God	1 Kings 3:4, 9	1 Corinthians 1:30
Temple Builder	1 Kings 5, 6, 7, 8	Ephesians 2:20-22
Greater than Solomon	1 Kings 10	Matthew 12:42
The Prophet/God's Word	1 Kings 13:1-3	John 1:14
King of King/Lord of Lords	1 Kings 22:19	Revelation 19:16
CHRIST Revealed in 2 KINGS		
The Righteous King	2 Kings 3:12	1 Corinthians 1:30
The Man of God	2 Kings 1:12	Luke 23:47
Word of the Lord in Person	2 Kings 3:12	John 1:14
CHRIST Revealed in 1 CHRONICLES		
The Greater King David	1 Chronicles 11:1-3	Matthew 1:1; Revelation 22:16
CHRIST Revealed in 2 CHRONICLES		Hebrews 9:11; 2:17
Prophet/Priest/King	2 Chronicles 20:14-21	Revelation 19:16
Temple Cleanser	2 Chronicles 1:11, 12; 7:29	Matthew 2:6
Reformer	2 Chronicles 29:1-19	Hebrews 9:10

THE BOOK	Christ in the Old Testament Continued OLD TESTAMENT Chapters	NEW TESTAMENT Chapters
CHRIST Revealed in EZRA	Ezra 6:7	Hebrews 5:1-5
Governor/Priest	Ezra 10:10	Matthew 2:6
Scribe and Restorer	Ezra 6:2-7	Isaiah 58:12 with Acts 3:20-21
CHRIST Revealed in NEHEMIAH	Nehemiah 5:14	Matthew 2:6
Governor of Judah	Nehemiah 2:4-8	John 17
Man of Prayer and Work	Nehemiah 3:1-10	Matthew 16:18
CHRIST Revealed in ESTHER		
Great King and His Bride	Esther 1:1-8; 2-17	Revelation 19:7
CHRIST Revealed in JOB		
Patient Suffering Priest	Job 1:20-22; 20:8, 10	Hebrews 5:1-5
CHRIST Revealed in PSALMS		Hebrews 9:11; 2:17
Beloved Shepherd/King The Sweet Singer/ Worshiper	Psalm 23 Psalm 139-145	John 3:16; 10:11-14 Hebrews 2:12
CHRIST Revealed in PROVERBS		
The Wisdom of God	Proverbs 1, 2	1 Corinthians 1:20,24; Colossians 2:3

THE BOOK	Christ in the Old Testament Continued OLD TESTAMENT Chapters	NEW TESTAMENT Chapters
CHRIST Revealed in ECCLESIASTES		
The Preacher in Jerusalem	Ecclesiastes 1:1	Luke 4:18-20
The Son of David	Ecclesiastes 1:1	Matthew 1:1
The Wisdom of God	Ecclesiastes 1:1	1 Corinthians 1:30
The King "from above"	Ecclesiastes 1:1	Galatians 4:26
CHRIST Revealed in SONG OF SOLOMON		
King of Peace/Bridegroom lover	Song of Solomon 1-8	John 14:27; Ephesians 5:23-32
CHRIST Revealed in ISAIAH		
The Holy One of Israel	Isaiah 30:11,12,15,29	Mark 1:24
Our Salvation	Isaiah 12	Matthew 1:21
Our Righteousness	Isaiah 51:4-8	1 Corinthians 1:30
Our Comfort	Isaiah 51:3, 66:13	John 14:16, 18
The True Judge	Isaiah 2:4	John 5:22
CHRIST Revealed in JEREMIAH		
The Appointed Prophet	Jeremiah 1:5	Acts 3:22-24
The Righteous Branch/King	Jeremiah 23:5	1 Corinthians 1:30
The Lord our Righteousness	Jeremiah 23:4-6	1 Corinthians 1:30

THE BOOK	Christ in the Old Testament Continued OLD TESTAMENT Chapters	NEW TESTAMENT Chapters
CHRIST Revealed in LAMENTATIONS		
The Weeping Prophet	Lamentations 1:16	Luke 19:41-44
The Man of Sorrows	Lamentations 1:12, 18	Matthew 23:37, 38
CHRIST Revealed in EZEKIEL		
The Son of Man	Ezekiel 2:1-8; 3:1-4	John 1:51
The Shekinah Glory	Ezekiel 43:1-4	John 1:14-18
CHRIST Revealed in DANIEL		
The Son of Man	Daniel 7:13	John 1:51
The Crushing Stone	Daniel 2:34-35	Matthew 21:42-44
The Kingdom of God in Person	Daniel 7:27	Romans 14:17
King of Kings/Lord of Lords	Daniel 7:27	Revelation 19:16
CHRIST Revealed in HOSEA		
Prophet of Law and Love	Hosea 1, 2	Acts 3:22,23; Matthew 5:17, 18; John 3:16
CHRIST Revealed in JOEL		
Jehovah-God, Promiser and Baptizer in the Holy Spirit	Joel 2:28-32	Luke 24:49; Acts 2:33; John 1:31-33

THE BOOK	Christ in the Old Testament Continued OLD TESTAMENT Chapters	NEW TESTAMENT Chapters
CHRIST Revealed in AMOS		
Burden bearer and the Judge/Punisher of nations	Amos 1	2 Thessalonians 1:7-9
Builder of David's Tabernacle	Amos 9:11-15	Matthew 16:18, 19; Acts 15:15-18
CHRIST Revealed in OBADIAH		
Servant/Worshiper and Executor of Divine Wrath	Obadiah 15, 17, 21	Hebrews 2:12; 2 Thessalonians 1:6-10
CHRIST Revealed in JONAH		
The Greater than Jonah	Jonah 1:17	Matthew 12:39-41
CHRIST Revealed in MICAH		
Heavenly Micah, "Like God"	Micah 7:17, 18	Hebrews 1:2-4
Rejected King of the Jews	Micah 5:1	John 19:15
Establisher of His House	Micah 4:1, 2	Hebrews 3:6
CHRIST Revealed in NAHUM		
Prophet of Comfort and Vengeance	Nahum 1:2-7, 15; 2:2	John 14:16; 2 Thessalonians 1:1-8

Christ in the Old Testament Continued

THE BOOK	OLD TESTAMENT Chapters	NEW TESTAMENT Chapters
CHRIST Revealed in HABAKKUK		
Judge of Babylon	Habakkuk 1:5-11	Revelation 17,18
The Rewarder of Faith	Habakkuk 2:1-4	Hebrews 10:38; 11:16
CHRIST Revealed in ZEPHANIAH		
The Jealous God and Executor of God's Wrath	Zephaniah 1:18	2 Corinthians 11:2; Romans 2:5, 6
CHRIST Revealed in HAGGAI		
Prophet/Priest/Prince and Builder of the Lord's House	Haggai 1, 2, 3	Matthew 16:18; Hebrews 1:1, 2; 3:1-4
CHRIST Revealed in ZECHARIAH		
Whom Jehovah Remembers	Name Interpreted	
The Branch	Zechariah 3:8	Matthew 2:23
Jehovah's Servant	Zechariah 3:8	Philippians 2:7-9
The Smitten Shepherd	Zechariah 13:7	Mark 14:27
King-Priest/Temple Builder	Zechariah 6:9-12	Hebrews 5:5,6; Ephesians 2:20-22
King over all the earth	Zechariah 14:9	Revelation 19:16
CHRIST Revealed in MALACHI		
Messenger of Covenant, Refiner/Purifier/Cleanser of the Temple	Malachi 3:1-3	Matthew 3:11; 21:12-14; 26:26-28; John 2:13-17

APPENDIX C

DIVISION THEOLOGY AND REPLACEMENT THEOLOGY

Division Theology suggests that Israel and the Church are two different peoples who have different roles in God's plan. That perspective, typically, also suggest that each will have different roles and destinies in the latter days of the Endtimes. I would be the first to agree that the ethnic, physical people of Israel and the Church are two different peoples.

However, a distinction must be carefully made regarding the terminology and semantics involved. Those who trust in Him, whether in the Old or the New Testament, are His own. If they have saving faith, by God's grace, then they are members of the spiritual family of God. As is shown throughout this book, it is very important to note that there is a "physical Israel" and there is a "spiritual Israel".

Every human who has lived, or who will ever live, is the physical **_creation of God_**. Being created by God, however, does not equate to being a **_spiritual child of God_**. Only those who have a faith relationship with God are seen by Him as being a **_member of His spiritual family_**. There never has been a division within God's family. From Adam and Eve until the last soul to be saved in the Endtimes, those with saving faith are in God's spiritual family. No division can separate them from one another. Division Theology erroneously divides New Testament believers from Old Testament believers. (See Chapters 9, 11, 19, 20, and 21 for a clear understanding.) This *Division Theology* concept brings confusion to the truths of the overall redemptive work of Christ, which He accomplished in the giving of His body, shedding His blood, and His resurrection.

Replacement Theology, on the other hand, is the belief that the Church, primarily seen today as a Gentilized Church, has replaced Israel as God's chosen people. This is a grave misunderstanding and error. (See Chapters 9, 11, 19, 20, and 21 to gain a clear understanding of this vital subject.) While most Bible-believing Christians repudiate *Replacement Theology*, many have fallen prey to the perverse, confusing and unbiblical idea of *Division Theology*.

About the Author

Joe Lutz is president of ENDlighten Ministries. ENDlighten Ministries facilitates biblical prophecy seminars in churches and for the general public regarding the Endtimes; develops publications for the same; and engages media, Christian and secular, regarding global and prophetic events and issues.

Mr. Lutz holds a degree in theology and is a recipient of an honorary doctorate of jurisprudence. He has held ministerial positions, including pastoral, international missions outreach, evangelism, and Endtimes seminars. Fifty-years of interest and study in biblical prophecy has provided him with an in-depth knowledge of biblical prophecy topics. He has traveled all fifty states in the USA and to thirteen foreign countries.

He and his wife, Colleen, have five grown children and six grandchildren. They enjoy traveling and reading, and he enjoys golf.

- For obtaining information for scheduling an ENDlighten Ministries Endtimes Seminar, please email your interest and request to seminars@ENDlightenMinistries.org.

- For a talk radio, television, print or internet media interview regarding biblical prophecy, or for a promotional interview regarding this book, please email your request to media@ENDlightenMinistries.org

- Submit questions to info@ENDlightenMinistries.org.

For further information, please visit the ministry's website:

www.ENDlightenMinistries.org

In the Fall of 2017, *The Incredible Key* won the First Place award in the End Times category of the Christian Author Awards sponsored by Xulon Press.

Made in the USA
Lexington, KY
17 May 2018